Readings in Feminist Rhetorical Theory

Readings in Feminist Rhetorical Theory

• Sonia Johnson • Cheris Kramarae • bell hooks • Gloria Anzaldúa • Mary Daly • Starhawk • Paula Gunn Allen • Trinh T. Minh-ha • Sally Miller Gearhart •

Karen A. Foss
University of New Mexico

Sonja K. Foss
University of Colorado at Denver

Cindy L. Griffin
Colorado State University

Editors

SAGE Publications
International Educational and Professional Publisher
Thousand Oaks ▪ London ▪ New Delhi

Copyright © 2004 by Sage Publications, Inc.

All rights reserved. No part of this book may be reproduced or utilized in any form or by any means, electronic or mechanical, including photocopying, recording, or by any information storage and retrieval system, without permission in writing from the publisher.

For information:

Sage Publications, Inc.
2455 Teller Road
Thousand Oaks, California 91320
E-mail: order@sagepub.com

Sage Publications Ltd.
6 Bonhill Street
London EC2A 4PU
United Kingdom

Sage Publications India Pvt. Ltd.
B-42, Panchsheel Enclave
Post Box 4109
New Delhi 110 017 India

Printed in the United States of America

Library of Congress Cataloging-in-Publication Data

Readings in feminist rhetorical theory/Karen A. Foss, Sonja K. Foss, and Cindy L. Griffin, editors.
    p. cm.
Includes bibliographical references and index.
ISBN 0-7619-3015-9 (pbk.)
  1. Feminist theory. 2. Rhetoric. I. Foss, Karen A. II. Foss, Sonja K. III. Griffin, Cindy L.
HQ1190.R434 2004
305.42′01—dc22   2003018551

Printed on acid-free paper

03 04 05 06 07 08 09 10 9 8 7 6 5 4 3 2 1

Acquiring Editor:	Todd R. Armstrong
Editorial Assistant:	Veronica K. Novak
Production Editor:	Claudia A. Hoffman
Typesetter:	C&M Digitals (P) Ltd.
Cover Designer:	Janet Foulger

Contents

	Acknowledgments	vii
1.	Introducing Feminist Rhetorical Scholarship	1
2.	Introduction to Cheris Kramarae	7
	2.1 Proprietors of Language	9
	2.2 Women as a Muted Group	19
	2.3 A Visiting Scholar	27
	2.4 Do We Really Want More Control of Technology?	34
	2.5 Feminist Theories of Communication	39
3.	Introduction to bell hooks	45
	3.1 Feminism: A Movement to End Sexist Oppression	47
	3.2 Feminist Politicization: A Comment	57
	3.3 Back to the Avant-Garde: The Progressive Vision	63
	3.4 Design: A Happening Life	71
4.	Introduction to Gloria Anzaldúa	75
	4.1 Speaking in Tongues: A Letter to 3rd World Women Writers	77
	4.2 La conciencia de la mestiza: Towards a New Consciousness	85
	4.3 Del otro lado	97
	4.4 Beyond Traditional Notions of Identity	100
5.	Introduction to Mary Daly	105
	5.1 A Call for the Castration of Sexist Religion	107
	5.2 Gyn/Ecology: Spinning New Time/Space	119
	5.3 Sin Big	123
	5.4 Spiraling into the Nineties	130
6.	Introduction to Starhawk	141
	6.1 Witchcraft as Goddess Religion	143
	6.2 *Truth or Dare*	149
	Magic and Its Uses	149
	The Three Types of Power	151
	Roots of the Three Types of Power	153
	6.3 Ritual as Bonding: Action as Ritual	162
	6.4 *The Spiral Dance*	170
	6.5 Roundtable Discussion: Backlash	175

7.	Introduction to Paula Gunn Allen	179
	7.1 All the Good Indians	181
	7.2 Grandmother of the Sun: Ritual Gynocracy in Native America	184
	7.3 Some Like Indians Endure	199
	7.4 Essentially, It's Spring	204
	7.5 Haggles	206
8.	Introduction to Trinh T. Minh-ha	213
	8.1 Not You/Like You: Post-Colonial Women and the Interlocking Questions of Identity and Difference	215
	8.2 Yellow Sprouts	220
	8.3 The Totalizing Quest of Meaning	225
9.	Introduction to Sally Miller Gearhart	239
	9.1 The Womanization of Rhetoric	241
	9.2 The Gatherstretch	248
	9.3 The Chipko	259
	9.4 Notes from a Recovering Activist	266
10.	Introduction to Sonia Johnson	271
	10.1 The Bursting of the File	273
	10.2 Who's Afraid of the Supreme Court?	282
	10.3 Ship Ahoy	294
	10.4 Meet My Needs, Make Me Happy	297
	10.5 The Bears and Anarchy	304
	Index	313
	About the Editors	319

Acknowledgments

We are delighted that Sage Publications has chosen to support the compilation of the works of the feminist theorists featured in this book. We believe their voices, added to the conversation about rhetorical theory, will greatly expand our options for being in the world. Special thanks to Todd R. Armstrong, senior editor for communication and cultural studies at Sage, who was a supportive advocate and enjoyable partner in this effort. We also appreciate the expeditious way in which he turned our idea into a printed book.

We are particularly grateful to the nine theorists whose works are featured in this collection: Cheris Kramarae, bell hooks, Gloria Anzaldúa, Mary Daly, Starhawk, Paula Gunn Allen, Trinh T. Minh-ha, Sally Miller Gearhart, and Sonia Johnson. In many cases, the women worked with us to support the selection of the pieces that best exemplify the trajectory of their ideas. Most important, their transformative ideas about rhetoric continue to renew and inspire us.

Five reviewers responded to the proposal for the book with valuable suggestions, and we appreciate their input in this project: Barry Brummett, University of Texas at Austin; Lisa A. Flores, University of Utah; Charlotte Kroløkke, University of Southern Denmark; Mark McPhail, Miami University; and Kent A. Ono, University of Illinois.

Finally, this project reminded the three of us of how much fun it can be to work together. We value the trust, insights, and expansion that come from feminist collaboration.

—*Karen A. Foss*
—*Cindy L. Griffin*
—*Sonja K. Foss*

1

Introducing Feminist Rhetorical Scholarship

Over the past several decades, feminist rhetorical scholarship has followed a trajectory that is both linear and spiral in nature. In its most linear form, feminist ideas and theories entered the scholarly conversation with a kind of foreshadowing—a few radical essays that cracked the stronghold that traditional scholarship had on our journals and presses. These essays challenged us to think in new ways and hinted at the potential of feminist communication scholarship to transform our intellectual homes.[1] What followed—often called the *inclusion stage*[2]—was scholarship that recognized women as legitimate subjects of study, opening the doors for examining their words, actions, and theories. Once included, feminist communication scholars began a careful critique of traditional forms of scholarship, suggesting that our methods of discovery, artifacts of study, and criteria for the assessment of scholarship be reconsidered and revised. This third stage was closely followed by attempts to define and refine feminist perspectives and to name scholarly approaches, subjects of study, and methods that legitimately and uniquely could be labeled *feminist*. This fourth stage was quickly accompanied by a fifth, in which feminist communication scholars began to revision and reconceptualize traditional constructs, transforming disciplines and offering new theories, insights, and explanations for the phenomena they study.[3]

As we trace our roots and discuss our lineage, the spiral-like nature of feminist communication scholarship also becomes apparent. As we work, we regularly pause, recognizing that as we advance ideas and move forward, we return again and again to earlier approaches to borrow from the insights produced, revise or highlight a past discovery, clarify and contextualize a recent finding, and even refine or challenge a new theory. Such "spiraling" suggests that we have come to a place of maturity as feminist scholars, a place from which we can survey large bodies of work and decades of ideas and arguments that help us understand our world and explain our subjects of study. Unlike many of the women in our not-too-distant-past, more and more of our ideas and insights have been recorded and preserved.[4] As a result, we now can begin to make more comprehensive and systematic claims about where we've been, what we've named as important, and how we've explained our places in the world. Our goal in compiling this reader is to capture this maturity and make accessible an important part of the history of feminist theorizing about communication. We suggest that this scholarship is now at a place where a diverse enough group of scholars has been writing and theorizing for a long enough period of time that, once again, we can spiral back, reflect, and critique where we have been and where we are going.

Definitions of *Rhetoric*, *Theory*, and *Feminism*

We define *rhetoric* as any kind of human symbol use that functions in any realm—public, private, and anything in between. We do not see rhetoric as separate or distinct from communication. The terms are synonymous for us, and we think this allows for a more complex and comprehensive understanding of human symbol use, particularly as we attempt to understand and make sense of the symbols that are generated by individuals who traditionally have been devalued or underrepresented in our society.

We define a *theory* as a way of framing an experience or event—an effort to understand and account for something and the way it functions in the world.[5] We do not see theory as some mysterious activity that generates obscure explanations with little apparent connection to our daily lives. Instead, we define theory as something individuals do as they try to "figure out answers for, develop explanations about, and organize what is happening in their worlds."[6]

Although all of the scholars included in this reader theorize about rhetoric and communication, most do not overtly label themselves as rhetorical or communication theorists. We recognize that this may cause confusion and that our selection of these scholars raises the question of who actually is a rhetorical or communication theorist. Although a *rhetorical theorist* certainly can be a person who self-identifies as a rhetorical theorist, the rhetorical tradition has a long history of calling, studying, and using rhetorical and communication theorists who never avow (or avowed) that identity. Kenneth Burke, Jürgen Habermas, Jean Baudrillard, Michel Foucault, Edward Said, and Terry Eagleton represent such a group, and there are many others. Even Stephen Toulmin came late to the label *rhetorical theorist*. We suggest that considering scholars rhetorical theorists only when they identify as such is far too limiting. We define a rhetorical theorist as a person who is offering coherent and systematic explanations of the ways symbols work to create, exchange, and negotiate meanings. The theorists we have selected for this reader fit into this broader conceptualization of a rhetorical theorist—a conceptualization that allows us to work with and learn from diverse and important feminist communication theories.

We recognize that the definitions of feminism and feminist are quite varied and that it is a complex ideology. With Julia Wood, we define feminism as "an active commitment to equality and respect for life."* Similar to bell hooks, we ground our feminism in the "effort to end sexist oppression" but see feminism as much larger than the effort to eliminate the oppression of women. For us, feminism is the effort to disrupt the ideology of domination that pervades our culture and many of our relationships. It is the effort, in other words, to eliminate relationships of domination,

---

*Julia T. Wood, *Gendered Lives: Communication, Gender, and Culture*, 4th ed, (Belmont, CA: Wadsworth, 2001), p. 5.

oppression, and elitism and the creation instead of relationships of self-determination, affirmation, mutuality, equality, and respect. Feminism, then, is a commitment to eliminate relations of oppression and domination in general, whether of women, African Americans, old people, lesbians, gay men, family members, friends, acquaintances, or co-workers. What we and other feminists are trying to do is to transform relationships and the larger culture so that they reflect more humane and enriching ways to live.[7]

Criteria for Inclusion of Theorists

We used three criteria to select the nine theorists whose work is included in this volume: a comprehensive body of scholarship that contains both depth and breadth, diversity, and accessibility. All of the nine theorists we have included—Cheris Kramarae, bell hooks, Gloria Anzaldúa, Mary Daly, Starhawk, Paula Gunn Allen, Trinh T. Minh-ha, Sally Miller Gearhart, and Sonia Johnson—have produced a substantial body of work in which they have articulated feminist theories that are relevant to rhetoric and communication. Their work displays both depth—they theorize extensively about communication constructs—and breadth—their theories encompass a wide range of communication constructs. Among this group, the first essay was published in 1974 and all, with the exception of Sonia Johnson, continue to write, produce, and publish today. Combined, their work totals more than 400 articles, books, short stories, collections of poetry, films, and musical compositions; spans more than four decades; and addresses over 100 different communication constructs.

The nine scholars we have included also represent enormous diversity—an important component of feminist scholarship and our second criterion for the selection of theorists to include. These scholars represent years of study in an impressive range of disciplines: philosophy and theology, literature and poetry, languages, communication, cultural studies, and environmental and spiritual venues. They are teachers, writers, filmmakers, and activists; lesbian, bisexual, and heterosexual; as well as a multiracial mix of Native American, Lebanese, Latina, Vietnamese, African American, and European American. They represent perspectives and positions on feminism and communication that vary across race and ethnicity, sexual orientation, and economic position and that allow for a truly diverse explanation of the ways symbols can work in our society.

A final criterion we used for inclusion in this volume is accessibility. With bell hooks, we ask, "of what use is feminist theory . . . that leaves [women] stumbling bleary-eyed from classroom settings" as they attempt to make sense of jargon and overly complex sentences that mask the meaning, if not the potential, of the theory?[8] As hooks explains, "many women have responded to [inaccessible] feminist theory that does not speak clearly to us by trashing theory, and, as a consequence, further promoting the false dichotomy between theory and practice."[9] Rather than select theorists who have the potential to keep individuals distanced from and struggling with feminist theory, we have included scholars who enact accessibility in their work.

In compiling this volume, we recognize that, while we have highlighted the work of nine scholars who have been writing and theorizing for decades, many other feminist scholars have not been included in this reader. For example, theorists such as Judith Butler, Hélène Cixous, and Gyatri Spivak are not included in this volume. Although we acknowledge and recognize the important and positive impact each of these scholars has had on feminist theorizing, our criteria of accessibility (and, to some extent, the scope of their bodies of work) prevented us from including them. Although their work is enormously important, we selected nine other theorists who met all three of the criteria we used—scope and depth of work, diversity, and accessibility. Scholars such as Barbara Bieseker, Karlyn Kohrs Campbell, Celeste Condit, Melissa Deem, and Lisa Flores, among many, many others, also are not included. Again, we want to state clearly that the work of these feminist scholars is enormously important. Although their work is diverse and accessible, its scope is not as broad or as extensive at this point as the nine scholars we selected. The work of third-wave feminists also has not been included. Our goal is not to negate these important and emerging voices; we recognize their enormous value and contributions to feminist communication scholarship. However, a single volume such as this reader cannot simultaneously feature the work of scholars who have been theorizing for decades while also recording the work of newer feminist theorists, and we chose as our focus the former.

In summary, our goal is not to negate, erase, or silence the voices of feminists we were not able to include. Rather, it is to offer a collection of essays that helps us recognize that a comprehensive, diverse, and accessible body of work now exists upon which we can build and about which we should know if we are to have a thorough understanding of our options as symbol users. We offer this text as a collection of work for understanding symbol use from feminist perspectives. It highlights various aspects of our thinking and theorizing that are not always visible in traditional theories about rhetoric and communication. We acknowledge that this book constitutes only one way of framing feminist work, celebrate this framing as a legitimate one, and actively seek out other ways to frame, teach, honor, critique, and record feminist communication theories.

Ways to Use this Book

From the more than 400 options from which we had to choose, we have identified a small sample of work from each theorist for inclusion—three to five essays, chapters, short stories, and/or poems per theorist. For each theorist, our selections represent her work both historically (including earlier work as well as more recent ideas) and conceptually (illustrating key concepts within the theorist's body of work). We have arranged the selections of each theorist chronologically to show the historical development, but they clearly can be read in any order. We introduce each theorist with a brief biography and a short discussion of the key ideas in the selections that follow. We have arranged the theorists and their works along a continuum, with the first scholars in this reader (Kramarae and hooks) describing the difficulties feminists encounter as they work and live in the dominant culture. Our second grouping (Anzaldua, Daly, Starhawk, and Gunn Allen) describes two worlds or systems, one grounded in patriarchy and the second grounded in feminist principles. Our final three theorists (Trinh, Gearhart, and Johnson) suggest new worlds or systems that attempt to break completely with patriarchal principles and practices.

Because of the range of ideas presented here, we suggest that this reader can be used in a number of ways. One option is to use it as a companion volume to *Feminist Rhetorical Theories*[10] or other volumes that explore the theories of the scholars represented here, offering samples of the original work by these theorists to provide a more in-depth understanding of their ideas. A second option is to highlight the different perspectives on feminism offered by these scholars, discussing the diversity of feminisms and the different implications, strengths, and weaknesses of each. With this approach, readers also can begin to trace the evolution of feminist thought and see where feminist scholars have been and how we might continue to advance feminist theories.

A third option is to use the theories of these scholars as a basis to discuss the ways in which feminist scholarship transforms traditional communication concepts such as ethos, audience adaptation, identification, ideology, the scope or function of rhetoric, power, exigency, rationality, and even the definition of rhetoric. When compared to traditional explanations of these constructs, the ideas offered by the theorists included here allow for a more complex and comprehensive discussion of many communication constructs that are foundational to our discipline. All of the theorists included discuss social change and address questions of how change happens, the strategies available to promote change, and the consequences of changing patriarchal practices and constructs. As such, a third use of this reader is to explore feminist theories of social change via these readings.

As feminist rhetorical scholarship continues to flourish, adds to the rhetorical tradition, expands familiar constructs, and identifies new principles and practices, our work as scholars of communication continues to be enriched. We offer this reader in this spirit of enrichment and look forward to many lively discussions as we continue to explore rhetoric, theory, and feminism.

Notes

1. See, for example, Karlyn Kohrs Campbell, "The Rhetoric of Women's Liberation: An Oxymoron," *Quarterly Journal of Speech* 59 (1973): 74-86; Cheris Kramer, "Women's Speech: Separate but Unequal?" *Quarterly Journal of Speech* 60 (1974): 14; Robin Lakoff, *Language and Woman's Place* (New York: Harper Colophon, 1975); and Sally Miller Gearhart, "The Womanization of Rhetoric," *Women's Studies International Quarterly* 2 (1979): 195-201.
2. Carole Spitzack and Kathryn Carter, "Women in Communication Studies: A Typology for Revision," *Quarterly Journal of Speech* 73 (1987): 401-413.
3. For a detailed survey of these stages, see Karen A. Foss, Sonja K. Foss, and Cindy L. Griffin, *Feminist Rhetorical Theories* (Thousand Oaks, CA: Sage, 1999), pp. 17-32.
4. For an insightful discussion of the ways women's ideas are erased, see Dale Spender, *Women of Ideas and What Men Have Done to Them* (Boston: Pandora, 1988).
5. Foss, Foss, and Griffin, p. 7.
6. Foss, Foss, and Griffin, p. 8.
7. bell hooks, *Feminist Theory: From Margin to Center* (Boston: South End, 1984), p. 24.
8. bell hooks, *Teaching to Transgress: Education as the Practice of Freedom* (New York: Routledge, 1994), p. 65. See also our explanation of the criterion of accessibility in Foss, Foss, and Griffin, pp. 10-11.
9. hooks, 65.
10. Foss, Foss, and Griffin.

2

Introduction to Cheris Kramarae

Through her work in the areas of language, power, and technology, Cheris Kramarae develops communication theory that accurately reflects women's experiences. Born in 1938 in South Dakota, Kramarae earned a B.S. degree in journalism and English from South Dakota State University in 1959, an M.S. degree in journalism and English from Ohio University in 1963, and a Ph.D. in speech communication from the University of Illinois in 1975. Kramarae spent most of her academic career teaching in the Speech Communication Department at the University of Illinois.

The focus of Kramarae's work is the structure and use of language that results in the privileging of the perceptions, experiences, and modes of expression of men. As a result, language does not serve the needs of women and men equally, as Kramarae explains in an excerpt from "Women as a Muted Group," a chapter in *Women and Men Speaking*. In "Proprietors of Language," Kramarae attributes the persistence of inaccurate stereotypes of women's and men's speech to men's greater proprietorship of language.

Kramarae defines feminism as the practice of disrupting the linguistic and other structures that create a hostile environment for women. For her, such disruption takes the form of critiquing language and speech, creating new linguistic knowledge by attending to the communication of women, and inventing and using words and definitions that feature women's experiences. "Do We Really Want More Control of Technology?" in which Kramarae critiques the term *control*, is an example of such disruption. In "Feminist Theories of Communication," Kramarae explains various feminist theories of communication designed to intervene in linguistic structures. The result of such new theories at the intersection of language and gender, as Kramarae explains in "A Visiting Scholar," is the creation of new ways of theorizing and practicing communication that can produce a more humane and hospitable world for both women and men.

From McConnell-Ginet, *Women & Language in Literature & Society,* pp. 58-68. Copyright © 1980 by Praeger Publishers. Reproduced with permission of Greenwood Publishing Group, Inc., Westport, CT.

2.1

Proprietors of Language

Cheris Kramarae

Women's speech has been described as polite, emotional, enthusiastic, gossipy, talkative, uncertain, dull, and chatty; men's speech, in contrast, as capable, direct, rational, illustrating a sense of humor, unfeeling, strong (in tone and word choice), and blunt. In recent years a great deal of research has attempted to translate such general stereotypes into specific linguistic terms so that "objective" measurements can be made to determine the nature and degree of sex differences in phonology, word choice, intonation, and syntax. While some differences have been found by these means, no evidence has emerged for many of the differences hypothesized on the basis of such stereotypes.[1]

To begin to explain the labels and the beliefs about women's and men's speech, we need to explore women's and men's different relationship to the means of expression, language itself—their different access to, different control over, and different involvement with the English code. By and large men have controlled the norms of use; and this control, in turn, has shaped the language system available for use by both sexes and has influenced the judgments made about the speech of women and men. Men have largely determined what is labeled, have defined the ordering and classifying system, and have in most instances created the words which are catalogued in our dictionaries and which are the medium of everyday speech. Thomas Hardy's heroine in *Far From the Madding Crowd* observes that "it is difficult for a woman to define her feelings in language which is chiefly made by men to express theirs."[2] Women have often had to fit their needs for self-expression to the vocabulary and thus the value-system of the other, custodian group. This different relationship to the language means that even similar speech by women and men might be perceived as being different.

It is not, of course, that women have played no role in the development of language systems. As Patricia Nichols documents, women are sometimes in the vanguard of linguistic change. And, as the major sources of adult linguistic influence on young children, women have undoubtedly helped chart the course of many developments in language, although we still understand relatively little about this process. But in such public and self-conscious matters as the "legitimizing" of new words and meanings and establishing their general currency throughout the language community, it is men's influence that has predominated.

Women and men are believed and expected to have different behavior. "We *see* a man doing what we would ordinarily think of as feminine, sitting still, and manage to think of it as masculine because a man is doing it. Some people manage even to continue to think of men standing up when in fact they are sitting down," writes Mary Ellmann.[3] Similarly, what we hear will be affected by what we expect to hear, that is, what is "appropriate" for females and for males.

Language, its uses and powers, has been a foremost concern for feminists. In 1973 Mary Daly called attention to women's relationship to language.

> In a sexist world, symbol systems and conceptual apparatuses have been male creations. These do not reflect the experiences of women, but rather function to falsify our own self-images and experiences. . . . It is necessary to grasp the fundamental fact that women have had the power of naming stolen from us. We have not been free to name ourselves, the world, or god.[4]

Dale Spender thinks the power so basic that she writes of the Namer and the Named. Femininity, writes Spender, is not a symbol of women's making in the way that masculinity is a symbol of man's making.[5] Shirley Ardener, in fact, suggests that the gender division itself is basically of male construction, and that "physical differentiations (whether 'real' or 'socially perceived') are merely arbitrary markers which have been useful for setting up social oppositions."[6] Women's speech "exists" because men have labeled it.

A few men have mentioned the differing involvement women and men have with the organization of the language. For example, in 1922 the influential linguist Otto Jespersen wrote that "as a rule women are more conservative than men, and . . . they do nothing more than keep to the traditional language which they have learnt from their parents and hand on to their children, while innovations are due to the innovations of men."[7] Brian Foster in *The Changing English Language* deals at length with the way the British language has been influenced by American men: "In the mind of many a young Briton and his girl, American speech is the hall-mark of the tough guy and the he-man."[8] (Although Foster's book is almost entirely about male involvement in language change, he includes no explicit discussion of the exclusion of women.)

In his preface to *Dictionary of American Slang*, Stuart Flexner initially defines slang as "the body of words and expressions frequently used by or intelligible to a rather large portion of the general American public" although not considered good formal usage by most people. Slang is highly transitory, and it comprises at any given time about 10 percent of the words an average American knows. For Flexner, slang comes from the "imagination, self-confidence, and optimism of our people," and its creation and use represent Americans' intellectual, spiritual, and emotional restlessness and vitality. Thus, "by and large, the man who uses slang is a forceful, pleasing, acceptable personality." Furthermore, adds Flexner, "most American slang is created and used by males."[9] Many of the slang expressions become a part of standard usage in a continuous linguistic and social process from which women have been largely excluded. Women have been especially cautioned through at least 150 years of etiquette books to avoid the use of slang.[10]

Women are more likely to be isolated from each other or restricted to jobs which do not encourage or reward imagination, self-confidence, and optimism. Their homes, jobs, clothing, cars, and kitchen utensils are usually created and named by men. Or so it appears. It should be noted that one important factor here may be our scant documentation of women's actual contributions to material and linguistic culture. Inadequate histories of women's activities and relations to one another, coupled with prevalent assumptions of women's passivity and men's active creativity, may have obscured the real extent and nature of women's role in shaping our common heritage. Nonetheless, women and men do not have exactly the same heritage. The woman who would be a public speaker already violates norms, for there is "a trans-class prejudice against women as speakers at all." The limits to women's speaking rights seem to place women "in a special relation to language which becomes theirs as a consequence of being human, and at the same time not theirs as a consequence of being female."[11]

These restrictions are not, of course, new. In an essay first written in 1881—"Women and the Alphabet: Ought Women to Learn It?"—Thomas Higginson notes that women learn that it is proper for them to sing but indelicate to speak in public.[12] The stereotypes of "appropriate" verbal behavior for males and females are themselves restrictions on the idea that women could have something to contribute to the continuing creation of the English language. Certainly not all males are equally involved in the evolution of new words or in the setting of standards of usage. But, in general, it is men's and not women's interests, activities, and perceptions which have been recorded.

Evidence that the words and meanings of our general discussions are men's formations and more closely represent their and not women's experiences and perceptions comes from a variety of sources. In *Keywords*, Raymond Williams lists 155 words which he considers significant in formulating the way we see and discuss many of our "cultural experiences";[13] the first 12 entries suggest the types of concepts included—aesthetic, alienation, art, behavior, bourgeois, bureaucracy, capitalism, career, charity, city, civilization, and class. The publisher's book jacket presents Williams' work as showing "the complex interaction between the changed meanings of words, how these changes affect people's concepts and how people's concepts are once again changed by the changes." In his accounts of the evolution of certain words, Williams cites hundreds of people who were influential in forming, modifying, or redefining the meanings. Only a few of those hundreds mentioned are women; for instance, Jane Austen and Lady Bradshaugh are named under "Sensibility."

Williams' own preferences account for the material selected for his book, and his preferences may reflect a gender-biased interest. He also might very well have overlooked or underestimated women's influence in determining the formation and meaning of these and other "keywords." In any case, reviewers of Williams' book did not notice women's virtual absence and thus evidently found this representation of male dominance neither startling nor inaccurate.

Those who hold important positions in political and cultural institutions, from Washington, D.C., to Madison Avenue, have particular power to coin and to give wide circulation to new words or phrases.[14] Because they rarely occupy top positions, women are seldom involved in the promotion of new expressions which gain currency, yet women are nonetheless inevitably affected by new language. Many people have argued that our perception of social reality is shaped by our particular language; we will not see, hear, or think concepts except as our language allows. Whether or not language determines thought in any significant way, it seems plausible that language can at least *constrain* concept formation, and that gender-biased language may constrain the perception and expression of women, as well as men who do not conform to heterosexual male norms or are in other ways outside the "mainstream."

Women's experience when recorded has usually been recorded by men and through the medium of a language developed by men. About the resulting version of "reality," the women of the [British] feminist/philosophy writing collective ask:

> Is it possible that the language developed by one group in society within an oppressive relationship can simultaneously serve the purpose for the oppressed group?

> We would like to suggest that there is a problem both of concept formation within an existing male-constructed framework of thought and a problem of language use in developing and articulating an authentic understanding of the world and one's relationship to it.[15]

Betty Friedan in *The Feminine Mystique* talked of the problem, experienced by most housewives, which had no name; the lack of the name was, of course, one of the reasons the problem seemed so difficult to describe in 1963.[16] As Peter Berger and Thomas Luckmann write, "The subjective reality of something that is never talked about comes to be shaky."[17] It comes as no surprise then that feminists often suffer category confusion, "an inability to know how to classify things," for they suffer "a double ontological shock"—first the awareness that what is actually happening is quite different from what many others around them believe is happening, and second, their difficulty in categorizing what is really happening.[18]

Although there is little empirical study of how language helps us order our world, there is considerable reason to suppose that labels can help. First, having an "established" word means that there is no need for a personal narrative to explain the concept to others. Second, having a word legitimates the concept. Third, having a shared word helps establish a bond, a link with others for whom the concept is meaningful. An anecdotal illustration: one English woman described to a group of women a recurring frustrating experience. She and her husband both worked outside the home and would arrive home about the same time each evening. He would seldom do any kitchen work, saying, "I'd be glad to do it, but you do it so much better than I." She would go to the kitchen rather pleased at the compliment, but also rather upset and tired. She had some difficulty determining what was wrong, before eventually realizing that he was using flattery to keep her in her place. She said, "I need to be able to tell you—and to tell him—succinctly, in a word, what he is when he does this."[19] (A flatterpressor; or, more sonorously, *tyrannus adulatorius?*)

An essay by Jennifer Williams and Howard Giles suggests that Henri Tajfel's theory of intergroup behavior can be utilized to examine the *changing* relationship between women and men.[20] The Tajfel approach posits that our social identity, part of our self-concept, is derived from our knowledge of the social groups we belong to and the values we believe other groups hold. Tajfel is particularly interested in "inferior" groups—that is, groups which are negatively evaluated by many—and in the methods members of such groups employ to achieve a positive self-image.

Williams and Giles suggest that one strategy women are using today is to refuse to accept the negative definition of themselves that has been organized and perpetuated by men. Women concerned with language cull dictionaries, fiction, and conversations for the terms used to define women, in order to document the type and extent of the linguistic putdown of women.[21] While the old dictionaries remain a disturbingly accurate picture of the usage of many speakers, Ruth Todasco's introduction to an alternative dictionary, the *Feminist English Dictionary,* reminds us that "a general awareness of their sexism can weaken their authority," and thus promote the spread of ways of speaking that do not devalue women.[22] She argues that openly talking about words which have been men's property (for example, the many epithets for women) destroys some of their power.

In addition to pointing out and analyzing the manner in which women have been negatively defined by men, a number of women are also concerned to define themselves and their interests. Early in the contemporary women's liberation movement, many feminists began consciously developing a vocabulary to deal with their concerns. For example, a 1970 article in the *Long Island Press* lists 13 new expressions—including *sexist, male chauvinism, sexegration*—in use by feminists.[23]

Definition and redefinition have recently become the central concerns of many women who are investigating the interrelationships of people and their institutions from a variety of viewpoints. Mary Daly, feminist philosopher and theologian, writes that her book *Gyn/Ecology* is about "mind/spirit/body pollution inflicted through patriarchal myth and language" and about ways of creating new words and searching the rich etymology of old words such as *hag, harpy, crone, fury,* and *spinster*.[24] Similarly, in a panel discussion she spoke of the importance of overcoming "this inherited vocabulary of idiotology" in order to understand and break patriarchy. On the same panel, linguist Julia Penelope Stanley discussed the need to reclaim English in order to better serve women's purposes: "With language, I can claim aspects of myself that I've denied, express ideas that have been suppressed and tabooed for a long time . . . define my life as real, and I can act to change my life"; and poet Adrienne Rich talked about taboos, about what and where women, both black and white, have been forbidden to speak, and about women's recent "coming to language out of silence," naming themselves and their interests.[25]

As some recent research has shown, women in the past have been involved in at least some types of linguistic innovation.[26] We are now collecting the clues of such activity and building on our foremothers' language to create new modes of language use for ourselves. The impact this new writing and speaking will have is suggested by the interest which has been shown; *Gyn/Ecology* sold more than 10,000 copies in its first three weeks after publication.[27]

Additionally, women are not limiting their discussion to their own groups, but are asserting themselves in previously male-dominated spheres. They have pressured publishing companies into establishing guidelines for writers, suggesting new ways to avoid sexist terms. Feminists have published their own dictionaries challenging the views of language use codified by "standard" lexicographers. An entry in *A Woman's New World Dictionary* reads:

MAN. [Generic] 1. An absurd assumption still accepted by some that both sexes are included when the word "man" is used. 2. A mis-statement of fact. 3. An egotistical male distortion, legitimized in the language, that "man" could/should represent both sexes. 4. A false hope. See WO/MAN.[28]

That standard dictionaries do not give an accurate picture of the actual usage and interpretation of so-called "generic masculines" by either women or men is clear from such empirical research as that of Wendy Martyna. Feminist groups are publishing their own journals, financing their own presses, and making public recommendations about how labeling should be changed. For example, in a *New York Times* essay, Ethel Strainchamps suggests that, instead of discussing the alteration of the titles of women (for example, using *Ms.*), editors should, for once, consider that men might make an adjustment and begin to label themselves according to *their* marital history (perhaps *Master/Mister?*).[29]

Some women are also reconsidering and reevaluating structural and functional patterns of discourse. It has been argued that cooperation rather than competition is the prime pattern of communicative interaction within many women's groups.[30] Women's greater willingness to reach agreement and to avoid conflict has been traditionally evaluated as a weakness.[31] But today the "very 'male' pattern," that of vying with each other for individual attention, is being challenged, and the standards used by many men in evaluating both women and men are being forcefully questioned.[32]

As might be expected, women's challenges to male supremacy have brought strong reactions. The linguistic changes women advocate have, for example, often been redefined or put in a different context so that the meaning of the change is diminished or lost. For example, *chairperson* is used primarily to refer to females, while *chairman* is still used frequently to refer to males. So *chairperson*, proposed as a neutral term, has tended to become gender-specific.

Stanley argues that laughter is a strategy many men use to avoid considering viewpoints that are inimical to their interpretation of reality. Analysis at the intergroup level suggests that laughter and ridicule can also be a defensive response through which a dominant group seeks to protect its threatened social identity. Especially in the early 1970s many columnists and writers of letters to editors played with the feminists' complaints about the so-called generic *man* and *he* by writing essays in which *person* was substituted for each *man* resulting in strings of sentences like the following: "It was interesting to see how a group with obviously persongled egos were able to personipulate an organization the size of ours into looking like a pack of fools. 'Chairperson' indeed!"[33]

Women who write for the public eye risk being considered "deviant" almost as much as those who adopt the "masculine" public speaking role. At the very least, their writing is seldom judged by the same criteria as men's. As many feminist critics have noted, women writers are often split off from "writers" and reviewed separately, with their sex and their marital status often prime considerations in the evaluation of their books. For example, the (London) *Sunday Times* reviewer concludes his comments on Erica Jong's novel *How to Save Your Own Life*, "It is not so much a case of Women's Lib as Women's Glib," and continues:

> So it was that when I took up *The Golden Honeycomb* I suffered some misgivings to find it was by another woman author, Kamala Markandaya, but my uneasiness quickly vanished, for soon after I began the book I realized I was reading a novelist of rare quality. Her insights are not prejudiced by her gender; her art is to report the truth and life of things.[34]

One suspects that in her historical saga she is not advocating changes threatening to the male reviewer.

Women who implicitly or explicitly recommend change in the relationship between women and men are often accused of intellectual deviancy. They are said, for example, to be making "childish war" on language, or to write "from a very subjective point of view."[35] One man suggested to the editors of the *Feminist English Dictionary* that they include a male adviser to provide an "objective view."[36] The Macmillan Publishing Company guidelines for more egalitarian standards in the representation of females and males in children's stories have been described as "a willful exercise in intellectual dishonesty."[37] The British feminist publishing house, Virago, is accused of "contemplating social follies and injustices from an arbitrarily feminist point of view which makes its literature not only non-serious but, worse, humourless."[38]

As Jessica Bernard, and Dot Griffiths and Esther Saraga, have noted, the kinds, extent, conclusions, and explanations of research on gender differences vary depending upon what issues are politically and socially useful for the dominant group at any particular time.[39] Seventeen members of Harvard's linquistics department replied to students asking for a ban on the use of *man* and masculine pronouns to refer to all people: "The fact that the masculine is the unmarked gender in English (or that the feminine is unmarked in the language of the Tunica Indians) is simply a feature of grammar.... There is really no cause for anxiety or pronoun-envy on the part of those seeking such changes."[40] Stefan Kanfer in a *Time* essay entitled "Sispeak: A Msguided Attempt to Change Herstory" warns that the women's liberation movement has "a touching, almost mystical trust in words" and sees in the feminist attack on words "only another social crime—one against the means and the hope of communication."[41] John Condon questions with paternal concern the wisdom of the women who are talking about male bias in language:

> Sometimes blaming language habits is a rhetorically effective way to alert us to and dramatize a social problem. But also, sometimes attempting to change some conventional habits is not very effective in changing the attitudes and behavior which are at fault. We must be careful that our efforts are not misguided and wasted.[42]

When women take steps to change the language structure and their own uses of language, they are in fact acting to change their status in society; they are challenging the legitimacy of the dominant group. By calling the challengers and their proposals for language change silly, unnatural, irrational, and simplistic, the dominant group tries to reaffirm its threatened social identity.

To return to our initial question: given that popular stereotypes of women's and men's speech bear little direct relation to the actualities of women's and men's ways of speaking, how can we explain their persistence?

An understanding of the strategies employed by women concerned with language use and structure, and a look at the types of responses by their critics, provide a means of interpreting the perceptions people have of women's and men's speech. The long tradition of male control of language, determining both the symbols which are developed and the norms for usage for women and men, means that women's speech will not be evaluated the same way as men's speech. Our understanding of what women say, of what men say, depends in part upon our understanding of the limits to what women do/should/can say and what men do/should/can say. Women's speech is not like men's speech even when the same words and grammatical constructions are used.

Recognition of traditional restrictions on women as language users can help explain the finding by several investigators of different labels for similar behavior. In a study involving the same child, identified for some observers as a boy and for some a girl, John Condry and Sandra Condry report that the child's crying was labeled "anger" if the infant was thought to be a boy, and "fear" if the infant was thought to be a girl.[43] D. W. Addington found that the changes in the tone of voice of males affect the evaluation of their personalities differently than do similar changes in female voices.[44] Meredith Gall et al. found that for women verbal fluency is negatively evaluated while for men it is positively evaluated.[45]

In an essay appropriately entitled "Truth Is a Linguistic Question," Dwight Bolinger suggests that linguists and others should show more concern not only with the way language is used—and with questions of appropriateness—but also with the way language *is*—and with questions of the fitness of language to the perceptions of speakers. Bolinger further adds:

> Women are taught their place . . . by the implicit lies that language tells about them. Now you can argue that a term is not a proposition; therefore merely having the words does not constitute a lie about anybody. . . . People may be liars but words are not. This argument has a familiar ring. We hear it every time Congress tries to pass legislation restricting the possessions of guns. . . . [However,] lots of casualties, some crippling ones, result from merely having weapons around.[46]

He suggests that students of language consider not only the meaning of the parts—the individual words and sentences—occurring in discourse, but also the meaning of the whole, the language code from which we draw. Of course, in actual social settings, meaning will be negotiated to some extent by the participants. But women will not be equal participants or successful negotiators if the language code does not serve them equally. Dell Hymes begins a similar argument and suggests that women are "communicatively second-class citizens" because of the restrictions on what they may say, when and where they may say it, and what conceptions of themselves are presented in the English code.[47]

If successful, the feminist challenge to the myths of linguistic "propriety" will undermine the basis of any group's claim to "proprietorship" and thus will improve the chances for a class-free citizenry in the speech community.

Notes

1. The above issues are discussed in detail in *The Sociology of the Languages of American Women,* ed. Betty Lou Dubois and Isabel Crouch (San Antonio, Texas: Trinity University, 1976); Howard Giles, Philip M. Smith, and Jennifer A. Williams, "Women Speaking: The Voices of Perceived Androgyny and Feminism" (Paper presented at the International Conference on Sex-Role Stereotyping, at Cardiff, Wales, July 1977); Cheris Kramarae "Folklinguistics," *Psychology Today* 8 (June 1974): 82–85; Cheris Kramarae, "Stereotypes of Women's Speech: The Word from Cartoons," *Journal of Popular Culture* 8 (1974): 622–38; Cheris Kramarae, "Perceptions of Female and Male Speech," *Language and Speech* 20 (April–June 1977): 151–61; Cheris Kramarae, "Women's and Men's Rating of Their Own and Ideal Speech," *Communication Quarterly* 26 (Spring 1978): 2–11; William Labov, *The Social Stratification of English in*

New York City (Washington, D.C.: Center for Applied Linguistics, 1966); Robin Lakoff, "Language and Woman's Place," *Language in Society* 2 (1973): 45–79; Peter Trudgill, "Sex, Covert Prestige and Linguistic Change in the Urban British English of Norwich," *Language in Society* 1 (1972): 179–95.

2. One of the anonymous reviewers of this book drew attention to the Hardy quotation.
3. Mary Ellmann, *Thinking about Women* (New York: Harcourt Brace Jovanovich, 1968), p. 6.
4. Mary Daly, *Beyond God the Father: Towards a Philosophy of Women's Liberation* (Boston: Beacon Press, 1973), pp. 7–8.
5. Dale Spender, "The Namer and the Named," manuscript (University of London).
6. Shirley Ardener, "Introduction," *Perceiving Women*, ed. Shirley Ardener (London: Malaby Press, 1975), p. xviii.
7. Otto Jespersen, *Language: Its Nature, Development and Origin* (London: Allen & Unwin, 1922), p. 242.
8. Brian Foster, *The Changing English Language* (London: Macmillan, 1976), p. 14.
9. Stuart Flexner, "Preface," *Dictionary of American Slang*, eds. Harold Wentworth and Stuart Berg Flexner, 2nd supplemental ed. (New York: Thomas Y. Crowell, 1975), pp. vi, viii.
10. Cheris Kramarae, "Excessive Loquacity: Women's Speech as Represented in American Etiquette Books" (paper presented at the Speech Communication Association Summer Conference in Austin, Texas, July 1975).
11. Cora Kaplan, "Language Gender," *Papers on Patriarchy* (London: Women's Publishing Collective, 1976), pp. 28, 29.
12. Thomas Wentworth Higginson, *Woman and the Alphabet* (Boston and New York: Houghton Miffin, 1900; reprinted ed. New York: Arno Press, 1972), p. 33.
13. Raymond Williams, *Keywords: A Vocabulary of Culture and Society* (New York: Oxford University Press, 1976), p. 13.
14. See the collection of essays ed. Hugh Rank, *Language and Public Policy* (Urbana, Ill.: National Council of Teachers of English, 1974).
15. feminist/philosophy writing collective, "Cutting through Phallic Morality," manuscript (London), n.p.
16. Betty Friedan, *The Feminine Mystique* (New York: Norton, 1963).
17. Peter Berger and Thomas Luckmann, *The Social Construction of Reality* (Harmondsworth, Middlesex, England: Penquin, 1975), p. 173.
18. Sandra Lee Bartky, "Toward a Phenomenology of Feminist Consciousness," in *Feminism and Philosophy,* ed. Mary Vetterling-Braggin, Frederick Elliston, and Jane English (Totowa, N.J.: Littlefield, Adams, 1977), p. 29.
19. This narration took place during a language-and-gender study group meeting in London, May 1977.
20. Jennifer Williams and Howard Giles, "The Changing Status of Women in Society: An Intergroup Perspective," in *Studies in Intergroup Behavior,* ed. Henri Tajfel (London: Academic Press, 1978). See also Henri Tajfel, "Social Identity and Intergroup Behavior," *Social Sciences Information* 13 (1974): 65–93.
21. This is the technique used by, for example, the Bristol [England] Women's Liberation Group, "Definitions," *Enough* (n.d.), pp. 23–24; the editors of the *Feminist English Dictionary: An Intelligent Woman's Guide to Dirty Words* (Chicago: Loop Center YWCA, 1973); Alleen Pace Nilsen, "Sexism as Shown through the English Vocabulary," in *Sexism and Language,* ed. Alleen Pace Nilsen, Haig Bosmajian, H. Lee Gershuny, and Julia P. Stanley (Urbana, Ill.: National Council of Teachers of English, 1977); Julia P. Stanley, "Paradigmatic Woman: The Prostitute," *Papers in Language Variation*, ed. David L. Shores and Carol P. Hines (Birmingham: University of Alabama, Press, 1977): and Varda One, "Manglish," *Everywoman* 1 (31 July 1970).

22. Ruth Todasco, "Introduction," *Feminist English Dictionary,* p. iii.
23. Gay Pauley, "Women's Lib Lingo Replaces Girl Talk," *Long Island Press,* 21 November 1970, p. 8.
24. Mary Daly, *Gyn/Ecology* (Boston: Beacon Press, 1978), p. 9.
25. Mary Daly, in "The Transformation of Silence into Language and Action," *Sinister Wisdom,* 6 (Summer 1978): 9; Julia Penelope Stanley, p. 5; and other panel participants were Adrienne Rich, p. 21, Audre Lorde, and Judith McDaniel.
26. See the essay by Patricia Nichols in this volume.
27. Ann Marie Lipinski, "The Selling of Women Takes a Scholarly Twist in Publishing," *Chicago Tribune* (Lifestyle section), 21 January 1979, pp. 1, 4.
28. "A Woman's New World Dictionary," *A Paper of Joyful Noise for the Majority Sex* 2 (1973): 3.
29. Ethel Strainchamps, "Ethel Strainchamps Wrote This," *New York Times,* 4 October 1971, p. 39.
30. For example, Susan Kalčik, "'. . . Like Ann's gynecologist or the time I was almost raped': Personal Narratives in Women's Rap Groups," *Journal of American Folklore* 88 (January–March 1975): 3–11.
31. See Alice H. Eagly, "Sex Differences in Influenceability," *Psychological Bulletin* 85: (1978): 86–116, for a review of some of the literature on "persuasibility."
32. "A Continuation of the Story of the Collective That Has No Name," *Ain't I a Woman* 1 (30 October 1970): 9.
33. Edmund Shimberg, Letter in the *APA Monitor,* October 1971, p. 9.
34. Ronald Harwood, "Confessions of a Trans-Sexual Lover," [London] *Sunday Times,* 1 May 1977, p. 41.
35. Jacques Barzun, "A Few Words on a Few Words," *The Columbia Forum* (Summer 1974): 18; "Bookshelf" [review of Carolyn Faulder, Christine Jackson, and Mary Lewis, *The Women's Directory*], [London] *Sunday Times,* 3 October 1976, p. 43.
36. Reported by Alice Klement, "Sex Life of Words Spelled Out," manuscript filed at the Women's Collection, Northwestern University Library, Evanston, Illinois.
37. James J. Kilpatrick, "And Some Are More Equal than Others." *The American Sociologist* 2 (May 1976): 85.
38. "Virago Salvo," *New Society* (27 January 1977): 164.
39. Jessie Bernard, *Sex Differences: An Overview,* MSS Module 26 (n.p.: MSS Modular Publications, 1973), pp. 1–18; Dot Griffiths and Esther Saraga, "'. . . fundamentally suited to different social roles': Sex Differences in a Sexist Society," *Women, Biology and Ideology* (forthcoming).
40. Quoted in Casey Miller and Kate Swift, *Words and Women* (Garden City, N.Y.: Doubleday [Anchor], 1976), p. 76.
41. Stefan Kanfer, "Sispeak: A Misguided Attempt to Change Herstory," *Time,* 23 October 1972, p. 79.
42. John Condon, *Semantics and Communication,* 2nd ed. (New York: Macmillan, 1975), p. 68.
43. John Condry and Sandra Condry, "Sex Differences: A Study of the Eye of the Beholder," *Child Development* 47 (1976): 812–19.
44. D. W. Addington, "The Relationship of Selected Vocal Characteristics to Personality Perception," *Speech Monographs* 35 (1968): 492–503.
45. Meredith Gall, Amos Hobb, and Kenneth Craik, "Non-linguistic Factors in Oral Language Productivity," *Perceptual and Motor Skills* 29 (1969): 871–74.
46. Dwight Bolinger, "Truth Is a Linguistic Question," in *Language and Public Policy,* ed. Hugh Rank (Urbana, Ill.: National Council of Teachers of English, 1974), p. 164.
47. Dell Hymes, *Foundations in Sociolinguistics: An Ethnographic Approach* (Philadelphia: University of Pennsylvania Press, 1974), p. 205.

From Kramarae, C. "Women as a muted group," in *Women and Men Speaking: Frameworks for Analysis*. Copyright © 1981. Reprinted with permission.

2.2

Women as a Muted Group

Cheris Kramarae

Two women who began working together in 1966, the early days of the present women's movement, write, "We didn't have the words to describe what we believed in; Women's Liberation didn't exist. We called ourselves radical women, coming out of the experience of the civil rights and student movements.... At that time, *sexism* wasn't yet a word in the language, and we were trying to identify and figure out what to do with the problem that had no name, the so-called 'women's issue'" (Naomi Weisstein and Heather Booth, 1978:27).

The muted group theory provides the following explanation and expansion of their experience: The language of a particular culture does not serve all its speakers equally, for not all speakers contribute in an equal fashion to its formulation. Women (and members of other subordinate groups) are not as free or as able as men are to say what they wish, when and where they wish, because the words and the norms for their use have been formulated by the dominant group, men. So women cannot as easily or as directly articulate their experiences as men can. Women's perceptions differ from those of men because women's subordination means they experience life differently. However, the words and norms for speaking are not generated from or fitted to women's experiences. Women are thus "muted." Their talk is often not considered of much value by men—who are, or appear to be, deaf and blind to much of women's experiences. Words constantly ignored may eventually come to be unspoken and perhaps even unthought.

The muted group theory provides a way of conceptualizing and visualizing two types of structure: the underlying "template structures" of a group of people (the mesh of beliefs and categories that comprise their world view) and the "structure of realization" (the articulation of their world view). The underlying structures cannot be directly known; we can know them only by their reflections through language and other signs. Edwin Ardener (1975) states that groups that are on top of the social hierarchy determine to a great extent the dominant communication system of a society. Subordinate groups (such as children and women) are made "inarticulate" (pp. 21, 22).

A visual representation of the relationship women and men have to language (a modification of a diagram by E. Ardener [1975:26]) will make clearer how women, according to this theory, adapt their ideas and expressions in order to speak through the communicative modes of men.

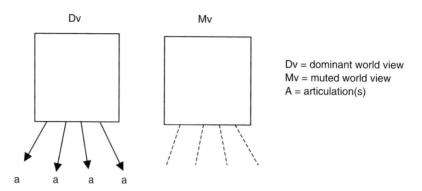

According to this theory, women are "inarticulate" because the language they use is derivative, having been developed largely out of male perception of reality. A system of division of labor between males and females means that the ingredients of everyday life will differ for women and men—and thus their perceptions will also differ. The public areas of life—and public discourse—in most societies appear to be controlled by males. The work, interests, and talk of women are not considered as important to men as men's own work, interests, and talk. Women do, of course, speak. However, in public discourse especially, "the appropriate language registers often seem to have been 'encoded' by males, [and thus] women may be at a disadvantage when wishing to express matters of peculiar concern to them." Unless their views are presented in a form acceptable to men, and to women brought up in the male idiom, they will not be given a proper hearing (S. Ardener, 1975:ix). The male system of perception, which is represented in the language used by both men and women, does not provide a good "fit" for the women's expression of their experiences. While individual men may have difficulty in expressing their model, there is presumed a close correspondence between the men's position in the society and the dominant model. Women are a "muted group" in that some of their perceptions cannot be stated, or at least not easily expressed, in the idiom of the dominant structure. To give a rather specialized example, but one that provides a clear instance of a misfit between the models of women and the idiom of the dominant structure: for nuns it becomes almost impossible to describe accurately one's "marriage" to Christ because the usual terms for marriage are inappropriate in the context (see Drid Williams, 1975 [in S. Ardener]).

Another example is offered by Hilary Callan (1978), who writes of the manner in which women are muted by a language structure that incorporates men's but not women's experience. She writes of language as a "conceptual toolbag" which contains terms such as dominance, hierarchy, status, control, and possession, which describe a traditional male authority pattern. The description of the organization of female groups in those terms often makes it easy to see female groups as incompetent, as poor imitations of the male groups. Callan writes of the problems nurses, for example, have in defining themselves. They have been defined by others as angels of mercy and as battle-axes, depending upon whether they are seen as accepting a supporting, nurturing role or whether they are seen as renouncing "femininity" (p. 211). The language imposes its structure on the way the nurses and the observers of nurses describe them, although that language code may not include terms that reflect interaction patterns of nurses or the important aspects of their own professional training or professional history.

The discussion of muted groups was initially inspired by a debate about the methods of social anthropologists (Edwin Ardener, 1973). The framework can be applied, Edwin Ardener argues, with equal validity to research about any groups in society, including all-male groups (e.g., blacks and whites; children and adults; working class and middle class), in which members of one group are in an asymmetrical power relationship with members of another contrasting group. The concept of mutedness is partly a means of conveying the manner in which boundaries of perception are defined by the experiences of the members of the groups, and the manner in which the dominant group engulfs the subordinate group and "blocks the power of actualization of the other" (E. Ardener, p. 25). Of course, not every member of a group will have the same perceptions as every other member; but common experiences will lead to some general, if sometimes not explicit, agreement as to what constitutes reality.[1]

Because the gender division is so basic to the organization of our society, because the assignment to a gender category is made at birth, usually for a lifetime, and because men are dominant in so many areas of public life, the discussion of the mutedness of women is of particular concern.

The basic assumptions of the muted group theory pertaining to the relationship of women and men appear to be:

1. Women perceive the world differently from men because of women's and men's different experiences and activities rooted in the division of labor.

2. Because of their political dominance, the men's system of perception is dominant, impeding the free expression of the women's alternative models of the world.

3. In order to participate in society women must transform their own models in terms of the received male system of expression.[2]

The proponents of the muted group theory hold that a language reflects a world view. They argue that over the years a dominant group may generate a communication system that supports its conception of the world and then call it *the* language of the society, while at the same time subjecting others to experiences that are not reflected in that language. Edwin Ardener writes: "The muted structures are 'there' but cannot be 'realized' in the language of the dominant structure" (p. 22).

Although the authors of the essays in *Perceiving Women* (S. Ardener, 1975) do not, except in very general terms, deal with the method by which the dominant/subordinate relationship between men and women was established and is perpetuated, I think their argument could reasonably be expanded along these lines: Society and its communication system are defined by men. The importance of the male/female division itself is likely a product of the male definition of the social structure. Some features of women's experience cannot be expressed or expressed easily within this social structure. The resulting relative "inarticulateness" of women presently aids in consigning them to positions of little freedom or power; women and their concerns continue to be of marginal importance in men's perception.

Below I list several hypotheses, concerning female and male expression, which I think are suggested by the muted theory.[3]

1. Females are more likely to have difficulty expressing themselves fluently within dominant (public) modes of expression.

2. Males have more difficulty than females in understanding what members of the other gender mean.

3. Females are likely to find ways to express themselves outside the dominant public modes of expression used by males in both their verbal conventions and their nonverbal behavior.

4. Females are more likely to state dissatisfaction with the dominant public modes of expression.

5. Women refusing to live by the ideas of social organizations held by the dominant group (example: women who are active in the modern Women's Liberation movement) will change dominant public modes of expression as they consciously and verbally reject those ideas.

6. Females are not as likely to coin the words that become widely recognized and used by both men and women.

7. Females' sense of humor—what relationships between persons, places, and things they consider incongruous—will differ from males' sense of humor.

The discussions below are designed to explore the evidence for the existence of different men's and women's world views.

Shirley Ardener and Edwin Ardener and the other authors of the essays in *Perceiving Women* (S. Ardener, 1975) (as well as others who have been involved in the women's anthropology group seminar at Oxford) are concerned with the value of this general theoretical approach for research in several cultures, including British. Their work provides valuable evidence for the usefulness of this approach as a tool for social anthropology work.[4] Here, my interests are more limited; I am primarily interested in what questions the theory raises and what explanations it may provide for the communication patterns among and between women and men in Great Britain and the United States.

In this chapter I consider the first, second, third, fourth, and fifth hypotheses above; and in the following two chapters I include material relevant to the sixth and seventh hypotheses.

Verbal Skills of Women and Men

That females will have more difficulty than males expressing themselves seems implicit in the muted group theory. Most of the information available on sex differences and verbal skills does not seem to support such an hypothesis. But experiences common to many women suggest an area of inarticulateness that has not yet received much research attention. Women are writing of their "silencing" because the tools of expression have been shaped by men. And men also often suffer, and cause others to suffer, from an inability or unwillingness to self-disclose, to discuss feelings, and to do interaction support work. References to these specific topics are found in a variety of sources, from academic journals to writings coming from men's consciousness-raising groups and from feminist periodicals.

Eleanor Emmons Maccoby and Carol Nagy Jacklin (1974) state that "female superiority on verbal tasks has been one of the more solidly established generalizations in the field of sex differences" (p. 75). Their generalizations are based almost entirely on data from studies of children and young adults. Girls are found to show more maturation in verbal abilities in the first years of life. Few differences have been found in the preschool to early adolescence years but at about age eleven females begin to outscore males at a wide variety of verbal skills—spelling, punctuation, vocabulary, fluency, comprehension of written tests including complex logical material, and various tests of verbal creativity (p. 84).

As always, the way the studies are set up makes a difference as to what results are found and how they are interpreted. The confidence with which generalizations can be made about the linguistic skills of very young children is in question, since studies of the past two decades in this area have been concerned with the linguistic skills of only a few, carefully selected groups (Maccoby and Jacklin, p. 77). Not much information on the linguistic skills of adults is available—at least not in academic linguistic studies.

Furthermore, the gender of the researcher appears to have had some bearing on study results regarding differences. At least in pre-1960s studies, research teams composed partly of males were more likely to find male superiority on various measures while teams of women were more likely to find female superiority. (Barrie Thorne and Nancy Henley, 1975: 286–287. See their annotated bibliography, and Henley, Thorne, and Kramarae, in preparation, for reports of studies of gender differences in some aspects of verbal ability.) So some caution is important in making generalizations. However, a comparison of study results now available reveals that when gender differences have been found among children and young adults, usually females have slightly higher test scores and are said to have "superior" overall linguistic abilities. Differences in phonology seem solidly established. Studies by Lewis Levine and Harry Crockett (1966), Roger Shuy, Walter Wolfram, and William Riley (1967), Wolfram (1969), William Labov (1972), Peter Trudgill (1975), Jenny Cheshire (1978), and Patricia Nichols (1978) show females are more likely to use "standard" or "higher prestige" pronunciations. (However, the particular conditions and work opportunities for the women and the men studied must be considered before such generalizations can be drawn for the people in any geographical area [Nichols, 1978]. Maryann Hartman [1976] has begun a study of the language use of Maine women and men over seventy years of age, a study that has found occupation an important factor.)

Multiple explanations have been offered: Girls' neurological systems are more mature at birth; they are more responsive to sounds and thus perhaps get a head start on language learning. Stuttering and reading disorders are more frequent among males; perhaps genetic factors enable girls to handle language more easily (Cinthia Lee Gannett Conrad, 1978). Girls are more social, and spend more time interacting with friends. (Maccoby and Jacklin [1974:349] call the latter statement "unfounded belief.") Roger Abrahams (1972) suggests that groups with relatively little power may learn to place a high value on verbal skills in order ro present themselves verbally in a way not to create offense. Perhaps women use what they perceive as "correct" speech in order to compensate for lack of status in other areas of their lives (Trudgill, 1975). Nancy Henley (1977) writes that underlings must be more circumspect, more correct, in following the rules of proper speaking than those people in dominant positions (pp. 84–86). Ronald K. S. Macaulay (1978) points out that test differences between males and females are usually slight; they have been, he writes, overemphasized and misinterpreted.

The muted group theory itself would not predict that adult females are more fluent. If females have to speak through a social system and a language structure which to a large extent overlook females or consider their interests subordinate to the interests of males, we could expect that females would be less fluent, perhaps particularly after puberty and through the teens when gender differences, social expectations for boys and girls, and relationships between boys and girls are given so much attention by the teens themselves (often with the encouragement of the media, teachers, and parents). Yet, as indicated, evidence of female linguistic superiority is strongest in studies concerning males and females eleven years and older. Perhaps females are *not* particularly handicapped by the dominant communication system. Perhaps females are forced to monitor their speech in a way boys are not, that is, to develop superior verbal facility and a consciousness that recognizes multiple perceptions and interpretations of the world. Perhaps care by, primarily, female teachers in the lower grades (as well as care by mothers at home) gives girls a chance to develop language skills within a structure that is supportive of girls' linguistic expression. Teachers are more likely to underestimate the abilities of boys in the early teens, especially boys from working-class homes, and to reprimand them more (Sara Delamont, 1976:57). The school systems in the United States and Great Britain may *expect* girls to develop better reading and writing skills (Dale Spender, 1979), to be correct in their writing and speaking; and that expectation might enable girls to have a positive approach to some aspects of language learning.

Studies of the brain organization for speech and writing skills indicate women, in general, might have a biological predisposition toward linguistic processing which uses both hemispheres of the brain—the left hemisphere with its linear, sequential, analytical, and externally focused mode of processing and the right with its holistic, gestaltist, imagistic, and inner-focused mode. Men's language processing appears more lateralized in the left hemisphere (Conrad, 1978; but for a countering argument see Anthony W. H. Buffery and Jeffrey A. Gray, 1972). Relatively slightly different predispositions at birth, perhaps strengthened by cultural experiences, might explain some of the perceived differences between females' writing and speech styles and males' styles.[5]

Although females, at least young females, appear to have an edge in many types of language skills, perhaps researchers have not looked at other salient characteristics of speech behavior. For example, we know little about the importance male and female school children place on their language. Perhaps males do not care as much about developing linguistic skills, at least within the school system. Perhaps what are considered important skills by the academic researchers are not considered to be important by the boys. Perhaps girls, who are evidently somewhat more sensitive to negative comments (Maccoby and Jacklin, 1974:158), are more concerned about performing in the "right" way ordained by the teachers. Perhaps we are too ready to equate "superior control of language" to the "appropriate language behavior of the classroom." Young black males put great value on verbal skills developed outside the school—skills that are not likely to be highly evaluated by teachers. Researchers have paid little attention, however, to the verbal skills of black or white *girls* outside the school.

As this discussion indicates, the muted group theory, as I have outlined it, offers little help in explaining the sex differences that have been found in "verbal ability" in the types of empirical studies completed in recent years. On the other hand, the empirical studies have worked with the language common to both genders; they do not consider the possibility implicit in the muted group theory that experiences peculiar to the subordinate group have not yet been encoded in a language. I have attended seminars (in Great Britain and in the United States) that had as the explicit topic for discussion the limitations of language for women. The women attending discussed shared experiences for which there are no labels, and lists were drawn up of the things, relationships, and experiences for which there are no labels. For example, one woman talked about a common occurrence in her life which needed a label. She and her husband, both working full-time outside the home, usually arrive home at about the same time. She would like him to share the dinner-making responsibilities but the job always falls upon her. Occasionally he says, "I would be glad to make dinner. But you do it so much better than I." She was pleased to receive this compliment but as she found herself in the kitchen each time she realized that he was using a verbal strategy for which she had no word and thus had more difficulty identifying and bringing to his awareness. She told the people at the seminar, "I had to tell you the whole story to explain to you how he was using flattery to keep me in my female place." She said she needed a word to define the strategy, or a word to define the person who uses the strategy, a word which would be commonly understood by both women and men. Then, when he tried that strategy she could explain her feelings by turning to him and saying, "You are _____," or "What you are doing is called _____."

Spender (1977), who organized one of the seminars, set out to collect perceived gaps in the language, experiences of women that need a name: A term for normal sexual power in women (a counterpart for *potent*); a term for *a woman* that connotes an individual, an autonomous human being rather than a qualifying term which calls attention to the woman/man division (Simone de Beauvoir [1964] writes that "woman represents only the negative . . . it is vexing to hear a man say: 'You think thus and so because you are a woman.' . . . It would be out of the question to reply: 'And you think the contrary because you are a man'; for it is understood that the fact of being a man is no peculiarity" [p. xv]); a word equivalent to *effeminate* for a woman with "manly" qualities; a word for a man who takes a woman's *No* to mean *Yes* and appears to think this is clever; a word for a woman who is not flattered by male propositions (the last example mentioned is by Julia Stanley, 1974); and a positive word to take the place of the phrase "not sexist." As I indicate in later sections, many women are now working to name themselves and their activities; and they are very conscious that this action is not traditionally women's action. Many of them speak of having been "silenced" by men who have been the definers of the worlds of both men and women. Their discussions indicate how language, the symbolic system, is closely tied to a patriarchal social structure.

Notes

1. A French anthropologist, Nicole-Claude Mathieu (1973 [trans. by D. M. Leonard Barker, 1978]), has taken issue with some aspects of E. Ardener's analysis and with

some of his assumptions about the relationship of women and men anthropologists. Her critique of the E. Ardener essay "Belief and the Problem of Women" and his reply (in S. Ardener, ed., 1975) to her critique will be valuable for anyone wishing to explore further the participation of women and of men in determining the focus and boundaries of the discipline of social anthropology.
2. Debate continues over the constraints a particular language places on its speakers' perception of the world. I use "constraints" rather than "determination" since most people writing today about the Humbolt-Whorf-Lee-Sapir hypothesis (which states that language determines the way we think) argue that although the concept/articulation capabilities of any particular language do influence what speakers of a language are able to "see" and to think about, people are able to perceive things outside their particular language.
3. Edwin Ardener and Shirley Ardener (conversation, 1977) warn that the underlying structures of women's and men's models of the world cannot be easily detected and that if they are elicited the difference between women's and men's models may be found to be quite small—although perhaps very important in male/female interaction. Further, they warn that talking about the theory as a way of listing and testing several hypotheses brings an element of reduction into the discussion of the theory. While, as they point out, the women/men relationship appears to be an extremely clear example of a relationship between dominant and subordinate groups, the muted group theory is designed to look at the relationship between all asymmetrical groups.
4. The study of woman by social anthropologists has continued with the publication of *Defining Females: The Nature of Women in Society*, edited by Shirley Ardener (1978). Some of the papers in that collection also make use of the theory that posits that there are dominant modes of expressions in any society (generated by dominant groups) which cause the "muting" of the subordinate groups. In that work, S. Ardener writes, "The 'mutedness' of one group may be regarded as the inverse of the 'deafness' of the dominant group, as the 'invisibility' of the former's achievements is an expression of the 'blindness' of the latter. Words which continually fall upon deaf ears may, of course, in the end become unspoken, or even unthought" (p. 20).
5. I am, however, very reluctant to suggest biological imperatives as answers to our questions about female/male differences in behavior. The possibilities, limitations, and dangers of a biosocial perspective (which at present is built on little solid data from either primates or humans) have been recently evaluated by many (including eight writers in *Signs: Journal of Women in Culture and Society*, 1979, 4 (4), 695-717). Rather than focusing on "innate differences" we might do well to listen to many women talk about their perceptions of the degree, costs, and types of asymmetry in our human relationships. Those perspectives have been largely missing in previous research on and discussions of women's and men's nature and behavior—research and discussions that too often in the past have been basically arguments for the status quo of the social structure.

Previously published in *CSWS Review*, 1988, pp. 13-16. Reprinted with permission.

2.3

A Visiting Scholar

How Feminism Has and Has Not Influenced My Field

Cheris Kramarae

Fifteen years ago I set out to write what I hoped would be a fairly comprehensive review of language and sex (as it was called then) research. I had checked new and old bibliographies, and used all the customary library reference sources. The material I found fit quickly and easily into an article of 25 typed pages. But I didn't know about the many relevant observations and studies of women in the nineteenth and early twentieth centuries. From my research review it appeared that feminists in the late 1960s and early 1970s were the first to see and hear language and communication norms as related to girls' and women's oppression. I didn't know!

I know a little more today. In every research field, women have had to rediscover the actions and influence of the work of those "disappointed" but very active women, since the standard current educational materials do not record it.

When I published my first review in 1974, I didn't know about all the feminist scholarship that *should* have influenced language studies, but *did not* because it was neither mentioned in textbooks nor cited in articles of the "experts." One of my current concerns is to refind the important feminist research that had no lasting influence on language and communication studies and work to have that material included in contemporary histories and perspectives.

Some of this work can be recovered by careful searches, some of it by chance encounters. For example, working in the library stacks one day 10 years ago, I pulled a dusty 1913 book off a shelf because the title looked interesting: *The Old-Fashioned Woman: Primitive Fancies About the Sex*. It contained a marvelous discussion of what the author, Elsie Clews Parsons, labeled "sex dialects." The topics she covered anticipated the work of sociolinguists in the 1970s, who began (for the first time we thought) to study the way language reflects and maintains the separation of females and males. The book's title springs from Parsons' belief that women were living by antiquated societal rules.

Parsons became a research project for me as I traced her through teaching positions, travels, publications (148 books, articles, and reviews) under her own name and more under pseudonyms. *Religious Chastity*, for example, was published under a male pseudonym, possibly to make more persuasive her enumeration of the ways religious practices reflect the general unbalanced social status of men and women.

At the time of her death in 1941, Parsons was president of the American Anthropological Association. Her 25 years of fieldwork among the Pueblo Indians and her publications based on that work brought her recognition from other anthropologists. I wonder if the praise given to her publications based on that fieldwork, writings still cited in anthropological studies, is the reason that her earlier work even survives on the library shelf.

Her earlier work was concerned with the importance of freeing people from societal constraints based on sex or racial division, age, or economic or political class. Critics and biographers immediately after her death described it as containing "patient, impersonal, drily ironic evidence," as being criticism done with a "generalizing approach," and as showing more concern with intellectual criticism of fundamental forms of modern ways of life than with factual accuracy. One critic praised her later work by saying that it showed she had learned "the difficulties of a purely intellectual attack upon catch phrases and meaningless symbols." This criticism is similar to modern criticism that is often directed toward those who write of their concern with the way the English language manhandles women or with the extent of the difference in the ways that women and men use words, and with the implications of the differences.

The topics Parsons mentions (for example, differential use of swearing, exclamations, and slang; and differential control of topics of conversation) are some of the very topics that have recently been "discovered," and made the focus of theoretical and empirical research. More than 70 years later, the same types of linguistic differences are being heard and discussed. Although in many respects social conditions have changed during those years, the ways in which women's speech is thought to differ from men's speech remain much the same. If Parsons' work had not been disregarded or disparaged by the "experts," sociolinguists could have moved on more quickly with our analyses.

Yet even now, seeing Parsons' work does provide us with insights. Her writings on language and sex illustrate the way that one's perspective and basic assumptions determine what is seen and heard. The linguist Otto Jespersen wrote in 1922 about some of the same topics in his chapter, "The Woman," that Parsons had covered earlier in her chapter, "Sex Dialects." But even as the titles indicate, while Jespersen treats women's speech separately, as an aberrant form of men's speech, Parsons discusses the two "dialects" as coexisting phenomena although recognizing that men do not hold women's speech in high favor. In her chapter, Parsons discusses the differential control of topics in North America, with men but not women talking shop, politics, and sports. In the same section she discusses the taboos of some tribes that prohibit speech between husband and wife for two months after marriage or which require women to address men using differing terms than those they use for each other. She thus questions the "logic" of our culture, in a manner that she must have hoped would be academic enough in tone to seem an acceptable, impersonal, presentation of data. However, the material and tone did not win her book a place in men's bibliographies, and thus until recently it was also lost to feminists.

Recent Changes in Communication Research and Practice

For all the inattention of malestream research to the feminist scholarship that *should* have influenced all communication work, we can still see that we all owe a great deal to early women's rights theorists and reformers working on language use and speaking rights. I will now mention just a few issues here that are not usually discussed in the communication text or theory books and articles in the field of communication. Opportunities are opening to women, but are still more likely to be open to white, middle-class women, than Black or Hispanic working-class women.

Access to some on-air broadcasting jobs. Broadcast officials for many years refused to consider women as possible candidates for broadcasting jobs.

Access to lecture halls. After a few women first gave public speeches in the early nineteenth century, many others also attempting to address women and men were denied the use of platforms in schoolhouses or civic halls as well as churches.

The right to retain their full birth name after marriage. The system of patronymic naming still has firm hold in this culture, though women are now legally allowed to keep their name. This does not mean, of course, that others will call us by our full birth names. In the first place, women in many settings and situations are called more often by their first name than are men. The confusion about what to call a woman, sometimes sincere but often an attempt to make sure we remain "other," leads to some strange address forms. Recently, assigned to a committee as the "I suppose we need a woman" representative, I heard the meeting called to order this way: "Cheris and Gentlemen."

Access to literacy and a literature of our own. The women's presses and women's studies divisions of large publishing companies still lead precarious lives, and their publications are not often distributed widely. However, a middle-class reader, at least, can find a wealth of feminist information, debates, and challenges. True, we must gather it quickly since it will likely be erased by "established" critics and ignored by most library and documentation centers. Still, at the moment, we even have feminist books available that chronicle *that* process (e.g., Dale Spender's *Women of Ideas and What Men Have Done to Them*).

Temporary and limited access to some lecterns at universities and in churches. These are still largely governed by men who can thus control the number of women allowed in.

Current feminist research on language and gender. The dozens of books and many hundreds of articles on this topic are read, discussed, and cited by activists, students, scholars, and others engaged in many other occupations (mostly women). This impact, however, is not what is usually meant by questions asking how much influence feminist work has had. What is usually meant is "How have men changed their thinking and research because of feminist work?" But the importance of feminist research to women should not be trivialized. One of the difficulties of seeing what impact women's work is having on academic disciplines is that if men pay mind to it, they are likely to co-opt the work without acknowledging it as feminist work. For example, feminists' concern and experimentation with, and theorizing about language have had an (usually unacknowledged) influence on the talking, writing, and thinking of many men.

Current Research in Language and Communication

Increasingly in or across all disciplines feminists are working with such questions as "What can we learn about the structure of power through studying diversity of language use?," "How are discourses altered as economic situations and institutions evolve?," "What changes are in order and possible for women who say that English is unsatisfactory for explaining their lives?," "How are our experiences shaped by the words and syntax available?," "What other codes can be or have been used for expression of anger and protest?" Increasingly, we are making it clear that language is not as simple as the traditional dictionaries have it. In fact, language is not as Webster has it at all!

In the past 15 years, feminists have effected changes in the vocabulary and structure of the language we use to talk about ourselves. But work such as *A Feminist Dictionary* does indicate the extensive redefining that has been going on among women of all social classes. Suzette Haden Elgin has published a grammar and dictionary of Láadan, a language constructed precisely to enable women to talk about chunks of their reality that previously had no names, and thus were difficult to accept as reality (e.g., *radíidin:* nonholiday, a time allegedly a holiday but actually so much a burden of work and preparations that it is a dreaded occasion . . . *A First Dictionary and Grammar of Láadan,* Box 1624, Madison, WI 53701-1624). While several women, including linguist Julia Penelope, have pointed out that the Láadan language at present is inadequate for talking about, for example, male violence or homosexual love, it is in conception a very important project that can illustrate problems in "our" English language and offer language possibilities. So studying language and gender has led to questions of dictionary formation, and language construction and change.

It has also led to close analysis of conversations. Feminist researchers have, for example, been very conscious of the conversational work done by women in many female-male conversations. In initial studies of white, middle-class speakers, women in conversations with men were more likely to follow up on the topics raised by men and to offer supportive "uh huhs" encouraging a speaker to continue. And women were more likely to be interrupted when they were talking. Jack Whalen, University of Oregon, and Marilyn Whalen, University of California at Santa Barbara, are doing close analysis of the conversations of girls and boys. These researchers are alert to the possibilities of similar interaction patterns. Dominance might be accomplished in other ways among boys and girls, or men and women, with different cultural heritage and economic backgrounds. The point is that feminists are encouraging the analysis of features of talk and relationships that were once considered uninteresting or incidental to language study. Much of their work has recently been on the constraints on talk between doctors and, especially, women patients, constraints which contribute to structuring doctor-patient power relationships. Elizabeth Holloway at the

University of Oregon is one of the researchers working on conversational analysis of the doctor-patient relationship, building on her earlier research in the counseling process.

How Feminism Has Affected My Research

While feminist theory has a sometimes presence (irritating or funny or dangerous) for many masculinist communication researchers, for me it has provided sensible approaches to experiencing and explaining the world, including the world of research. A linguist friend of mine told me she was glad that she received her last degree in the 1960s before she had heard much about feminism or had begun "thinking"; now she identifies herself as a feminist, lesbian, separatist linguist, and she thinks she would be unable to sit obediently through the courses and ideology required for anyone wishing to obtain a Ph.D. at most universities.

On the other hand, I returned to graduate work in 1972 *because* of the people and ideas of the feminist movement. Trying to provide a nourishing environment for a husband with a career and for two young children eager to grow up and out had many good moments, and teaching (as a "faculty wife") several sections of the same course on a yearly temporary basis gave me some income along with valued time with students. But blessed as I was, I was a "disappointed" woman who worried that 20 years later, if I was *lucky*, the children would have left home and I would still be teaching the same course over and over again. My advocacy of the practices and ideas of the feminist movement had encouraged two of my friends to go back to graduate programs. I joined them but I was still very fearful that, since no teacher had ever encouraged me to work for a Ph.D., perhaps I wasn't smart enough to manage taking graduate courses *and* teach full time. (I didn't dare give up my teaching job because I knew I might otherwise find myself with a Ph.D. but no job.)

I saved time and effort in one way. I entered all of the courses and began all of my term papers with attention to language—looking critically at the assumptions of the lecturer and assigned authors about the characteristics of women's and men's thought and talk, and assumptions about whose talk is worth studying and in what settings. My feminist critiques were continually at odds with the overwhelmingly male-oriented and male-decreed research questions and standards. But I was able to turn my dissatisfaction with the curriculum into critiques that gave me intellectual satisfaction, university credit, and eventually a degree and publications. I was fortunate to be in a program that allowed some credit for challenging critiques. At the same time, I remember too well the ridicule my feminism received, and I heard from a female faculty friend that several male professors regularly "gossiped and prattled" about what they called my "hysterical" ideas. It was not a particularly supportive atmosphere. There was no women's studies program at the university until after I received my Ph.D., but by giving myself linking assignments dealing with sexism, language, and the superstructure of our culture, I could find material of value in most graduate courses.

My colleagues continue to give me lessons about the content and functions of sexism. I try periodically—say at every twelfth instance—to provide them with mini-lessons also, by pointing out their outrageous sexist, racist, and homophobic remarks and "humor." Once, hearing yet another Jessica Hahn joke at an official administrative meeting, I remarked on the sexism a colleague was expressing. His response was,

"Lighten up, Cheris. We aren't all as interested as you are in constantly talking about sex differences and in making everything into some sex-division problem." I realized at the moment of his paternalistic comment that while I thought I was calling attention to the pervasiveness of men's sexualizing and trivializing women (by just occasionally pointing out a few of the ways men portray women's words and other activities as different, sexual, and silly), he and many others might really think that I was, by such an act, increasing the division. *I* already felt the effects of the division, of course. But until I spoke, *he* didn't. So if I spoke and made him uncomfortable by asking him to reconsider his actions as discriminatory, the question still remains, which of us was *really* the problem?

So my colleagues continue to educate me and provide me with unintended research questions and analytic approaches. I began my research with what I thought was a single research thread—language use. But the thread soon became a tangle as I discovered that following it led to work done and issues raised by community activists and by researchers in literature, sociology, linguistics, social psychology, and anthropology.

The Future Influence of Feminist Scholarship on Language and Communication

Because of bold feminist analysis, we are ready now to stop using *sex* or *gender* as a term to describe a distinct, unchanging social and personal characteristic of a person and to begin using *gender* as a term to describe an inequity and hierarchy that also interacts in the construction of race, age, and class divisions. The use of these as seemingly separate *variables* (which are added on, or not, in any particular communication study) obscures rather than reveals relationships. We need, rather, to look at the connections—at, for example, the ways that a gender hierarchy is deeply embedded in race, class, age, and sexual orientation divisions and inequities. Gender then, appears as a political and thus possibly temporary division. When we study gender issues from this perspective, we will be better able to see the connections and divisions among women, whether white or Black or Third World. We can then better see whose purpose the political polarities (male-female, white-of color, West-East) serve.

Why, for example, are the verbal "games" played by young Black males often based on who can say the most demeaning, outrageous things about the other's mother? Why do so many people ridicule gay men in terms also used to describe and ridicule women? We need to study the many ways dominant groups use genderizing terms to organize and divide people into subordinate groups. Traditional communication studies are built on the assumption that separate variables can be usefully studied, say, two or three at a time. Feminist theory can be used as the basis of an argument that class, age, race, sexual orientation, and gender are not autonomous academic categories but essentially interrelated political hierarchies.

Lucy Stone said that she had been a disappointed woman most of her life. She was at the same time an optimistic woman who worked in many ways to change the conditions of women's lives. A feminist in communication studies is still thought, as was Lucy Stone, to have a wild tongue; we are still heavily censored. But we are still introducing our world views, describing our relationships, and providing ways of addressing the dominant society's perception of difference and antagonism.

Suggested Readings

Elgin, Suzette Haden. *Native Tongue.* New York: DAW. 1984.

Kramarae, Cheris, and Paula Treichler, with assistance of Ann Russo. *A Feminist Dictionary.* Boston and London: Pandora Press. 1985.

Spender, Dale. *Women of Ideas and What Men Have Done to Them: From Aphra Behn to Adrienne Rich.* London: Routledge & Kegan Paul. 1982.

Thorne, Barrie, Cheris Kramarae, and Nancy Henley, eds., *Language, Gender and Society.* Rowley, Massachusetts: Newbury House. 1983.

West, Candace. *Routine Complications: Trouble with Talk Between Doctors and Patients.* Bloomington: Indiana University Press. 1984.

In 1855, Lucy Stone insisted on keeping her own name after marriage, challenging the laws and conventions that made husband and wife one, and that one the husband. Her action helped encourage others—including Jane Grant—to challenge the naming restrictions. Grant, who founded the Lucy Stone League, also envisioned a fund for the study of women and their accomplishments. After her death, her husband, William Harris, arranged for her money to be used in supporting what is now called the Center for the Study of Women in Society at the University of Oregon, which promises to continue supporting "disappointed" and resourceful, courageous, and accomplishing women.

Previously published in Maramatsu, Y. U. (Ed.), *The Proceedings of the 1988 Tokyo Symposium on Women*, 1989. Reprinted with permission.

2.4

Do We Really Want More Control of Technology?

Cheris Kramarae

At first glance and hearing, and even second, the answer to the question "Do women really want more control of technological processes?" seems a clear yes. Many women have used analyses and direct actions to argue that if women are to reach their various goals they need much better access and control to many new technologies, especially the new communications technologies. While we have become increasingly skeptical of promises that technology will *fix* the many forms of inequalities women experience, we have at the same time been increasingly interested in the possibilities of supportive interaction, including the sharing of information, that will be available if we can have much greater access to, and can dictate the uses of, communications technology. We would seem to need more control and use of communication technology just to ensure that the current inequality of women and men does not become greater.

But in order to be emphatic about saying yes, that what we most need is to own and run our own bits and bytes, we should be sure that we have specified the nature of the problem we face, and our long term goals.

I begin with attention to several areas where feminists[1] have called for social adjustment of technological change, in order to repair damages done to women through oversight and plan. Then I will try to extend and critique those analyses and actions, by suggesting a relocation of theory and practice. Listening to the words and watching the programs of ecofeminists, *I want to suggest that our new efforts focus more on relationships of people and earth, rather than on control of nature through technological processes.*

This may seem a sweeping, idealistic statement of little value to us here today. Certainly, there are important impediments to our even considering a major change in the way we think and talk about women, communication and technology. Most events, policies and theories around us restrict our being able to easily think in this more holistic way about technology. (For example, there are many unexamined assumptions not only about technology but also about our relationship to each other and the rest of the earth.) In addition, I think we all believe that we need to work quickly to solve immediate problems involving the lives of isolated or exploited women and men, especially in the Third World (including those in the so-called "developing" countries). However, I also think that we can look at our past research and see that feminist analysis has already been moving toward a recognition of the bonds we all have with each other and the rest of the earth and recognition of the life-destroying problems that have been created by a focus on *control*. We have recognized that many of the problems women have with communication processes arise from our acceptance of the tactics of controlling globe-trotting multinationals, including military organizations. The solutions to these problems also need to be global.

Around the world, women have had a variety of proposed and active projects involving communication technology. I will review a few of these contemporary projects before suggesting new questions and approaches.

Important (but perhaps too limiting) Projects Which Stress Control and Access

1. Organizations for Satellite Communication. Many women are convinced that satellite communication is vital for women's communication of the future, and are determined that women and their projects will be included in the funding and planning of satellite communication. For example, The Women's Task Force for Satellite Communication, associated with the [U.S.] Women's Institute for Freedom of the Press, states:

> It is [our position] that progress for women is—and has always been throughout history—directly correlated with our ability to reach each other and the public with our information. If satellites are the communication system of the future, as the printed press was the communication system at the time the U.S. Constitution was written, then our Constitutional right to "freedom of the press" should assure us equal opportunity to communicate through this modern 'press'—that is, with government protection of our right, not government abridgement of it. (*Media Report to Women*, July 1, 1978, 6; also see Women's Institute for Freedom of the Press, 1979)

I give this as an example of the increasing number of declarations of women's right to communicate. Here it is the right to communication via satellite communication, but this declaration is related to other discussions of the "right to communication."

2. Organizations Working for More Access to Electronic Communication Technology. Many women in the "First World" and the "Third World" (I stress the quotation marks around these words) discuss the importance to women of *access* to all new electronic communication technologies. Otherwise, the argument goes, women will have to exchange messages delivered by foot and use old manual typewriters and retype mailing lists and use ancient mimeograph machines while men are using photocopying machines and zipping their messages around via the use of secretaries and long distance telephone, fax machines, electronic mail, videotex systems and

computers. If we are left with only the machinery which men reject as too slow and out of date, we are then left with the prospect of much repetitive, time consuming work. So some women's groups are working to help women maintain large networks and learn how various technological innovations can be used. For example, in the U.S. the National Women's Mailing List is a non-profit project of the Women's Information Exchange, dedicated to providing information on technology for use in networking and resource sharing among women.

These organizations and actions to help women keep up with new equipment and processes are certainly beneficial. But our concern with *control* and *access* directs our attention away from other important considerations. I mention several here.

A first suggestion: We can reconsider what types of connections we wish for women. Women working with communication and technology issues have placed a lot of stress on ways to improve communication among women around the world by increasing our ability to quickly and inexpensively contact each other and our research centers and libraries. Certainly we are in general agreement that if women are to help each other we have to be able to hear each other. However, we should not at the same time ignore the kinds of relationships women throughout the world already have. I am typing this on a computer, parts of which were assembled in other countries, most likely by women. Communication technology "progress" is built on the lives of women working as "factory girls" in assembly lines, at very low pay in bad conditions. The equipment they work on will be sold for the benefit of people, mostly in other countries, for the profit of corporate men.

For example, the many thousands of women working in electronic plants in Mexico are regularly exposed to toxic chemicals. One plant manager in Ciudad Juarez explained that the women's health and safety concerns are not important issues: "We don't worry too much about these matters; these girls don't stay on the job long enough to get sick." Of course, many of the women are required to sign temporary work contracts, without social security or health benefits or the possibility of acquiring seniority and increased salaries. The employers often require that new employees have perfect vision—but most of the women soon need glasses and many develop chronic conjunctivitis and other eye problems (Fuentes and Ehrenreich 1984, 31). These women are producing equipment which can provide ease of communication for some other more privileged women in other places, but the equipment is seldom used to expose and communicate information about the ways the equipment is being manufactured at women's expense. What men call technological progress often turns out to be more exploitation of "Third World" workers, women in particular.

Aiding information exchange among "Third World" and "First World" activists could be an important strategy for change in women's lives (see discussion in Fuentes and Ehrenreich)—and does not necessarily require use of the latest electronic communication devices. As we continue to talk about the importance of setting up women's networks we need to talk about what function the networks will serve. Will we deal with what "technological progress" is doing to women? To do this we need to listen to what information is already available from "Third World" women in the U.S. and elsewhere. Black women and women of color, as Audre Lorde points out, "operate in the teeth of a system for which racism and sexism are primary, established, and necessary props of profit" (1984, 129).

A second suggestion: We can take a closer look at and make a reevaluation of the technological aids women are already using to communicate with each other in many situations in many places. The new technological devices may not be the best for our needs. We have been very creative and often very effective in using "primitive" methods of communicating. For example, women working for National Broadcasting Corporation, a major U.S. broadcasting company, have used messages on washroom mirrors as well as more conventional methods of sending information (reported in *Media Report to Women* March, 1978, 4). In other places women have organized music festivals (and Batya Weinbaum [1987] writes of the disruptive, creative, transformative political action of these festivals). Others have used wall newspapers, mimeographed leaflets, loudspeakers, tape recorders, puppet shows. Others have used itinerant information vans, street theatre—not high tech, but sometimes very effective methods of communicating (especially for the half billion women unable to read and write). Women who are frustrated with what is being said by individuals and groups using these low tech forms can more easily form spin-off groups than they could if all the focus is put on talking about satellite networks and high tech equipment.

A third suggestion: Perhaps most important of all, we can benefit from a critique of the language we are using to discuss communication and technology issues. We talk a lot about *rights*—for example, discussions of equal access rights to communication technological equipment, and processes, and discussions of equal right to communicate. Discussions about equal rights to communicate are heard increasingly as women extend the traditional listing of "human rights" to include and stress the importance of communication. Talking about and working to establish each person's "right to communicate" as a basic human right would seem to be powerful conception and goal for women (see discussions in Finlay [1987] and Unesco [1980]). Yet, as some women working with an ecofeminist approach suggest, the language of "rights" is problematic, because such discussions are based on a concept of *individual* human rights, obscuring the webs of connection that makes continued existence on this earth possible (Diamond and Quinby 1988, 194). This language of individual *rights* comes from a masculinist ideology and vision of *control*, not a feminist ideology and vision of *interconnectedness*.

In sum, we need to rethink what we mean and want when we talk about *control*. At times, malestream communication "experts" would seem to use words and terms that sound promising to us. They at times use words that would seem to involve our thinking and our lives—*exploitation, free and balanced flow of information, participatory democracy, user-oriented communication models,* and so on. But if we look closely, we note that information about women's activities and goals have still not been integrated into their communication research. And we note that the malestream discussions about communication focus still focus on *control* rather than on *community*.

Women do not, of course, have a single, shared vision of what we wish for the world. But most of us agree on the need to provide new voices, values, and visions into traditional discussions of communication and technology. I do not suggest that we stop talking about *control*. In fact, I suggest we talk *more* about control, analyzing how it has come to be such a central issue and how it has shaped our discussions and our lives. And then we will be better prepared to talk about alternatives.

Note

1. I realize that "feminist" and "feminists" do not have the same meaning to all women in all communities. I use it here to describe the women and the activities which challenge the exploitation of women. (See discussion in Cheris Kramarae and Paula Treichler, with assistance of Ann Russo, 1985.)

Bibliography

Diamond, Irene, and Lee Quinby. 1988. American Feminism and the Language of Control. In Irene Diamond and Lee Quinby, eds. *Feminism & Foucault: Reflection on Resistance.* Boston: Northeastern University Press, 193–206.

Finlay, Marike. 1987. *Powermatics: A Discursive Critique of New Communications Technology.* London and New York: Routledge & Kegan Paul.

Fuentes, Annette, and Barbara Ehrenreich. 1984. *Women in the Global Factory.* Boston: South End Press.

Kramarae, Cheris, ed. 1988. *Technology and Women's Voices: Keeping in Touch.* London and New York: Routledge & Kegan Paul.

Kramarae, Cheris, and Paula Treichler, with assistance of Ann Russo. *A Feminist Dictionary.* London: Routledge/Pandora Press.

Lorde, Audre. 1984. *Sister Outsider: Essays and Speeches.* Trumansburg, N.Y.: The Crossing Press.

Machung, Anne. 1988. "Who Needs a Personality to Talk to a Machine?": Communication in the Automated Office. In Cheris Kramarae, ed., 62–81.

Turkle, Sherry. 1988. Computational Reticence: Why Women Fear the Intimate Machine. In Cheris Kramarae, ed., 41–61.

Unesco. 1980. *Many Voices, One World: Towards a More Just and More Efficient World Information and Communication Order.* London: Kegan Page.

Weinbaum, Batya. 1987. Music, Dance, and Song: Women's Cultural Resistance in Making Their Own Music. *Heresies* 22, 18–21.

Women's Institute for Freedom of the Press. 1979. The first annual conference on planning a national and international communications system for women, April 7–8, National Press Club: A Report. Women's Institute for Freedom of the Press, 3306 Ross Place, N. W., Washington, DC 20008.

From *International Encyclopedia of Communications, 4 Volumes,* edited by Erik Barnouw, copyright © 1989 by the Trustees of the University of Pennsylvania. Used by permission of Oxford University Press, Inc.

2.5

Feminist Theories of Communication

Cheris Kramarae

Feminist communication theory is nurtured and critiqued by feminist theory as it has developed in the large intercultural and international feminist movements. The histories, questions, analytical tools, and boundaries of feminist communication theory are reviewed, revised, reinterpreted, and written in ways that are themselves challenges to traditional communication theory. Although there is no general agreement about the categories of feminist communication study and theory (or even about the need for agreement), some topics are common to many of the analyses.

Feminist theory. Feminists consider most theories of communication inadequate, misleading, and dangerous because they distort women's experiences, ideas, and concerns. One problem is with what has traditionally been labeled theory. Australian feminist theorist Dale Spender argues that in a society in which men have named only themselves as theorists their theories have often been used to mystify, intimidate, and oppress others while justifying the status quo. Male theorizing has too often been used to construct divisions between those "who know" and those who don't. Spender points out that much theorizing is based on the honoring of great men: entire systems of books, courses, and dialectics have been erected around individual men whose names are used to label theoretical frameworks. In communication research there is, for example, Marxist theory, Foucauldian theory, McLuhanism, and Lacanian theory. It is no accident that there is no (Mary) Dalyist theory, no (Julia) Penelopeian theory, no (Suzette) Elginist theory, no (Adrienne) Richist theory, no (Monique) Wittigian theory—even though these theorists have written extensively about communications issues, bringing together and expanding our knowledge of language and interaction and suggesting new problems, methodologies, and interpretations. To validate this work by labeling the theories with women's names would acknowledge that these women are experts and have created serious, impressive, contending theories. For feminists, even though recognizing the need to discover and rediscover the women whose names and intellectual work have been distorted, appropriated, or elided by men's histories, the problems with associating theories with individual names are complex. U.S. scholar Nancy Hartsock and others argue that theory is not the activity of a few but the articulation, open to all, of our practical, knowing activities; theory can be considered as making conscious the philosophy embedded in our lives—"theory in the flesh." Feminism itself is not a theory, a set of hypotheses, an institution, or a collection of principles; it is a movement, a renouncement of obedience to the systems erected by men, a search for answers to new questions, a collective process.

Thus feminists recognize that there is not a single human way of understanding interactions. U.S. philosopher Sandra Harding is joined by others in suggesting that innovative theorists welcome a plurality of perspectives to encourage the instability of analytical categories and to encourage the use of these instabilities as resources for thinking and action. Harding points out that this approach to theorizing incorporates what some believe to be a distinctive emphasis that many women put on contextual thinking and decision making, a focus on the importance and usefulness of talk, connectedness, and relationships. Such a perspective is exemplified by U.S. psychologist Carol Gilligan's *In a Different Voice* (1982), an influential and controversial study positing the existence of a distinctively female process of moral development based on intimacy and caring rather than on the more abstract principles of fairness or justice often characterizing male moral decisions.

Silencing of women. Many studies have uncovered the ways in which women's discourse is subject to male control and censorship. For example, research conducted in the United States and elsewhere shows that in male-female gatherings men talk more and interrupt more than women. It is telling that men's talkativeness and interruptive tendencies are not among men's stereotypes about male interaction.

Formal educational structures and possibilities differ for women and men, leading to the stifling of women's creative reading, writing, and speaking. U.S. writer Alice Walker asks, "What did it mean for a Black woman to be an artist in our grandmothers' time?"—that is, an artist given no training in reading or writing, no books or other resources. UNESCO figures report that the gap between male and female literacy is growing in many societies. In some countries when women are permitted to go to universities they are segregated from male students and often are not allowed to participate in discussion. Women often are not permitted to study abroad. In many countries—for example, even in Japan, where the literacy rate is close to 100 percent—women have been excluded from many literary jobs and honors and are encouraged to express their subordination through "feminine" words, voice, and syntax. In all formal education what is taught is men's knowledge; the silencing of active, theorizing women takes place in almost all educational formats. U.S. theorist Berenice Carroll notes that men apply gender-specific terms to evaluate men's and women's intellectual achievements. Terms such as *original, innovative, first rank,* and *excellent* are used to exclude women, whose intellectual contributions are called derivative, unoriginal, popular.

Women are also silenced or threatened by the application of deviancy labels. Spender documents that women, particularly knowledgeable, witty women, who question or rebel against patriarchy are called aberrations, unnatural, unattractive, unsexed, unnaturally sexed, and man-haters. Women writing in the Indian journal

Manushi, for example, frequently analyze the ways in which the labeling of women makes it very costly, in terms of reputation and economic sanctions, for women to speak out on social issues. Such analysis often concerns how assessments of a woman's behavior are based on the relations she is believed to have with men and on the deviation of her behavior from the ideal of the loyal, obedient wife.

The ultimate exercise of personal and political power is through violence. Although this has long been an issue for feminists concerned with the victimization of women through rape and domestic abuse, some theorists have begun to acknowledge that the threat of male violence, implicit and explicit, restricts women's activities in every sphere and thus underlies all aspects of human communication.

Heteropatriarchal semantics. U.S. theorist Julia Penelope and others have explored the ways in which language itself is a conceptual frame governing how and what we think. In a heteropatriarchal society such as the United States, for example, heterosexuality and male dominance are assumed to be natural and "male" and "female" to be natural, eternal categories rather than the expression of concepts essential to the maintenance of the heteropatriarchy. Similarly, French novelist Monique Wittig asserts that the fact of oppression created the categories rather than vice versa. Masculine/feminine and male/female are language categories concealing the social and political differences between men and women. A materialist feminist approach argues that although race and sex are seen as the cause or origin of oppression, they are actually the sign or mark imposed by the oppressor. Sex, race, and class are not individual characteristics but in many countries constitute the conceptual terminology supporting a white, middle-class, male elite. The categories are thus closely related in function. A major feminist contribution to social scientific theory has been the replacement of *sex* by the terms *gender* or *sex/gender system,* reflecting the fact that such categories are culturally and not biologically determined. Most feminist theorists focus on gender differences in order to draw attention to how that divisive system is socially constructed and maintained.

Feminist communication theorists consider language problematic in a way that much mainstream communication theory does not. Traditional Marxism, for example, assumes the relation "women/men" to be a natural one, outside the social order; in much Marxist theorizing women are assigned to classes of men, bourgeoisie or proletariat, an assumption that hides the class conflict between men and women. Instead of viewing language primarily as a tool for the transmission of information, the feminist approach treats language as a basically man-made construction that constricts the ways we can make meaning. In feminist linguistic work, for example, dictionaries are studied as representative of male symbol systems and prejudices. Many feminists are engaged in recovering and inventing ways of defining, speaking, and writing female experiences and perceptions.

Writing the body. This expression is most frequently associated with some French feminists who argue in part that women need to learn to write from their bodies, their pleasures, and their experiences. A major focus is again on silences, on the absence of women's voices caused by the overpowering voices of masculinity in the structure and use of language. Rather than focusing on, for example, the documentation of a past in which women have been vocal or arguing that speech differences are grounded in sex, race, or class differences (which some French feminists find to be inadequate and traditionally North American problem-solving approaches), writers such as Hélène Cixous suggest that we write a feminine language with "mother's milk" or "the blood's language." That is, women can begin with the immediate specificity of their bodies and their psychosexuality to create a new reality.

Other feminists have criticized this particular psychoanalytical perspective for being ahistorical, ignoring or paying little attention to differences established by race and class, and overlooking the social/political institutions that support the oppression of women. Other, multilingual feminists question the existence of a single language of the body because women think and speak in different ways about their bodies depending on the categories and relationships available in various languages.

Some believe a more useful approach than neo-Freudian psychoanalytic theories is emerging in the writings of feminists who describe their multiple, shifting, often seemingly self-contradictory identities. Objecting to the ready labels often applied to them (e.g., "white," "middle class," "black," or "Hispanic"), these women claim for themselves others as well, such as "intellectual," "feminist," and "anti-imperialist." They also question the assumption that there exist, for our theorizing of language and communication, separate homes within feminism based on the imposed divisions among racial, ethnic, religious, sexual, or national identities. Used separately these labels too often leave unchallenged such polar concepts as East/West or white/nonwhite, which themselves leave unchallenged the idea that communication theory based on analyses of the situation of women in the West can be adequate for the West when they do not deal with the hierarchical East/West divide. Similarly, others point to how such concepts as "capitalism" and "Christianity" construct many of the analytical terms in communication theory.

Technologies. Feminist scholars have been very interested in the differing consequences of technologies for the construction and employment of males and females. One research area concerns the methods that are used to speak and write to others: who may or must interact with whom and how. Some feminist theorists have given explanations and implications of women's exclusions from the social histories of the technological processes involved in communication—printing, radio, television, and so on. A related area of research presents the evidence that technological processes, developed and analyzed primarily by men, have had profound and largely unexplored consequences for women's communication. The resources available to women structure the time, place, and content of their interactions.

The media as industry. Feminist criticism of the media has a long history. In the United States in 1870 Susan B. Anthony and Elizabeth Cady Stanton were conscious of how very different the structure and policies of their weekly newspaper, *The Revolution*, were from those of most newspapers. Anthony and Stanton wanted to publish primarily women's words because "masculine ideas have ruled the race for 6,000 years," and they insisted that women's words appear under their own names. In the late twentieth century the establishment and expansion, primarily in Europe and North America, of women's periodicals, publishing collectives, press networks, and professional organizations have been part of an unprecedented effort to provide women with access to information sources and networks. Despite such attempts, however, media industries remain largely under male control, and women remain vastly underrepresented in media management and production worldwide.

In countries with high illiteracy rates for women and with prominent gender differences in work experience, mobility, and media access, much feminist criticism involves the documentation and analysis of the values carried by media messages, including the representation of physical ideals of beauty and femininity against which all women are evaluated and the portrayal of housework and childcare as female duties. Many of these particular messages come from Europe and the United States, a fact that raises important questions about media practices and ideology. Who is allowed to make cultural productions, and how are they used? How are media practices in the dominant cultures involved in social and political dominance throughout the world?

Feminist theorists have begun to address such issues by expanding on the perspectives and approaches characteristic of traditional mass communications. The impact has been felt in various fields as studies examine the ways in which women's participation in the production of art and literature has been ignored or restricted and how biased and distorted media images—or the absence of images—have contributed to the silencing of women and the perpetuation of dangerous stereotypes.

Public and private. The opposition of the concepts "public" and "private" is central to many communication histories and theories. In many cultures these concepts support a capitalist status quo and an extensive sex/gender system. Within this system the minds and words of women are considered complementary, and inferior, to those of men; masculine intellect is seen in contrast to and as transcending the feminine character, which is biologically driven and firmly bound to the body and the home. Men make the move away from the body and the home to reason and public activities.

This public/private division is present throughout mainstream communication theorizing, which is itself often divided into the study of interpersonal communication—focusing on such topics as male/female, intimacy, sex roles, role playing, friendships, body image, empathy and healthy interaction, styles of listening, perception processes, self-concept, and identity—and mass communication—concerned with such issues as competition, producers and consumers, technology, political power, audience, content, history, institutions, persuasion, and policymakers. Interpersonal communication study is the "small world" approach dealing with relationships among individuals. Much interpersonal communication research begins with an assumption of equality in the private world. Mass media study, however, is the "big world" of communication structures and policies and deals with significant political issues.

There are other areas of study that do not fit neatly into this dichotomy. Yet most cultural studies, with interest in forms of communication as everyday activities and with concern for the misuse of media, have not provided critiques of the controlling dichotomy or incorporated women's communication experiences as represented in feminist scholarship and theory. Notable exceptions include U.S. scholar Janice Radway's analysis of readers' uses of romance novels and British scholar Angela McRobbie's critique of the exclusion of girls from men's cultural studies of the working class.

Feminists have written about the dichotomy between public and private not as a natural or convenient division of labor but as a paradigm convenient for posing separate sexual spheres of activity and for exaggerating gender differences in political life. Men cannot possess a public, political life unless there is also posited a separate private, apolitical life. For centuries women have criticized masculinist assumptions in many cultures about a "women's sphere." For example, Westerners often are critical of purdah, the man-made rules and sanctions that seclude women, govern their behavior toward men, and control their speech and movement in the home and community. Yet related rules and sanctions can be seen to operate in many forms in all patriarchal societies, even in men's harassment of women in "public" streets throughout the world. The history of women's attempts to "make sense"—to speak and write for themselves, to control their own knowledge, and to transmit this knowledge to others—has been virtually ignored in men's histories. Feminist communication theory exposes that divisive, distorting category system of private and public and offers a more diversified, holistic understanding of communication.

Bibliography

Donna Allen, ed., *Media Report to Women,* Washington, D.C., 1972.
Katherine Fishburn, *Women in Popular Culture,* Westport, Conn., 1982.
Carol Gilligan, *In a Different Voice: Psychological Theory and Women's Development,* Cambridge, Mass., 1982.
Fran P. Hosken, ed., *Women's International Network,* Lexington, Mass., 1975.
Cheris Kramarae and Paula Treichler, with Ann Russo, *A Feminist Dictionary,* New York, 1985.
Cheris Kramarae, ed., *Technology and Women's Voices: Keeping in Touch,* London, 1987.
Teresa de Lauretis, ed., *Feminist Studies/Critical Studies,* Bloomington, Ind., 1986.
Toril Moi, *Sexual/Textual Politics: Feminist Literary Theory,* London and New York, 1985.
Cherríe Moraga and Gloria Anzaldúa, eds., *This Bridge Called My Back: Writings by Radical Women of Color,* Watertown, Mass., 1981.
Dale Spender, *Women of Ideas and What Men Have Done to Them: From Aphra Behn to Adrienne Rich,* London, 1982.
Barrie Thorne, Cheris Kramarae, and Nancy Henley, eds., *Language, Gender, and Society,* Rowley, Mass., 1983.

3

Introduction to bell hooks

To live and act in a way that challenges systems of domination is the commitment that characterizes the work of bell hooks, who prefers her name in lowercase to focus attention on her ideas rather than on herself. She seeks to intervene in the culture of domination that characterizes Western culture, which she calls *white supremacist capitalist patriarchy*, a label that suggests the interlocking structures of sexism, racism, class elitism, capitalism, and heterosexism. Born in 1952 in Kentucky, hooks earned her degrees in English—a B.A. from Stanford University in 1973, an M.A. from the University of Wisconsin in 1976, and a Ph.D. from the University of California at Santa Cruz in 1983. She taught at various universities, including Yale University, Oberlin College, and the City College of the City University of New York, before leaving academia to focus exclusively on writing.

Feminism, which hooks defines as a struggle to eradicate the ideology of domination, is a primary means for transforming white supremacist capitalist patriarchy. In "Feminism: A Movement to End Sexist Oppression," hooks explains her perspective on feminism and its potential for cultural transformation.

Hooks offers a number of strategies for intervention in domination or the process of decolonization by which marginalized groups develop a critical consciousness that enables them to stop internalizing their inferiority. Three readings illustrate such strategies. In "Feminist Politicization," hooks discusses confession and suggests that it must be linked to critical consciousness to be effective. "Back to the Avant-Garde" illustrates hooks's concern with visual representations as a site for intervening in the ideology of domination. In "Design: A Happening Life," hooks suggests that design shapes how individuals live, and she sees in design the means for creating a life of joy and peace.

From hooks, b., "Feminism: A movement to end sexist oppression," in *Feminist Theory: From Margin to Center*, pp. 17-31. Copyright © 1984. Reprinted with permission from South End Press.

3.1

Feminism

A Movement to End Sexist Oppression

bell hooks

A central problem within feminist discourse has been our inability to either arrive at a consensus of opinion about what feminism is or accept definition(s) that could serve as points of unification. Without agreed upon definition(s), we lack a sound foundation on which to construct theory or engage in overall meaningful praxis. Expressing her frustrations with the absence of clear definitions in a recent essay, "Towards A Revolutionary Ethics," Carmen Vasquez comments:

> We can't even agree on what a "Feminist" is, never mind what she would believe in and how she defines the principles that constitute honor among us. In key with the American capitalist obsession for individualism and anything goes so long as it gets you what you want. Feminism in American has come to mean anything you like, honey. There are as many definitions of Feminism as there are feminists, some of my sisters say, with a chuckle. I don't think it's funny.

It is not funny. It indicates a growing disinterest in feminism as a radical political movement. It is a despairing gesture expressive of the belief that solidarity between women is not possible. It is a sign that the political naïveté which has traditionally characterized women's lot in male-dominated culture abounds.

Most people in the United States think of feminism or the more commonly used term "women's lib" as a movement that aims to make women the social equals of men. This broad definition, popularized by the media and mainstream segments of the movement, raises problematic questions. Since men are not equals in white supremacist, capitalist, patriarchal class structure, which men do women want to be equal to? Do women share a common vision of what equality means? Implicit in this simplistic definition of women's liberation is a dismissal of race and class as factors that, in conjunction with sexism, determine the extent to which an individual will be

47

discriminated against, exploited, or oppressed. Bourgeois white women interested in women's rights issues have been satisfied with simple definitions for obvious reasons. Rhetorically placing themselves in the same social category as oppressed women, they were not anxious to call attention to race and class privilege.

Women in lower class and poor groups, particularly those who are non-white, would not have defined women's liberation as women gaining social equality with men since they are continually reminded in their everyday lives that all women do not share a common social status. Concurrently, they know that many males in their social groups are exploited and oppressed. Knowing that men in their groups do not have social, political, and economic power, they would not deem it liberatory to share their social status. While they are aware that sexism enables men in their respective groups to have privileges denied them, they are more likely to see exaggerated expressions of male chauvinism among their peers as stemming from the male's sense of himself as powerless and ineffectual in relation to ruling male groups, rather than an expression of an overall privileged social status. From the very onset of the women's liberation movement, these women were suspicious of feminism precisely because they recognized the limitations inherent in its definition. They recognized the possibility that feminism defined as social equality with men might easily become a movement that would primarily affect the social standing of white women in middle and upper class groups while affecting only in a very marginal way the social status of working class and poor women.

Not all the women who were at the forefront of organized women's movement shaping definitions were content with making women's liberation synonymous with women gaining social equality with men. On the opening pages of *Woman Power: The Movement for Women's Liberation,* Cellestine Ware, a black woman active in the movement, wrote under the heading "Goals":

> Radical feminism is working for the eradication of domination and elitism in all human relationships. This would make self-determination the ultimate good and require the downfall of society as we know it today.

Individual radical feminists like Charlotte Bunch based their analyses on an informed understanding of the politics of domination and a recognition of the interconnections between various systems of domination even as they focused primarily on sexism. Their perspectives were not valued by those organizers and participants in women's movement who were more interested in social reforms. The anonymous authors of a pamphlet on feminist issues published in 1976, *Women and the New World,* make the point that many women active in women's liberation movement were far more comfortable with the notion of feminism as a reform that would help women attain social equality with men of their class than feminism defined as a radical movement that would eradicate domination and transform society:

> Whatever the organization, the location or the ethnic composition of the group, all the women's liberation organizations had one thing in common: they all came together based on a biological and sociological fact rather than on a body of ideas. Women came together in the women's liberation movement on the basis that we were women and all women are subject to male domination. We saw all women as being our allies and all men as being the

oppressor. We never questioned the extent to which American women accept the same materialistic and individualistic values as American men. We did not stop to think that American women are just as reluctant as American men to struggle for a new society based on new values of mutual respect, cooperation and social responsibility.

It is now evident that many women active in feminist movement were interested in reform as an end in itself, not as a stage in the progression towards revolutionary transformation. Even though Zillah Eisenstein can optimistically point to the potential radicalism of liberal women who work for social reform in *The Radical Future of Liberal Feminism,* the process by which this radicalism will surface is unclear. Eisenstein offers as an example of the radical implications of liberal feminist programs the demands made at the government-sponsored Houston conference on women's rights issues which took place in 1978:

> The Houston report demands as a human right a full voice and role for women in determining the destiny of our world, our nation, our families, and our individual lives. It specifically calls for (1) the elimination of violence in the home and the development of shelters for battered women, (2) support for women's business, (3) a solution to child abuse, (4) federally funded nonsexist child care, (5) a policy of full employment so that all women who wish and are able to work may do so, (6) the protection of homemakers so that marriage is a partnership, (7) an end to the sexist portrayal of women in the media, (8) establishment of reproductive freedom and the end to involuntary sterilization, (9) a remedy to the double discrimination against minority women, (10) a revision of criminal codes dealing with rape, (11) elimination of discrimination on the basis of sexual preference, (12) the establishment of nonsexist education, and (13) an examination of all welfare reform proposals for their specific impact on women.

The positive impact of liberal reforms on women's lives should not lead to the assumption that they eradicate systems of domination. Nowhere in these demands is there an emphasis on eradicating the politic of domination, yet it would need to be abolished if any of these demands were to be met. The lack of any emphasis on domination is consistent with the liberal feminist belief that women can achieve equality with men of their class without challenging and changing the cultural basis of group oppression. It is this belief that negates the likelihood that the potential radicalism of liberal feminism will ever be realized. Writing as early as 1967, Brazilian scholar Heleith Saffioti emphasized that bourgeois feminism has always been "fundamentally and unconsciously a feminism of the ruling class," that:

> Whatever revolutionary content there is in petty-bourgeois feminist praxis, it has been put there by the efforts of the middle strata, especially the less well off, to move up socially. To do this, however, they sought merely to expand the existing social structures, and never went so far as to challenge the status quo. Thus, while petty-bourgeois feminism may always have aimed at establishing social equality between the sexes, the consciousness it represented has remained utopian in its desire for and struggle to bring about a partial transformation of society; this it believed could be done without disturbing the foundations on which it rested ... In this sense, petty-bourgeois feminism is not feminism at all; indeed it has helped to consolidate class society by giving camouflage to its internal contradictions ...

Radical dimensions of liberal women's social protest will continue to serve as an ideological support system providing the necessary critical and analytical impetus for the maintenance of a liberalism that aims to grant women greater equality of opportunity within the present white supremacist capitalist, patriarchal state. Such liberal women's rights activism in its essence diminishes feminist struggle. Philosopher Mihailo Markovic discusses the limitations of liberalism in his essay, "Women's Liberation and Human Emancipation":

> Another basic characteristic of liberalism which constitutes a formidable obstacle to an oppressed social group's emancipation is its conception of human nature. If selfishness, aggressiveness, the drive to conquer and dominate, really are among defining human traits, as every liberal philosopher since Locke tries to convince us, the oppression in civil society—i.e. in the social sphere not regulated by the state—is a fact of life and the basic civil relationship between a man and a woman will always remain a battlefield. Woman, being less aggressive, is then either the less human of the two and doomed to subjugation, or else she must get more power-hungry herself and try to dominate man. Liberation for both is not feasible.

Although liberal perspectives on feminism include reforms that would have radical implications for society, these are the reforms which will be resisted precisely because they would set the stage for revolutionary transformation were they implemented. It is evident that society is more responsive to those "feminist" demands that are not threatening, that may even help maintain the status quo. Jeanne Gross gives an example of this co-optation of feminist strategy in her essay "Feminist Ethics from a Marxist Perspective," published in 1977:

> If we as women want change in all aspects of our lives, we must recognize that capitalism is uniquely capable of coopting piecemeal change . . . Capitalism is capable of taking our visionary changes and using them against us. For example, many married women, recognizing their oppression in the family, have divorced. They are thrown, with no preparation of protection, into the labor market. For many women this has meant taking their places at the row of typewriters. Corporations are now recognizing the capacity for exploitation in divorced women. The turnover in such jobs is incredibly high. "If she complains, she can be replaced."

Particularly as regards work, many liberal feminist reforms simply reinforced capitalist, materialist values (illustrating the flexibility of capitalism) without truly liberating women economically.

Liberal women have not been alone in drawing upon the dynamism of feminism to further their interests. The great majority of women who have benefited in any way from feminist-generated social reforms do not want to be seen as advocates of feminism. Conferences on issues of relevance to women, that would never have been organized or funded had there not been a feminist movement, take place all over the United States and the participants do not want to be seen as advocates of feminism. They are either reluctant to make a public commitment to feminist movement or sneer at the term. Individual African-American, Native American Indian, Asian-American, and Hispanic American women find themselves isolated if they support feminist movement. Even women who may achieve fame and notoriety (as well as increased economic income) in response to attention given their work by large numbers of women who support feminism may deflect attention away from their engagement with feminist movement. They may even go so far as to create other terms that express their concern with women's issues so as to avoid using the term feminist. The creation of new terms that have no relationship to organized political activity tend to provide women who may already be reluctant to explore feminism with ready excuses to explain their reluctance to participate. This illustrates an uncritical acceptance of distorted definitions of feminism rather than a demand for redefinition. They may support specific issues while divorcing themselves from what they assume is feminist movement.

In a recent article in a San Francisco newspaper, "Sisters—Under the Skin," columnist Bob Greene commented on the aversion many women apparently have to the term feminism. Greene finds it curious that many women "who obviously believe in everything that proud feminists believe in dismiss the term "feminist" as something unpleasant; something with which they do not wish to be associated." Even though such women often acknowledge that they have benefited from feminist-generated reform measures which have improved the social status of specific groups of women, they do not wish to be seen as participants in feminist movement:

> There is no getting around it. After all this time, the term "feminist" makes many bright, ambitious, intelligent women embarrassed and uncomfortable. They simply don't want to be associated with it.
> It's as if it has an unpleasant connotation that they want no connection with. Chances are if you were to present them with every mainstream feminist belief, they would go along with the beliefs to the letter—and even if they consider themselves feminists, they hasten to say no.

Many women are reluctant to advocate feminism because they are uncertain about the meaning of the term. Other women from exploited and oppressed ethnic groups dismiss the term because they do not wish to be perceived as supporting a racist movement; feminism is often equated with white women's rights effort. Large numbers of women see feminism as synonymous with lesbianism; their homophobia leads them to reject association with any group identified as pro-lesbian. Some women fear the word "feminism" because they shun identification with any political movement, especially one perceived as radical. Of course there are women who do not wish to be associated with women's rights movement in any form so they reject and oppose feminist movement. Most women are more familiar with negative perspectives on "women's lib" than the positive significations of feminism. It is this term's positive political significance and power that we must now struggle to recover and maintain.

Currently feminism seems to be a term without any clear significance. The "anything goes" approach to the definition of the word has rendered it practically meaningless. What is meant by "anything goes" is usually that any woman who wants social equality with men regardless of her political perspective (she can be a conservative right-winger or a nationalist communist) can label herself feminist. Most attempts at defining feminism reflect the class nature of the movement. Definitions are usually liberal in origin and focus on the individual woman's right to freedom and self-determination. In Barbara Berg's *The Remembered Gate: Origins of American Feminism,* she defines feminism as a "broad movement embracing numerous phases of woman's emancipation." However, her emphasis is on women gaining greater individual freedom. Expanding on the above definition, Berg adds:

> It is the freedom to decide her own destiny; freedom from sex-determined role; freedom from society's oppressive restrictions; freedom to express her thoughts fully and to convert them freely into action. Feminism demands the acceptance of woman's right to individual conscience and judgment. It postulates that woman's essential worth stems from her common humanity and does not depend on the other relationships of her life.

This definition of feminism is almost apolitical in tone; yet it is the type of definition many liberal women find appealing. It evokes a very romantic notion of personal freedom which is more acceptable than a definition that emphasizes radical political action.

Many feminist radicals now know that neither a feminism that focuses on woman as an autonomous human being worthy of personal freedom nor one that focuses on the attainment of equality of opportunity with men can rid society of sexism and male domination. Feminism is a struggle to end sexist oppression. Therefore, it is necessarily a struggle to eradicate the ideology of domination that permeates Western culture on various levels as well as a commitment to reorganizing society so that the self-development of people can take precedence over imperialism, economic expansion, and material desires. Defined in this way, it is unlikely that women would join feminist movement simply because we are biologically the same. A commitment to feminism so defined would demand that each individual participant acquire a critical political consciousness based on ideas and beliefs.

All too often the slogan "the personal is political" (which was first used to stress that woman's everyday reality is informed and shaped by politics and is necessarily political) became a means of encouraging women to think that the experience of discrimination, exploitation, or oppression automatically corresponded with an understanding of the ideological and institutional apparatus shaping one's social status. As a consequence, many women who had not fully examined their situation never developed a sophisticated understanding of their political reality and its relationship to that of women as a collective group. They were encouraged to focus on giving voice to personal experience. Like revolutionaries working to change the lot of colonized people globally, it is necessary for feminist activists to stress that the ability to see and describe one's own reality is a significant step in the long process of self-recovery; but it is only a beginning. When women internalized the idea that describing their own woe was synonymous with developing a critical political consciousness, the progress of feminist movement was stalled. Starting from such incomplete perspectives, it is not surprising that theories and strategies were developed that were collectively inadequate and misguided. To correct this inadequacy in past analysis, we must now encourage women to develop a keen, comprehensive understanding of women's political reality. Broader perspectives can only emerge as we examine both the personal that is political, the politics of society as a whole, and global revolutionary politics.

Feminism defined in political terms that stress collective as well as individual experience challenges women to enter a new domain—to leave behind the apolitical stance sexism decrees is our lot and develop political consciousness. Women know from our everyday lives that many of us rarely discuss politics. Even when women talked about sexist politics in the heyday of contemporary feminism, rather than allow this engagement with serious political matters to lead to complex, in-depth analysis of women's social status, we insisted that men were "the enemy," the cause of all our problems. As a consequence, we examined almost exclusively women's relationship to male supremacy and the ideology of sexism. The focus on "man as enemy" created, as Marlene Dixon emphasizes in her essay, "The Rise and Demise of Women's Liberation: A Class Analysis," a "politics of psychological oppression" which evoked world views which "pit individual against individual and mystify the social basis of exploitation." By repudiating the popular notion that the focus of feminist movement should be social equality of the sexes and emphasizing eradicating the cultural basis of group oppression, our own analysis would require an exploration of all aspects of women's political reality. This would mean that race and class oppression would be recognized as feminist issues with as much relevance as sexism.

When feminism is defined in such a way that it calls attention to the diversity of women's social and political reality, it centralizes the experiences of all women, especially the women whose social conditions have been least written about, studied, or changed by political movements. When we cease to focus on the simplistic stance "men are the enemy," we are compelled to examine systems of domination and our role in their maintenance and perpetuation. Lack of adequate definition made it easy for bourgeois women, whether liberal or radical in perspective, to maintain their dominance over the leadership of the movement and its direction. This hegemony continues to exist in most feminist organizations. Exploited and oppressed groups of women are usually encouraged by those in power to feel that their situation is hopeless, that they can do nothing to break the pattern of domination. Given such socialization, these women have often felt that our only response to white, bourgeois, hegemonic dominance of feminist movement is to trash, reject, or dismiss feminism. This reaction is in no way threatening to the women who wish to maintain control over the direction of feminist theory and praxis. They prefer us to be silent, passively accepting their ideas. They prefer us speaking against "them" rather than developing our own ideas about feminist movement.

Feminism is the struggle to end sexist oppression. Its aim is not to benefit solely any specific group of women, any particular race or class of women. It does not privilege women over men. It has the power to transform in a meaningful way all our lives. Most importantly, feminism is neither a lifestyle nor a ready-made identity or role one can step into. Diverting energy from feminist movement that aims to change society, many women concentrate on the development of a counter-culture, a woman-centered world wherein participants have little contact with men. Such attempts do not indicate a respect or concern for the vast majority of women who are unable to integrate their cultural expressions with the visions offered by alternative woman-centered communities. In *Beyond God the Father*, Mary Daly urged women to give up "the securities offered by the patriarchal system" and create new space that would be woman-centered. Responding to Daly, Jeanne Gross pointed to the contradictions that arise when the focus of feminist movement is on the construction of new space:

> Creating a "counterworld" places an incredible amount of pressure on the women who attempt to embark on such a project. The pressure comes from the belief that the only true resources for such an endeavor are ourselves. The past which is totally patriarchal is viewed as irredeemable . . .

If we go about creating an alternative culture without remaining in dialogue with others (and the historical circumstances that give rise to their identity) we have no reality check for our goals. We run the very real risk that the dominant ideology of the culture is re-duplicated in the feminist movement through cultural imperialism.

Equating feminist struggle with living in a counter-cultural, woman-centered world erected barriers that closed the movement off from most women. Despite sexist discrimination, exploitation, or oppression, many women feel their lives as they live them are important and valuable. Naturally the suggestion that these lives could be simply left or abandoned for an alternative "feminist" lifestyle met with resistance. Feeling their life experiences devalued, deemed solely negative and worthless, many women responded by vehemently attacking feminism. By rejecting the notion of an alternative feminist "lifestyle" that can emerge only when women create a subculture (whether it is living space or even space like women's studies that at many campuses has become exclusive) and insisting that feminist struggle can begin wherever an individual woman is, we create a movement that focuses on our collective experience, a movement that is continually mass-based.

Over the past six years, many separatist-oriented communities have been formed by women so that the focus has shifted from the development of woman-centered space towards an emphasis on identity. Once woman-centered space exists, it can be maintained only if women remain convinced that it is the only place where they can be self-realized and free. After assuming a "feminist" identity, women often seek to live the "feminist" lifestyle. These women do not see that it undermines feminist movement to project the assumption that "feminist" is but another pre-packaged role women can now select as they search for identity. The willingness to see feminism as a lifestyle choice rather than a political commitment reflects the class nature of the movement. It is not surprising that the vast majority of women who equate feminism with alternative lifestyle are from middle class backgrounds, unmarried, college-educated, often students who are without many of the social and economic responsibilities that working class and poor women who are laborers, parents, homemakers, and wives confront daily. Sometimes lesbians have sought to equate feminism with lifestyle but for significantly different reasons. Given the prejudice and discrimination against lesbian women in our society, alternative communities that are woman-centered are one means of creating positive, affirming environments. Despite positive reasons for developing woman-centered space, (which does not need to be equated with a "feminist" lifestyle) like pleasure, support, and resource-sharing, emphasis on creating a counter-culture has alienated women from feminist movement, for such space can be in churches, kitchens, etc.

Longing for community, connection, a sense of shared purpose, many women found support networks in feminist organizations. Satisfied in a personal way by new relationships generated in what was called a "safe," "supportive" context wherein discussion focused on feminist ideology, they did not question whether masses of women shared the same need for community. Certainly many black women as well as women from other ethnic groups do not feel an absence of community among women in their lives despite exploitation and oppression. The focus on feminism as a way to develop shared identity and community has little appeal to women who experience community, who seek ways to end exploitation and oppression in the context of their lives. While they may develop an interest in a feminist politic that works to eradicate sexist oppression, they will probably never feel as intense a need for a "feminist" identity and lifestyle.

Often emphasis on identity and lifestyle is appealing because it creates a false sense that one is engaged in praxis. However, praxis within any political movement that aims to have a radical transformative impact on society cannot be solely focused on creating spaces wherein would-be-radicals experience safety and support. Feminist movement to end sexist oppression actively engages participants in revolutionary struggle. Struggle is rarely safe or pleasurable.

Focusing on feminism as political commitment, we resist the emphasis on individual identity and lifestyle. (This should not be confused with the very real need to unite theory and practice.) Such resistance engages us in revolutionary praxis. The ethics of Western society informed by imperialism and capitalism are personal rather than social. They teach us that the individual good is more important then the collective good and consequently that individual change is of greater significance than collective change. This particular form of cultural imperialism has been reproduced in feminist movement in the form of individual women equating the fact that their lives have been changed in a meaningful way by feminism "as is" with a policy of no change need occur in the theory and praxis even if it has little or no impact on society as a whole, or on masses of women.

To emphasize that engagement with feminist struggle as political commitment we could avoid using the phrase "I am a feminist" (a linguistic structure designed to refer to some personal aspect of identity and self-definition) and could state "I advocate feminism." Because there has been undue emphasis placed on feminism as an identity or lifestyle, people usually resort to stereotyped perspectives on feminism. Deflecting attention away from stereotypes is necessary if we are to revise our strategy and direction. I have found that saying "I am a feminist" usually means I am plugged into preconceived notions of identity, role, or behavior. When I say "I advocate feminism" the response is usually "what is feminism?" A phrase like "I advocate" does not imply the kind of absolutism that is suggested by "I am." It does not engage us in the either/or dualistic thinking that is the central ideological component of all systems of domination in Western society. It implies that a choice has been made, that commitment to feminism is an act of will. It does not suggest that by committing oneself to feminism, the possibility of supporting other political movements is negated.

As a black woman interested in feminist movement, I am often asked whether being black is more important than being a woman; whether feminist struggle to end sexist oppression is more important than the struggle to end racism and vice-versa. All such questions are rooted in competitive either/or thinking, the belief that the self is formed in opposition to an other. Therefore one is a feminist because you are not something else. Most people are socialized to think in terms of opposition rather than compatibility. Rather than see anti-racist work as totally compatible with working to end sexist oppression, they are often seen as two movements competing for first place. When asked "Are you a feminist?" it appears that an affirmative answer is translated to mean that one is concerned with no political issues other than feminism. When one is black, an affirmative response is likely to be heard as a devaluation of struggle to end racism. Given the fear of being misunderstood, it has been difficult for black women and women in exploited and oppressed ethnic groups to give expression to their interest in feminist concerns. They have been wary of saying "I am a feminist." The shift in expression from "I am a feminist" to "I advocate feminism" could serve as a useful strategy for eliminating the focus on identity and lifestyle. It could serve as a way women who are concerned about feminism as well as other political movements could express their support while avoiding linguistic structures that give primacy to one particular group. It would also encourage greater exploration in feminist theory.

The shift in definition away from notions of social equality towards an emphasis on ending sexist oppression leads to a shift in attitudes in regard to the development of theory. Given the class nature of feminist movement so far, as well as racial hierarchies, developing theory (the guiding set of beliefs and principles that become the basis for action) has been a task particularly subject to the hegemonic dominance of white academic women. This has led many women outside the privileged race/class group to see the focus on developing theory, even the very use of the term, as a concern that functions only to reinforce the power of the elite group. Such reactions reinforce the sexist/racist/classist notion that developing theory is the domain of the white intellectual. Privileged white women active in feminist movement, whether liberal or radical in perspective, encourage black women to contribute "experiential" work, personal life stories. Personal experiences are important to feminist movement but they cannot take the place of theory. Charlotte Bunch explains the special significance of theory in her essay, "Feminism and Education: Not By Degrees":

> Theory enables us to see immediate needs in terms of long-range goals and an overall perspective on the world. It thus gives us a framework for evaluating various strategies in both the long and the short run and for seeing the types of changes that they are likely to produce. Theory is not just a body of facts or a set of personal opinions. It involves explanations and hypotheses that are based on available knowledge and experience. It is also dependent on conjecture and insight about how to interpret those facts and experiences and their significance.

Since bourgeois white women had defined feminism in such a way as to make it appear that it had no real significance for black women, they could then conclude that black women need not contribute to developing theory. We were to provide the colorful life stories to document and validate the prevailing set of theoretical assumptions.* Focus on social equality with men as a definition of feminism led to an emphasis on discrimination, male attitudes, and legalistic reforms. Feminism as a movement to end sexist oppression directs our attention to systems of domination and the inter-relatedness of sex, race, and class oppression. Therefore, it compels us to centralize the experiences and the social predicaments of women who bear the brunt of sexist oppression as a way to understand the collective social status of women in the United States. Defining feminism as a movement to end sexist oppression is crucial for the development of theory because it is a starting point indicating the direction of exploration and analysis.

The foundation of future feminist struggle must be solidly based on a recognition of the need to eradicate the underlying cultural basis and causes of sexism and other forms of group oppression. Without challenging and changing these philosophical structures, no feminist reforms will have a long range impact. Consequently, it is now necessary for advocates of feminism to collectively acknowledge that our struggle cannot be defined as a movement to gain social equality with men; that terms like "liberal feminist" and "bourgeois feminist" represent contradictions that must be resolved so that feminism will not be continually co-opted to serve the opportunistic ends of special interest groups.

---

*An interesting discussion of black women's responses to feminist movement may be found in the essay "Challenging Imperial Feminism" by Valerie Amos and Pratibha Parmar in the Autumn 1984 issue of *Feminist Review*.

From hooks, b., "Feminist politicization: A comment," in hooks, b., & Watkins, G. (eds.) *Talking Back: Thinking Feminist, Thinking Black*, copyright © 1989. Reprinted with permission from South End Press.

3.2

Feminist Politicization

A Comment

bell hooks

Always a part of my inner listening self closes down when I hear the words "the personal is political." Yes, I understand them. I understand that aspect of early feminist consciousness-raising that urged every listening woman to see her problems, especially problems she experienced as the outcome of sexism and sexist oppression, as political issues. To begin on the inside and move outside. To begin with the self as starting point, then to move beyond self-reflection to an awareness of collective reality. This was the promise these words held. But that promise was all too easily unfulfilled, broken. A culture of domination is necessarily narcissistic. To take woman to the self as starting point for politicization, woman who, in white-supremacist, capitalist patriarchy, is particularly made, socially constructed, to think only me—my body—I constitute a universe—all that truly matters. To take her—this woman—to the self as starting point for politicization is necessarily risky.

We see now the danger in "the personal is political." The personal most known as private, as that space where there is no intervention from the outside, as that which can be kept to the self, as that which does not extend beyond. Knowing the way this culture conceives the personal; the promise was to transform the meaning by linking it with the political, a word so associated in the minds of even small school children with government, with a world of affairs outside the body, the private, the self. We see now the danger. "The personal is political." No sense of connection between one's person and a larger material reality—no sense of what the political is. In this phrase, what most resonates is the word personal—not the word political. Unsure of the political, each female presumes knowledge of the person—the personal. No need then to search for the meaning of political, simpler to stay with the personal, to make synonymous the personal and the political. Then the self does not become that which one moves into to move beyond, or to connect with. It stays in place, the starting point from which one need never move. If the personal and the political are one and the same, then there is no politicization, no way to become the radical feminist subject.

Perhaps these words are too strong. Perhaps some of you remember the poignancy, the depth, the way this slogan reached into your life, grasped hold of your experience—and you did move. You did understand better the link between personal experience and political reality. The ways individual women were able to concretely find the deep structure of this slogan, use it to radicalize consciousness, need not be denied. Still, to name the danger, the ways it led feminist politics into identity politics, is crucial for the construction of a social space, a radical front wherein politicization of consciousness, of the self, can become real in everyday life.

This slogan had such power because it insisted on the primacy of the personal, not in a narcissistic way, but in its implied naming of the self as a site for politicization, which was in this society a very radical challenge to notions of self and identity. The challenging meaning behind the slogan, however, was not consistently conveyed. While stating "the personal is political" did highlight feminist concern with self, it did not insist on a connection between politicization and transformation of consciousness. It spoke most immediately to the concerns women had about self and identity. Again, the radical insistence on the primacy of a politicized self was submerged, subsumed within a larger cultural framework wherein focus on identity was already legitimized within structures of domination. Obsessive, narcissistic concern with "finding an identity" was already a popular cultural preoccupation, one that deflected attention away from radical politics. Feminist focus on self was then easily linked not to a process of radical politicization, but to a process of de-politicization. Popularly, the important quest was not to radically change our relationship to self and identity, to educate for critical consciousness, to become politically engaged and committed, but to explore one's identity, to affirm and assert the primacy of the self as it already existed. Such a focus was strengthened by an emphasis within feminist movement on lifestyle, on being politically correct in one's representation of self rather than being political.

Exasperated with identity politics, Jenny Bourne begins her essay, "Homelands of the Mind: Jewish Feminism and Identity Politics," with the assertion:

> Identity Politics is all the rage. Exploitation is out (it is extrinsically determinist). Oppression is in (It is intrinsically personal). What is to be done has been replaced by who am I. Political culture has ceded to cultural politics. The material world has passed into the metaphysical. The Blacks, the Women, the Gays have all searched for themselves. And now combining all their quests, has arrived the quest for Jewish feminist identity.

Bourne's essay speaks to the crisis of political commitment and engagement engendered by relentless focus on identity. I wholeheartedly affirm her effort to expose the ways identity politics has led to the construction of a notion of feminist movement that is, as she sees it, "separatist, individualistic, and inward-looking." She asserts: "The organic relationship we tried to forge between the personal and the political has been so degraded that now the only area of politics deemed legitimate is the personal." However, I think it essential not to mock or ridicule the metaphysical but to find a constructive point of connection between material struggle and metaphysical concerns. We cannot oppose the emphasis on identity politics by inverting the logic and devaluing the personal. It does not further feminist movement to ignore issues of identity or to critique concern with self without posing alternative approaches, without addressing in a dialectical manner the issue of feminist politicization—the link between efforts to socially construct self, identity in an oppositional framework, one that resists domination, and allows for the greatest degree of well-being.

To challenge identity politics we must offer strategies of politicization that enlarge our conception of who we are, that intensify our sense of intersubjectivity, our relation to a collective reality. We do this by reemphasizing how history, political science, psychoanalysis, and diverse ways of knowing can be used to inform our ideas of self and identity. Politicization of the self can have its starting point in an exploration of the personal wherein what is first revolutionized is the way we think about the self. To begin revisioning, we must acknowledge the need to examine the self from a new, critical standpoint. Such a perspective, while it would insist on the self as a site for politicization, would equally insist that simply describing one's experience of exploitation or oppression is not to become politicized. It is not sufficient to know the personal but to know—to speak it in a different way. Knowing the personal might mean naming spaces of ignorance, gaps in knowledge, ones that render us unable to link the personal with the political.

In *Ain't I a Woman*, I pointed to the distinction between experiencing a form of exploitation and understanding the particular structure of domination that is the cause. The opening paragraph of the chapter on "Racism and Feminism: The Issue of Accountability" begins:

> American women of all races are socialized to think of racism solely in the context of race hatred. Specifically in the case of black and white people. For most women, the first knowledge of racism as institutionalized oppression is engendered either by direct personal experience or through information gleaned from conversations, books, television, or movies. Consequently, the American woman's understanding of racism as a political tool of colonialism and imperialism is severely limited. To experience the pain of race hatred or to witness that pain is not to understand its origin, evolution, or impact on world history.

Many women engaged in feminist movement assumed that describing one's personal experience of exploitation by men was to be politicized. Politicization necessarily combines this process (the naming of one's experience) with critical understanding of the concrete material reality that lays the groundwork for that personal experience. The work of understanding that groundwork and what must be done to transform it is quite different from the effort to raise one's consciousness about personal experience even as they are linked.

Feminist critiques of identity politics which call attention to the way it undermines feminist movement should not deny the importance of naming and giving voice to one's experience. It must be continually stressed that this is only part of the process of politicization, one which must be linked to education for critical consciousness that teaches about structures of domination and how they function. It is understanding the latter that enables us to imagine new possibilities, strategies for change and transformation. The extent to which we are able to link radical self-awareness to collective struggle to change and transform self and society will determine the fate of feminist revolution.

Focus on self in feminist movement has not been solely the province of privileged white women. Women of color, many of whom were struggling to articulate and name our experience for the first time, also began to focus attention on identity in static and non-productive ways. Jenny Bourne focuses on individual black women who promoted identity politics, calling attention to a statement by the Combahee River Collective which reads: "The most profound and potentially the most radical politics come directly out of our own identity as opposed to working to end somebody else's oppression." This statement asserts the primacy of identity politics. Coming from radical black women, it served to legitimize the emphasis in feminist movement on identity—that to know one's needs as an individual is to be political. It is in many ways a very problematic statement. If one's identity is constructed from a base of power and privilege gained from participation in and acceptance of structures of domination, it is not a given that focus on naming that identity will lead to a radicalized consciousness, a questioning of that privilege, or to active resistance. It is possible to name one's personal experience without committing oneself to transforming or changing that experience.

To imply, as this statement does, that individuals cannot successfully radicalize their consciousness and their actions as much by working in resistance struggles that do not directly effect their lives is to underestimate the power of solidarity. It is only as allies with those who are exploited and oppressed, working in struggles for liberation, that individuals who are not victimized demonstrate their allegiance, their political commitment, their determination to resist, to break with the structures of domination that offer them personal privilege. This holds true for individuals from oppressed and exploited groups as well. Our consciousness can be radicalized by acting to eradicate forms of domination that do not have direct correspondence with our identities and experiences. Bourne states:

> Identity politics regards the discovery of identity as its supreme goal. Feminists even assert that discovering an identity is an act of resistance. The mistake is to view identity as an end rather than a means... Identity is not merely a precursor to action, it is also created through action.

Indeed, for many exploited and oppressed peoples the struggle to create an identity, to name one's reality is an act of resistance because the process of domination—whether it be imperialist colonization, racism, or sexist oppression—has stripped us of our identity, devalued language, culture, appearance. Again, this is only a stage in the process of revolution (one Bourne seems to deny has any value), but it must not be denigrated, even if people of privilege repeat this gesture so often that it has no radical implications. For example: the slogan "black is beautiful" was an important popular expression of resistance to white supremacy (of course that expression loses meaning and power if it is not linked to a process of politicization where black people learn to see ourselves as subjects rather than as objects, where as an expression of being subjects we act to transform the world we live in so that our skin no longer signifies that we will be degraded, exploited). It would be a grave mistake to suggest that politicization of self is not part of the process by which we prepare ourselves to act most effectively for radical social change. Only when it becomes narcissistic or when, as Bourne states, it naively suggests that "structural, material issues of race, class, and power, would first be resolved in terms of personal consciousness" does it diminish liberatory struggle.

When I chart a map of feminist politicization, of how we become more politically self-aware, I begin with the insistence on commitment to education for critical consciousness. Much of that education does start with examining the self from a new, critical perspective. To this end, confession and memory can be used constructively to illuminate past experiences, particularly when such experience is theorized. Using confession and memory as ways of naming reality enables women and men to talk about personal experience as part of a process of politicization which places such talk in a dialectical context. This allows us to discuss personal experience in a different way, in a way that politicizes not just the telling, but the tale. Theorizing experience as we tell personal narrative, we have a sharper, keener sense of the end that is desired by the telling. An interesting and constructive use of memory and confession is narrated in the book, *Female Sexualization: A Collective Work of Memory*, edited by Frigga Haug. Collectively, the women who speak work not just to name their experience but to place that experience in a theoretical context. They use confession and memory as tools of intervention which allow them to unite scientific knowledge with everyday experience. So as not to place undue emphasis on the individual, they consistently link individual experience to collective reality. Story-telling becomes a process of historicization. It does not remove women from history but enables us to see ourselves as part of history. The act of writing autobiographical stories enabled the women in the Haug book to see themselves form a different perspective, one which they describe as a "politically necessary form of cultural labor." They comment, "It makes us live our lives more consciously." Used constructively, confession and memory are tools that heighten self-awareness; they need not make us solely inward-looking.

Feminist thinkers in the United States use confession and memory primarily as a way to narrate tales of victimization, which are rarely rendered dialectically. This focus means that we do not have various and diverse accountings of all aspects of female experience. As we struggle to learn more about how women relate to one another, to men, and to children in everyday life, how we construct strategies of resistance and survival, it is useful to rely on confession and memory as documentary sources. We must, however, be careful not to promote the construction of narratives of female experience that become so normative that all experience that does not fit the model is deemed illegitimate or unworthy of investigation.

Rethinking ways to constructively use confession and memory shifts the focus away from mere naming of one's experience. It enables feminist thinkers to talk about identity in relation to culture, history, politics, whatever and to challenge the notion of identity as static and unchanging. To explore identity in relation to strategies of politicization, feminist thinkers must be willing to see the female self anew, to examine how we are gendered critically and analytically from various standpoints. In early feminist consciousness-raising, confession was often the way to share negative traumas, the experience of male violence for example. Yet there remain many unexplored areas of female experience that need to be fully examined, thereby widening the scope of our understanding of what it is to be female in this society. Imagine a group of black women working to educate ourselves for critical consciousness, exploring our relation to radical politics, to left politics. We might better understand our collective reluctance to commit ourselves to feminist struggle, to revolutionary politics or we might also chart those experiences that prepare and enable us to make such commitments.

There is much exciting work to be done when we use confession and memory as a way to theorize experience, to deepen our awareness, as part of the process of radical politicization. Often we experience pleasure and joy when we share personal stories, closeness, intimacy. This is why the personal has had such a place in feminist discourse. To reaffirm the power of the personal while simultaneously not getting trapped in identity politics, we must work to link personal narratives with knowledge of how we must act politically to change and transform the world.

Copyright © 1996 from *Reel to Real* by Watkins, G. Reproduced by permission of Routledge/Taylor & Francis Books, Inc.

3.3

Back to the Avant-Garde

The Progressive Vision

bell hooks

Whether or not progress has been made in representing race, sex, and class holistically in film can be gauged if we take a critical look at the ways black females are represented in both mainstream and independent cinema. Rarely do I see compelling representations of black females. Although there are films that represent black womanhood in ways that I enjoy and respect, constructing "positive" images, on a deeper level these images do not convey the complexity of black female experience that I hope one day to see interpreted on cinematic screens in the United States. It troubles me that for a long time I have had difficulty finding words to articulate what these images might be, ways I desire to see black females depicted. It troubles me that when I talk to other black women, I hear them speaking of the same wistful yearning and of the same difficulty naming what they want to see.

Certainly I want to see images that are more diverse and exploratory. I like the representation of the black woman character in Woody Allen's *The Purple Rose of Cairo*. In the film within the film she plays the traditional part of the fat mammy-maid that was such a stock character in presixties Hollywood dramas. That moment when she walks off the screen to express her dissatisfaction with her job, with her dominating white mistress, and with her overall filmic role delighted me. It was a brief, pleasurable moment of cinematic resistance. Her few seconds of "talking back" to the screen required audiences to really take a good look at her—to stop rendering her image invisible by keeping their gaze always and only fixed on the white female star. Allen's subversive moment (an uncommon one in his films, which tend to give us witty versions of old racist, sexist stereotypes when representing black womanhood) felt like an experiment.

There are so few images of blackness that attempt in any way to be subversive that when I see one like this, I imagine all the myriad ways conventional representations of black people could be disrupted by experimentation. I am equally moved by that moment in Jim Jarmusch's *Mystery Train* when the young Japanese couple arrive in the

63

train station in Memphis only to encounter what appears to be a homeless black man, a drifter, but who turns to them and speaks in Japanese. The interaction takes only a moment, but it deconstructs and expresses so much. It reminds us that appearances are deceiving. It made me think about black men as travelers, about black men who fight in armies around the world. This filmic moment challenges our perceptions of blackness by engaging in a process of defamiliarization (the taking of a familiar image and depicting it in such a way that we look at it and see it differently). Way before Tarantino was dabbling in "cool" images of blackness, Jarmusch had shown in *Down by Law* and other work that it was possible for a white-guy filmmaker to do progressive work around race and representation. And then there is that magic moment in Charles Burnett's film *Killer of Sheep* when the black heterosexual couple dances in their front room—no words, just the curious shadows their bodies make on the wall.

My passion for movies was not engendered by conventional cinema. I was obsessed with watching "foreign" films and drawn visually to avant-garde experimental work in the United States. Early on I developed a passion for Stan Brakhage's work that has been sustained. Coming to work by women filmmakers through explorations of feminist art practices, I was and continue to be fascinated by the work of filmmakers like Yvonne Rainer, Beth B., Leslie Thornton, Kathleen Collins, Julie Dash, and, of course the work of theorist and filmmaker Trinh T. Minh-ha, a longtime comrade and friend. Among this collective work, Minh-ha has centrally highlighted representations of blackness. At times she has been critiqued for this focus, interrogated about her choices. We have had long talks about the way in which white audiences and critics usually act as though an entire range of images constituted their purview but the moment an artist of color goes wherever their vision takes them, their right to such movement is questioned. In Minh-ha's case she was also often questioned by black people who were not "comfortable" with her work, with the images of Africa they saw in *Reassemblage* or *Naked Spaces*. Often these individuals approach her work from the standpoint of racial essentialism. Similar critiques about the construction of Africa etc. are rarely leveled at black filmmakers. The images I saw as a consumer of foreign films and experimental works in the United States shaped my visual expectations. Whenever I brought those expectations to bear on representations of blackness, I was sorely disappointed. I wanted a complexity that never was. Since feminist thinking informed my looking relations I was no more satisfied with what I saw in black films than the work of their white counterparts.

Indeed, patriarchal cinematic practices (ways narratives are constructed, images are shot) inform so much of what is identified as black film that it does not then become a location where blackness is represented in a liberatory manner, where we can see decolonized images. This is one of the dilemmas we face when our understanding of black experience is shaped solely by a focus on race, when the ways sex and class mediate racial identity are ignored. It has served the interests of contemporary black male filmmakers in the United States to look past the ways their relations are shaped by cinematic pedagogy in terms of both their technical training and what they are accustomed to seeing. Ironically, there are infinitely more transgressive visionary images of black femaleness in the work of a filmmaker like Oscar Micheaux than there are in that of most black male directors, precisely because Micheaux was not seeing through the lens of white longings and expectations. When contemporary black filmmakers, particularly males, offer audiences the same white supremacist aesthetics that we see in mainstream white cinema (making their lighter-skinned characters more feminine, more desirable; glorying in thin bodies; imaging black female sexuality as whorish), they are not making critical interventions. And very few critics, male or female, have wanted to openly interrogate why it was that films that were most talked about as breaking new ground for black cinema in the United States (*Sweet Sweetback's Baadassss Song* [1971], *Bush Mama* [1975], *Passing Through* [1977]), all made by black men at the onset of contemporary feminist movement, simply imposed on representations of black sexuality, and black female sexuality in particular, a pornographic, patriarchal frame. One film that was not usually talked about as much was progressive in the ways it depicted race, sex, and class—that film was Charles Burnett's *Killer of Sheep*. While every black person and his mother, too, knew about *Sweet Sweetback*, whether they were alive when the film first came out or not, few black audiences knew of Burnett's film. There is a continuum in the patriarchal imagination that informs these early works and the films made by black filmmakers today, whether independent or mainstream. This continued allegiance to patriarchy has made it easier for black male filmmakers who are in no way inventive when it comes to their construction of gender to make it in Hollywood.

While the making and production of Haile Gerima's film *Sankofa* was presented as an act of resistance, a challenge to Hollywood's white supremacist aesthetic practices, all the representations of black womanhood in the film were quite consistent with Hollywood narratives. In many talks Gerima proclaimed that the purpose of this film "was to disrupt Hollywood, . . . to disrupt their sense of movies." Yet this film broke its pact with Hollywood only in the way it challenged audiences to see slavery from the standpoint of the pain and anguish of the enslaved. Overall, the filmic narrative valorized hierarchies—that of male over female particularly, more powerful male over less powerful male, positioned black women as positive mother figures or sexual victims redeemed only as they seek healing from the wise black male. The two leading black women "stars" in this movie appear in roles that are so in keeping with Hollywood narratives that it is mind-boggling. Mother Nunu's character was just a contemporary remake of Annie in *Imitation of Life*, only here her sacrifices and martyrdom are for her biracial son. The other female, Shola, is an African American model, who in the present has become a willing paid sex object for massa and in slavery is the victim of a brutal rape (surprise, surprise). If mainstream cinema's dominant representations of black women have been as "mammy or ho," the images in *Sankofa* follow this same continuum, only the end result is different. Shola changes her wicked wicked ways to affirm blackness. This depiction of the sexual black woman as a betrayer of blackness is common in the works of successful contemporary mainstream black filmmakers. It seems both white and black audiences are more comfortable watching black women when we are kept in our place by sexist, racist characterizations.

Filmmaker Haile Gerima states in an interview published in a newsletter entitled the *Gaither Reporter* that he "didn't think about male and female. I just thought about slavery and black people—African people. So I was not really into gender, women and men. . . . For me, all of them are supposed to come as human beings fighting to change a brutal circumstance." This comment seems completely disingenuous, since resisting representations of individual black men in *Sankofa* do indeed break with mainstream norms. Obviously the filmmaker thought about gender but not about the need to give audiences progressive, nonsexist images of black womanhood. Despite its positive construction of Africa as a common symbolic homeland for black people, *Sankofa* is conservative in its narrative, its construction of blackness, and its overall technique. Celebrated by black audiences from all classes, to some extent this film reinstitutionalizes an outmoded black aesthetic that sees black film as existing primarily as a tool in the liberation struggle. Gerima comments: "For me, film is not a playing toy. Film is used for social change. Film is not to duplicate our reality. Film is used to interpret our reality, to do something about our condition, to activate people, to even make people rise up against a system that is racist and make it change." Few black filmmakers would disagree with the idea that film can further liberation, but that cannot be its only purpose. Such a concept of the medium ignores the place of pleasure in relation to the visual and the need for diverse representations of our experience in the world, an experience that is defined by blackness even as it transcends it.

Focusing solely on representation and race tends to distort the perspective of black artists. Indeed, if more black male filmmakers were looking at the ways race, sex, and class converge, then their articulations of black experience might offer us more daring, complex interpretations—among them representations of black masculinity. Until black male artists challenge and change sexist thinking, their work will never have the power to engage black women and men fully in the work of liberation. The patriarchal cinema, whether black or white, is fundamentally distorted and can only give us incomplete images of males and females. If all sexist black male filmmakers (and their female counterparts) would abandon the patriarchal cinematic pedagogy, we would begin to see a visual revolution, for the images that would emerge from this new consciousness would necessarily be different.

Creating new and different representations of blackness should not be seen as the sole responsibility of black artists, however. Ostensibly, any artist whose politics lead him or her to oppose imperialism, colonialism, neocolonialism, white supremacy, and the everyday racism that abounds in all our lives would endeavor to create images that do not perpetuate and sustain domination and exploitation. The fact that progressive nonblack artists who make films, especially experimental work, challenge themselves around this issue is vital to the formation of a cultural climate in which different images can be introduced. Avant-garde/experimental work is central to the creation of alternative visions. Yet when black filmmakers embrace the realm of the experimental, they are often seen as practicing elitism, as turning their backs on the struggle to create liberatory visions.

In all areas of cultural production black artists confront barriers when we seek to do work that is not easily accessible, that does not have a plot or a linear narrative. My perspective on these issues has been informed by the dilemmas I have faced as a creative writer trying to gain acceptance for my own experimental work, which is not written in language that is as clear and plain as much of my critical writing. This creative writing is often poetic, abstract, nonlinear. In a similar vein, no matter how many essays I write that do not use abstract or heavily academic language, those few I choose to write using academic language tend to be harshly critiqued for not being clear enough. As a black artist who works with words and who makes visual art now and then, I am acutely aware of the way in which our longing to experiment, to create from a multiplicity of standpoints, meets with resistance from those whose interest in that work is primarily commercial, from audiences, and from critics. Whether we are talking about book production or the making of films, everyone wants more of what sells. Experimental work is always risky, all the more so in an area like film where the costs of production are so high. In his interview with *Border/Lines* filmmaker John Akomfrah shared his sense that "personal, reflective black cinema has been eclipsed in a way by a much more aggressive, marketed cinema."

Usually the relative dearth of experimental work in cinema by black artists in the United States is explained by the evocation of economic constraints. Filmmaker Julie Dash, who has made movies that mix the experimental and the conventional, says that the commercial "industry tells you there is no room for the avant-garde." In agreement with other black filmmakers I have spoken with, she reiterates that most people view the choice to be avant-garde as one that "ensures that you will be a struggling artist for the rest of your life." While it is obvious that economic constraints inform the artistic choices that black filmmakers make, that fact does not preclude an interrogation of the many other factors that inhibit and/or prohibit the creative expression of black artists.

Despite the differences between writing books and producing films, the fact that the incredible success of contemporary black writers has not created a climate in which more experimental writing by black artists can be published suggests that there is still an unwillingness on the part of producers and audiences to engage work by black artists that challenges conventional representations, whether in style or content, irrespective of the cost of production. Books are relatively cheap to produce, yet publishers still act as though there is no audience for unconventional work. The fact that publishing such work is not at all risky does not open up the cultural space for certain types of books to be mass-marketed, even as experimental writings by white authors garner acclaim. Actually, when a black writer gains widespread success with work that is conventional, it does not open spaces for a variety of standpoints and styles of writing to emerge. It usually happens that individual writers are encouraged to reproduce what already has been proven to sell. Hardly anybody talks about the significance of writing that has not been composed with the marketplace in mind. The few black writers I know who do experimental work have jobs that allow them to self-publish, or seek alternative publishing; they never intended to make money from this work. Despite the success of my critical essays, I still find that publishers and editors are reluctant to engage writing that is unconventional.

A culture that is not ready for black writers to experiment with the written word will be all the more closed to the idea of engaging experimental images. No matter what a filmmaker dreams of doing in his or her imagination, there has to be a reality base where those dreams are realized. It is hard for black filmmakers to let their imaginations soar when they face a culture that is still so closed. Many filmmakers feel they are still trying to convince mainstream culture that they can actually make standard films. Doing experimental work has little appeal. That is why director-cinematographer Arthur Jaffa raises the issue of "sacrifice" in relation to artistic vision. If there is not a growing body of black artists who are committed to exploring experimentally, then we will never really see truly revolutionary or even radical images of blackness on the screen.

To a grave extent the formation of a critical black cinema has been undermined by the cultural obsession with mainstream success that overdetermines the direction of artistic work, especially the work of black artists. Spike Lee's success in conventional cinema means that lots of young black filmmakers see no reason to engage independent filmmaking at all. They want to find the easiest route to the money and the fame. Many folks thought Julie Dash would have it made after the success of *Daughters of the Dust*, but of course she still has difficulty getting support for projects that are not conventional. The assumption that success in the mainstream makes it possible for other venues to emerge, for the unconventional to be affirmed is utterly false. In all areas of cultural production in this society those black artists who gain conventional success often act to censor and police art-making practices that they are not interested in. Until black artists and critics find ways to support and affirm the continual creation of experimental black cinema, visionary images will not emerge that will enable us to move to another level.

Black audiences have wrong-mindedly believed that the push for more "positive" images would necessarily lead to diverse representations of blackness. Yet the very insistence on positive images automatically acts to constrict and limit what can be created. The work of black artists in all arenas of cultural production in the United States is subject to heavy policing by consumers around whether or not that work is authentic, whether it is positive, and so on. All these efforts to impose a vision on the artist are restrictive. This is most evident in the filmmaking context.

Audiences who watched *Daughters of the Dust* (which merges the conventional and the unconventional) at an early screening witnessed resisting spectatorship. To a grave extent the film had to be positioned aesthetically before many viewers could see and appreciate it on its own terms. When viewers came looking for conventional cinema and did not find it, many were disappointed and enraged. The way in which black consumers hold black artists accountable for satisfying their conventional visual desire wrongly places incredible burdens on us. Again, this is especially true for filmmakers.

A vital dimension of critical black cinema will be lost if all black filmmakers abandon a passion for independent filmmaking to seek success in mainstream cinema. Until there are lots of black filmmakers who are willing to work as struggling artists to produce a variety of representations that emerge from unfettered imaginations, we will never really witness a cultural transformation of representations of blackness. The mainstream will never create images that perpetually intervene and subvert the stereotypes. While there are minor interventions here and there (and certainly Spike Lee has created some of those cinematic moments), they occur rarely, usually in only one scene, and thus are not apt to alter the visual impact of an entire picture.

One difficulty black artists encounter when they attempt to create unconventional films is that the more commonly accepted markers of avant-garde filmmaking may be too restrictive for work that endeavors to engage the politics of representation. Trinh T. Minh-ha found that the criteria conventionally used to determine whether work is avant-garde often do not conform to the strategies she deploys. To her a film might set itself apart "because it exposes its politics of representation instead of seeking to transcend representation in favor of visionary presence and spontaneity, which often constitute the prime criteria for what the avant-garde considers to be Art." Indeed, it is equally possible that a narrow vision of avant-garde practices leads black filmmakers to assume that they must conform to styles of working that disallow critical engagement with representations of blackness. If so, then another dimension of the work to be done involves expanding that vision. Audiences have been rigidly socialized to see cinema in fixed and narrow ways, especially when it comes to looking at representations of blackness. Again and again the persistent desire on the part of black audiences of all classes to see "realistic" and/or familiar images on the screen acts to curtail the imaginative scope of artists who do not wish to ignore those audiences or make films that they never engage. As a consequence, individual black filmmakers doing experimental work must join forces with critics to teach viewers a different aesthetic, to share new ways of looking.

At the same time, while it is crucial for black filmmakers to consider issues of accountability and the politics of representation, it is equally crucial that artists sustain the integrity of their vision. It should be seen as not only fine but essential to the assertion of liberated black subjectivity that there will indeed be black artists in all areas of cultural production who do work that will not be easily accessible. I long ago made a commitment to writing that would reach a larger audience, even as I continued to actively produce work that does not necessarily have wide appeal. Often black artists are encouraged to believe that the value of what we create is determined by audience acceptance. To expand the scope of creative possibility, we need to know that there is room for all types of cultural production, that artistic diversity is essential, and that some exceptional work will have mass appeal and some of it won't. To the extent that black audiences and black artists passively endorse the binary opposition between what sells big and what doesn't, the nature of artistic production will suffer. It should be possible for artists in every cultural sphere to do experimental work alongside conventional work if they choose, or to devote themselves to one or the other.

Overall, black artistic production will be severely damaged if the values of the marketplace overdetermine what we create. There are individual black filmmakers who have access to funds that would allow them to do short experimental works. Yet not enough folks are ready to take the leap. Calling attention to those artists who are fully self-determining with regard to their work is one way to show that it is possible to choose alternative strategies for artistic fulfillment and lead a satisfying life, even if there is not a lot of cash flow. Camille Billops has certainly created her own space in which to work. The rewards are different from those she would receive if she had chosen to focus on being commercially successful, but they are rewards nonetheless. Arthur Jaffa has been raising funds to make an independent experimental film. He does other work to make money. There is a growing number of independent black filmmakers charting different journeys. Only a few are seriously committed to experimental films, however.

If we long to transform the culture so that the conventional mass media are not the only force teaching people what to like and how to see, then we have to embrace the avant-garde/the experimental. Here is where we'll find radical possibility. We can deconstruct the images in the mainstream white supremacist capitalist patriarchal cinema for days and it will not lead to cultural revolution. For too long black people and everyone else in this culture have been socialized to see the avant-garde solely as a marginal place where art that only a few understand resides. The time has come to rethink our assumptions. When we embrace the avant-garde as a necessary matrix of critical possibility, acknowledging that it is a context for cultural revolution, new and exciting representations of blackness will emerge.

Imagine a film that dares to show us the naked black female form in a pro-sex narrative that does not begin with rape as the central metaphor of our existence and as the boundary of our sexual landscape. Or a film working with images of elderly black women. And how about a radical visual conceptualization of black heterosexual relationships? I dream of seeing a documentary film about a woman writer and the filmmaker she loved that would use still images, a voice-over with love letters. No conventional story—a fragmented narrative, maybe a sound track with Celtic music or Coltrane or Sufi chants. When we are willing to dare, to risk, to stretch the bounds of the visual, moving our imaginations all over the place, all will be possible. There will be nothing that cannot be seen.

Previously published in *The Shambhala Sun*, July 1998. Reprinted with permission.

3.4

Design

A Happening Life

bell hooks

All my life I have been obsessed by the pleasure of design. There is no human being in the world who is not born into a happening life who is not born with the will to endlessly design. My girlhood fantasy was to become an architect, and to this day I wish I had kept the plans for a dream house envisioned back then.

Distinguished architect Harwell Hamilton Harris described Frank Lloyd Wright's work as the revelation of architecture as art . . . not the art of books or of classrooms, but the art that proceeds from the very fiber of things. An art from within; filling the imagination with a swirling stream of living images; arousing an intense desire to body them forth in living buildings; energizing their possessor with a feeling of the reality of the self; making him part of the living stream; sensitive to the aliveness of things; projecting himself unconsciously into all things; feeling the oneness and continuity of all things; delighting in the rediscovery of his own self in these expressions; delighting in the richness and mutliplicity of being of which he finds himself capable.

This vision of architecture evokes a world of interbeing. It is the longing to make such a world that has been mostly forsaken as everything in our culture is subordinated to the maintenance of systems of exploitation and/or oppression, to white supremacist capitalist patriarchy.

Today design has little meaning for masses of people for whom interbeing seems only a romantic dream as they scramble to fulfill materialistic fantasies, believing, as everything teaches them to, that consuming is the only way to ecstasy. Sorrow stirs in me every time I face the myriad ways in which advanced capitalism removes the cultural conditions that would enable everyone, including the poor, to have access to learning an aesthetic appreciation of design.

I learned an aesthetic appreciation from Baby, my mother's mother, who could not read or write. Design was visible in the quilts she made, both the crazy-pieced ones and those carefully constructed from patterns. Sadly the ability to recognize beauty does not seem to be innate. Even as it is clear that some individuals are born gifted with an acute aesthetic sensibility, most of us must learn how to see beauty. And even those folks who are gifted must practice the art of looking to maintain their gifts.

When I wander around the West Village and enter shops selling to those who are well-off the artifacts (furniture, dishes, candleholders, lamps, etc.) that were once in lower middle class and middle class homes, I think about the way in which class often over-determines our relationship to design. It is hard to imagine that as late as the fifties it was still possible for families without much money to own an exquisitely designed chair or table.

Today, there is no design for everybody. Design is primarily for those who can afford it and/or the people who are taught to think about aesthetics. Simply because people have money does not mean that they will have an eye for design, but there is an everyday pedagogy of design in our culture. Its lessons are brought to those of us with class privilege who know the right magazines to look at, the right stores to go to, the best designers to hire. Many popular magazines draw a map for those who want to know where to go to buy well-made beautifully designed objects.

Once again I ponder how the artifacts that are more likely to be in poor and lower class homes these days are bereft of design and artistry, such as the cheap chairs that are not real wood and that easily fall apart from too much use. Sometimes in those high-priced stores I see skillfully designed artifacts that were in our working class home; we did not value them because our desiring minds were already reaching for the next materialistic status symbol.

This points not to a failure on the part of poor and working class people to invest in cultural capital but rather to those problematic historical moments when the desire for material status alters the capacity to appreciate the value of an object. For example, growing up we all had beautiful hand-made quilts on our bed. While our grandmother saw them as objects of beauty, her children looked forward to the day when they could remove those old-fashioned quilts and replace them with store bought blankets and comforters. However, as materially privileged consumers began to register through mass media their sense of quilts as meaningful valuable objects, members of my family begin to change their way of seeing these artifacts. The heart of the matter was not really aesthetic value but material status.

Ultimately, cheaply made reproductions of old style quilts do not enhance the aesthetic sensibility of those who buy them. Whether we are talking about sub-standard housing or teakettles, coffeepots and quilts, it is clear that corporate-run economics ensures that most individuals will accept the notion that status derived from conspicuous consumption is more important for individual happiness than aesthetics.

In such a corrupt world the vision of design Harwell Hamilton Harris described must struggle to have meaning. Speaking to a graduating class in the fifties he shared these insights: Don't let design become routine. Begin each new design with an air of excitement, with the confidence that out of it will come a wholly new thing, not a made-over one. It is a life of discovery, discovery of your own nature and discovery of the nature of the universe. It is the means by which you grow personally. I am not talking about architecture as a means of making a living; I am talking about architecture as living.

To realize this vision we would have to see design as shaping how we live, as having spiritual value. We would have to really live. When life is happening, design has meaning. In such a world every design that we encounter strengthens our recognition of the value of being alive, of being able to experience joy and peace. In my life the primary principle that has guided and sustained me as I have approached the issue of design (whether drawing up primitive blueprints for the renovation of living space, book covers, or just the way I choose to create designs for folders) has been the practice of finding delight and pleasure in that which is simple.

I am a fan of the bumper sticker which urges us to live simply so that others may simply live. Often the call to be mindful of that which is simple is misunderstood, heard only as a demand that we live without beauty or luxury, without appreciation of the finer things.

For me it has always been a call to search for the beauty that is beyond that which can be made most easily apparent, to find beauty in the everyday. My decision to move towards elegance in simplicity was stirred by an effort to throw off the bondage of excess. This included traditional ways of thinking about design, which seemed to cloud my aesthetic vision.

Japanese sculptor and designer Isamu Noguchi's devotion to finding a simple essence led him to articulate a vision of a world beyond art. With quiet daring he was able to declare, The work that contains only what is really necessary would scarcely exist. It would almost disappear. In a sense it would be an invisible work. I have not yet reached that point, but I would like to go so far. Such a work would not claim itself to be art. It has nothing conspicuous and might look as if it simply fell from heaven. . . .

In such a vision lies our hope. It is the dream of a world where design enables us to live and die fully, to come close to paradise, to know that heavenly splendor is always here for us. We have only to design and endlessly design a life where that vision is there for everyone to see and realize.

Introduction to Gloria Anzaldúa

Born in 1942, Gloria Anzaldúa grew up in Texas on the border between Mexico and the United States, the daughter of a Mexican mother and an Anglo father. The first member of her family to move out of the valley and pursue a higher education, Anzaldúa earned a B.A. in English in 1969 from Pan-American University in Edinburgh, Texas, and an M.A. in literature and education from the University of Texas–Austin. She has taught creative writing, Chicano/a studies, and feminist studies at the University of Texas–Austin, San Francisco State University, and the University of California at Santa Cruz.

Anzaldúa's writing is directed at theorizing the Borderlands—literal and psychological—as a place where cultures and identities clash. The beginning selection is her poem, "Del Otro Lado," which describes the literal and social Borderlands of Anzaldúa's life. In "Speaking in Tongues," she confronts the need for women who inhabit the Borderlands to move beyond blaming others for the Borderlands and to assume responsibility for its possibilities. In "La Conciencia de la *mestiza*," Anzaldúa describes the new consciousness she believes the Borderlands can produce, led by the *mestiza* in a struggle that, for Anzaldúa, is a feminist one. Anzaldúa uses the metaphor of the *mestiza*, a woman of mixed blood, to show how anyone can potentially make use of multiple and contradictory conditions to create a new hybrid that is strong, tenacious, and capable of changing the world. In "Beyond Traditional Notions of Identity," Anzaldúa suggests reframing as an approach for moving from the disorientation of the Borderlands to the new *mestiza* consciousness. Reframing includes the rhetorical processes of abandoning old unworkable metaphors in favor of new ones and telling different stories that move from victimhood to agency.

From *Words In Our Pockets* (Bootlegger: San Francisco), the Feminist Writers' Guild Handbook. Used by permission.

4.1

Speaking in Tongues

A Letter to 3rd World Women Writers

Gloria Anzaldúa

21 mayo 80

Dear mujeres de color, companions in writing —

I sit here naked in the sun, typewriter against my knee trying to visualize you. Black woman huddles over a desk in the fifth floor of some New York tenement. Sitting on a porch in south Texas, a Chicana fanning away mosquitos and the hot air, trying to arouse the smouldering embers of writing. Indian woman walking to school or work lamenting the lack of time to weave writing into your life. Asian American, lesbian, single mother, tugged in all directions by children, lover or ex-husband, and the writing.

It is not easy writing this letter. It began as a poem, a long poem. I tried to turn it into an essay but the result was wooden, cold. I have not yet unlearned the esoteric bullshit and pseudo-intellectualizing that school brainwashed into my writing.

How to begin again. How to approximate the intimacy and immediacy I want. What form? A letter, of course.

My dear *hermanas*, the dangers we face as women writers of color are not the same as those of white women though we have many in common. We don't have as much to lose—we never had any privileges. I wanted to call the dangers "obstacles" but that would be a kind of lying. We can't *transcend* the dangers, can't rise above them. We must go through them and hope we won't have to repeat the performance.

Unlikely to be friends of people in high literary places, the beginning woman of color is invisible both in the white male mainstream world and in the white women's feminist world, though in the latter this is gradually changing. The *lesbian* of color is not only invisible, she doesn't even exist. Our speech, too, is inaudible. We speak in tongues like the outcast and the insane.

Because white eyes do not want to know us, they do not bother to learn our language, the language which reflects us, our culture, our spirit. The schools we attended or didn't attend did not give us the skills for writing nor the confidence that we were correct in using our class and ethnic languages. I, for one, became adept at, and majored in English to spite, to show up, the arrogant racist teachers who thought all Chicano children were dumb and dirty. And Spanish was not taught in grade school. And Spanish was not required in High School. And though now I write my poems in Spanish as well as English I feel the rip-off of my native tongue.

> I *lack imagination* you say
> *No.* I lack language.
> The language to clarify
> my resistance to the literate.
> Words are a war to me.
> They threaten my family.
>
> To gain the word
> to describe the loss
> I risk losing everything.
> I may create a monster
> the word's length and body
> swelling up colorful and thrilling
> looming over my *mother,* characterized.
> Her voice in the distance
> *unintelligible illiterate.*
> These are the monster's words.[1]
>
> —Cherríe Moraga

Who gave us permission to perform the act of writing? Why does writing seem so unnatural for me? I'll do anything to postpone it—empty the trash, answer the telephone. The voice recurs in me: *Who am I, a poor Chicanita from the sticks, to think I could write?* How dare I even considered becoming a writer as I stooped over the tomato fields bending, bending under the hot sun, hands broadened and calloused, not fit to hold the quill, numbed into an animal stupor by the heat.

How hard it is for us to *think* we can choose to become writers, much less *feel* and *believe* that we can. What have we to contribute, to give? Our own expectations condition us. Does not our class, our culture as well as the white man tell us writing is not for women such as us?

The white man speaks: *Perhaps if you scrape the dark off of your face. Maybe if you bleach your bones. Stop speaking in tongues, stop writing left-handed. Don't cultivate your colored skins nor tongues of fire if you want to make it in a right-handed world.*

"Man, like all the other animals, fears and is repelled by that which he does not understand, and mere difference is apt to connote something malign."[2]

I think, yes, perhaps if we go to the university. Perhaps if we become male-women or as middleclass as we can. Perhaps if we give up loving women, we will be worthy of having something to say worth saying. They convince us that we must cultivate art for art's sake. Bow down to the sacred bull, form. Put frames and metaframes around the writing. Achieve distance in order to win the coveted title "literary writer" or "professional writer." Above all do not be simple, direct, nor immediate.

Why do they fight us? Because they think we are dangerous beasts? Why *are* we dangerous beasts? Because we shake and often break the white's comfortable stereotypic images they have of us: the Black domestic, the lumbering nanny with twelve babies sucking her tits, the slant-eyed Chinese with her expert hand—"They know how to treat a man in bed," the flat-faced Chicana or Indian, passively lying on her back, being fucked by the Man *a la* La Chingada.

The Third World woman revolts: *We revoke, we erase your white male imprint. When you come knocking on our doors with your rubber stamps to brand our faces with DUMB, HYSTERICAL, PASSIVE PUTA, PERVERT, when you come with your branding irons to burn MY PROPERTY on our buttocks, we will vomit the guilt, self-denial and race-hatred you have force-fed into us right back into your mouth. We are done being cushions for your projected fears. We are tired of being your sacrificial lambs and scapegoats.*

I can write this and yet I realize that many of us women of color who have strung degrees, credentials and published books around our necks like pearls that we hang onto for dear life are in danger of contributing to the invisibility of our sister-writers. "La Vendida," the sell-out.

The danger of selling out one's own ideologies. For the Third World woman, who has, at best, one foot in the feminist literary world, the temptation is great to adopt the current feeling-fads and theory fads, the latest half truths in political thought, the half-digested new age psychological axioms that are preached by the white feminist establishment. Its followers are notorious for "adopting" women of color as their "cause" while still expecting us to adapt to *their* expectations and *their* language.

How dare we get out of our colored faces. How dare we reveal the human flesh underneath and bleed red blood like the white folks. It takes tremendous energy and courage not to acquiesce, not to capitulate to a definition of feminism that still renders most of us invisible. Even as I write this I am disturbed that I am the only Third World woman writer in this handbook. Over and over I have found myself to be the only Third World woman at readings, workshops, and meetings.

We cannot allow ourselves to be tokenized. We must make our own writing and that of Third World women the first priority. We cannot educate white women and take them by the hand. Most of us are willing to help but we can't do the white woman's homework for her. That's an energy drain. More times than she cares to remember, Nellie Wong, Asian American feminist writer, has been called by white women wanting a list of Asian American women who can give readings or workshops. We are in danger of being reduced to purveyors of resource lists.

Coming face to face with one's limitations. There are only so many things I can do in one day. Luisah Teish addressing a group of predominantly white feminist writers had this to say of Third World women's experience:

"If you are not caught in the maze that (we) are in, it's very difficult to explain to you the hours in the day we do not have. And the hours that we do not have are hours that are translated into survival skills and money. And when one of those hours is taken away it means an hour not that we don't have to lie back and stare at the ceiling or an hour that we don't have to talk to a friend. For me it's a loaf of bread."

> Understand.
> My family is poor.
> Poor. I can't afford
> a new ribbon. The risk
> of this one is enough
> to keep me moving
> through it, accountable.
> The repetition like my mother's
> stories retold, *each* time
> reveals more particulars
> gains more familiarity.
>
> You can't get me in your car so fast.[3]
>
> —Cherríe Moraga

"Complacency is a far more dangerous attitude than outrage."[4]

—Naomi Littlebear

Why am I compelled to write? Because the writing saves me from this complacency I fear. Because I have no choice. Because I must keep the spirit of my revolt and myself alive. Because the world I create in the writing compensates for what the real world does not give me. By writing I put order in the world, give it a handle so I can grasp it. I write because life does not appease my appetites and hunger. I write to record what others erase when I speak, to rewrite the stories others have miswritten about me, about you. To become more intimate with myself and you. To discover myself, to preserve myself, to make myself, to achieve self-autonomy. To dispel the myths that I am a mad prophet or a poor suffering soul. To convince myself that I am worthy and that what I have to say is not a pile of shit. To show that I *can* and that I *will* write, never mind their admonitions to the contrary. And I will write about the unmentionables, never mind the outraged gasp of the censor and the audience. Finally I write because I'm scared of writing but I'm more scared of not writing.

Why should I try to justify why I write? Do I need to justify being Chicana, being woman? You might as well ask me to try to justify why I'm alive.

The act of writing is the act of making soul, alchemy. It is the quest for the self, for the center of the self, which we women of color have come to think as "other"—the dark, the feminine. Didn't we start writing to reconcile this other within us? We knew we were different, set apart, exiled from what is considered "normal," white-right. And as we internalized this exile, we came to see the alien within us and too often, as a result, we split apart from ourselves and each other. Forever after we have been in search of that self, that "other" and each other. And we return, in widening spirals and never to the same childhood place where it happened, first in our families, with our mothers, with our fathers. The writing is a tool for piercing that mystery but it also shields us, gives a margin of distance, helps us survive. And those that don't survive? The waste of ourselves: so much meat thrown at the feet of madness or fate or the state.

24 mayo 80

It is dark and damp and has been raining all day. I love days like this. As I lie in bed I am able to delve inward. Perhaps today I will write from that deep core. As I grope for words and a voice to speak of writing, I stare at my brown hand clenching the pen and think of you thousands of miles away clutching your pen. You are not alone.

> Pen, I feel right at home in your ink doing a pirouette, stirring the cobwebs, leaving my signature on the window panes. Pen, how could I ever have feared you. You're quite house-broken but it's your wildness I am in love with. I'll have to get rid of you when you start being predictable, when you stop chasing dustdevils. The more you outwit me the more I love you. It's when I'm tired or have had too much caffeine or wine that you get past my defenses and you say more than what I had intended. You surprise me, shock me into knowing some part of me I'd kept secret even from myself.
>
> —*Journal entry*

In the kitchen Maria and Cherríe's voices falling on these pages. I can see Cherríe going about in her terry cloth wrap, barefoot washing the dishes, shaking out the tablecloth, vacuuming. Deriving a certain pleasure watching her perform those simple tasks, I am thinking *they lied, there is no separation between life and writing.*

The danger in writing is not fusing our personal experience and world view with the social reality we live in, with our inner life, our history, our economics, and our vision. What validates us as human beings validates us as writers. What matters to us is the relationships that are important to us whether with our self or others. We must use what is important to us to get to the writing. *No topic is too trivial.* The danger is in being too universal and humanitarian and invoking the eternal to the sacrifice of the particular and the feminine and the specific historical moment.

The problem is to focus, to concentrate. The body distracts, sabotages with a hundred ruses, a cup of coffee, pencils to sharpen. The solution is to anchor the body to a cigarette or some other ritual. And who has time or energy to write after nurturing husband or lover, children, and often an outside job? The problems seem insurmountable and they are, but they cease being insurmountable once we make up our mind that whether married or childrened or working outside jobs we are going to make time for the writing.

Forget the room of one's own—write in the kitchen, lock yourself up in the bathroom. Write on the bus or the welfare line, on the job or during meals, between sleeping or waking. I write while sitting on the john. No long stretches at the typewriter unless you're wealthy or have a patron—you may not even own a typewriter. While you wash the floor or clothes listen to the words chanting in your body. When you're depressed, angry, hurt, when compassion and love possess you. When you cannot help but write.

Distractions all—that I spring on myself when I'm so deep into the writing when I'm almost at that place, that dark cellar where some "thing" is liable to jump up and pounce on me. The ways I subvert the writing are many. The way I don't tap the well nor learn how to make the windmill turn.

Eating is my main distraction. Getting up to eat an apple danish. That I've been off sugar for three years is not a deterrent nor that I have to put on a coat, find the keys and go out into the San Francisco fog to get it. Getting up to light incense, to put a record on, to go for a walk—anything just to put off the writing.

Returning after I've stuffed myself. Writing paragraphs on pieces of paper, adding to the puzzle on the floor, to the confusion on my desk making completion far away and perfection impossible.

26 mayo 80

Dear mujeres de color, I feel heavy and tired and there is a buzz in my head—too many beers last night. But I must finish this letter. My bribe: to take myself out to pizza.

So I cut and paste and line the floor with my bits of paper. My life strewn on the floor in bits and pieces and I try to make some order out of it working against time, psyching myself up with decaffeinated coffee, trying to fill in the gaps.

Leslie, my housemate, comes in, gets on hands and knees to read my fragments on the floor and says, "It's good, Gloria." And I think: *I don't have to go back to Texas, to my family of land, mesquites, cactus, rattle-snakes and roadrunners. My family, this community of writers. How could I have lived and survived so long without it. And I remember the isolation, re-live the pain again.*

"To assess the damage is a dangerous act,"[5] writes Cherríe Moraga. To stop there is even more dangerous.

It's too easy, blaming it all on the white man or white feminists or society or on our parents. What we say and what we do ultimately comes back to us, so let us own our responsibility, place it in our own hands and carry it with dignity and strength. No one's going to do my shitwork, I pick up after myself.

It makes perfect sense to me now how I resisted the act of writing, the commitment to writing. To write is to confront one's demons, look them in the face and live to write about them. Fear acts like a magnet; it draws the demons out of the closet and into the ink in our pens.

The tiger riding our backs (writing) never lets us alone. *Why aren't you riding, writing, writing?* It asks constantly till we begin to feel we're vampires sucking the blood out of too fresh an experience; that we are sucking life's blood to feed the pen. Writing is the most daring thing I have ever done and the most dangerous. Nellie Wong calls writing "the three-eyed demon shrieking the truth."[6]

Writing is dangerous because we are afraid of what the writing reveals: the fears, the angers, the strengths of a woman under a triple or quadruple oppression. Yet in that very act lies our survival because a woman who writes has power. And a woman with power is feared.

> What did it mean for a black woman to be an artist in our grandmother's time? It is a question with an answer cruel enough to stop the blood.[7]
>
> —Alice Walker

I have never seen so much power in the ability to move and transform others as from that of the writing of women of color.

In the San Francisco area, where I now live, none can stir the audience with their craft and truthsaying as do Cherríe Moraga (Chicana), Genny Lim (Asian American), and Luisah Teish (Black). With women like these, the loneliness of writing and the sense of powerlessness can be dispelled. We can walk among each other talking of our writing, reading to each other. And more and more when I'm alone, though still in communion with each other, the writing possesses me and propels me to leap into a timeless, spaceless no-place where I forget myself and feel I am the universe. *This* is power.

It's not on paper that you create but in your innards, in the gut and out of living tissue—*organic writing* I call it. A poem works for me *not* when it says what I want it to say and *not* when it evokes what I want it to. It works when the subject I started out with metamorphoses alchemically into a different one, one that has been discovered, or uncovered, by the poem. It works when it surprises me, when it says something I have repressed or pretended not to know. The meaning and worth of my writing is measured by how much *I* put myself on the line and how much nakedness I achieve.

> Audre said we need to speak up. Speak loud, speak unsettling things and be dangerous and just fuck, hell, let it out and let everybody hear whether they want to or not.[8]
>
> —*Kathy Kendall*

I say mujer magica, empty yourself. Shock yourself into new ways of perceiving the world, shock your readers into the same. Stop the chatter inside their heads.

Your skin must be sensitive enough for the lightest kiss and thick enough to ward off the sneers. If you are going to spit in the eye of the world, make sure your back is to the wind. Write of what most links us with life, the sensation of the body, the images seen by the eye, the expansion of the psyche in tranquility: moments of high intensity, its movement, sounds, thoughts. *Even though we go hungry we are not impoverished of experiences.*

> I think many of us have been fooled by the mass media, by society's conditioning that our lives must be lived in great explosions, by "falling in love," by being "swept off our feet," and by the sorcery of magic genies that will fulfill our every wish, our every childhood longing. Wishes, dreams, and fantasies are important parts of our creative lives. They are the steps a writer integrates into her craft. They are the spectrum of resources to reach the truth, the heart of things, the immediacy and the impact of human conflict.[9]
>
> —*Nellie Wong*

Many have a way with words. They label themselves seers but they will not see. Many have the gift of tongue but nothing to say. Do not listen to them. Many who have words and tongue have no ear, they cannot listen and they will not hear.

There is no need for words to fester in our minds. They germinate in the open mouth of the barefoot child in the midst of restive crowds. They wither in ivory towers and in college classrooms.

Throw away abstraction and the academic learning, the rules, the map and compass. Feel your way without blinders. To touch more people, the personal realities and the social must be evoked—not through rhetoric but through blood and pus and sweat.

Write with your eyes like painters, with your ears like musicians, with your feet like dancers. You are the truthsayer with quill and torch. Write with your tongues of fire. Don't let the pen banish you from yourself. Don't let the ink coagulate in your pens. Don't let the censor snuff out the spark, nor the gags muffle your voice. Put your shit on the paper.

We are not reconciled to the oppressors who whet their howl on our grief. We are not reconciled.

Find the muse within you. The voice that lies buried under you, dig it up. Do not fake it, try to sell it for a handclap or your name in print.

Love,
Gloria

Notes

1. Cherríe Moraga's poem, "It's the Poverty" from *Loving In The War Years*, an unpublished book of poems.
2. Alice Walker, editor, "What White Publishers Won't Print," *I Love Myself When I am Laughing—A Zora Neale Hurston Reader*, (New York: The Feminist Press, 1979), p. 169.
3. Moraga, *Ibid.*
4. Naomi Littlebear, The Dark of the Moon, (Portland: Olive Press, 1977) p. 36.
5. Cherríe Moraga's essay, see "La Guera."
6. Nellie Wong, "Flows from the Dark of Monsters and Demons: Notes on Writing," *Radical Women Pamphlet*, (San Francisco, 1979).
7. Alice Walker, "In Search of Our Mothers' Gardens: The Creativity of Black Women in the South," MS, May, 1974, p. 60.
8. Letter from Kathy Kendall, March 10, 1980, concerning a writer's workshop given by Audre Lorde, Adrienne Rich, and Meridel LeSeur.
9. Nellie Wong, *Ibid.*

From *Making Face, Making Soul: Hacienda Caras.* Copyright © 1990 edited by Gloria Anzaldúa. Reprinted by permission of Aunt Lute Books.

4.2

La conciencia de la mestiza

Towards a New Consciousness

Gloria Anzaldúa

> *Por la mujer de mi raza*
> *hablará el espíritu.*[1]

Jose Vasconcelos, Mexican philosopher, envisaged *una raza mestiza, una mezcla de razas afines, una raza de color—la primera raza síntesis del globo.* He called it a cosmic race, *la raza cósmica,* a fifth race embracing the four major races of the world.[2] Opposite to the theory of the pure Aryan, and to the policy of racial purity that white America practices, his theory is one of inclusivity. At the confluence of two or more genetic streams, with chromosomes constantly "crossing over," this mixture of races, rather than resulting in an inferior being, provides hybrid progeny, a mutable, more malleable species with a rich gene pool. From this racial, ideological, cultural and biological cross-pollinization, an "alien" consciousness is presently in the making—a new *mestiza* consciousness, *una conciencia de mujer.* It is a consciousness of the Borderlands.

Una lucha de fronteras/A Struggle of Borders

> Because I, a *mestiza,*
> continually walk out of one culture
> and into another,
> because I am in all cultures at the same time,
> *alma entre dos mundos, tres, cuatro,*
> *me zumba la cabeza con lo contradictorio.*
> *Estoy norteada por todas las voces que me hablan*
> *simultáneamente.*

The ambivalence from the clash of voices results in mental and emotional states of perplexity. Internal strife results in insecurity and indecisiveness. The *mestiza*'s dual or multiple personality is plagued by psychic restlessness.

In a constant state of mental nepantilism, an Aztec word meaning torn between ways, *la mestiza* is a product of the transfer of the cultural and spiritual values of one group to another. Being tricultural, monolingual, bilingual or multilingual, speaking a patois, and in a state of perpetual transition, the *mestiza* faces the dilemma of the mixed breed: which collectivity does the daughter of a darkskinned mother listen to?

El choque de un alma atrapado entre el mundo del espíritu y el mundo de la técnica a veces la deja entullada. Cradled in one culture, sandwiched between two cultures, straddling all three cultures and their value systems, *la mestiza* undergoes a struggle of flesh, a struggle of borders, an inner war. Like all people, we perceive the version of reality that our culture communicates. Like others having or living in more than one culture, we get multiple, often opposing messages. The coming together of two self-consistent but habitually incompatible frames of reference[3] causes *un choque,* a cultural collision.

Within us and within *la cultura chicana,* commonly held beliefs of the white culture attack commonly held beliefs of the Mexican culture, and both attack commonly held beliefs of the indigenous culture. Subconsciously, we see an attack on ourselves and our beliefs as a threat and we attempt to block with a counterstance.

But it is not enough to stand on the opposite river bank, shouting questions, challenging patriarchical, white conventions. A counterstance locks one into a duel of oppressor and oppressed; locked in mortal combat, like the cop and the criminal, both are reduced to a common denominator of violence. The counterstance refutes the dominant culture's views and beliefs, and, for this, it is proudly defiant. All reaction is limited by, and dependent on, what it is reacting against. Because the counterstance stems from a problem with authority—outer as well as inner—it's a step towards liberation from cultural domination. But it is not a way of life. At some point, on our way to a new consciousness, we will have to leave the opposite bank, the split between the two mortal combatants somehow healed so that we are on both shores at once and, at once, see through serpent and eagle eyes. Or perhaps we will decide to disengage from the dominant culture, write it off altogether as a lost cause, and cross the border into a wholly new and separate territory. Or we might go another route. The possibilities are numerous once we decide to act and not react.

A Tolerance For Ambiguity

These numerous possibilities leave *la mestiza* floundering in uncharted seas. In perceiving conflicting information and points of view, she is subjected to a swamping of her psychological borders. She has discovered that she can't hold concepts or ideas in rigid boundaries. The borders and walls that are supposed to keep the undesirable ideas out are entrenched habits and patterns of behavior; these habits and patterns are the enemy within. Rigidity means death. Only by remaining flexible is she able to stretch the psyche horizontally and vertically. *La mestiza* constantly has to shift out of habitual formations; from convergent thinking, analytical reasoning that tends to use rationality to move toward a single goal (a Western mode), to divergent thinking,[4] characterized by movement away from set patterns and goals and toward a more whole perspective, one that includes rather than excludes.

The new *mestiza* copes by developing a tolerance for contradictions, a tolerance for ambiguity. She learns to be an Indian in Mexican culture, to be Mexican from an Anglo point of view. She learns to juggle cultures. She has a plural personality, she operates in a pluralistic mode—nothing is thrust out, the good, the bad and the ugly, nothing rejected, nothing abandoned. Not only does she sustain contradictions, she turns the ambivalence into something else.

She can be jarred out of ambivalence by an intense, and often painful, emotional event which inverts or resolves the ambivalence. I'm not sure exactly how. The work takes place underground—subconsciously. It is work that the soul performs. That focal point or fulcrum, that juncture where the *mestiza* stands, is where phenomena tend to collide. It is where the possibility of uniting all that is separate occurs. This assembly is not one where severed or separated pieces merely come together. Nor is it a balancing of opposing powers. In attempting to work out a synthesis, the self has added a third element which is greater than the sum of its severed parts. That third element is a new consciousness—a *mestiza* consciousness—and though it is a source of intense pain, its energy comes from a continual creative motion that keeps breaking down the unitary aspect of each new paradigm.

En unas pocas centurias, the future will belong to the *mestiza*. Because the future depends on the breaking down of paradigms, it depends on the straddling of two or more cultures. By creating a new mythos—that is, a change in the way we perceive reality, the way we see ourselves and the ways we behave—*la mestiza* creates a new consciousness.

The work of *mestiza* consciousness is to break down the subject-object duality that keeps her a prisoner and to show in the flesh and through the images in her work how duality is transcended. The answer to the problem between the white race and the colored, between males and females, lies in healing the split that originates in the very foundation of our lives, our culture, our languages, our thoughts. A massive uprooting of dualistic thinking in the individual and collective consciousness is the beginning of a long struggle, but one that could, in our best hopes, bring us to the end of rape, of violence, of war.

La encrucijada/The Crossroads

> A chicken is being sacrificed
> at a crossroads, a simple mound of earth
> a mud shrine for *Eshu*,
> *Yoruba* god of indeterminacy,
> who blesses her choice of path.
> She begins her journey.

Su cuerpo es una bocacalle. La mestiza has gone from being the sacrificial goat to becoming the officiating priestess at the crossroads.

As a *mestiza* I have no country, my homeland cast me out; yet all countries are mine because I am every woman's sister or potential lover. (As a lesbian I have no race, my own people disclaim me; but I am all races because there is the queer of me in all races.) I am cultureless because, as a feminist, I challenge the collective cultural/religious male-derived beliefs of Indo-Hispanics and Anglos; yet I am cultured because I am participating in the creation of yet another culture, a new story to explain the world and our participation in it, a new value system with images and symbols that connect us to each other and to the planet. *Soy un amasamiento,* I am an act of kneading, of uniting and joining that not only has produced both a creature of darkness and a creature of light, but also a creature that questions the definitions of light and dark and gives them new meanings.

We are the people who leap in the dark, we are the people on the knees of the gods. In our flesh, (r)evolution works out the clash of cultures. It makes us crazy constantly, but if the center holds, we've made some kind of evolutionary step forward. *Nuestra alma el trabajo,* the opus, the great alchemical work; spiritual *mestizaje,* a "morphogenesis,"* an inevitable unfolding. We have become the quickening serpent movement.

Indigenous like corn, like corn, the *mestiza* is a product of crossbreeding, designed for preservation under a variety of conditions. Like an ear of corn—a female seed-bearing organ—the *mestiza* is tenacious, tightly wrapped in the husks of her culture. Like kernels she clings to the cob; with thick stalks and strong brace roots, she holds tight to the earth—she will survive the crossroads.

Lavando y remojando el maíz en agua de cal, despojando el pellejo. Moliendo, mixteando, amasando, haciendo tortillas de masa.** She steeps the corn in lime, it swells, softens. With stone roller on *metate,* she grinds the corn, then grinds again. She kneads and moulds the dough, pats the round balls into *tortillas.*

> We are the porous rock in the stone *metate*
> squatting on the ground.
> We are the rolling pin, *el maíz y agua,*
> *la masa harina. Somos el amasijo.*
> *Somos lo molido en el metate.*
> We are the *comal* sizzling hot,
> the hot *tortilla,* the hungry mouth.
> We are the coarse rock.
> We are the grinding motion,
> the mixed potion, *somos el molcajete.*

---

* To borrow chemist Ilya Prigogine's theory of "dissipative structures." Prigogine discovered that substances interact not in predictable ways as it was taught in science, but in different and fluctuating ways to produce new and more complex structures, a kind of birth he called "morphogenesis," which created unpredictable innovations.[5]

** *Tortillas de masa harina:* corn tortillas are of two types, the smooth uniform ones made in a tortilla press and usually bought at a tortilla factory or supermarket, and *gorditas,* made by mixing *masa* with lard or shortening or butter (my mother sometimes puts in bits of bacon or *chicharrones*).

We are the pestle, the *comino, ajo, pimienta,*
We are the *chile colorado,*
the green shoot that cracks the rock.
We will abide.

El camino de la mestiza/The Mestiza Way

Caught between the sudden contraction, the breath sucked in and the endless space, the brown woman stands still, looks at the sky. She decides to go down, digging her way along the roots of trees. Sifting through the bones, she shakes them to see if there is any marrow in them. Then, touching the dirt to her forehead, to her tongue, she takes a few bones, leaves the rest in their burial place.

She goes through her backpack, keeps her journal and address book, throws away the muni-bart metromaps. The coins are heavy and they go next, then the greenbacks flutter through the air. She keeps her knife, can opener and eyebrow pencil. She puts bones, pieces of bark, *hierbas,* eagle feather, snakeskin, tape recorder, the rattle and drum in her pack and she sets out to become the complete *tolteca.*

Her first step is to take inventory. *Despojando, desgranando, quitando paja.* Just what did she inherit from her ancestors? This weight on her back—which is the baggage from the Indian mother, which the baggage from the Spanish father, which the baggage from the Anglo?

Pero es difícil differentiating between *lo heredado, lo adquirido, lo impuesto.* She puts history through a sieve, winnows out the lies, looks at the forces that we as a race, as women, have been a part of. *Luego bota lo que no vale, los desmientos, los desencuentos, el embrutecimiento. Aguarda el juicio, hondo y enraízado, de la gente antigua.* This step is a conscious rupture with all oppressive traditions of all cultures and religions. She communicates that rupture, documents the struggle. She reinterprets history and, using new symbols, she shapes new myths. She adopts new perspectives toward the darkskinned, women and queers. She strengthens her tolerance (and intolerance) for ambiguity. She is willing to share, to make herself vulnerable to foreign ways of seeing and thinking. She surrenders all notions of safety, of the familiar. Deconstruct, construct. She becomes a *nahual,* able to transform herself into a tree, a coyote, into another person. She learns to transform the small "I" into the total Self. *Se hace moldeadora de su alma. Según la concepción que tiene de sí misma, así será.*

Que no se nos olvide los hombres

"Tú no sirves pa' nada—
you're good for nothing.
Eres pura vieja."

"You're nothing but a woman" means you are defective. Its opposite is to be *un macho.* The modern meaning of the word "machismo," as well as the concept, is actually an Anglo invention. For men like my father, being "macho" meant being strong enough to protect and support my mother and us, yet being able to show love. Today's macho has doubts about his ability to feed and protect his family. His "machismo" is an adaptation to oppression and poverty and low self-esteem. It is the result of hierarchical male dominance. The Anglo, feeling inadequate and inferior and powerless, displaces or transfers these feelings to the Chicano by shaming him. In the Gringo world, the Chicano suffers from excessive humility and self-effacement, shame of self and self-deprecation. Around Latinos he suffers from a sense of language inadequacy and its accompanying discomfort; with Native Americans he suffers from a racial amnesia which ignores our common blood, and from guilt because the Spanish part of him took their land and oppressed them. He has an excessive compensatory hubris when around Mexicans from the other side. It overlays a deep sense of racial shame.

The loss of a sense of dignity and respect in the macho breeds a false machismo which leads him to put down women and even to brutalize them. Coexisting with his sexist behavior is a love for the mother which takes precedence over that of all others. Devoted son, macho pig. To wash down the shame of his acts, of his very being, and to handle the brute in the mirror, he takes to the bottle, the snort, the needle and the fist.

Though we "understand" the root causes of male hatred and fear, and the subsequent wounding of women, we do not excuse, we do not condone and we will not longer put up with it. From the men of our race, we demand the admission/acknowledgement/disclosure/testimony that they wound us, violate us, are afraid of us and of our power. We need them to say they will begin to eliminate their hurtful put-down ways. But more than the words, we demand acts. We say to them: we will develop equal power with you and those who have shamed us.

It is imperative that *mestizas* support each other in changing the sexist elements in the Mexican-Indian culture. As long as woman is put down, the Indian and the Black in all of us is put down. The struggle of the *mestiza* is above all a feminist one. As long as *los hombres* think they have to *chingar mujeres* and each other to be men, as long as men are taught that they are superior and therefore culturally favored over *la mujer,* as long as to be a *vieja* is a thing of derision, there can be no real healing of our psyches. We're halfway there—we have such love of the Mother, the good mother. The first step is to unlearn the *puta/virgen* dichotomy and to see *Coatlapopeuh—Coatlicue* in the Mother, *Guadalupe.*

Tenderness, a sign of vulnerability, is so feared that it is showered on women with verbal abuse and blows. Men, even more than women, are fettered to gender roles. Women at least have had the guts to break out of bondage. Only gay men have had the courage to expose themselves to the woman inside them and to challenge the current masculinity. I've encountered a few scattered and isolated gentle straight men, the beginnings of a new breed, but they are confused, and entangled with sexist behaviors that they have not been able to eradicate. We need a new masculinity and the new man needs a movement.

Lumping the males who deviate from the general norm with man, the oppressor, is a gross injustice. *Asombra pensar que nos hemos quedado en ese pozo oscuro donde el mundo encierra a las lesbianas. Asombra pensar que hemos, como feministas y lesbianas, cerrado nuestros corazónes a los hombres, a nuestros hermanos los jotos, desheredados y marginales como nosotros.* Being the supreme crossers of cultures, homosexuals have strong bonds with the queer white, Black, Asian, Native American, Latino and with the queer in Italy, Australia and the rest of the planet. We come from all colors, all classes, all races, all time periods. Our role is to link people with each other—the Blacks with Jews with Indians with Asians with whites with extraterrestrials. It is to transfer ideas and information from one culture to another. Colored homosexuals have more knowledge of other cultures; have always been at the forefront (although sometimes in the closet) of all liberation struggles in this country; have suffered more injustices and have survived them despite all odds. Chicanos need to acknowledge the political and artistic contributions of their queer. People, listen to what your *jotería* is saying.

The *mestizo* and the queer exist at this time and point on the evolutionary continuum for a purpose. We are a blending that proves that all blood is intricately woven together, and that we are spawned out of similar souls.

Somos una genta

> *Hay tantísimas fronteras*
> *que dividen a la gente,*
> *pero por cada frontera*
> *existe también un puente.*
>
> —Gina Valdés[6]

Divided Loyalties. Many women and men of color do not want to have any dealings with white people. It takes too much time and energy to explain to the downwardly mobile, white middle-class women that it's okay for us to want to own "possessions," never having had any nice furniture on our dirt floors or "luxuries" like washing machines. Many feel that whites should help their own people rid themselves of race hatred and fear first. I, for one, choose to use some of my energy to serve as mediator. I think we need to allow whites to be our allies. Through our literature, art, *corridos* and folktales we must share our history with them so when they set up committees to help Big Mountain Navajos or the Chicano farmworkers or *los Nicaragüenses* they won't turn people away because of their racial fears and ignorances. They will come to see that they are not helping us but following our lead.

Individually, but also as a racial entity, we need to voice our needs. We need to say to white society: we need you to accept the fact that Chicanos are different, to acknowledge your rejection and negation of us. We need you to own the fact that you looked upon us as less than human, that you stole our lands, our personhood, our self-respect. We need you to make public restitution: to say that, to compensate for your own sense of defectiveness, you strive for power over us, you erase our history and our experience because it makes you feel guilty—you'd rather forget your brutish acts. To say you've split yourself from minority groups, that you disown us, that your dual consciousness splits off parts of yourself, transferring the "negative" parts onto us. (Where there is persecution of minorities, there is shadow projection. Where there is violence and war, there is repression of shadow.) To say that you are afraid of us, that to put distance between us, you wear the mask of contempt. Admit that Mexico is your double, that she exists in the shadow of this country, that we are irrevocably tied to her. Gringo, accept the doppelganger in your psyche. By taking back your collective shadow the intracultural split will heal. And finally, tell us what you need from us.

By Your True Faces We Will Know You

I am visible—see this Indian face—yet I am invisible. I both blind them with my beak nose and am their blind spot. But I exist, we exist. They'd like to think I have melted in the pot. But I haven't, we haven't.

The dominant white culture is killing us slowly with its ignorance. By taking away our self-determination, it has made us weak and empty. As a people we have resisted and we have taken expedient positions, but we have never been allowed to develop unencumbered—we have never been allowed to be fully ourselves. The whites in power want us people of color to barricade ourselves behind our separate tribal walls so they can pick us off one at a time with their hidden weapons; so they can whitewash and distort history. Ignorance splits people, creates prejudices. A misinformed people is a subjugated people.

Before the Chicano and the undocumented worker and the Mexican from the other side can come together, before the Chicano can have unity with Native Americans and other groups, we need to know the history of their struggle and they need to know ours. Our mothers, our sisters and brothers, the guys who hang out on street corners, the children in the playgrounds, each of us must know our Indian lineage, our afro-*mestisaje,* our history of resistance.

To the immigrant *mexicano* and the recent arrivals we must teach our history. The 80 million *mexicanos* and the Latinos from Central and South America must know of our struggles. Each one of us must know basic facts about Nicaragua, Chile and the rest of Latin America. The Latinoist movement (Chicanos, Puerto Ricans, Cubans and other Spanish-speaking people working together to combat racial discrimination in the market place) is good but it is not enough. Other than a common culture we will have nothing to hold us together. We need to meet on a broader communal ground.

The struggle is inner: Chicano, *indio,* American Indian, *mojado, mexicano,* immigrant Latino, Anglo in power, working class Anglo, Black, Asian—our psyches resemble the bordertowns and are populated by the same people. The struggle has always been inner, and is played out in the outer terrains. Awareness of our situation must come before inner changes, which in turn come before changes in society. Nothing happens in the "real" world unless it first happens in the images in our heads.

El día de la Chicana

> I will not be shamed again
> Nor will I shame myself.

I am possessed by a vision: that we Chicanas and Chicanos have taken back or uncovered our true faces, our dignity and self-respect. It's a validation vision.

Seeing the Chicana anew in light of her history. I seek an exoneration, a seeing through the fictions of white supremacy, a seeing of ourselves in our true guises and not as the false racial personality that has been given to us and that we have given to ourselves. I seek our woman's face, our true features, the positive and the negative seen clearly, free of the tainted biases of male dominance. I seek new images of identity, new beliefs about ourselves, our humanity and worth no longer in question.

Estamos viviendo en la noche de la Raza, un tiempo cuando el trabajo se hace a lo quieto, en el oscuro. El día cuando aceptamos tal y como somos y para en donde vamos y porque—ese día será el día de la Raza. Yo tengo el conpromiso de expresar mi visión, mi sensibilidad, mi percepción de la revalidación de la gente mexicana, su mérito, estimación, honra, aprecio y validez.

On December 2nd when my sun goes into my first house, I celebrate *el día de la Chicana y el Chicano*. On that day I clean my altars, light my *Coatlalopeuh* candle, burn sage and copal, take *el baño para espantar basura*, sweep my house. On that day I bare my soul, make myself vulnerable to friends and family by expressing my feelings. On that day I affirm who we are.

On that day I look inside our conflicts and our basic introverted racial temperament. I identify our needs, voice them. I acknowledge that the self and the race have been wounded. I recognize the need to take care of our personhood, of our racial self. On that day I gather the splintered and disowned parts of *la gente mexicana* and hold them in my arms. *Todas las partes de nosotros valen.*

On that day I say, "Yes, all you people wound us when you reject us. Rejection strips us of self-worth; our vulnerability exposes us to shame. It is our innate identity you find wanting. We are ashamed that we need your good opinion, that we need your acceptance. We can no longer camouflage our needs, can no longer let defenses and fences sprout around us. We can no longer withdraw. To rage and look upon you with contempt is to rage and be contemptuous of ourselves. We can no longer blame you, nor disown the white parts, the male parts, the pathological parts, the queer parts, the vulnerable parts. Here we are weaponless with open arms, with only our magic. Let's try it our way, the *mestiza* way, the Chicana way, the woman way.

On that day, I search for our essential dignity as a people, a people with a sense of purpose—to belong and contribute to something greater than our pueblo. On that day I seek to recover and reshape my spiritual identity. *¡Anímate! Raza, a celebrar el día de la Chicana.*

El retorno

> All movements are accomplished in six stages,
> and the seventh brings return.
>
> —*I Ching*[7]

> *Tanto tiempo sin verte casa mía,*
> *mi cuna, mi hondo nido de la huerta.*
>
> —"*Soledad*"[8]

I stand at the river, watch the curving, twisting serpent, a serpent nailed to the fence where the mouth of the Rio Grande empties into the Gulf.

I have come back. *Tanto dolor me costó el alejamiento.* I shade my eyes and look up. The bone beak of a hawk slowly circling over me, checking me out as potential carrion. In its wake a little bird flickering its wings, swimming sporadically like a fish.

In the distance the expressway and the slough of traffic like an irritated sow. The sudden pull in my gut, *la tierra, los aguaceros.* My land, *el viento soplando la arena, el lagartijo debajo de un nopalito. Me acuerdo como era antes. Una región desértica de vasta llanuras, costeras de baja altura, de escasa lluvia, de chaparrales formados por mesquites y huizaches.* If I look real hard I can almost see the Spanish fathers who were called "the cavalry of Christ" enter this valley riding their burros, see the clash of cultures commence.

Tierra natal. This is home, the small towns in the Valley, *los pueblitos* with chicken pens and goats picketed to mesquite shrubs. *En las colonias* on the other side of the tracks, junk cars line the front yards of hot pink and lavender-trimmed houses—Chicano architecture we call it, self-consciously. I have missed the TV shows where hosts speak in half and half, and where awards are given in the category of Tex-Mex music. I have missed the Mexican cemeteries blooming with artificial flowers, the fields of aloe vera and red pepper, rows of sugar cane, of corn hanging on the stalks, the cloud of *polvareda* in the dirt roads behind a speeding truck, *el sabor de tamales de rez y venado.* I have missed *la yequa colorada* gnawing the wooden gate of her stall, the smell of horse flesh from Carito's corrals. *He hecho menos las noches calientes sin aire, noches de linternas y lechuzas* making holes in the night.

I still feel the old despair when I look at the unpainted, dilapidated, scrap lumber houses consisting mostly of corrugated aluminum. Some of the poorest people in the U.S. live in the Lower Rio Grande Valley, an arid and semi-arid land of irrigated farming, intense sunlight and heat, citrus groves next to chaparral and cactus. I walk through the elementary school I attended so long ago, that remained segregated until recently. I remember how the white teachers used to punish us for being Mexican.

How I love this tragic valley of South Texas, as Ricardo Sánchez calls it; this borderland between the Nueces and the Rio Grande. This land has survived possession and ill-use by five countries: Spain, Mexico, the Republic of Texas, the Confederacy, and the U.S. again. It has survived Anglo-Mexican blood feuds, lynchings, burnings, rapes, pillage.

Today I see the Valley still struggling to survive. Whether it does or not, it will never be as I remember it. The borderlands depression that was set off by the 1982 peso devaluation in Mexico resulted in the closure of hundreds of Valley businesses. Many people lost their homes, cars, land. Prior to 1982, U.S. store owners thrived on retail sales to Mexicans who came across the borders for groceries and clothes and appliances. While goods on the U.S. side have become 10, 100, 1000 times more expensive for Mexican buyers, goods on the Mexican side have become 10, 100, 1000 times cheaper for Americans. Because the Valley is heavily dependent on agriculture and Mexican retail trade, it has the highest unemployment rates along the entire border region; it is the Valley that has been hardest hit.***

*** Out of the twenty-two border counties in the four border states, Hidalgo County (named for Father Hidalgo who was shot in 1810 after instigating Mexico's revolt against Spanish rule under the banner of *la Virgen de Guadalupe*) is the most poverty-stricken county in the nation as well as the largest home base (along with Imperial in California) for migrant farmworkers. It was here that I was born and raised, I am amazed that both it and I have survived.

"It's been a bad year for corn," my brother, Nune, says. As he talks, I remember my father scanning the sky for a rain that would end the drought, looking up into the sky, day after day, while the corn withered on its stalk. My father has been dead for 29 years, having worked himself to death. The life span of a Mexican farm laborer is 56—he lived to be 38. It shocks me that I am older than he. I, too, search the sky for rain. Like the ancients, I worship the rain god and the maize goddess, but unlike my father I have recovered their names. Now for rain (irrigation) one offers not a sacrifice of blood, but of money.

"Farming is in a bad way," my brother says. "Two to three thousand small and big farmers went bankrupt in this country last year. Six years ago the price of corn was $8.00 per hundred pounds," he goes on. "This year it is $3.90 per hundred pounds." And, I think to myself, after taking inflation into account, not planting anything puts you ahead.

I walk out to the back yard, stare at *los rosales de mamá*. She wants me to help her prune the rose bushes, dig out the carpet grass that is choking them. *Mamagrande Ramona también tenía rosales.* Here every Mexican grows flowers. If they don't have a piece of dirt, they use car tires, jars, cans, shoe boxes. Roses are the Mexican's favorite flower. I think, how symbolic—thorns and all.

Yes, the Chicano and Chicana have always taken care of growing things and the land. Again I see the four of us kids getting off the school bus, changing into our work clothes, walking into the field with Papí and Mamí, all six of us bending to the ground. Below our feet, under the earth lie the watermelon seeds. We cover them with paper plates, putting *terremotes* on top of the plates to keep them from being blown away by the wind. The paper plates keep the freeze away. Next day or the next, we remove the plates, bare the tiny green shoots to the elements. They survive and grow, give fruit hundreds of times the size of the seed. We water them and hoe them. We harvest them. The vines dry, rot, are plowed under. Growth, death, decay, birth. The soil prepared again and again, impregnated, worked on. A constant changing of forms, *renacimientos de la tierra madre.*

>This land was Mexican once
> was Indian always
>   and is.
>   And will be again.

—*From* Borderlands/
La Frontera: The New Mestiza

Notes

1. This is my own "take-off" on Jose Vasconcelos' idea. Jose Vasconcelos, *La Raza Cósmica: Missión de la Raza Ibero-Americana* (México: Aguilar S.A. de Ediciones, 1961).
2. Vasconcelos.

3. Arthur Koestler termed this "bisociation." Albert Rothenberg, *The Creative Process in Art, Science, and Other Fields* (Chicago, IL: University of Chicago Press, 1979), 12.
4. In part, I derive my definitions for "convergent" and "divergent" thinking from Rothenberg, 12–13.
5. Harold Gilliam, "Searching for a New World View," *This World* (January, 1981), 23.
6. Gina Valdés, *Puentes y Fronteras: Coplas Chicanas* (Los Angeles, CA: Castle Lithograph, 1982), 2.
7. Richard Wilhelm, *The I Ching or Book of Changes,* trans. Cary F. Baynes (Princeton, NJ: Princeton University Press, 1950), 98.
8. "*Soledad*" is sung by the group Haciendo Punto en Otro Son.

From Ramos, J., & Ramps, J. (Eds.), *Companeros: Latina Lesbians (An Anthology)*. Copyright © 1994 Routledge, a member of the Taylor and Francis Group. Reprinted with permission.

4.3

Del otro lado

Gloria Anzaldúa

She looks at the Border Park fence
posts are stuck into her throat, her navel,
barbwire is shoved up her cunt.
Her body torn in two, half a woman on the other side
half a woman on this side, the right side
And she went to the North American university,
excelled in the Gringo's tongue
learned to file in folders.
But she remembered the other half
strangled in Aztec villages, in Mayan villages, in Incan villages.

She watched her land made hostile
and she a stranger, an 80,000 year old illegal alien
Go back to where you came from, she is told.
She is spanked for speaking her natal tongue
She is laughed at for eating her mother's tortillas and chiles
She is ridiculed for wearing her bright shawls.
The ancient dances beaten back inside her,
the old song choked back into her throat

At night when no one is looking
She sings the song of the wounded
The wind carried her wails into the cities and the deserts.

The half of her that's on the other side
walks lost through the land
dropping bits of herself, a hand,
a shoulder, a chunk of hair.
Her pieces scattered over the deserts,
the mountains and valleys.
Her mute voice whispers through grass stems.
She sings the song of the wounded,
she howls her pain to the moon
no time to grieve, no time to heal

Hers is a struggle of the flesh, a struggle of borders.
An inner war.

She remembers
The horror in her sister's voice,
"Eres una de las otras,"
The look in her mother's face as she says,

"I am so ashamed, I will never
be able to raise my head in this pueblo."
The mother's words are barbs digging into her flesh.
De las otras. Cast out. Untouchable.
"But I'm me," she cries, "I've always been me."
"Don't bring your queer friends into my house,
my land, the planet. Get away.
Don't contaminate us, get away."

Away, she went away.
But every place she went
they pushed her to the other side
and that other side pushed her to the other side
of the other side of the other side
Kept in the shadows of other.
No right to sing, to rage, to explode.
You should be ashamed of yourself.
People are starving in Ethiopia,
dying in Guatemala and Nicaragua
while you talk about gay rights and orgasms.

Pushed to the edge of the world
there she made her home on the edge
of towns, of neighborhoods, blocks, houses,
Always pushed toward the other side.
In all lands alien, nowhere citizen.
Away, she went away
but each place she went
pushed her to the other side, al otro lado.

From Anzaldúa, G., & Keating, A. (Eds.), *this bridge we call home: radical visions for transformation.* Copyright © 2002 Routledge, a member of the Taylor and Francis Group. Reprinted with permission.

4.4

Beyond Traditional Notions of Identity

Gloria Anzaldúa

At sunset I walk along the bluffs gazing at the shifting sea, a hammered sheet of silver. A full moon rises over the cliffs of Natural Bridges State Beach in California like an opalescent ball. Under my feet pressure and heat are continuously changing the layers of sedimentary rock formed 100,000 years ago. It took the waves thousands of years to cut out remnant headlands and thousands more to wear holes or arches through its flanks and shape three stone bridges. Year after year these same waves expanded the arches, until the weight of the overlying rock collapsed the outermost bridge 21 years ago. In a few seconds the 1989 Loma Prieta earthquake brought down the innermost bridge. Today only the middle one remains, a lone, castlelike seastack with an arched hole for an eye.

Whenever I glimpse the arch of this bridge my breath catches. Bridges are thresholds to other realities, archetypal, primal symbols of shifting consciousness. They connote transitioning, crossing borders, and changing perspectives. Transformations occur in this in-between space, an unstable, unpredictable, precarious, always-in-transition space lacking clear boundaries.

Most of us dwell in this space so much of the time that it's become a sort of "home." Though it links us to other ideas, people, and worlds, we feel threatened by these new connections and the change they engender. I think of how feminist ideas and movements are attacked, called unnatural by the ruling powers, when in fact they are ideas whose time has come, ideas as relentless as the waves carving and later eroding stone arches. Change is inevitable; no bridge lasts forever.

More than two decades ago, Cherríe Moraga and I edited a multigenre collection giving voice to radical women of color, *This Bridge Called My Back*. Every generation that reads *This Bridge Called My Back* rewrites it. Like the trestle bridge, and other things that have reached their zenith, it will decline unless we attach it to new growth or append new growth to it. In a new collection of writings and art, *this bridge we call home*, AnaLouise Keating and I, together with our contributors, attempt to continue the dialogue of the past 21 years, rethink the old ideas, and germinate new theories. We move from focusing on what has been done to us (victimhood) to a more extensive level of agency, one that questions what we're doing to each other, to those in distant countries, and to the earth's environment.

Twenty-one years ago we struggled with the recognition of difference within the context of commonality. Today we grapple with the recognition of commonality within the context of difference. While *This Bridge Called My Back* displaced whiteness, this bridge we call home carries that displacement further. It questions the terms white and women of color by showing that whiteness may not be applied to all whites, because some possess women-of-color consciousness, just as some women of color bear white consciousness. We intend to change notions of identity, viewing it as part of a more complex system covering a larger terrain, and demonstrating that the politics of exclusion based on traditional categories diminishes our humanness.

Today categories of race and gender are more permeable and flexible than they were for those of us growing up before the 1980s. Today we need to move beyond separate and easy identifications, creating bridges that cross race and other classifications among different groups via intergenerational dialogue. Rather than legislating and restricting racial identities, we hope to make them more pliant.

We must learn to incorporate additional underrepresented voices; we must attempt to break the impasse between women of color and other groups. By including women and men of different "races," nationalities, classes, sexualities, genders, and ages in our discussions, we complicate the debates within feminist theory both inside and outside the academy and inside and outside the United States.

Our goal is not to use differences to separate us from others, but neither is it to gloss over those differences. Many of us identify with groups and social positions not limited to our ethnic, racial, religious, class, gender, and national classifications. Though most people self-define by what they exclude, we define who we are by what we include—what I call the new tribalism. I fear that many mujeres de color will not want whites or men to join the dialogue. We risk the displeasure of those women. There are no safe spaces. "Home" can be unsafe and dangerous because it bears the likelihood of intimacy and thus thinner boundaries.

I recall the internal strife that flared in the postings of the listserv that we had set up for contributors to our book. I think the online conflict, too, masked feelings of fear—this supposedly safe space was no longer safe. The contentious debates among Palestinian women and Jews of Latina, Native, and European ancestry churned a liquid fire in our guts.

Conflict, with its fiery nature, can trigger transformation, depending on how we respond to it. Often, delving deeply into conflict, instead of fleeing from it, can bring an understanding (conocimiento) that will turn things around.

A bridge is not just about one set of people crossing to the other side; it's also about those on the other side crossing to this side. And ultimately, it's about doing away with demarcations like "ours" and "theirs." Diversity of perspectives expands and alters the dialogue, not in an add-on fashion but through a multiplicity that's transformational, such as in mestiza consciousness. To include whites is not an attempt to restore the privilege of white writers, scholars, and activists; it is a refusal to continue walking the color line. To include men is to collapse the gender line. These inclusions challenge conventional identities and promote more expansive configurations of identities—some of which will, in turn, soon become cages and have to be dismantled.

Ours is the responsibility of marking the journey and passing on the torches left by those who have already crossed many types of bridges. We honor those whose backs are the bedrock we stand on, even as our shoulders become the ground for the generations that follow, and their bodies then become the next layer.

I descend down the steep bluffs to the tide-pool terraces between sea and cliffs. Squatting, I stare at a sea anemone in a pocket of water on the pitted rock. I prod the anemone; it shudders and shakes, contracting into a protective ball. We all respond to pain and pleasure in similar ways. Imagination, a function of the soul, has the capacity to extend us beyond the confines of our skin, situation, and condition so we can choose our responses. It enables us to reimagine our lives, rewrite the self, and create guiding myths for our times. As I walk back home along the cliffs, a westerly wind buffeting my back, the crashing breakers scour the shoulders of the bluffs, slowly hewing out keyholes, fledgling bridges in the making.

You struggle each day to know the world you live in, to come to grips with the problems of life. Motivated by the need to understand, you crave to be what and who you are.

Many are witnessing a major cultural shift in their understanding of what knowledge consists of and how we come to know, a shift from the kinds of knowledge valued now to the kinds that will be desired in the 21st century, a shift away from knowledge contributing to both military and corporate technologies and the colonization of our lives by TV and the Internet, to the inner exploration of the meaning and purpose of life. You attribute this shift to the feminization of knowledge, a way of knowing and acting on ese saber you call conocimiento. Those carrying conocimiento refuse to accept spirituality as a devalued form of knowledge, and instead elevate it to the same level occupied by science and rationality.

You're strolling downtown. Suddenly the sidewalk buckles and rises before you. Bricks fly through the air. Your thigh muscles tense to run, but shock holds you in check. Dust rains down all around you, dimming your sight, clogging your nostrils, coating your throat. In front of you the second story of a building caves into the ground floor. Just as suddenly the earth stops trembling. People with pallid faces gather before the collapsed building. Near your feet a hand sticks out of the rubble.

Coasting over the cracked bridge and pits in the pavement, you drive home at five miles an hour. The apartment manager comes to check and tells you, "No te puedes quedar aquí. You have to evacuate, the gas lines are not secure, there's no electricity, and the water's contaminated." You want to salvage your books, your computer, and three years' worth of writing. "I'm staying home," you reply.

You boil water, sweep up the broken cups and plates. Just when you think the ground beneath your feet is stable, the two plates again grind together along the San Andreas Fault. The seismic rupture moves the Monterey Peninsula three inches north. It shifts you into the crack between the worlds, shattering the mythology that grounds you.

Three weeks after the doctor confirms your diagnosis, you cross the trestle bridge near the wharf, your shortcut to downtown Santa Cruz. As you listen to your footsteps echoing on the timber, the reality of having a disease that could cost you your feet... your eyes... your creativity... the life of the writer you've worked so hard to build... life itself... finally penetrates, arresting you in the middle del puente.

You're furious with your body for limiting your artistic activities, for its slow crawl toward the grave. You're infuriated with yourself for not living up to your expectations, not living your life fully. You realize that you use the whip of your ideals to flagellate yourself, and the masochist in you gets pleasure from your suffering.

Tu, la consentida, the special one, thought yourself exempt from living like ordinary people. Self-pity swamps you, que suerte maldita! Self-absorbed, you're unable to climb out of the pit that's yourself. Feeling helpless, you draft the script of victimization and retreat from the world, withdraw from your body. You count the bars of your cage, refusing to name your demons.

Taking a deep breath, you close your eyes and sense parts of your soul returning to your body. Challenging the old self's orthodoxy is never enough; you must submit a sketch of an alternative self.

You fly in from another speaking gig on the East Coast, arriving at the feminist academic conference late. Hayas un desmadre. A racist incident has unleashed flames of anger held in check for decades. Like most feminist conferences, this one begins as a bridge, a place of mutual access where thousands crisscross, network, share ideas, and struggle together to resolve women's issues. After 15 years of struggle, of putting their trust on this common space, of waiting for the organization to deal with racism as it's promised, the women of color and some Jewish, working-class, and progressive white allies feel betrayed by their white middle-class sisters.

They're tired of being treated as outsiders. They feel that whites still view issues of racism as the concern of women of color alone, anti-Semitism the concern only of Jewish women, homophobia the concern of lesbians, and class the concern of working-class and poor women. White women accuse women of color and their allies of emotionalism—after all, this is the academy. Feeling unjustly attacked, they adamantly proclaim they're not racist.

Caught in the middle of the power struggle, you're forced to take sides, forced to negotiate another identity crisis. Being coerced to turn your back on one group/person and favor the other feels like a knife to the heart. It reminds you of the '70s when other lesbians reprimanded you and urged you to abandon your friendships with men.

What takes a bashing is not so much you but who you think you are, an illusion you're hellbent on protecting and preserving at all costs. You think you've made progress, gained a new awareness, found a new version of reality, created a workable story, fulfilled an obligation, and followed your own conscience. But when you cast to the world what you've created and put your ideals into action, the contradictions explode in your face.

When creating a personal narrative, you also co-create the group/cultural story. You examine the description handed to you of the world, picking holes in the paradigms currently constructing reality. You doubt that traditional Western science is the best knowledge system, the only true, impartial arbiter of reality. You turn the established narrative on its head, seeing through, resisting, and subverting its assumptions. Again, it's not enough to denounce the culture's old account—you must provide new narratives embodying alternative potentials.

You examine the contentions accompanying the old cultural narratives: Your ethnic tribe wants you to isolate, insisting that you remain within race and class boundaries. The dominant culture prefers that you abandon your roots and assimilate, insisting that you leave your Indianness behind and seek shelter under the Hispanic or Latino umbrella.

The temptation to succumb to these assimilationist tactics and escape the stigma of being Mexican stalls you on the bridge between isolation and assimilation. But both are debilitating. How can you step outside ethnic and other labels while cleaving to your identity? Your identity has roots you share with all people and other beings—spirit, feeling, and body compose a greater identity category.

Reframing the old story points to another option besides assimilation and separation—a "new tribalism." You pick and choose views, cultures with transformational potential—a partially conscious selection, not a mestizaje imposed on you, but one whose process you can control. A retribalizing mestizaje becomes your coping mechanism, your strategy of resistance to both acculturating and inculturating pressures.

Tussling con remolinos (whirlwinds) of different belief systems builds the muscles of mestiza consciousness, enabling it to stretch. Being Chicana (or indigenous, Mexican, Basque, Spanish, Berber-Arab, Gypsy) is no longer enough; being female, woman of color, patlache (queer) no longer suffices. Your resistance to identity boxes leads you to a different tribe, a different story (of mestizaje), enabling you to rethink yourself in global-spiritual terms instead of conventional categories of color, class, career.

It calls you to retribalize your identity to a more inclusive one, redefining what it means to be una mexicana de este lado, an American in the United States, a citizen of the world, classifications reflecting an emerging planetary culture. In this narrative, national boundaries dividing us from the "others" (nos/otras) are porous, and the cracks between worlds serve as gateways.

Through the act of writing you call, like the ancient chamana, the scattered pieces of your soul back to your body. You commence the arduous task of rebuilding yourself, composing a story that more accurately expresses your new identity. You seek out allies and, together, begin building spiritual/political communities that struggle for personal growth and social justice. By compartiendo historias, ideas, we forge bonds across race, gender, and other lines, creating a new tribalism.

For you, writing is an archetypal journey home to the self, un proceso de crear puentes (bridges) to the next phase, next place, next culture, next reality. The thrust toward spiritual realization, health, freedom, and justice propels you to help rebuild the bridge to the world when you return "home." You realize that "home" is that bridge, the in-between place of constant transition, the most unsafe of all spaces. You remove the old bridge from your back, and though afraid, allow diverse groups to collectively rebuild it, to buttress it with new steel plates, girders, cable bracing, and trusses.

Introduction to Mary Daly

Born in 1928 in New York, Mary Daly holds an M.A. in English from the Catholic University of America in Washington, D.C., a Ph.D. in religion from St. Mary's College in South Bend, Indiana, and two Ph.D.s—in philosophy and theology—from the University of Fribourg in Switzerland. In 1966, Daly began teaching at Boston College, becoming the school's first female theology professor. Her theories reflect her determination, spirit, and energy as she journeys into the Outercourse, which she defines as moving beyond the imprisoning mental, physical, emotional, and spiritual walls of patriarchy.

Daly's early work addressed the sexism she saw in all patriarchal religions. In "A Call for the Castration of Sexist Religion," Daly names this sexism, describing a sexual caste system inherent in all forms of Christianity. She offers solutions to this hierarchy, identifying God as the Verb of Verbs and thus making a space for women to participate in religion. As Daly's theories evolved, she rejected her earlier attempts to make a space for women in Christianity, calling instead for women to move into an entirely different spiritual realm. This new realm is introduced in *Gyn/Ecology: Spinning New Time/Space*, where Daly describes the misogynistic forces she sees in the world and urges women to journey into a life-loving and life-affirming state of Be-ing.

In "Gyn/Ecology," Daly begins to alter the ways in which her work is read, and in "Sin Big," which summarizes her experiences at Boston College, Daly continues to develop her unusual writing style (she uses slashes, capitalization, hyphens, and the redefinition of familiar words to create an alternative universe in her work). "Spiraling Into the Nineties" illustrates the full integration of this unique writing style as well as Daly's radical feminist approach to change.

From *The Unitarian Universalist Christian*, 27, (Autumn/Winter 1972), pp. 22-37. Reprinted with permission.

5.1

A Call for the Castration of Sexist Religion

Theology After the Demise of "God the Father"

Mary Daly

The basic presuppositions of this essay have been proposed in some detail first of all in my book, *The Church and the Second Sex*, which was published four years ago, and more recently and far more radically in a number of articles that have been published over the course of the past few years.[1] I shall briefly review some of these before proceeding to the basic work of this article, which is to explore the potential of the women's revolution for transforming what I shall for the time being call theological consciousness.

Basic to the work at hand is my conviction that there exists a worldwide sexual caste system involving birth-ascribed hierarchically ordered groups, and that this system is masked by sex role segregation, which is harder to perceive than spatial segregation, as in a ghetto. This caste system is also masked by women's duality of status, for women have a derivative status stemming from relationships with men, which tends to hide our infrahuman condition *as women*. Finally, it is hidden by ideologies and institutions that alienate women from our true selves, deluding us with false identifications, sapping our energies, deflecting our anger and our hope.

Patriarchal religion has made it more difficult to see through the injustices of the system by legitimating and reinforcing it. The long history of legitimation of sexism by Christianity is by now too well known to require detailed repetition here. I need not allude to the misogynism of the church Fathers—for example, Tertullian, who informed women in general: "You are the devil's gateway," or Augustine, who opined that women are not made to the image of God. I can omit reference to Thomas Aquinas and his numerous commentators and disciples who defined women as misbegotten males. I can pass over Karl Barth's proclamation that woman is ontologically subordinate to man and Dietrich Bonhoeffer's insistence that women should be subordinate to their husbands. All of this is well known. The point has been made: patriarchal religion supports and perpetuates patriarchy.

There are other axioms in my present thinking that are fundamental. I think it is certain that the bonding phenomenon among women, generally referred to as sisterhood, has deeply spiritual dimensions, even if those experiencing it would not always be inclined to use religious jargon to describe the experience. This spiritual quality of the women's revolution is grounded in our confrontation with non-being. As the ultimate aliens, perennial outsiders in "a man's world," women are beginning to be able to allow ourselves and each other to experience nothingness—to see that the entire social structure, meaning structure, language structure bequeathed to us essentially excludes us as fully human beings. This places us consciously in a marginal situation. We become recognizable to ourselves as extra-environmentals. This seeing requires existential courage, and women in our time are in a special way called to be the bearers of this courage, which expresses itself in sisterhood.

Sisterhood, I maintain, is both revolutionary and revelatory. By refusing, together, to be objects—to accept the role of "the Other"—women are beginning to break down the credibility of sex role stereotyping and bring about a genuine psychic revolution in the direction of what I have called "the sisterhood of man," that is, in the direction of an androgynous society. By the same token, sisterhood is revelation. The breakdown of the idols of patriarchal religion is happening in women's new consciousness. Out of our courage to be in the absence of these idols—in the face of the experience of non-being—can emerge a new sense of transcendence, that is, a new and more genuine spiritual consciousness. This means that a transvaluation of values can take place.

Sisterhood, then, is in a very real sense an anti-church. In creating a counterworld to the society endorsed by patriarchal religion, women are at war with sexist religion *as sexist*. This is true whether we concern ourselves directly with religion or not. Women whose consciousness has been raised are spiritual exiles whose sense of transcendence is seeking alternative expressions to those available in institutional religion. At the same time, sisterhood is functioning as church, proclaiming dimensions of truth which organized religion fails to proclaim. It is a space set apart, in which we can be ourselves. It is also a charismatic community, in which women experience prophecy and healing. It is a community with a mission to be a counterforce to male-dominated society. Finally it is an *exodus* community based upon the promise in women ourselves.

These, then, are some basic axioms to my approach to the problem of theology after the demise of God the Father. It cannot be stressed too strongly that the system and the entire conceptual apparatus of Christian theology, developed under the conditions of patriarchy, have been the products of males and that in large measure these serve the interests of sexist society. Given these conditions it is not surprising that women who are attempting to challenge the structures, symbols, and values of Christianity are at times not radical and daring enough, stopping at the goal of mere reformism within pre-established social structures and/or semantic structures that reflect the latter. To get beyond this requires a resurrection experience—beginning to hear and to speak new words. This means real cerebral work but the work ahead is hardly a merely cerebral exercise. It is a growing that has to go on—a growing that takes place *on the boundary* of patriarchal institutions and their legitimations.

I: What has to be done?

It would in a sense be true but also in a sense misleading to describe what is happening among women (in specific ways among women with "theological training" as it is called) as "the creation of a new theology." It would be misleading if it were taken to mean that the basic assumptions of patriarchal religion, most specifically of Christianity, will go unchallenged—as is generally the case in works that attempt to construct "new theologies"—even new radical theologies. I would therefore be very hesitant to call what I believe has to be done "a theology of women's liberation," which would mean placing it within the category of theology as presently understood, even "radically." Rather, what I am concerned with is the problem of how the women's revolution can transform Western spiritual consciousness, its symbolizations and its values.

On the other hand, it would be true to speak of the work at hand as the creation of a new theology if the word could be torn free of its traditional limiting associations with patriarchal religion. For its burden is to show how the women's revolution insofar as it is true to its own essential dynamics, is a deeply spiritual revolution pointing beyond the idolatries of sexist religion and society and sparking creative action toward transcendence. It has a dynamic that extends outward from the becoming of women toward universal human becoming. If it is not short-circuited this fundamental impulse to which the women's movement is giving expression has spiritual and religious meanings. It has to do with the search for ultimate meaning and reality, which some would call God.

It should be recognized that women have been extra-environmentals in society. Not only have we been excluded from decision-making, but also we have had no essential role in the creation of thought. Under the conditions of patriarchy—which are the only conditions within historical memory—the entire symbol system and conceptual apparatus has been developed by men. It does not adequately reflect or take into account the experience of women and in fact functions to falsify our own self-image and experience. Educated women have often resolved the problems raised by the situation by simply not seeing it, that is, by screening out experience and responding only to the questions considered meaningful and licit within the prevailing thought structures. Women who have perceived the reality of sexual oppression, on the other hand, as Simone de Beauvoir sadly notes, usually exhaust themselves in breaking through to discovery of their own humanity, with little energy left for constructing their own interpretation of the universe. Therefore, the various ideological constructs, among them theology, cannot be imagined to reflect a balanced or adequate perspective. What is required of women at this point in history is a radical refusal to limit our perspectives, our questioning, our creativity to any of the preconceived patterns of a male-dominated culture. When the positive products of the emerging awareness, questioning, and creativity of women express dimensions of the search for ultimate meaning, they can indeed be called theological, but in the sense of theology that demands the death of the God of patriarchal religion.

As I have indicated elsewhere, theology may be oppressive to women in a number of ways. First, it may be overtly and explicitly oppressive, proclaiming women's subordination as God's will. Second, theology is oppressive even in the absence of explicitly oppressive statements, when exclusively masculine symbolism for God, for the notion of divine "incarnation" in human nature, and for the human relationship to

God reinforces sexual hierarchy. Third, even when its basic assumptions appear to be incompatible with sexism and when its language is somewhat purified of fixation upon maleness, theology is damaging if it encourages detachment from the reality of the human struggle against oppression in its concrete manifestations. That is, the lack of explicit relevance of intellection to the fact of oppression in its precise forms, such as sexual hierarchy, is itself oppressive. This is the case, for example, when theologians write long treatises on creative hope, political theology, or revolution without any specific acknowledgment of or application to the problem of sexism. Tillich's ontological theology, too, even though it is potentially liberating in a very radical sense, fails to be adequate in this regard. The specific relevance of "power of being" to the fact of sexual oppression is not indicated. Moreover, just as Tillich's discussion of God is "detached," so also is the rest of his systematic theology. His discussion of "estrangement," for example, when he "breaks" the myth of the Fall, fails to take specifically into account the malignant view of the man-woman relationship which the androcentric myth itself inadvertently "reveals" and perpetuates. He simply generalizes and "goes beyond" the problem. Since the residue of this specific content of the myth still deeply affects Western culture in its attitudes, customs, and laws (e.g. concerning prostitution and abortion), I would suggest that this approach is not adequate.

II: The Problem of "Method"

The question arises, therefore, of the method that I propose for dealing with questions of religious symbols and concepts, and with ethical problems. I will begin my description of this with some indications of what my method is *not*. First of all it obviously is not that of a "kerygmatic theology," which supposes some unique and changeless revelation peculiar to Christianity.[2] Neither is my approach that of a disinterested observer who claims to have an "objective" knowledge "about" reality.[3] Nor is it an attempt to correlate with the existing cultural situation "eternal truths" which are presumed to have been captured as adequately as possible in a fixed and limited set of symbols. Such a correlation process would not be adequate even if understood as *relativizing* of the Christian symbols—that is, even if it included recognition that these symbols need not be seen in a fundamentalist or literalist way.[4] None of these approaches is adequate to express the revolutionary potential of women's liberation for changing religious consciousness and for challenging the forms in which this consciousness incarnates itself.

The method that is required is a method not of correlation but of *liberation*. Even the term "method" must be reinterpreted and in fact wrenched out of its usual semantic field, for the emerging theological creativity in women is by no means a merely cerebral process. In order to understand the implications of this process it is necessary to grasp the fundamental fact that women have had the power of *naming* stolen from us. We have not been free to use our own power to name ourselves, the world, or God. The old naming was not the product of dialogue—a fact inadvertently admitted in the Genesis myth of Adam naming the animals and the woman. Women are now realizing that this imposing of words was false because partial. That is, partial and inadequate words have been taken as adequate.

To exist humanly is to name the self, the world, and God.[5] The "method" of the evolving spiritual consciousness of women is nothing less than this beginning to speak humanly—a reclaiming of the right to speak.

It would be a mistake to imagine that the new speech of women can be equated simply with women speaking men's words. What is happening is that women are *hearing* each other and ourselves for the first time, and out of this supportive hearing emerge *new words*.[6] This is not to say necessarily that an entirely new set of words is coming into being full blown in a material sense, i.e., new sounds or combinations of letters on paper. Rather, words which, materially speaking, are identical with the old become new in a semantic context that emerges from qualitatively new experience. The word *exodus* as applied to the new community of women, exemplifies this phenomenon.[7] The meaning is stripped of the patriarchal context of the Biblical writings. So also the word *sisterhood* when heard with new ears no longer means a subordinate semi-brotherhood, but an authentic bonding of women on a wide scale for the first time in recorded history.

Moreover, this liberation of language from its old semantic context implies a breakthrough to new semantic fields. The new context has its source and its verification in the rising consciousness women have of ourselves and of our situation. Since this consciousness contradicts the established sense of reality which is reflected in the prevailing social and linguistic structures, its verbal expressions involve apparent contradictions. This is especially the case since, as I have pointed out, the new words do not constitute a new language in a material sense, but a new set of meanings that clashes with the old. The new words of women's becoming, then, function in such a way that they raise questions and problems, and at the same time give clues to the resolution of the problems. When, for example, I write of "the sisterhood of man" there is involved an apparent contradiction and a jarring of images. "Intellectually" everyone "knows" that "man" is a generic term. However, in view of the fact that we live in a world in which full humanity is attributed only to males, and in view of the significant fact that "man" also means male, the term does not come through as truly generic. For this reason many feminists would like to erase the specious generic term "man" from the language. What "sisterhood of man" does, however, is something else. It gives a generic weight to "sisterhood" which the term has never before been called on to bear. At the same time it emasculates the pseudo-generic "man." The expression, then, raises the problem of a sexually imbalanced world and it signals other possibilities.

The method of liberation, then, involves a castrating of language and images that reflect and perpetuate the structures of a sexist world. It *castrates* precisely in the sense of cutting away the phallus-centered value system imposed by patriarchy, in its subtle as well as in its more manifest expressions. As aliens in a man's world who are now rising up to name—that is, to create—our own world, women are beginning to recognize that the value system that has been thrust upon us by the various cultural institutions of patriarchy has amounted to a kind of gang rape of minds and bodies.

Feminists are accustomed to enduring such labels as "castrating females." Some have rightly retorted that if "to castrate" essentially means to deprive of power, potency, creativity, ability to communicate, then indeed it is women who have been castrated by a sexist society. However, I would push the analysis a bit further. It is also true that men are castrated by such a social system in which destructive competitiveness treats men who are low on the totem pole (e.g. Black males, poor males, non-competitive males,

Third World males, etc.) *like women*. Yet all of these can still look down upon the primordially castrated beings—women. What is happening now is that these primordial eunuchs are rising up to castrate the system that castrates—that great "God-Father" of us all which indulges senselessly and universally in the politics of rape.

The cutting away of this phallus-centered value system in its various incarnations amounts also to a kind of exorcism that essentially must be done by women, who are in a position to experience the demonic destructiveness of the super-phallic society in our own being. The *machismo* ethos that has the human psyche in its grip creates a web of projections, introjections, and self-fulfilling prophecies. It fosters a basic alienation within the psyche—a failure to lay claim to that part of the psyche that is then projected onto the "Other." It is essentially demonic in that it cuts off the power of human becoming.

The method of liberation-castration-exorcism, then, is a becoming process of the "Other"—women—in which we hear and speak our own words. The development of this new hearing faculty and of the new speech involves the dislodging of images that reflect and reinforce the prevailing social arrangements. This happens in one way when women assume active, creative, leadership roles. I am not referring to "role models" in the commonly accepted sense of patriarchy's "models," rather to the emergence of a kind of contagious freedom—a point which I will develop later.

The dislodging process requires a refusal of the false identity of tokenism. This often implies the necessity for dramatic action, which is many-dimensional in meaning. There is no single prescription for such symbolic acts. They grow organically out of particular situations. They are revelatory, since they not only unmask the fact of sexism but also give signals and clues of future transcendence.[8]

III: The Unfolding of God

It has sometimes been argued that anthropomorphic symbols for "God" are important and even necessary because the fundamental powers of the cosmos otherwise are seen as impersonal. One of the insights characteristic of the "rising woman consciousness" (as Nelle Morton aptly calls it) is that this kind of dichotomizing need not be. That is, it is not necessary to anthropomorphize or to reify transcendence in order to relate to this personally. The dichotomizing-reifying-projecting syndrome has been characteristic of patriarchal consciousness, making "the Other" the repository of the contents of the lost self. Since women are now beginning to recognize in ourselves the victims of such dichotomizing processes, the insight extends to other manifestations of the pathological splitting off of reality into falsely conceived opposites. Why indeed must "God" be a noun? Why not a verb—the most active and dynamic of all? Hasn't the naming of "God" as a noun been an act of murdering that dynamic Verb? And isn't the Verb infinitely more personal than a mere static noun? The anthropomorphic symbols for God may be intended to convey personality, but they fail to convey that God is Being. Women now who are experiencing the shock of non-being and the surge of self-affirmation against this are inclined to perceive transcendence as the Verb in which we participate—live, move, and have our being.

This Verb—the Verb of Verbs—is intransitive. It has no object to limit its dynamism. That which it is over against is non-being. Women in the process of liberation are enabled to perceive this because our liberation consists in refusing to be "the Other" and asserting instead "I am"—without making another "the Other." Unlike Sartre's "us versus a third" (the closest approximation to love possible in his world) the new sisterhood is saying "us versus non-being." When this kind of community-consciousness is present, there are clues and intimations of the God without an over-against—who is Be-ing. The unfolding of the woman consciousness is an intimation of the endless unfolding of God.

IV: New Space: New Time

The unfolding of God, then, is an event in which women participate as we participate in our own revolution. The process involves the creation of new space, in which women are free to become who we are, in which there are real and significant alternatives to the prefabricated identities provided within the enclosed spaces of patriarchal institutions. As opposed to the foreclosed identity allotted to us within those spaces, there is a diffused identity—an open road to discovery of the self and of each other. The new space is located always "on the boundary." Its center is on the boundary of patriarchal institutions, such as churches, universities, national and international politics, families. Its center is the lives of women, whose experience of becoming wrenches the locus of the center for us by putting it on the boundary of all that has been considered central. In universities and seminaries, for example, the phenomenon of women's studies is becoming widespread, and for many women involved this is the very heart of thought and action. It is perceived as the core of intellectual and personal vitality, often as the only part of the "curriculum" which is not dead. By contrast, many male administrators and faculty perceive "women's studies" as peripheral, even trivial, perhaps hardly more serious than the "ladies' page" of the daily newspaper. Most "good" administrators do sense that there is something of vitality there, of course, and therefore tolerate or even encourage women's studies—but it remains "on the boundary." So, too, the coming together of women on the boundary of "the church" is for us the center of spiritual community, unrecognized by institutional religion.

The new space, then, has a kind of invisibility to those who have not entered it. It is therefore to some degree, inviolate. At the same time it communicates power which, paradoxically, is experienced both as power of presence and power of absence. It is not political power understood as the phallic power of patriarchy that objectifies and dehumanizes. Rather it is a flow of energy which is participation in the power of being. For women who are becoming conscious, this participation is made possible initially by casting off the role of "the Other" which is the disguised nothingness imposed by a sexist world. The burst of anger and creativity made possible in the presence of one's sisters is an experience of becoming whole, of overcoming the division within the self that makes nothingness block the dynamism of being. Instead of settling for being half a person, which is equivalent to a self-destructive non-person, the emerging woman is casting off the role definitions and moving toward androgynous being. This is not a mere "becoming equal to men in a man's world"—which would mean settling for footing within patriarchal space. It is, rather, something like God speaking forth God's self in women. While life in the new space may be "dangerous" in that it means living without the securities offered by the patriarchal system in return for docility to its rules, it offers a deeper security that can absorb risks that such living demands. This safety is participation in *being*, as opposed to inauthenticity, alienation, non-identity—in a word, non-being.

The power of presence that is experienced by those who have begun to live in the new space radiates outward, attracting others. For those who are fixated upon patriarchal space it apparently is threatening. Indeed this sense of threat is frequently expressed. For those who are thus threatened, the presence of women to each other is experienced as an absence. Such women are no longer empty receptacles to be used as "the Other," and are no longer internalizing the projections that cut off the flow of being. Men who need such projection screens experience the power of absence of such "objects" and are thrown into the situation of perceiving nothingness. Sometimes the absence of women that elicits this anxiety is in fact physical. For example, when women deliberately stay away from meetings, chapel services, etc., in order to be free to do what is important to ourselves, there is sometimes an inordinate response of protest. Sometimes the absence is simply non-cooperation, refusal to "play the game" of sex roles, refusal to flatter and agree, etc. This too hints at presence of another space that women have gone off to and the would-be users are left with no one to use. Sometimes, of course, the absence of women takes the form of active resistance. Again, it throws those who would assume the role of exploiters back into their sense of nothingness.

In this way then, women's confrontation with the experience of nothingness invites men to confront it also. Many, of course, respond with hostility. The hostility may be open or, in some cases, partially disguised both from the men who are exercising it and from the women against whom it is directed. When disguised, it often takes seductive forms, such as invitations to "dialogue" under conditions psychologically loaded against the woman, or invitations to a quick and easy "reconciliation" without taking seriously the problems raised. Other men react with disguised hostility in the form of being "the feminist's friend," not in the sense of really hearing women but as paternalistic supervisors, analysts, or "spokesmen" for the movement. Despite the many avenues of non-authentic response to the threat of women's power of absence, some men do accept the challenge to confront the experience of nothingness that offers itself when "the Other" ceases to be "the Other" and stands back to say "I am." In so doing men can liberate themselves toward wholeness, that is, toward androgynous being. This new participation in the power of being becomes possible for men when women move into the new space.

Entry into the new space whose center is on the boundary of the institutions of patriarchy also involves entry into new time. To be caught up in these institutions is to be living in time past. This is strikingly evident in the liturgies and rituals that legitimate them. By contrast, when women live on the boundary, we are vividly aware of living in time present/future. Participation in the unfolding of God means also this time breakthrough. The center of the new time is on the boundary of patriarchal time. What it is, in fact, is women's *own* time. It *is* whenever we are living out of our own sense of reality, refusing to be possessed, conquered, and alienated by the linear, measured out, quantitative time of the patriarchal system. Women, insofar as we are becoming who we are, are living in a qualitative, organic time that escapes the measurements of the system. For example, women who sit in institutional committee meetings without surrendering to the purposes and goals set forth by the male-dominated structure, are literally working on our own time while perhaps appearing to be working "on company time." The center of our activities is organic, in such a way that events are more significant than clocks. This boundary living is a way of being in and out of "the system." It entails a refusal of false clarity. Essentially it is being alive *now*, which in its deepest dimension is participation in the unfolding of God.

It should be apparent, then, that for women entrance into our own space and time is another way of expressing integration and transformation. For women, to stay in patriarchal space is to remain in time past. The appearance of change is basically only cyclic movement. Breaking out of the circle requires anger, which enables us to burst out of the alienative circle. Since women are dealing with demonic power relationships, that is, with structured evil, rage operates as a positive force, making possible a breakthrough. It can trigger movement from the experience of nothingness to participation in being. When this happens, the past is changed, that is, its significance for us is changed. Thus the past is no longer static: it too is on the boundary. When women take positive steps to move out of patriarchal space and time there is a surge of new life. I would analyze this as participation in God the Verb that cannot be broken down simply into past, present, and future time, since it is a form-destroying, form-creating, transforming power that makes all things new.

V: New Being

Elizabeth Cady Stanton, who was probably the boldest thinker of the first generation of feminists, expressed an insight that is important to our present understanding of our situation. She wrote:

> Take the snake, the fruit-tree and the woman from the tableau, and we have no fall, nor frowning Judge, no Inferno, no everlasting punishment—hence no need of a Savior. Thus the bottom falls out of the whole Christian theology. Here is the reason why in all the Biblical researches and higher criticisms, the scholars never touch the position of women.[9]

Stanton in this passage has pointed out very accurately the key role of the myth of feminine evil as a foundation for the entire structure of phallic Christian ideology. This myth takes on cosmic proportions when the male's biased viewpoint is metamorphosed into God's viewpoint. With the assurance of this divine disapproval of women, Christianity was able to perpetuate the mechanisms of "blaming the victim" and scapegoat psychology.

Out of the rising woman consciousness is coming a realization that patriarchal religion's treatment of the mystery of evil has been out of focus and therefore that its deepest dimensions have never been really confronted. In dislodging ourselves from the role of "the Other" women are dislodging the problem from this false context. We are thus also moving the question of healing into a new perspective.

The healing process, we are beginning to understand, requires that women cast forth "the Other" within our divided selves, so that the internalized "eternal feminine" image can no longer hold down the authentic self. This process is also in effect an invitation to men to lay claim to their own complete identity. The invitation to wholeness that women are issuing to men has nothing to do with easy reconciliation or cheap grace. Rather, it takes the form of a positive refusal of co-optation.

Since the mystery of evil has been dislocated in patriarchal religious consciousness, it is logical to ask whether the Christian "solution" suffers from a comparable and consequent dislocation. I have already suggested that the idea of a divine incarnation in a male savior may be seen as one more legitimation of male superiority. Indeed, I think it can be seen now as a perpetuation of the "original sin" rather than as salvation. To put it rather bluntly, I propose that Christianity itself should be castrated by cutting away the products of supermale arrogance: the myths of sin and salvation that are simply two diverse symptoms of the same disease.

I further suggest that when Paul Tillich conceived of the Christ as the New Being he was enunciating a partial truth which has to be dislodged from its context. As in the case of his treatment of the myth of the Fall, he abstracts from the specific content of the symbol—which specific content in fact functions to justify societal structures that oppress us. It is indeed true that our psyches cry out for New Being. However, under the conditions of patriarchy it is most improbable, I think, that a male symbol can function adequately as the bearer of New Being. Inevitably it lends itself to some degree to reinforcement of the structures that oppress, even though, of course, there is an ambivalence about this. I think, rather that the bearers of New Being have to be those who live precariously on the boundary of patriarchal space—the primordial aliens: women. The story of Adam and Eve has been described as the hoax of the millenia. So also now the idea of the God-Man (God-Male, on the imaginative level)—the dogma of the hypostatic union—is beginning to be perceived by some women as a kind of cosmic joke. Under the conditions of patriarchy the role of liberating the human race from the original sin of sexism would seem to be precisely the role that a male symbol *cannot* perform. I am suggesting that the idea of salvation uniquely by a male savior perpetuates the problem of patriarchal oppression. I see two problems connected with this. First, the symbol itself is one-sided, as far as sexual identity is concerned, and it is precisely on the wrong side, functioning to glorify maleness. Those who would argue that the Christ symbol "can be used" oppressively but need not be used that way, should ponder the message that the unique maleness of the symbol itself conveys. When one has grasped this problem, it is natural to speculate that the doctrine of the Second Coming might be a way to salvage tradition—whether this be conceived as appearing in the form of a woman or a group of women or in terms of so-called "feminine" characteristics. However, this presupposes that a *first* Coming actually has occurred. Before moving into the use of this kind of language it would be important to be well aware of what we are about—which brings me to a second problem connected with the traditional doctrine of the "Incarnation," namely that a symbol has functioned as a model for human perfection. We have come to recognize that it is not adequate for us to accept the manner in which personal symbol-model figures have functioned in patriarchal religion and attempt to change the "content." This takes us, then, to the question of models.

VI: Jesus was a feminist, but so what?

In an admirable and scholarly article Leonard Swidler marshals historical evidence to show convincingly that Jesus was a feminist.[10] What I think I perceive happening in the rising woman consciousness is an affirmation that goes something like this: "Fine. Wonderful. But even if he wasn't, *I am.*" Professor Swidler's work has the advantages of striving for historical accuracy and of seeking to maintain continuity with tradition. At the same time, I would have some serious difficulties with him on at least two scores: First, there are difficulties involved in his thesis that one can extract "religious truth" from "time-conditioned categories." Implicit in this seems to be the idea that we can shuck off the debris of past oppressiveness and get back to the pristine purity of the original revelation. The core of my difficulty with this, I think, is that it seems backward-looking, assuming at least implicitly that we should give priority to the past over present experience. My second difficulty is interrelated with this, namely, that there seems to be in this approach an assumption that there *are* adequate models in the past. The traditional idea of *imitatio Christi* seems to be the not-so-hidden agenda of this method.

In contrast to this, I think women are perceiving that patriarchal religion is indeed patriarchal and are choosing to give priority to what we find valid in our own experience without needing to look to the past for legitimations of this. I am suggesting, first, that there are no adequate models in the past to guide us in our present situation. Second, I am proposing that the very idea of model, as commonly understood, is one of those conceptual tools of patriarchy that we need to wrench from its old semantic field. We may use the same term, materially speaking, but what we are in fact about, I think, is breaking models. It seems to have been a part of the patriarchal mind-set to imitate slavishly a master or father-figure (witness the apprentice system in universities) with an almost blind devotion and then to reject this figure in order to be oneself. (It is significant, perhaps, that the Latin term *modulus* means a small measure.) This imitation-rejection syndrome is not what is going on with women now. Rather, there is a contagious freedom in the air. Women who are living in the new space which is on the boundary of patriarchy, spark in others existential courage to affirm their own unique being.

As the idea of "model" is torn free from the male context, women call forth in each other the courage to enter the exodus community. "Exodus," too, we are beginning to hear with new ears. It means going *away* from the land of our fathers. We are going away because of a promise. The promise is not something handed down by a hypostatized God-Father, but rather something that we recognize—that we *hear*—in ourselves and in each other. It is the unfulfilled potentiality of our *foremothers* whose largely unrecorded history we are now assuming into our present/future. It is the promise in our sisters whose voices have been stolen from them. It is in our own potentiality that we are finding it. In finding it we are participating in the Verb Who is the most active of all verbs.

Notes

1. See Mary Daly, *The Church and the Second Sex* (New York: Harper and Row, 1968.) See also especially the following articles that I have published in 1971–72:
"After the Death of God the Father," *Commonweal,* March 12, 1971, pp. 7–11.
"The Courage to See," *The Christian Century,* Sept. 22, 1971, pp. 1108–1111.

"Abortion and Sexual Caste," *Commonweal,* Feb. 4, 1972, pp. 415–419.
"The Spiritual Revolution: Women's liberation as Theological Re-education," *Andover Newton Quarterly,* March 1972.
"The Women's Movement: An Exodus Community," *Religious Education* Sept.–Oct., 1972.

2. Karl Barth is of course well known for this approach to theology, which holds as sacred the presuppositions of patriarchy. However, I am using the expression in a broader sense, to apply to modern Christian apologists who are attempting to absorb the anger and insight of women without acknowledging the depth of the problem. An example of this is Robin Scroggs, "Paul: Chauvinist or Liberationist?" *The Christian Century,* March 15, 1972, pp. 307–309. Professor Scroggs is concerned to distinguish Paul's own views from those expressed in the pseudepigraphical writings attributed to him. For women this is too little and too late. The women's critique is not of a few passages but of a universe of sexist suppositions.
3. Male authors who are now claiming that they can write accurately "about women" give away the level of their comprehension by the use of this expression. The new consciousness of women is not mere "knowledge about," but an emotional-intellectual-volitional rebirth. An example of the products of such male claims is Donald McDonald, "The Liberation of Women," *The Center Magazine,* May–June, 1972.
4. This is Paul Tillich's method. Although I find it less inadequate than the methods of other systematic theologians of this century, it clearly does not offer the radical critique of patriarchal religion that can only come from women, the primordial outsiders.
5. See Paulo Freire, *Pedagogy of the Oppressed* (New York: Herder and Herder, 1970). Freire wrote acutely of the namelessness of the oppressed without acknowledging in this book the prototypical namelessness of women.
6. Nelle Morton gives a profound and moving analysis of this in her article "The Rising Woman Consciousness in a Male Language Structure," *Andover Newton Quarterly,* March, 1972, pp. 172–190.
7. This is the sense in which "exodus" was applied to the historic walk-out from Harvard Memorial Church called for in my sermon of November 14, 1971. See Mary Daly, "The Women's Movement: An Exodus Community," *Religious Education,* Sept. 1972. This article contains the sermon and reflections upon the event by some women who participated.
8. See "The Women's Movement: An Exodus Community," *Ibid.* The Harvard Exodus and its continuing aftermath exemplifies this process, involving refusal of tokenism, breaking with the past, dramatic action, and movement toward the really new.
9. Elizabeth Cady Stanton, Letter to the Editor, The Critic (1896), cited in *Up from the Pedestal,* edited by Aileen S. Kraditor (Chicago: Quadrangle Books, 1968), p. 119.
10. See Leonard Swidler, "Jesus Was a Feminist," *The Catholic World,* January, 1971, pp. 177–183.

From *The Politics of Women's Spirituality: Essays on the Rise of Spiritual Power within the Feminist Movement,* edited by Charlene Spretnak, 1982. Reprinted with permission.

5.2

Gyn/Ecology

Spinning New Time/Space

Mary Daly

In the course of The Second Passage, Crone-ographers who have survived dis-covering the various manifestations of Goddess-murder on this patriarchal planet have become aware of the deep and universal intent to destroy the diving spark in women. We have seen that the perpetrators of this planetary atrocity are acting out the deadly myths of patriarchy and that this ritual enactment of the sado-myths has become more refined with the "progress of civilization." This refinement includes an escalation of violence and visibility and at the same time a decrease of visibility to those mesmerized by the Processions of fathers, sons, and holy ghosts.

The know-ing of this deadly intent has been necessary for our a-mazing process of exorcism. It is equally necessary for moving on the Labyrinthine Journey of Ecstasy, for this process is damaged/hindered by not knowing/acknowledging the dangers, traps, deceptions built into the terrain. As long as "knowledge" of the horrors of androcracy is fragmented, compartmentalized, belittled, we cannot integrate this into our know-ing process. We then mistake the male-made maze for our Self-centering way.

Since we have come through the somber Passage of recognizing the alien/alienating environment in which woman-hating rituals vary from *suttee* to gynecological iatrogenesis, we can begin to tread/thread our way in new time/space. This knowing/acting/Self-centering Process is itself the creating of a new, woman-identified environment. It is the becoming of Gyn/Ecology. This involves the dis-spelling of the mind/spirit/body pollution that is produced out of man-made myths, language, ritual atrocities, and meta-rituals such as "scholarship," which erase our Selves. It also involves dis-covering the sources of the Self's original movement, hearing the moving of this movement. It involves speaking forth the New Words which correspond to this deep listening, speaking the words of our lives.

Breaking out of the patriarchal processions into our own Gyn/Ecological process is the specific theme of this, The Third Passage. In a general sense, our movement through the preceding Passages has all been and is Gyn/Ecological Journeying. Moreover, since our movement is not linear but rather resembles spiraling, we continue to re-member/re-call/re-claim the knowledge gained in the preceding Passages, assuming this into our present/future. Hence, there is no authentic way in which the preceding Passages can be dissociated from the Third. Thus, Gyn/Ecology is not the climax or linear end point in time of the Journey, but rather it is a defining theme/thread in our Labyrinthine Journey of the inner ear, in the course of which we constantly hear deeper and deeper reverberations from all of the Passages and learn to be attuned to echoes, subtleties, and distinctions not attended to before. Yet, Gyn/Ecology is the proper name for The Third Passage, for it names the patterns/ designs of the moving Female-identified environment which can only be heard/seen after the Journeyer has been initiated through The First and The Second Passages.

As the Spinster spins into and through this Passage she is encouraged by her strengthened powers of hearing and seeing. By now she has begun to develop a kind of multidimensional/multiform power of sensing/understanding her environment. This is a Self-identified *synaesthesia:* It is woman-identified *gynaesthesia*. It is a complex way of perceiving the interrelatedness of seemingly disparate phenomena. It is also a pattern-detecting power which may be named positive paranoia. Far from being a debilitating "mental disease," this is a strengthening and realistic dis-ease in a polluted and destructive environment. Derived from the Greek terms *para,* meaning beyond, outside of, and *nous,* meaning mind, the term *paranoia* is appropriate to describe movement beyond, outside of, the patriarchal mind-set. It is the State of Positively Revolting Hags.

Moving through all three Passages is moving from the state of anaesthesia to empowering gynaesthesia, as dormant senses become awake and alive. Since, in The Second Passage, the Voyager became more aware not only of the blatancy and interconnectedness of phallocratic evil, but also of its reality, she is enabled to detect and name its implicit presence and therefore to overcome roadblocks in her dis-covery of be-ing. Empowered with positive paranoia she can move with increasing confidence.

We have seen that this is the age of holy ghosts, with particular reference to gynecology. It is an age of manipulation through/by invisible and *almost* insensible presences. Some of these might be called physical, such as radiation and "white noise." Others more properly may be said to belong to the realm of the spirit, of "ghost." We are dealing here with the realm of implicit or subliminal manipulation, of quiet, almost indiscernible, intent on the part of the manipulators and quiet, unacknowledged acceptance of their ghostly presences and messages by their victims. Hence, the first chapter of this Passage will be concerned with Spooking. The Haggard Journeyer will not be astonished to find that Spooking is multileveled. Women are spooked by patriarchal males in a variety of ways; for example, through implicit messages of their institutions, through body language, through the silences and deceptive devices of their media, their grammar, their education, their professions, their technology, their oppressive and confusing fashions, customs, etiquette "humor," through their subliminal advertising and their "sublime" music (such as Christmas carols piped into supermarkets that seduce the listener into identifying with the tamed Goddess who abjectly adores her son).

Women are also spooked by other women who act as instrumental agents for patriarchal males, concurring, with varying degrees of conscious complicity, in all of the above tactics. To the extent that any woman acts—or nonacts when action is required—in such complicity, she functions as a double agent of Spooking, for politically she *is* and *is not* functioning as a woman. Since Hags/Witches have expectations of her—righteous expectations which are almost impossible to discard without falling into total cynicism and despair—she spooks us doubly, particularly by her absences/silences/nonsupport. Finally, Spinsters are spooked by the alien presences that have been inspired (breathed into) our own spirits/minds. These involve fragments of the false self which are still acting/nonacting in complicity with the Possessors. They also take the shape of nameless fears, unbearable implanted guilt feelings for affirming our own being, fear of our newly discovered powers and of successful use of them, fear of dis-covering/releasing our own deep wells of anger, particularly fear of our anger against other women and against ourselves for failing our Selves. Spinsters are spooked by fear of the Ultimate Irony, which would be to become a martyr/scapegoat for feminism, whose purpose is to release women from the role of martyr and scapegoat.

Faced with being spooked, Spinsters are learning to Spook/Speak back. This Spinster-Spooking is also re-calling/re-membering/re-claiming our Witches' power to cast spells, to charm, to overcome prestige with prestidigitation, to cast glamours, to employ occult grammar, to enthrall, to bewitch. Spinster-Spooking is both cognitive and tactical. Cognitively, it means pattern-detecting. It means understanding the time-warps through which women are divided from each other—since each woman comes to consciousness through the unique events of her own history. It means also seeing the problems caused through space-warps—since Hags and potential Hags are divided from each other in separate institutional settings, disabled from sharing survival tactics in our condition of common isolation, spooked by our apparent aloneness. Tactically, Spooking means learning to refuse the seductive summons by the Passive Voices that call us into the State of Animated Death. It means learning to hear and respond to the call of the wild, learning ways of en-couraging and en-spiriting the Self and other Spinsters, learning con-questing, learning methods of dispossession, specifically of dis-possessing the Self of possession by the past and possession by the future. It means a-mazing the modern witchcraze, developing skills for unpainting the Painted Birds possessed through the device of tokenism, exposing the Thoroughly Therapeutic Society.

Since Spooking cannot always be done alone, and since it is a primary but not complete expression of Gyn/Ecology, the second chapter of this Passage is concerned with Sparking. In order to move on the con-questing Voyage, Spinsters need fire. It is significant that Witches and widows were burned alive, consumed by fire. For fire is source and symbol of energy, of gynergy. It is because women are known to be energy sources that patriarchal males seek to possess and consume us. This is done less dramatically in day-by-day draining of energy, in the slow and steady extinguishing of women's fire. Sparking is necessary to re-claim our fire. Sparking, like Spooking, is a form of Gyn/Ecology. Sparking is Speaking with tongues of fire. Sparking is igniting the divine Spark in women. Light and warmth, which are necessary for creating and moving, are results of Sparking. Sparking is creating a room of one's own, a moving time/spaceship of one's own, in which the Self can expand, in which the Self can join with other Self-centering Selves.

Sparking is making possible Female Friendship, which is totally Other from male comradeship. Hence, the Spinster will examine male comradeship/fraternity, in order to avoid the trap of confusing sisterhood with brotherhood, of thinking (even in some small dusty corner of the mind) of sisterhood as if it were simply a gender-correlative of brotherhood. She will come to see that the term *bonding*, as it applies to Hags/Harpies/Furies/Crones is as thoroughly Other from "male bonding" as Hags are the Other in relation to patriarchy. Male comradeship/bonding depends upon energy drained from women (its secret glue), since women are generators of energy. The bonding of Hags in friendship *for* women is not draining but rather energizing/gynergizing. It is the opposite of brotherhood, not essentially because Self-centering women oppose and fight patriarchy in a reactive way, but because we are/act for our Selves.

The term *comrade* is derived from a Middle French word meaning a group of soldiers sleeping in one room, or roommate. The concept of room here is spatial, suggesting links resulting from physical proximity, not necessarily from choice. The space is physical, not psychic, and it is definitely not A Room of One's Own. To the degree that it has been chosen, the choice has been made by another. The comrades do not choose each other for any inherent qualities of mind/spirit. Although this accidental and spatial "roommate" aspect does apply to all women insofar as all women are oppressed/possessed, it does not apply to the deep and conscious bonding of Hags in the process of be-ing. Since the core/the soul-spark of such deep bonding is friendship, it does not essentially depend upon an enemy for its existence/becoming.

At first, it is hard to generate enough sparks for building the fires of Female Friendship. This is particularly the case since patriarchal males, sensing the ultimate threat of Female Sparking, make every effort to put out women's fires whenever we start them. They try to steal the fire of Furies in order to destroy us in their perpetual witchcraze. Like Cinderellas, Hags stand among the cinders, but we know that they are cinders of our burned foresisters. We know that the cinders still Spark.

Sparking means building the fires of gynergetic communication and confidence. As a result, each Sparking Hag not only begins to live in a lighted and warm room of her own; she prepares a place for a loom of her own. In this space she can begin to weave the tapestries of her own creation. With her increasing fire and force, she can begin to Spin. As she and her sisters Spin together, we create The Network of our time/space.

Gyn/Ecological Spinning is essential for entry into our Otherworld. The Voyager who does not Spin is in mortal danger. She may become trapped in one of the blind alleys of the maze which has been uncovered in The Second Passage. That is, she may become fixated upon the atrocities of androcracy, "spinning her wheels" instead of spinning on her heel and facing in Other directions. Or the nonspinner may make the fatal mistake of trying to jump over the atrocities into pseudo-ecstasy. As a result of this escapism, this blind "leap of faith," she can only fall into a tailspin.

The force of Spinsters' Spinning is the power of spirit spiraling, whirling. As we break into The Third Passage, we whirl into our own world. Gyn/Ecology is weaving the way past the dead past and the dry places, weaving our world tapestry out of genesis and demise.

Previously published in *The New Yorker*, February 26/March 4, 1996, pp. 76-84. Reprinted with permission.

5.3

Sin Big

Mary Daly

The author created her own feminist lexicon and became a gleeful flamethrower in the world of academic theology.

Ever since childhood, I have been honing my skills for living the life of a Radical Feminist Pirate and cultivating the Courage to Sin. The word "sin" is derived from the Indo-European root "es-," meaning "to be." When I discovered this etymology, I intuitively understood that for a woman trapped in patriarchy, which is the religion of the entire planet, "to be" in the fullest sense is "to sin."

Women who are Pirates in a phallocratic society are involved in a complex operation. First, it is necessary to Plunder—that is, righteously rip off—gems of knowledge that the patriarchs have stolen from us. Second, we must Smuggle back to other women our Plundered treasures. In order to invent strategies that will be big and bold enough for the next millennium, it is crucial that women share our experiences: the chances we have taken and the choices that have kept us alive. They are my Pirate's battle cry and wake-up call for women who want to hear.

Piratic Preparations In Childhood

One day when I was about nine or ten, I was walking home from St. John the Evangelist parochial school in Schenectady, New York, accompanied by an obnoxious boy in my class who was gloating over the fact that he was an altar boy, while I could never "serve Mass," because I was only a girl. Although I had no interest in becoming an altar girl, this repulsive revelation of the sexual caste system that I would later learn to call "patriarchy" burned its way into my brain and kindled an unquenchable Rage. Since I soon found that I could not communicate this knowledge to those around me, I felt alone with it.

One day, a saleswoman came to our house taking orders for children's books. Her list included a book about ships, but when my mother tried to order it for me the woman embarrassed her by saying that it would be *silly* to order such a book for a little *girl*. This only increased my desire to find out about ships—especially pirate ships—and most especially the kind that could sail far up among the stars. In my mind, I began sprinting around Intergalactically, seeking my own homeland, which would be very different from this world of stupid restrictions. If that Otherworld did not exist, I would somehow conjure it up.

My father was a travelling salesman who sold ice-cream freezers. Our income was dependent upon his commissions, so I learned about living on the edge at a very early age.

My mother encouraged me unfailingly. She told me that she had loved school but had been "yanked out" of high school during her sophomore year. She wanted to give me everything that she had not been given in her own childhood. On those rare occasions when I volunteered to help with the household chores, she almost invariably said, "Go do your own work, dear!" So I had to find out what that work might be and try to do it.

When I was very small, I realized that I wanted to be a writer. This desire was inspired at least in part by a special box of books which I had seen around our house. The box contained copies of a book that had been written and published by my father long before I was born. The title of this volume, published in 1914, was "What Every Ice Cream Dealer Should Know."

My father had been forced to leave school after the eighth grade. I was deeply impressed that he had produced these red-covered books. I felt as if they were flashing a signal to me: "Do this! Carry on your heritage. Write!" But that left the question, "Write about *what?*"

In high school, I noticed the intellectual shortcomings of most of the boys in my classes, particularly in the areas of syntax and math. Because they were so obtuse, the teachers were obliged to move slowly when I felt ready to fly. I was becoming equipped to see through all the myths of male intellectual superiority.

There were also vital messages from nature. Especially important was a startling communication from a clover blossom one summer day when I was about fourteen. It said, with utmost simplicity, "I am." It was an experience that I would later call "an intuition of Be-ing, the Verb in which we all participate." Such invitations to my adolescent spirit were somehow intimately connected with the call of books. It was this encounter that launched me on my quest to become a Radical Feminist philosopher.

Onward by Degrees: Perfecting My Craft

After I graduated from college, my lust for learning and adventure led me to graduate school. First, I went to the Catholic University of America, in Washington, D.C., which had offered me a full-tuition scholarship while I studied for an M.A. in English. One night, after tedious hours of translating Middle English, I fell into a deep sleep and dreamed of green: Elemental, Be-dazzling Green. When I woke up, I had a revelation: "Study philosophy!" However, there was no scholarship money available there for a woman to study philosophy.

One day, when I was sitting in class, I suddenly had a vision of myself standing at a blackboard teaching *theology*. This was mystifying, since I had no ambition to pursue that subject. Moreover, such a thing was unheard of in 1952, when catholic women were still not allowed to teach or study theology.

Shortly after this unusual event, I "just happened" to see an ad for a School of Sacred Theology for women at St. Mary's College in Notre Dame, Indiana. I learned that this program had been initiated by the president of the college, Sister Madeleva. That fiery nun was exasperated that no university in this country would admit women to study catholic theology at the doctoral level. When I wrote to her, she immediately offered me a scholarship and a part-time teaching job to support my studies. Having armed myself with the M.A., I jumped at the chance. On the train headed for St. Mary's, I felt that I was riding a Great Wind.

At St. Mary's, I acquired the habit of thinking philosophically in a rigorously logical manner. Medieval theology, especially that of Aquinas, who became my teacher, was philosophy carried into an Other dimension. After earning my Ph.D. in religion at the ripe old age of twenty-five, I decided to keep on Searching. I applied to the University of Notre Dame, but I was refused admission to the doctoral program in philosophy solely on the basis of my sex. Moreover, I was unable to find a suitable teaching position, and found myself marooned for five years at a mediocre college in Brookline, Massachusetts. So, in 1959, I crossed the Atlantic to study at the University of Fribourg in Switzerland, where there was scholarship money available and where no obstacle was placed in the path of women who wanted to study for degrees in theology. My purpose was to obtain the highest of higher degrees in theology and philosophy, and between 1959 and 1965 I accumulated four degrees in Fribourg. I was getting ready to Sin Big.

The question may well arise: *Why did you go on and on pursuing doctorates— especially in theology?* Was I a learned lunatic? Well, sure. But what else could I do that would prepare me so adequately for my work in the women's movement that was soon to come?

Theology—especially medieval catholic theology—is a treasure chest containing archaic gems. By studying arduously, I equipped myself to reverse the reversals inherent in christian dogma and decode its doctrines with precision. Subsequently, I would take these myths, symbols, and "mysteries" out of their phallocentric framework and make them Visible in a woman-centered context. In my books "Beyond God the Father" (1973) and "Gyn/Ecology" (1978), the doctrines of the male-god and of the trinity are revealed as distorted reflections of ancient female images of divinity. So, also, the idea of the "virgin birth" of Jesus is exposed as both a pale derivative and a reversal of pre-patriarchal myths of parthenogenesis (which produces divine daughters, not sons).

During those years in Fribourg, I followed my own interior compass. In fact, I Plundered with a vengeance—flying to university classes on my Velosolex motor bicycle, teaching in three junior-year-abroad programs, and exploring Europe on a very skimpy shoestring. In 1964, I published an article in *Commonweal* magazine on women and the church, which led to a letter from a British publisher inviting me to write a book on the subject. My Smuggling career was about to begin, but I needed a great burst of inspiration, and within a few months that happened.

A Terrible Moment of Revelation

In the fall of 1965, I travelled to Rome for the Second Vatican Council of the Roman Catholic Church. One day, I borrowed a journalist's identification card and went into St. Peter's Basilica to sit in on a major session. In the distance, I saw a huge number of cardinals and bishops, old men in crimson dresses. In another section were the "auditors"—a group that included a few women, most of whom were nuns dressed in long black habits. The women sat docilely, listening to the senile, cracking whines of the men in red droning on in Latin, which the readers as well as the listeners barely comprehended. But what I found most appalling was the contrast between the arrogant bearing and colorful attire of the "princes of the church" and the humble, self-deprecating manner of the women. When the veiled nuns shuffled to the altar rail to receive "Holy Communion" from the hands of a priest, I felt that I was observing a string of lowly ants at a bizarre picnic. No Fellini movie could have outdone this unintended self-satire of catholicism.

I came to see that all of the so-called major religions—from buddhism and hinduism to islam, judaism, and christianity, as well as such secular derivatives as freudianism, jungianism, marxism, and maoism—are mere sects, infrastructures of the edifice of patriarchy. All are erected as parts of the male's shelter against anomie—that is, unpredictability and disorder. And the symbolic message is this: women are the dreaded anomie ("the enemy"). We are the real objects under attack in all the wars of patriarchy.

That moment of revelation in Rome continues to work subliminally, inspiring my humor and stoking the Fires of my Fury not merely against the catholic church and all the other religions and institutions that are the tentacles of patriarchy but against everything that dulls and diminishes women. Through me, it shouts messages meant for all women within Earshot: "Tell on them! Laugh out loud at their pompous penile processions! Reverse their reversals! Decode their 'mysteries'! Break their taboos! Spin tapestries of your own creation! Sin Big!"

Boom, Boom, Boomerang . . . Back and Ahead to Boston

In 1966, after seven years of glorious freedom in Europe, I spiralled back to the United States, anticipating the old dullness of the nineteen-fifties. But America was no longer the dead zone that I had fled in 1959.

I began teaching in what was ostensibly the liberal theology department at jesuit-run Boston College, which, over the years, would serve as my laboratory for the study of patriarchal tricks and for the development of Radical Feminist strategies. My first book, "The Church and the Second Sex," my reasonable and relatively mild book exposing the misogynism of "the church," was published in this country in 1968. Shortly after the publication and attendant publicity—including major television appearances—I was given a one-year terminal contract by Boston College; that is, I was fired. Although the university "bore-ocrats" gave no reason for their action, the students and the media understood the obvious connection between the book and the firing. An estimated fifteen hundred students—nearly all male—demonstrated on campus, and twenty-five hundred signed a petition. The administration building was decorated with brilliant red graffiti (still faintly but clearly legible in 1996). Television cameras rolled. My case received national/international/supernatural publicity.

In June, 1969, the embarrassed administration finally backed down, and I was ungraciously granted promotion and tenure. I began to see beyond this one university and its petty politics to the universal disease of "academentia." Tearing off the mind bindings that were strangling me, I moved into an invisible counter-university—the Feminist Universe.

Metamorphic Events and Strategies

In 1971, I became the first woman to be invited to preach the Sunday service at Harvard's Memorial Church. Had the invitation been issued ten or even five years earlier, it might have appeared as an acceptable honor. By that time, however, I was acutely aware of the trap of tokenism. If I accepted, I would be used to legitimize that church in particular and christianity in general. If I refused, I would be forfeiting an important opportunity for communication. I decided to "accept," with the intention of giving an anti-sermon that would be a clarion call to all to abandon patriarchal religion. I met with a few friends, and together we planned what came to be known as the Harvard Memorial Exodus. In order to deliver the "sermon," which would be a springboard for a walkout, I was obliged to sit in the sanctuary during the first part of the service. Misogynist scriptural passages were read by two of my Cohorts, thus paving the way for my anti-sermon.

I mounted the steps to the gigantic, phalluslike pulpit, and as I spoke I fervently hoped that afterward I would not have to endure the humiliation of being alone, except for six or seven staunch comrades, as I stalked out of the church. But the moment I finished, hundreds of women and some of the men began stampeding out of the church. By the time I managed to run down the steps of the enormous pulpit, half of the "flock" were pushing ahead of me. I just joined the crowd.

In 1975 I was refused a long-overdue promotion to the rank of full professor at Boston College. My response was to create, along with my female students and allies, an event known as the Forum on Women in Higher Education. Eight hundred women packed the large gymnasium, and the moderator of the forum, Robin Morgan, greeted them with the battle cry "Sisters, we meet on bloody jesuit ground!" By 1975, the backlash against feminism in universities and throughout society was well under way. Many women faculty and students spoke of the harassment they had experienced at their "home" institutions.

After that, I took an unpaid leave of absence in order to write "Gyn/Ecology," a book that explores patriarchal myths and the enactment of these in the form of atrocities against women. When the book was published in 1978, university administrators predictably reacted with "misterical" behavior. Monitors were sent to "observe" my classes, and various other mechanisms of mental torture were employed. While that institution has benefited from my name, attracting students and visiting faculty and gaining recognition for academic excellence and "liberality"/"liberalism," it has consistently fostered another kind of "name and fame." The grapevine blacklisting within the intricate buddy system that is the academic men's club is intended to manufacture a "no-win" situation for me as well as for all Radical Feminists, actual and potential.

From its inception, the decade of the nineteen-eighties was a time of creeping malaise in the United States. Gradually, many women became divided over every imaginable issue. Many could not see that the agents of androcracy were using their familiar strategy of "divide and conquer." Many women felt spooked. I did my best to convey optimism, and to name the agents of atrocities against women and nature through my teaching, public speaking, and writing. During this period, I published two books. The first, "Pure Lust: Elemental Feminist Philosophy" (1984), carries on where "Gyn/Ecology" leaves off. The other is "Websters' First New Intergalactic Wickedary of the English Language," a dictionary for Wicked women, which I conjured in cahoots with Jane Caputi in 1987.

In 1988–89, I decided to "blow the whistle" on B.C. by renewing my application for a promotion to full professor. My request was met with ridiculous rejection yet again. Colleagues from around the United States, Canada, and Europe sent outraged letters of protest. B.C. students and some of the faculty held five explosively original demonstrations on my behalf. For several months, loud chanting could be heard all across campus. Favorite chants included "Witch trial—jesuit style" and "Mary Daly refused again—academic freedom only for men." Another was "Barth [dean] and Monan [president], peas in a pod; keep women down in the name of God."

The Witches Return: Patriarchy on Trial

On May 14, 1989, hundreds of women poured into Sanders Theatre at Harvard University for an event that was billed as "A Dramatic Indictment of Gynocide, 1989." The opening address was given by Evelyn Wight, who spoke movingly of the murder of her sister, Rebecca. This atrocity had been perpetrated by a confirmed lesbian-hater while Rebecca was hiking on the Appalachian Trail with her partner, Claudia Brenner. At the conclusion of the speech, I pronounced a Nemesis Hex, thus setting the scene for a Dramatic Indictment.

A stern bailiff stalked to the lectern and shouted, "Wild Witches will now expose and condemn the massacre of women's minds, bodies, and spirits. Bring in the accused!" Accompanied by a thunderous beating of drums, black-robed members of the Witches' Chorus carried flamboyantly dressed, balloon-headed wooden dummies, representing agents of gynocide and biocide, down the aisle and onto the stage. Among the dummies were Jack the Ripper, figurehead for serial killers; Exxon, figurehead for Earth rapers of every kind; Sigmund Freud, figurehead for all professional mindfuckers; Boss-town College (dressed as a football wearing a roman collar), figurehead for the brain-drainers of academia.

After hearing the evidence in each case, the Witches of Boston (the whole audience) shouted: "Guilty!"

As High Chaircrone, I sentenced the dummies to de-heading. "Off with their heads!" shouted the women, as the jailers, flourishing sharp-edged labryses, descended upon the accused and popped their balloon heads. After this event, more than one woman said, "Patriarchy doesn't exist Here, Now."

Such relief, inspiration, and reinvigoration were desperately needed, for outside the Space we had created the war against women as escalating. That same year, a smiling man wearing hunting clothes gunned down and killed fourteen women in the engineering school at the University of Montreal with a semiautomatic rifle. After lining the women up in a classroom, he snarled, "You're all fucking feminists." This atrocity received very little media attention. The double phenomenon of increasing violence against women and erasure of this reality was to become commonplace in the decade that followed.

Roaring through the Nineteen-nineties: The Wrath of Nemesis is Here

The first Italian Lesbian Week was held in Bologna in 1991, shortly after "Beyond God the Father" was published in Italian. As part of the celebration, I gave a talk at the Sala dei Notai, the famed hall in the heart of Bologna. Nineteen ninety-two marked the publication of my philosophical autobiography, "Outercourse: The Be-Dazzling Voyage." In the late summer and early fall of 1994, I toured Switzerland and Germany with the German translation of the book. At the University of Fribourg, where, thirty years earlier, I had attended lectures delivered in Latin on medieval theology and philosophy, some women were actually studying and writing papers on "Gyn/Ecology." My heart skipped a beat when I learned this. But back in the United States, speaking around the country, I witnessed an upsurge of fear and rage, as gynocidal crimes became more numerous and more blatant. In December, 1994, Shannon Lowney, who had been one of my students, in 1989, in a course on feminist ethics, was murdered at a Planned Parenthood clinic in Brookline, Massachusetts, where abortions are performed, and where she worked as a receptionist.

During the course of this decade, it has become increasingly evident that "justice" under the asymmetric system of patriarchy is unattainable. It is even inconceivable. The prevailing order/ordure does not have the capacity to bestow the sought-after treasure. Yet there has been a surge of positive energy among women.

Justice under the patriarchal system is depicted as a blindfolded woman holding a sword and scales. In contrast, Nemesis, the Goddess of divine retribution, has her eyes open and uncovered—especially her Third Eye. Moreover, she is less concerned with retribution in the sense of an external meting out of rewards and punishments than with an internal judgment that sets in motion a disruption of the patriarchal balance of terror. A new psychic alignment of energy patterns accompanies this disruption, patterns I am now at work Dis-covering and analyzing for my new book, "Quintessence: Re-Calling the Outrageous, Contagious Courage of Women."

In this work, as in my Wickedary, I honor the work of Positively Revolting Hags. My definition of a true "Pro-Lifer" is "one who puts her Life on the line in the struggle against the necro-apocalyptic nobodies who are running/ruining the world."

5.4

Spiraling Into the Nineties

An Invitation to Outercourse

Mary Daly

As we move into the final decade of this millennium, how can women work to exorcize the evils that overwhelm us and at the same time Realize our capacity for ecstasy? Since there is no point in settling for anything less, this is the question I will attempt to address.

Uh, oh! I am hearing voices. "Who does she think she is, with her impossible questions and grandiose schemes? Why doesn't she just do re-search in academentia and leave the scheming to us?" Luckily I recognize those voices. They're coming from the old brotherhood of doubt demons who are always trying to undermine women's Self-confidence, and their cohorts the blah demons with their energy-draining "blah, blah, blah." The Time has come to switch them off. Now—That's better. To continue:

We have just come through a decade of escalating violence against women and all of the oppressed, and against earth, air, fire, water—the elements that sustain and constitute all Life. On the foreground level—the level of man-made horrors—this has been and continues to be a time not only of genocide and gynocide, but also of biocide—the devastation of all forms of Life. This level is very real.

Yet there are also Other levels, Other dimensions. I often refer to these simply as "the Background," meaning the Realm of Wild Reality, the Homeland of women's Selves and of all other Others—the Time/Space where auras of plants, planets, stars, animals, and all Other animate beings connect. As a philosopher, I would say that the Background *is* whenever/wherever we actively participate in Be-ing, the Verb of Verbs. In other words, it *is* when/where we are really Alive.

Re-membering my own Voyage as a Radical Feminist philosopher, I am intensely aware of the struggle to stay on my True Course, despite undermining by demons of distraction and fragmentation that have always attempted to pull me off course. These I gradually Dis-covered and learned to Name as agents and institutions of patriarchy, whose intent is to keep me—and indeed all living beings—within the strangle-hold of the foreground, that is, fatherland. My True Course was and is Outercourse—moving beyond the imprisoning mental, physical, emotional, spiritual walls of the state of possession. Insofar as I am focused on Outercoursing, naturally I am surrounded and aided by the benevolent forces of the Background.

This Voyage could also be called *Innercourse,* since it involves delving deeply into the process of communication with the Self and with Others—a process that demands profound and complex Passion, Remembering, Understanding. It could also be called *Countercourse,* since it requires Amazonian Acts of Courageous Battling. However, its primary/primal configuration is accurately Named *Outercourse,* for this is a Voyage of Spiraling Paths, Moving Out from the state of bondage. It is continual expansion of thinking, imagining, acting, be-ing.

I think I just heard someone say "That's fine for her, but I'm not a philosopher. I'm just . . ." Time to switch off the doubt demons again, dear reader. After all, a philosopher is really a lover of wisdom—a seeker—one who is on a Quest. If someone thinks she/he *has* wisdom, *owns* it, then she/he is not a philosopher. If you are a seeker, I am talking to you.

The Moments of Outercourse

The Spiraling Paths of Outercourse move from Moment to Moment. Unlike mere instants, Moments are Momentous. And they have Momentum. They have the Power to hurl us on an Intergalactic Voyage. Moments are Acts of Hope, Faith, and Biophilic Bounding. They are ontologically and politically significant, because they occur when a woman speaks and acts Courageously. Such speaking (Be-Speaking) and acting elicits responses from the world around her, to which she, in turn, is challenged to respond. She is challenged to move beyond foreground limitations.

Because the Moments of Outercourse are active in nature, I call them Moments/Movements of be-ing. For they propel Journeyers into ever more A-mazing Acts of Courage and Imagination. They are Metamorphic points of contact with one's Genius, one's Muse. They are similar to Virginia Woolf's "moments of being" in that they are revelatory; that is, they can be seen as windows or doors to the Background. But they are also something else, something E-motional. They are Acts of Qualitative Leaping *through* these portals further and further into the Background. I think that whenever a woman Leaps in this way she brings others with her—by example, by inspiration. Her Courage is contagious. Hence Moments/Movements of Outercourse are Political/ Metapolitical.

The Politics/Metapolitics of Outercourse: Piracy

Having been a Pirate for many years, I am speaking from a Piratic perspective. I have Righteously Plundered treasures of knowledge that have been stolen and hidden from women and I've struggled to Smuggle these back in such a way that they can be seen as distinct from their mindbinding trappings. After Voyaging for awhile, I began Reclaiming this stuff by Naming it in New ways, in order to render its liberating potential accessible to women. For example many light years ago I Plundered the christian idea of "the Second Coming" and transformed it to mean "the Second Coming of women." Since then, I have moved on to far more Daring and Disreputable Deeds.

There are many Other Sister Pirates Out there/here, with a great Diversity of Plundering and Smuggling skills. Take healing, for example. Pirates who are healers must range far and wide in order to Righteously rip off women's own healing tradition, which has been stolen, scattered, and partially destroyed. Then they have to sort it out from the poisonous distorting context in which it has been hidden and Smuggle it back to us.

This brings me to the subject of the Pirate's Craft. My Time Traveling adventures and my life as a Pirate have been possible because of my Craft. The word *craft* means, among other things, skill and cunning. Wild women sometimes refer to our strength, force, skill, and occupations as Witchcraft. My own particular Craft involves writing and the forging of philosophical theories.

Craft is etymologically related to the verb *crave*. Voyaging women Spiral with our Craft/Crafts because we crave something, because we have a strong longing for something. That "something" is the free unfolding and expansion of our be-ing. Propelled by Wonderlust, by Wanderlust, our Quest *is* the expansion of our be-ing.

Taking charge of our Crafts is a primary/primal task of women as Pirates, who are overcoming the "woman as vessel" motif that prevails in Stag-nation. Women under phallocratic rule are confined to the role of vessels/carriers, directed and controlled by men. Since that role is the basic base reversal of the very be-ing of Voyaging/Spiraling women, when we direct our own Crafts/Vessels we become reversers of that deadly reversal. In this process we become Crafty.

Crafty Pirates dare to sail across the vast Realm which I Now Name the Subliminal Sea. This contains deep Background knowledge, together with countless contaminants—the man-made subliminal and overt messages disseminated through the media and other patriarchal means for the purpose of mind manipulation. The heat generated by the Movement of our Crafts causes droplets from the Subliminal Sea to rise around us, forming a mist. Spiraling into the mist, we confront the contaminants and Dis-cover our buried Memories and tradition. This process is both exorcism and ecstasy. Indeed, it is Be-Dazzling, that is, eclipsing the foreground world by the brilliance of be-ing. In the Light of Be-Dazzling we are enabled to Dis-cover the hidden connections that make Sense of our Lives.

Time Traveling Now

Voyagers gifted with the Terrible Vision that rips through the mist of man-made mysteries/mystifications can Spiral full speed backward, around, and ahead with our Craft of the Fourth Dimension, which is the Craft of Time Travel. Having seen through the fabricated past, we can Envision our true Past. As the Past changes, the Present and the Future change.

For Now there is available a personal/political/historical context in which earlier Moments can be Re-membered. Hence the Present Moment can be Seen in a Be-Dazzling Light. Women who accept the Invitation to Outercourse accept the challenge to Spin and Weave the broken connections in our knowing, sensing, and feeling, becoming Alive again in our relationships to ourSelves and to each Other.

As I see our situation in the early Nineties, what is required is a Spiraling series of Victories over the fragmenters of women's Present and of our Memories, including our Memories of the Future. Such a series of Victories, that is, Moments of Spinning

Integrity, cannot be viewed as mere linear progression. When a Voyager Spirals into Outercourse she experiences Overlapping of the Moments of her earlier Travels—a conversation Now with those Moments. The repetitious aspect of Spiraling enriches her experience of Movement. There is an accumulation of Acts of Momentous Re-membering and thus she gathers Momentum for whirling ahead. Yet the most crucial Moments are always Now, and that is why Now is always the special target of the fragmenters of our lives.

Fragmentation often takes the form of enforced distracted busy-ness (a type of sloth imposed especially upon women), which is associated with psychic numbing. The encroachment of fragmentation, which manifests itself now in seemingly endless divisions within and among women, involves also the breakdown of nature by phallotechnocrats and the splitting of women from nature.

In this Age of Fragmentation, Sisterhood can seem like a lost and impossible dream. Much of the knowledge and many of the memories that were reclaimed in the so-called "second wave" of feminism have re-turned to a subliminal level in women's psyches. At this Time it is essential to Re-call our knowledge that all of our Spiraling Paths are interconnected. Herein lies the hope for resolving miscommunications arising from "generation gaps" and time warps, as well as from ethnic, cultural, and class differences. When Pirates Realize the interconnectedness among all our Spiraling Moments, it begins to become possible to respect and celebrate our Great Diversity, Secure in our understanding of our Common Quest, we can Dis-cover these rich variations as a Tremendous Treasure Trove, and as sources of fuel for the Voyage.

In Other words, I see hope that we can travel in Intergalactic Concordance!

At this High Moment of writing I am hearing voices again. "What 'concordance' is she talking about? There's nothing but discordance around here," they whine. "That Daffy Daly with her incurable absurd optimism, slashing and dashing all over the space—a lyrical lunatic, a Capitalizing crackpot!"

It's the tiresome crowd of spaced-out party poopers, trying to take the Wind out of my sails. Yep—Here come the doubt demons, still trying to keep up with my Craft, clinging to their colleagues the blah demons, attempting to give me the blahs.

Must I explain once again that I am indeed *proud* to be a member of the Lunatic Fringe? This I define as "Crackpot Crones in tune with the moon, propelled by Pure Lust, who dare to Spin Wildly, always." Indeed, from my Positively Peculiar Perspective, the Lunatic Fringe is the truly moving center of the women's movement, comprising those who choose always to Survive/Thrive on the Boundaries, refusing compromise.

The Invitation to Outercourse naturally implies a summons to Spiral into this Moving Center.

Entering the Age of Cronehood

The Impossible/Possible Dream of Radical Feminism has never died. It is true that for many, especially in the course of the decade of decadence we have just Survived, it seemed to fade. What happened, in fact, is that it receded, somewhat, into the depths of the Subliminal Sea. But Sister Pirates, who are also divers, have worked to retrieve it. Moreover, it is Surfacing again, seemingly of its own accord. I think that our Time is coming round again, as we enter the Nineties.

However, this re-surging of the Dream is no mere passive event, no spectator sport. It must be Realized. This is a Tremendous Challenge. I think that as Voyagers we now face the Challenge of entering the Age of Cronehood of Radical Feminism. It is probably the case that the so-called "first wave" of feminism, in the nineteenth century, did not surge into the Age of Cronehood, even though there lived individual Crones, such as Sojourner Truth and Matilda Joslyn Gage. For as a collective Movement, feminism became "stuck," and there was not the possibility then of fully seeing the multiracial, multiclass, and indeed planetary dimensions of the women's movement. Nor was it possible to know that our Sister Earth is in mortal danger.

In the "second wave," although there has been a dreary expenditure of energy reinventing the wheel, we are moving toward understanding that a Qualitative Leap into Cronehood is necessary for Survival.

It is a desperate time, but desperation, too, is a gift. Desperation combined with Furious Focus can hurl a significant New Cognitive Minority of women into the Age of Cronehood, the Time of Realizing the Fourth Dimension. While feminists have always been a minority under phallocratic rule, the New Cognitive Minority includes women who constitute a memory-bearing group—Crones who have "been around" and can Re-call earlier Moments, and who can *bear* the memories, learn from them, and open the way for change.

There is, of course, imminent danger of succumbing to psychic numbing. We could continue to drift as vessels driven by men in power. But we have the Power to Choose. We *can* seize the decade by taking charge of our Crafts. We *can* Move.

I recommend that we hasten to acquire New Virtues in order to Spiral into the Nineties. First, there is the Virtue of Rage. A Metamorphosing Sage rides her Rage. Rage is a transformative focusing force that awakens transcendent E-motion. When unleashed, it enables women as Furies to breathe Fire and fly into freedom.

The New Virtue of Courage takes many forms. Central to all of these is the Courage to Be through and beyond the state of negation, participating in the Unfolding of Be-ing, continuing on the Journey always. Such Courage is Outrageous. It transforms women into Positively Revolting Hags who reverse the reigning reversals, becoming ever more Offensive, more Tasteless.

Tasteless Travelers acquire the Courage to Leave hopeless institutions and other foreground fixations. We gain Courage to See—to become dis-illusioned. And all of this amounts to the Courage to Sin. I am not alluding here to the petty sort of sinning that is forbidden and therefore incited by the "major religions" of phallocracy. I am talking about Sinning Big. For a woman, to Sin is to Be. To Sin Big is to Be the Verb which is her Self-centering Self.

I suggest that women in the Age of Feminism's Cronehood need also to develop the Virtue of Disgust—the habit of feeling and expressing our profound revulsion at the conglomerates of toms, dicks, and harrys—and their henchwomen—who are hell-bent on destroying all Life.

Hand in hand with Disgust comes the Virtue of Laughing Out Loud. This is the Lusty habit of boisterous Be-Laughing women. It is our habit of cracking the hypocritical hierarchs' houses of mirrors, defusing their power of deluding Others.

The cackling of Crones together cracks the man-made universe. It creates a crack through which Cacklers can slip into Realms of the Wild. Laughing Out Loud is the Virtue of Crackpot Crones who know we have only Nothing to lose. We are the Nothing-losers.

"But it's so dangerous," whisper the doubt demons. "And so inappropriate," sniff the blah demons. Oh, those party poopers again.

"Get lost!" I say. And they do. Whew! It feels so fine to lose Nothing. Daring Intergalactic Sailors/Sisters, our Time has come—Time to find our own Space Out Here with the Sun.

Whoops—I Sense that my Craft is about to take off again, Spiraling farther Out. I wish you lots of Nothing-losing. It's an erratic, ecstatic experience—this hurling our Lives as far as we can go, Now, in the Be-Dazzling Nineties!

The Haggard Sense of Humor

by Mary Daly,
Conjured in cahoots with Jane Caputi

Women gifted with Horse Sense are often accused of "lacking a sense of humor." This accusation is predictable in the State of Reversal. Naturally, Hags possess a Haggard Sense of Humor. The word *haggard*, according to *Webster's*, means "intractable, willful, wanton." Intractable, Willful, Wanton women See, Hear, Taste, Touch, Smell through the deceptions of phallocracy. A Natural expression of such perceptions is Horselaughing. Indeed, Horsey women/Nags frequently indulge in Horselaughing.

The expression of our Haggard Sense of Humor is often condemned by means of such epithets as "tasteless, inappropriate, weird." Tasteless Hags gladly take on these words as Names. Some proclaim our-Selves as Weird as Gooneys. We invite the labelers to consult the *Wickedary* for a definition of the word *Gooney*, which is "an albatross: much maligned Weird bird who possesses an impeccable sense of humor and direction and who habitually wanders on long, tireless flights . . . a woman who participates in the qualities of a Gooney" (*Word-Web Two*).

Gooney Gossips proclaim that our impeccable Sense of Direction Implies a delicate balance between the Sense of Levity and the Sense of Gravity. This balance makes possible our long, tireless flights beyond the range of maps and compasses.

Battle-ax n ["slang: a quarrelsome, irritable, domineering woman"—*Webster's*]*
1: a Raging, Dreadless, Unconquerable Crone. *Example:* Carry Nation. 2: double-edged weapon of a Woman Warrior; Labrys wielded by an A-mazing Amazon

Be-Laughing: expression of Elemental humor carrying Lusty Laughers into the Background; ontological Laughing; be-ing Silly together; Laughing that cracks man-made pseudo-reality; Laughing that breaks the Terrible Taboo, Touching the spirits of women, enlivening auras, awakening Hope

---

*Editors' note: When Daly spells *Webster's* with an *'s*, she is referring to Webster's traditional dictionary. When she writes it *s'*, she is referring to Websters as she defines them in the *Wickedary*.

Be-Witching [*bewitch* "to attract or please to such a degree as to take away all power of resistance or considered reservation: ENCHANT, CHARM, FASCINATE (she bewitched King James no less than her first lover—*N.Y. Times*) (that time-honored privilege of saying foolish things in the grand manner which seems to have bewitched our gallant forefathers—Norman Douglas)"—*Webster's*] 1: breaking the rules/roles of boring bewitchingness; ontological Witching 2: leaping/hopping/flying inspired by Lust for Metamorphosis; Macromutational moments/movements of be-ing; Shape-shifting 3: the exercise of Labrys-like powers that ward off attacks and attract Elemental forces

Crabby *adj:* having the characteristics of a crab—active, pugnatious, tenacious, Self-sufficient, able to move in all directions. *Example:* Susan B. Anthony

Crone *n:* Great Hag of History, long-lasting one; Survivor of the perpetual witchcraze of patriarchy, whose status is determined not merely by chronological age, but by Crone-logical considerations; one who has Survived early stages of the Otherworld Journey and who therefore has Dis-covered depths of Courage, Strength, and Wisdom in her Self. *Examples: a:* Harriet Tubman, rescuer of slaves, psychically/physically fearless Foresister *b:* Ding Ling, twentieth-century feminist activist and author, Survivor of multiple political purges, one of China's best-known and most prolific female writers

Dike [**Dyke**] *n* ["a barrier preventing passage, especially protecting against or excluding something undesirable"—*Webster's*]: This definition has been awarded *Webster's* Intergalactic Seal of Approval

fembot *n:* female robot: the archetypical role model forced upon women throughout fatherland: the unstated goal/end of socialization into patriarchal womanhood: the totaled woman

Fumerist *n:* "a feminist humorist [who] makes light. . . . a sparking incendiary with blazes of light and insight. . . . [who] makes whys cracks"—Kate Clinton

fundamentalist *n* [*fundament* "the part of the body on which one sits: BUTTOCKS . . . anus"—*Webster's*]: one who sermonizes from the fundament, spreading the "word": WINDBAG; a bibliolater, esp. one affected with logorrhea

Glamour *n* ["a magic spell: BEWITCHMENT"—*Webster's*] 1: an Archimagical Spell by which Nixing Nags dispel phallic pseudopresence/absence.

Cockaludicrous Comment: We have already shown that they [Witches] can take away the male organ, not indeed by actually despoiling the human body of it, but by concealing it with some glamour. —Heinrich Kramer and James Sprenger,

Malleus Maleficarum 2: the Attracting/Magnetizing Powers of Hags 3: Word Magic: the Grammar of Wicked Websters N.B.: According to Walter W. Skeat: "The word *glamour* is a mere corruption of *gramarye* or *grammar*, meaning (1) grammar, (2) magic."

Glamour Eyes: Eyes of Eye-Biting Witches: Eyes that dispel the delusions of Witch prickers, danglers, and other deadfellows. *Cockaludicrous Comment:* For, according to S. Isidore . . . a glamour is nothing but a certain delusion of the senses, and especially of the eyes. —Heinrich Kramer and James Sprenger, *Malleus Maleficarum*

Glamourize *v:* to exercise the powers of Glamour Eyes: to exorcise the deceptive demons of phallocracy, reversing the reversals of mirrordom

Hag *n* [(derived fr. ME *hagge, hegge* . . . akin to MD *haghetise* witch, OHG *hagzissa, hagazussa* harpy witch all fr. a prehistoric WGmc compound whose components are akin respectively to OE *haga* hedge and to G dialect (Westphalia) *dus* devil]: "*archaic* a female demon: FURY, HARPY . . . an evil or frightening spirit . . . NIGHTMARE: . . . an ugly or evil-looking old woman"— *Webster's*]: *Archaic:* a Witch, Fury, Harpy, who haunts the Hedges/Boundaries of patriarchy, frightening fools and summoning Weird Wandering Women into the Wild . *Canny Comment:*

> Where Hags are, will be Spells.
> Where Women are, will be Spells.

> — Gaelic proverb

Laughing Out Loud, Virtue of: Lusty habit of boisterous Be-Laughing women: habit of cracking the hypocritical hierarchs' houses of mirrors, defusing their powers of deluding Others; cackling that cracks the man-made universe, creating a crack through with Cacklers can slip into the Realms of the Wild; Virtue of Crackpot Crones whose peals of laughter peel away the plastic passions and unpot the potted ones. *Canny Comment:*

> Firm in reliance, laugh a defiance,
> (Laugh in hope, for sure is the end)
> March, March many as one
> Shoulder to shoulder and friend to friend!

> —*Cicely Hamilton and Ethyl Smyth*

Nag *n*: a Scold with Horse Sense; a Biting Critic of cockocracy; one who has aquired the Virtue of Nagging

Nag *v* ["to affect with recurrent awareness, uncertainty, need for consideration or concern: make recurrently conscious of something (as a problem, solution, situation)"—*Webster's*]. This definition has been awarded *Websters'* Intergalactic Seal of Approval.

Numbot Chorus: images of "happy" fembots filing through the foreground of fatherdom's dumb shows/fantasies, erasing Rage, setting the stage for numberless mummified/numb-ified copies. Example: the Miss America Pageant.

Positively Revolting Hag: a stunning, beauteous Crone; one who inspires positive revulsion from phallic institutions and morality, inciting Others to Acts of Pure Lust

Shrew *n* ["a person, esp. (now only) a woman, given to railing or scolding or other perverse or malignant behavior"—*O.E.D.*]: an Untamed and Untamable Turbulent Termagant

Shrewd *adj* [(derived fr. ME *shrewe* . . . scolding woman—*Webster's*): "depraved, wicked . . . coming 'dangerously' near to the truth of the matter"—*O.E.D.*]: This definition has been awarded *Websters'* Intergalactic Seal of Approval.

Spinster *n:* a woman whose occupation is to Spin, to participate in the whirling movement of creation; one who has chosen her Self, who defines her Self by choice neither in relation to children nor to men; one who is Self-identified; a whirling dervish, Spiraling in New Time/Space

Virgin *n* [*virgin adj* "never captured: UNSUBDUED"—*Webster's*]: Wild, Lusty, Never captured, Unsubdued Old Maid; Marriage Resister

Webster *n* [(derived fr. OE *webbestre* female weaver—*Webster's*): "A weaver . . . as the designation of a woman"—*O.E.D.*]: a woman whose occupation is to Weave, esp. a Weaver of Words and Word-Webs. *N.B.:* The word *Webster* was Dis-covered by Judy Grahn, who has written: Webster is a word that formerly meant "female weaver," the "ster" ending indicating a female ancestor, or female possession of the word. The word-weavers of recent centuries who have given us the oration of Daniel Webster and the dictionary listings of Merriam-Webster stem from English family names that once descended through the female line. Some great-great-grandmother gave them her last name, *Webster*, she-who-weaves.

Wiles, Female [*wile* akin to OE *wigle* divination, sorcery—*Webster's*]: female powers of Divination and Witchcraft; Glamorous/Magnetizing powers of Hags and Glamour Pusses

W.I.T.C.H.: acronym for numberless Radical Feminist groups. *Examples: a:* Women's International Terrorist Conspiracy from Hell (New York Covens, 1969) *b:* Women's Inspirational Terrorist Conspiracy from Harvard (Cambridge, Mass., 1972–74) *c:* Wild Independent Thinking Crones and Hags (Cambridge, Mass., 1985–)

Editor's note: These excerpts are reprinted from *Websters' First New Intergalactic Wickedary of the English Language,* by Mary Daly, Conjured in cahoots with Jane Caputi (Boston: Beacon Press, 1987. Copyright © 1987 by Mary Daly. All rights reserved.)

Introduction to Starhawk

Starhawk's work reflects her belief in the sacredness of the earth and the healing powers available through the magic circle of life, which includes an orientation to the Goddess and acknowledgment of the immanent value of each person. Born Miriam Simos in 1951, Starhawk changed her name as a way of affirming her commitment to the Goddess and to new levels of her own power-from-within. "Witchcraft as Goddess Religion" explains this commitment and describes the Goddess religion and the importance of the Goddess to both women and men.

Starhawk identifies as a Witch, which she defines not as a woman flying around on a broom and brewing noxious potions but, instead, as someone committed to the Pagan tradition with the Goddess as the center. The term *Wicca* comes from the root word *wic*, meaning to bend or shape, so Witches bend energy and shape consciousness; they weave new possibilities. In the excerpt from the first chapter of *Truth or Dare*, Starhawk explores witchcraft, magic, and three types of power, two of which are rooted in the Pagan and Goddess traditions. Three rituals—"Relaxation," "Salt-Water Purification," and "The Cone of Power"—and two spells—"Anger Spell" and "The Indrinking Spell"—from *Spiral Dance* also are included to illustrate this weaving of new possibilities and the positive aspects of witchcraft and power in Starhawk's work.

Involved in political activism all her life, Starhawk sees feminism as political, however subtle or overt. "Ritual as Bonding: Action as Ritual" and an excerpt from a roundtable discussion on backlash illustrate the political nature of her feminism and the ways she uses ritual to affect change, demonstrating her interweaving of politics and spirituality.

From The Politics of Women's Spirituality: Essays on the Rise of Spiritual Power within the Feminist Movement, *edited by Charlene Spretnak, 1982. Reprinted with permission.*

6.1

Witchcraft as Goddess Religion

Starhawk

Witchcraft has always been a religion of poetry, not theology. The myths, legends, and teachings are recognized as metaphors for "That-Which-Cannot-Be-Told," the absolute reality our limited minds can never completely know. The mysteries of the absolute can never be explained—only felt or intuited. Symbols and ritual acts are used to trigger altered states of awareness, in which insights that go beyond words are revealed. When we speak of "the secrets that cannot be told," we do not mean merely that rules prevent us from speaking freely. We mean that the inner knowledge literally *cannot* be expressed in words. It can only be conveyed by experience, and no one can legislate what insight another person may draw from any given experience. For example, after participating in a certain ritual, a woman said, "As we were chanting, I felt that we blended together and became one voice; I sensed the oneness of everybody." Another woman said, "I became aware of how different the chant sounded for each of us, of how unique each person is." A man said simply, "I felt loved." To a Witch, all of these statements are equally true and valid. They are no more contradictory than the statements, "Your eyes are as bright as stars" and "Your eyes are as blue as the sea."

The primary symbol for "That-Which-Cannot-Be-Told" is the Goddess. The Goddess has infinite aspects and thousands of names—She is the reality behind many metaphors. She is reality, the manifest deity, omnipresent in all of life, in each of us. The Goddess is not separate from the world—She is the world, and all things in it: moon, sun, earth, star, stone, seed, flowing river, wind, wave, leaf and branch, bud and blossom, fang and claw, woman and man. In Witchcraft, flesh and spirit are one.

As we have seen, Goddess religion is unimaginably old, but contemporary Witchcraft could just as accurately be called the New Religion. The Craft, today, is undergoing more than a revival, it is experiencing a renaissance, a re-creation. Women are spurring this renewal, and actively reawakening the Goddess, the image of "the legitimacy and beneficence of female power."[1]

Since the decline of the Goddess religions, women have lacked religious models and spiritual systems that speak to female needs and experience. Male images of divinity characterize both Western and Eastern religions. Regardless of how abstract the underlying concept of God may be, the symbols, avatars, preachers, prophets, gurus, and Buddhas are overwhelmingly male. Women are not encouraged to explore their own strengths and realizations; they are taught to submit to male authority, to identify masculine perceptions as their spiritual ideals, to deny their bodies and sexuality, to fit their insights into a male mold.

Mary Daly, author of *Beyond God the Father*, points out that the model of the universe in which a male god rules the cosmos from outside serves to legitimize male control of social institutions. "The symbol of the Father God, spawned in the human imagination and sustained as plausible by patriarchy, has, in turn, rendered service to this type of society by making its mechanisms for the oppression of women appear right and fitting."[2] The unconscious model continues to shape the perceptions even of those who have consciously rejected religious teachings. The details of one dogma are rejected, but the underlying structure of belief is imbibed at so deep a level it is rarely questioned. Instead, a new dogma, a parallel structure, replaces the old. For example, many people have rejected the "revealed truth" of Christianity without ever questioning the underlying concept that truth is a set of beliefs revealed through the agency of a "Great Man," possessed of powers or intelligence beyond the ordinary human scope. Christ, as the "Great Man," may be replaced by Buddha, Freud, Marx, Jung, Werner Erhard, or the Maharaj Ji in their theology, but truth is always seen as coming from someone else, as only knowable secondhand. As feminist scholar Carol P. Christ points out, "Symbol systems cannot simply be rejected, they must be replaced. Where there is no replacement, the mind will revert to familiar structures at times of crisis, bafflement, or defeat."[3]

The symbolism of the Goddess is not a parallel structure to the symbolism of God the Father. The Goddess does not rule the world; She *is* the world. Manifest in each of us, She can be known internally by every individual, in all Her magnificent diversity. She does not legitimize the rule of either sex by the other and lends no authority to rulers of temporal hierarchies. In Witchcraft, each of us must reveal our own truth. Deity is seen in our own forms, whether female or male, because the Goddess has Her male aspect. Sexuality is a sacrament. Religion is a matter of relinking, with the divine within and with Her outer manifestations in all of the human and natural world.

The symbol of the Goddess is *poemagogic*, a term coined by Anton Ehrenzweig to "describe its special function of inducing and symbolizing the ego's creativity."[4] It has a dreamlike, "slippery" quality. One aspect slips into another: She is constantly changing form and changing face. Her images do not define or pin down a set of attributes; they spark inspiration, creation, fertility of mind and spirit: "One thing becomes another,/In the Mother . . . In the Mother . . ." (ritual chant for the winter solstice).

The importance of the Goddess symbol for women cannot be overstressed. The image of the Goddess inspires women to see ourselves as divine, our bodies as sacred, the changing phases of our lives as holy, our aggression as healthy, our anger as purifying, and our power to nurture and create, but also to limit and destroy when necessary, as the very force that sustains all life. Through the Goddess, we can discover our strength, enlighten our minds, own our bodies, and celebrate our emotions. We can move beyond narrow, constricting roles and become whole.

The Goddess is also important for men. The oppression of men in Father God-ruled patriarchy is perhaps less obvious but no less tragic than that of women. Men are encouraged to identify with a model no human being can successfully emulate: to be minirulers of narrow universes. They are internally split, into a "spiritual" self that is supposed to conquer their baser animal and emotional natures. They are at war with themselves: in the West, to "conquer" sin; in the East, to "conquer" desire or ego. Few escape from these wars undamaged. Men lose touch with their feelings and their bodies, becoming the "successful male zombies" described by Herb Goldberg in *The Hazards of Being Male:* "Oppressed by the cultural pressures that have denied him his feelings, by the mythology of the woman and the distorted and self-destructive way he sees and relates to her, by the urgency for him to 'act like a man,' which blocks his ability to respond to his inner promptings both emotionally and physiologically, and by a generalized self-hate that causes him to feel comfortable only when he is functioning well in harness, not when he lives for joy and personal growth."[5]

Because women give birth to males, nurture them at the breast, and in our culture are primarily responsible for their care as children, "every male brought up in a traditional home develops an intense early identification with his mother and, therefore, carries within him a strong feminine imprint."[6] The symbol of the Goddess allows men to experience and integrate the feminine side of their nature, which is often felt to be the deepest and most sensitive aspect of self. The Goddess does not exclude the male; She contains him, as a pregnant woman contains a male child. Her own male aspect embodies both the solar light of the intellect and wild, untamed animal energy.

Our relationship to the earth and the other species that share it has also been conditioned by our religious models. The image of God as outside of nature has given us a rationale for our own destruction of the natural order, and justified our plunder of the earth's resources. We have attempted to "conquer" nature as we have tried to conquer sin. Only as the results of pollution and ecological destruction become severe enough to threaten even urban humanity's adaptability have we come to recognize the importance of ecological balance and the interdependence of all life. The model of the Goddess, who is immanent in nature, fosters respect for the sacredness of all living things. Witchcraft can be seen as a religion of ecology. Its goal is harmony with nature, so that life may not just survive, but thrive.

The rise of Goddess religion makes some politically oriented feminists uneasy. They fear it will sidetrack energy away from direct action to bring about social change. But in areas as deeply rooted as the relations between the sexes, true social change can only come about when the myths and symbols of our culture are themselves changed. The symbol of the Goddess conveys the spiritual power both to challenge systems of oppression and to create new, life-oriented cultures.

Modern Witchcraft is a rich kaleidoscope of traditions and orientations. Covens, the small, closely knit groups that form the congregations of Witchcraft, are autonomous; there is no central authority that determines liturgy or rites. Some covens follow practices that have been handed down in an unbroken line since before the Burning Times. Others derive their rituals from leaders of modern revivals of the Craft—the two whose followers are most widespread are Gerald Gardner and Alex Sanders, both British. Feminist covens are probably the fastest-growing arm of the

Craft. Many are Dianic, a sect of Witchcraft that gives far more prominence to the female principle than the male. Other covens are openly eclectic, creating their own traditions from many sources. My own covens are based on the Faery Tradition, which goes back to the Little People of Stone Age Britain, but we believe in creating our own rituals, which reflect our needs and insights of today. In Witchcraft, a chant is not necessarily better because it is older. The Goddess is continually revealing Herself, and each of us is potentially capable of writing our own liturgy.

In spite of diversity, there are ethics and values that are common to all traditions of Witchcraft. They are based on the concept of the Goddess as immanent in the world and in all forms of life, including human beings.

Theologians familiar with Judeo-Christian concepts sometimes have trouble understanding how a religion such as Witchcraft can develop a system of ethics and a concept of justice. If there is no split between spirit and nature, no concept of sin, no covenant or commandments against which one can sin, how can people be ethical? By what standards can they judge their actions, when the external judge is removed from his place as ruler of the cosmos? And if the Goddess is immanent in the world, why work for change or strive toward an ideal? Why not bask in the perfection of divinity?

Love for life in all its forms is the basic ethic of Witchcraft. Witches are bound to honor and respect all living things, and to serve the life-force. While the Craft recognizes that life feeds on life and that we must kill in order to survive, life is never taken needlessly, never squandered or wasted. Serving the life-force means working to preserve the diversity of natural life, to prevent the poisoning of the environment and the destruction of species.

The world is the manifestation of the Goddess, but nothing in that concept need foster passivity. Many Eastern religions encourage quietism not because they believe the divine is truly immanent, but because they believe She/He is not. For them, the world is Maya, Illusion, masking the perfection of the Divine Reality. What happens in such a world is not really important; it is only a shadow play obscuring the Infinite Light. In Witchcraft, however, what happens in the world is vitally important. The Goddess is immanent, but She needs human help to realize Her fullest beauty. The harmonious balance of plant/animal/human/divine awareness is not automatic; it must constantly be renewed, and this is the true function of Craft rituals. Inner work, spiritual work, is most effective when it proceeds hand in hand with outer work. Meditation on the balance of nature might be considered a spiritual act in Witchcraft, but not as much as would cleaning up garbage left at a campsite or marching to protest an unsafe nuclear plant.

Witches do not see justice as administered by some external authority, based on a written code or set of rules imposed from without. Instead, justice is an inner sense that each act brings about consequences that must be faced responsibly. The Craft does not foster guilt, the stern, admonishing, self-hating inner voice that cripples action. Instead, it demands responsibility. "What you send, returns three times over" is the saying—an amplified version of "Do unto others as you would have them do unto you." For example, a Witch does not steal, not because of an admonition in a sacred book, but because the threefold harm far outweighs any small material gain. Stealing diminishes the thief's self-respect and sense of honor; it is an admission that one is incapable of providing honestly for one's own needs and desires. Stealing creates a climate of suspicion and fear, in which even thieves have to live. And, because we are all linked in the same social fabric, those who steal also pay higher prices for groceries, insurance, taxes. Witchcraft strongly imparts the view that all things are interdependent and interrelated and, therefore, mutually responsible. An act that harms anyone harms us all.

Honor is a guiding principle in the Craft. This is not a "macho" need to take offense at imagined slights against one's virility—it is an inner sense of pride and self-respect. The Goddess is honored in oneself, and in others. Women, who embody the Goddess, are respected, not placed on pedestals or etherealized, but valued for all their human qualities. The self, one's individuality and unique way of being in the world, is highly valued. The Goddess, like nature, loves diversity. Oneness is attained not through losing the self, but through realizing it fully. "Honor the Goddess in yourself, celebrate your self, and you will see that Self is everywhere."

In Witchcraft, "All acts of love and pleasure are My rituals." Sexuality, as a direct expression of the life-force, is seen as numinous and sacred. It can be expressed freely, so long as the guiding principle is love. Marriage is a deep commitment, a magical, spiritual, and psychic bond. But it is only one possibility out of many for loving, sexual expression.

Misuse of sexuality, however, is heinous. Rape, for example, is an intolerable crime because it dishonors the life-force by turning sexuality to the expression of violence and hostility instead of love. A woman has the sacred right to control her own body, as does a man. No one has the right to force or coerce another.

Life is valued in Witchcraft, and it is approached with an attitude of joy and wonder, as well as a sense of humor. Life is seen as the gift of the Goddess. If suffering exists, it is not our task to reconcile ourselves to it, but to work for change.

Magic, the art of sensing and shaping the subtle, unseen forces that flow through the world, of awakening deeper levels of consciousness beyond the rational, is an element common to all traditions of Witchcraft. Craft rituals are magical rites: They stimulate an awareness of the hidden side of reality, and awaken long-forgotten powers of the human mind.

The magical element in Witchcraft is disconcerting to many people. I would like to speak to the fear I have heard expressed that Witchcraft and occultism are in some way a revival of Nazism. There does seem to be evidence that Hitler and other Nazis were occultists—that is, they may have practiced some of the same techniques as others who seek to expand the horizons of the minds. Magic, like chemistry, is a set of techniques that can be put to the service of any philosophy. The rise of the Third Reich played on the civilized Germans' disillusionment with rationalism and tapped a deep longing to recover modes of experience Western culture had too long ignored. It is as if we had been trained, since infancy, never to use our left arms: The muscles have partly atrophied, but they cry out to be used. But Hitler perverted this longing and twisted it into cruelty and horror. The Nazis were not Goddess worshippers; they denigrated women, relegating them to the position of breeding animals whose role was to produce more Aryan warriors. They were the perfect patriarchy, the ultimate warrior cult—not servants of the life-force. Witchcraft has no ideal of a "superman" to be created at the expense of inferior races. In the Craft, all people are already seen as manifest gods, and differences in color, race, and customs are welcomed as signs of the myriad beauty of the Goddess. To equate Witches with Nazis because neither are

Judeo-Christians and both share magical elements is like saying that swans are really scorpions because neither are horses and both have tails.

Mother-Goddess is reawakening, and we can begin to recover our primal birthright, the sheer, intoxicating joy of being alive. We can open new eyes and see that there is nothing to be saved *from*, no struggle of life *against* the universe, no God outside the world to be feared and obeyed; only the Goddess, the Mother, the turning spiral that whirls us in and out of existence, whose winking eye is the pulse of being—birth, death, rebirth—whose laughter bubbles and courses through all things and who is found only through love: love of trees, of stones, of sky and clouds, of scented blossoms and thundering waves; of all that runs and flies and swims and crawls on her face; through love of ourselves; life-dissolving world-creating orgasmic love of each other; each of us unique and natural as a snowflake, each of us our own star, her Child, her lover, her beloved, her Self.

Notes

1. Carol P. Christ, "Why Women Need the Goddess," *Womanspirit Rising: A Feminist Reader in Religion*, Carol P. Christ and Judith Plaskow, eds. (San Francisco: Harper & Row, 1979), p. 278.
2. Mary Daly, *Beyond God the Father* (Boston: Beacon Press, 1973), p. 13.
3. Christ, *op. cit.*, p. 275.
4. Anton Ehrenzweig, *The Hidden Order of Art* (London: Paladin, 1967), p. 190.
5. Herb Goldberg, *The Hazards of Being Male* (New York: Signet, 1977), p. 4.
6. *Ibid.*, p. 39.

Selections from pages 6-16 from *Truth or Dare: Encounters with Power, Authority, and Mystery* by Starhawk. Copyright © 1987 by Miriam Simos. Reprinted by permission of HarperCollins Publishers, Inc.

6.2

Truth or Dare

Encounters with Power, Authority, and Mystery

Starhawk

Magic and Its Uses

Magic is a word that can be defined in many ways. A saying attributed to Dion Fortune is: "Magic is the art of changing consciousness at will." I sometimes call it the art of evoking power-from-within. Today, I will name it this: the art of liberation, the act that releases the mysteries, that ruptures the fabric of our beliefs and lets us look into the heart of deep space where dwell the immeasurable, life-generating powers.

Those powers live in us also, as we live in them. The mysteries are what is wild in us, what cannot be quantified or contained. But the mysteries are also what is most common to us all: blood, breath, heartbeat, the sprouting of seed, the waxing and waning of the moon, the turning of the earth around the sun, birth, growth, death, and renewal.

To practice magic is to tap that power, to burrow down through the systems of control like roots that crack concrete to find the living soil below.

We are never apart from the power of the mysteries. Every breath we take encompasses the circle of birth, death, and rebirth. The forces that push the blood cells through our veins are the same forces that spun the universe out of the primal ball of fire. We do not know what those forces are. We can invoke them, but we cannot control them, nor can we disconnect from them. They are our life, and when we die, decay, and decompose, we remain still within their cycle.

Yet somehow we human beings, made of the same materials as the stars, the eucalyptus, the jaguar, and the rose, we who inherit four billion years of survival have managed to create a culture in which the power of the mysteries has been denied and power itself has been redefined as power-over, as domination and control. Wielding that false and limited power, we create misery for each other and devastation for the other life forms that share this earth.

In a warped way, such an achievement is almost grimly inspiring. We are like a friend I had in the sixties who, while wheelchair-bound, paraplegic, and needing constant care, managed to deal drugs successfully until he killed himself with an overdose of heroin. We have overcome every handicap and surmounted every obstacle to self-destruction.

We are not particularly happy in this condition. We do not enjoy being the targets of nuclear warheads or developing cancer from our polluted environment. We do not enjoy starving, or wasting our lives in meaningless work, nor are we eager to be raped, abused, tortured, or bossed around. Whether the bosses enjoy their role is not the issue. The question is, How are the rest of us controlled? Or, even more to the point, How do we break control and set ourselves free?

This book is a text of magic, a liberation psychology. It holds tools, not answers, for the mysteries do not offer answers, but questions that in time, may change us.

Those who practice magic can be called many things: magicians, shamans, mystics. I myself am a Witch. *Witch* comes from the Anglo-Saxon root *wic*, meaning to bend or shape—to shape reality, to make magic. Witches bend energy and shape consciousness. We were—and are—shamans, healers, explorers of powers that do not fit the usual systems of control. Those powers are rightly perceived as dangerous to the established order, and so we have been taught to view them as evil or delusionary. We imagine Witches flying around on brooms or brewing up noxious potions.

Actually, Witchcraft is a mystery religion, based on ritual, on consciously structured collective experiences that allow us to encounter the immeasurable. It is the old, pre-Christian, tribal religion of Europe. Like other earth-based, tribal traditions, Withcraft sees the earth as sacred.

To Witches, the cosmos is the living body of the Goddess, in whose being we all partake, who encompasses us and is immanent within us. We call her Goddess not to narrowly define her gender, but as a continual reminder that what we value is life brought into the world. The great forces of the spirit are manifest in nature and culture. The Goddess is fertile earth and ripened fruit, and she is also the storehouse, where the earth's fruits are collected, guarded, and given out. She is the virgin grove of redwoods and also the carved shape that speaks through art of the wood's power. She is wildfire and hearthfire, the star's core, the forge, and the poetic fire of inspiration. She has infinite names and guises, many of them male: the Gods, her consorts, sons, companions. For what we call Goddess moves always through paradox, and so takes us into the heart of the mysteries, the great powers that can never be limited or defined.

However they name their Gods, tribal cultures across the world have always shared a common understanding: that the sacred is found here, where we are, immanent in the world. In Europe, long after Christianity had become the official faith, the more ancient understanding persisted in folk customs and beliefs, in ways of healing, and in the practices of the Witches, the dedicated few who preserved remnants of the Old Religion.

In the sixteenth and seventeenth centuries, the Catholic and Protestant churches began systematic Witch persecutions. Witches were accused by both Catholic and Protestant churches of worshiping the devil, but in reality our tradition has nothing to do with Satanism, a peculiarly Christian heresy.[1] Accused Witches were subjected to horrifying tortures and execution. The persecutions fractured peasant class solidarity, and marked off the domain of healing and midwifery as the preserve of upper-class, university-educated male "experts." The old organic worldview, the vision that saw sacred presence in all of life, was made illegitimate in Western culture. What remained of the value system of immanence was discredited. The living world became viewed as a machine, something made of non-living, atomized parts that could ultimately be completely known and controlled. That worldview in turn justified increased social control, isolation, and domination.[2]

Maligned and persecuted for four hundred years, the Craft went underground, became a closed and secret society that is only now reemerging.

I call myself a Witch even though I am fully aware that the word often produces fear.[3] Until we confront the fears and stereotypes evoked by the word, we cannot contact the powers that are also embedded there.

The word *Witch* throws us back into a world who is a being, a world in which everything is alive and speaking, if only we learn its language. The word brings us back to the outlawed awareness of the immanence of the sacred, and so it reeks of a holy stubbornness, an unwillingness to believe that the living milk of nurture we drink daily from the flowing world can be reduced to formula administered from a machine.

To be a Witch is to make a commitment to the Goddess, to the protection, preservation, nurturing, and fostering of the great powers of life as they emerge in every being. In these discussions of power, that, then, is my bias: I am on the side of the power that emerges from within, that is inherent in us as the power to grow is inherent in seed. As a shaper, as one who practices magic, my work is to find that power, to call it forth, to coax it out of hiding, tend it, and free it of constrictions. In a society based on power-over, that work inevitably must result in conflict with the forces of domination, for we cannot bear our own true fruit when we are under another's control.

To practice magic is to bear the responsibility for having a vision, for we work magic by envisioning what we want to create, clearing the obstacles in our way, and then directing energy through that vision. Magic works through the concrete; our ideals, our visions, are meaningless until they are in some way enacted. So, if our work is to evoke power-from-within, we must clearly envision the conditions that would allow that power to come forth, we must identify what blocks it, and create the conditions that foster empowerment. Given a world based on power-over, we must remake the world.

The Three Types of Power

The conflicts brewing today are only superficially questions of who will take power. Underneath is a deeper struggle: to change the nature of the power in which our society is rooted. The root question is, How do we define the world? For it is an old magical secret that the way we define reality shapes reality. Name a thing and you invoke it. If we call the world nonliving, we will surely kill her. But when we name of the world alive, we begin to bring her back to life.

Reality, of course, shapes and defines us. Only when we know how we have been shaped by the structures of power in which we live can we become shapers. A psychology of liberation can become our *athame*, our Witch's knife, the tool of magic that corresponds with the East, the element air: mind, clarity, vision. It is the knowledge and insight we need to carve out our own freedom.

Witches have a saying: "Where there's fear, there's power." It also works backward: "Where there's power, there's fear." We are afraid to look at power because one of the deepest prohibitions is that against seeing how power operates. Psychoanalyst Alice Miller, in her analysis of what she calls "poisonous pedagogy," shows "the overriding importance of our early conditioning to be obedient and dependent and to suppress our feelings."[4] "The more or less conscious goal of adults in rearing infants is to make sure they will never find out later in life that they were trained not to become aware of how they were manipulated."[5] We are afraid of the pain of seeing how deeply we have been shaped by systems of control.

Those systems and that power are built of the earth's charred bones and cemented with her stripped flesh. In this chapter, I will explore three types of power: power-over, power-from-within, and power-with. Power-over is linked to domination and control; power-from-within is linked to the mysteries that awaken our deepest abilities and potential. Power-with is social power, the influence we wield among equals.

Power-over comes from the consciousness I have termed estrangement: the view of the world as made up of atomized, nonliving parts, mechanically interacting, valued not for what they inherently are but only in relation to some outside standard. It is the consciousness modeled on the God who stands outside the world, outside nature, who must be appeased, placated, feared, and above all, obeyed. For, as we will see in chapter 2, power-over is ultimately born of war and the structures, social and intrapsychic, necessary to sustain mass, organized warfare. Having reshaped culture in a martial image, the institutions and ideologies of power-over perpetuate war so that it becomes a chronic human condition.

We live embedded in systems of power-over and are indoctrinated into them, often from birth. In its clearest form, power-over is the power of the prison guard, of the gun, power that is ultimately backed by force. Power-over enables one individual or group to make the decisions that affect others, and to enforce control.

Violence and control can take many forms. Power-over shapes every institution of our society. This power is wielded in the workplace, in the schools, in the courts, in the doctor's office. It may rule with weapons that are physical or by controlling the resources we need to live: money, food, medical care; or by controlling more subtle resources: information, approval, love. We are so accustomed to power-over, so steeped in its language and its implicit threats, that we often become aware of its functioning only when we see its extreme manifestations. For we have been shaped in its institutions, so that the insides of our minds resemble the battlefield and the jail.

In the Livermore action described in the opening of this chapter, we were relying on a different principle of *power*, one that I call power-from-within, or empowerment. The root of the word power means to be able. We were acting as if we were able to protect our friend. Our strength came not from weapons, but from our willingness to act.

Power-from-within is akin to the sense of mastery we develop as young children with each new unfolding ability: the exhilaration of standing erect, of walking, of speaking the magic words that convey our needs and thoughts.

But power-from-within is also akin to something deeper. It arises from our sense of connection, our bonding with other human beings, and with the environment.

Although power-over rules the systems we live in, power-from-within sustains our lives. We can feel that power in acts of creation and connection, in planting, building, writing, cleaning, healing, soothing, playing, singing, making love. We can feel it in acting together with others to oppose control.

A third aspect of power was also present in the jail at Camp Parks. We could call it power-with, or influence: the power of a strong individual in a group of equals, the power not to command, but to suggest and be listened to, to begin something and see it happen. The source of power-with is the willingness of others to listen to our ideas. We could call that willingness respect, not for a role, but for each unique person. We joined in the chanting begun by one woman in the jail because we respected her inspiration. Her idea felt right to us. She had no authority to command, but acted as a channel to focus and direct the will of the group.

In the dominant culture, power-with has become confused with power-over. When we attempt to create new structures that do not depend upon hierarchy for cohesion, we need to recognize power-with, so that we can work with it, share and spread, and also beware of it. For like the Witch's knife, the *athame,* power-with is double-bladed. It can be the seedbed of empowerment, but it can also spawn oppression. No group can function without such power, but within a group influence can too easily become authority.

Roots of the Three Types of Power

Power-over, power-from-within, and power-with are each rooted in a mode of consciousness and a worldview that can be identified. Each speaks in its own language and is supported by its own mythologies. Each depends upon distinct motivations.

The consciousness that underlies power-over sees the world as an object, made up of many separate, isolated parts that have no intrinsic life, awareness, or value. Consciousness is fragmented, disconnected. In *The Spiral Dance* I compared it to seeing by flashlight with a narrow beam that illumines one separate object at a time, but cannot reveal the fabric of space in which they interconnect. Relationships between objects are described by rules. We believe that we can, in the end, find rules to describe all things and their relationships, to predict what they will do, and allow us to control them.

The language of power-over is the language of law, of rules, of abstract, generalized formulations enforced on the concrete realities of particular circumstances.

In the worldview of power-over, human beings have no inherent worth; value must be earned or granted. The formulation of Fall/Redemption-oriented Christianity is that we are born in original sin and we can be saved only by grace.[6] In the secular world, the worth we acquire is constantly rated against that of others, in school, in the workplace, by potential mates and lovers. We internalize a primal insecurity about our own right to be, which drives us to compete for the tokens of pseudo-value.

Mechanistic science provides us with the technology of power-over. Technology gives us power entirely split from any questions of meaning or purpose. The nuclear bomb is perhaps the ultimate symbol of power-over and the ultimate irony, as nuclear physics has "proven" that the mechanistic model of the universe is overly simplistic.

Power-over motivates through fear. Its systems instill fear and then offer the hope of relief in return for compliance and obedience. We fear the force and violence of the system should we disobey, and we fear the loss of value, sustenance, comforts, and tokens of esteem.

In the jail story, our victory came when we ceased to act from fear. Systems of domination are not prepared to cope with fearlessness, because acts of courage and resistance break the expected patterns.

Power-from-within stems from a different consciousness—one that sees the world itself as a living being, made up of dynamic aspects, a world where one thing shape-shifts into another, where there are no solid separations and no simple causes and effects. In such a world, all things have inherent value, because all things are beings, aware in ways we can only imagine, interrelated in patterns too complex to ever be more than partially described. We do not have to earn value. Immanent value cannot be rated or compared. No one, nothing, can have more of it than another. Nor can we lose it. For we are, ourselves, the living body of the sacred. This is what Witches mean when we say, "Thou are Goddess," and also what mavericks and heretics have always read into the biblical account of the creation of the world in the image of God.

Immanent value does not mean that everyone is innately good, or that nothing should ever be destroyed. What is valued is the whole pattern, which always includes death as well as birth. I pull snails off the iris leaves and crush them—they are out of pattern here. They have no natural predators and devour the diversity of the garden. A hundred years ago they escaped from a Frenchman who brought them to California so he could continue to eat escargot. Now they ravage plants all up and down the West Coast. Yet I do not expect to completely kill them off. We will, at best, strike a balance, a new pattern. Nor will I put out poison, which disrupts larger patterns still. I will be predator, not poisoner.

The language of power-from-within is poetry, metaphor, symbol, ritual, myth, the language of magic, of "thinking in things," where the concrete becomes resonant with mysteries that go beyond its seeming solid form. Its language is action, which speaks in the body and to all the senses in ways that can never be completely conveyed in words.

The technology of power-from-within is magic, the art of changing consciousness, of shifting shapes and dimensions, of bending reality. Its science is a psychology far older than Freud, Jung, or Skinner. And its motivations are erotic in the broadest sense of the deep drives in us to experience and share pleasure, to connect, to create, to see our impact on others and on the world.

Power-with also embodies a particular consciousness, language, and set of motivations. It bridges the value systems of power-from-within and power-over. Power-with sees the world as a pattern of relationships, but its interest is in how that pattern can be shaped, molded, shifted. It values beings, forces, and people according to how they affect others and according to a history based on experience. It can recognize inherent worth, but can also rate and compare, valuing some more highly than others.

The language of power-with is gossip. Gossip has a bad reputation as being either malicious or trivial. But in any real community, people become interested in each others' relationships within the group, love affairs, quarrels, problems. The talking we do about each other provides us with invaluable information; it makes us aware of whom we can trust and whom we distrust, of whom to treat carefully and whom to confront, of what we can realistically expect a group to do together.

Gossip maintains the social order in a close-knit society more effectively than law. Margery Wolf describes how she observed women's informal groups working in rural

Taiwan: "A young woman whose mother-in-law was treating her with a harshness that exceeded village standards for such behavior told her woes to a work group, and if the older members of the group felt the complaint was justified, the mother-in-law would be allowed to overhear them criticizing her, would know that she was being gossiped about, and would usually alter her behavior toward her daughter-in-law. Every woman valued her standing within the women's circles because at some time in her life she might also need their support.... In the Taiwanese village I knew best, some women were very skilled at forming and directing village opinion toward matters as apparently disparate as domestic conflicts and temple organization. The women who had the most influence on village affairs were those who worked through the women's community."[7]

The art of wielding power-with, of gaining influence and using it creatively to empower, is probably intuitive to great and charismatic leaders. We can, however, observe and study it, both to improve our ability to use influence constructively and to identify the qualities we expect of those who assume leadership.

Developing a Psychology of Liberation

The skills, the descriptions, the tools of magic are road maps. I offer the principles of magic not as a belief system to be proved or disproved, but as an alternative descriptive system that can help us develop a psychology of liberation. An alternative is necessary because, in Audre Lorde's words, "the master's tools will never dismantle the master's house."[8] The way we describe the world determines how we will value and experience the world. The descriptive systems of psychology, of science, of patriarchal religion are not objective. Embedded in them are values. If we describe the world as being separate from God, we have devalued the world. If we say that only quantifiable experiences are true, we have not eliminated what cannot be measured, but we have devalued it. We are unlikely to encounter it in our texts or the works of the authorities, however often we may encounter it in our lives.

Language is political. A liberation psychology cannot be written in the standard jargon of the psychologists, because such language is designed to exclude those who do not have the approved training and credentials. For example: "In the less-structured personality, therefore, the technical problem is not to make the unconscious conscious, but to make the ego capable of coping with the drives by means of neutralizing libido and aggression, thereby making them available for the building of higher levels of object relations."[9] This statement could be roughly translated into advice for beginning therapists: "When you're dealing with someone who is really unstrung, don't delve into their dreams and fantasies, help them gain some self-control, at which point they might have hope of making friends or even attracting a lover." More than its content, the language and form of the statement embody attitudes about power, knowledge, and value. The statement reserves power for someone steeped in the training necessary to translate it. It assumes that knowledge can be conveyed separately from feeling, that the process of healing is directed and understood by the healer, not the patient. Furthermore, it presents itself as a statement of fact. Its abstracted language seems scientific but is not, in reality, either objective or verifiable. The statement actually is an unpoetic metaphor. It implies that the human psyche is constructed like a machine, fueled by twin drives of sex and aggression. If all the parts are not firmly bolted together, the fuel will spill out, possibly igniting explosions, and the engine will go nowhere.

An overt metaphor is a map, a description we may find useful or not, may accept or reject. A covert metaphor is an attempt to restructure our reality by leading us to accept the map as the territory without questioning where we are going or whose interests are being served.

A liberation psychology, like liberation theology, maintains an "option for the poor." It allies itself with the dispossessed, with those resisting oppression, not with the forces of control. It must be useful to those who may not have formal education, or state-issued licenses. Therefore, it must be understandable. It is not anti-intellectual, but it realizes that intellect divorced from feeling is itself part of our pain. Its insights are conveyed in a language that is concrete, a language of poetry, not jargon; of metaphors that clearly are metaphors; a language that refers back to the material world, that is sensual, that speaks of things that we can see and touch and feel. It is a vocabulary not of the elite but of the common, and its concepts can thus be tested by experience.

A psychology that can lead us to encounter the mysteries must be rooted in an earth-based spirituality that knows the sacred as immanent. What is sacred—whether we name it Goddess, God, spirit, or something else—is not outside the world, but manifests in nature, in human beings in the community and culture we create. Every being is sacred—meaning that each has inherent value that cannot be ranked in a hierarchy or compared to the value of another being. Worth does not have to be earned, acquired, or proven; it is inherent in our existence.

Earth-based spirituality values diversity, imposes no dogma, no single name for the sacred, no one path to the center. But at this moment in history, the mythology and imagery of the Goddess carry special liberating power. They free us from the domination of the all-male God who has so strongly legitimized male rule, and by extension, all systems of domination. The Goddess represents the sacredness of life made manifest. All of the symbols and practices associated with her reaffirm her presence in this world, in nature and culture, in life and death. She does not symbolize female rule over men—but freedom from rule. She herself has male aspects who are earth Gods, alive in nature, in the wildness and cycles of transformation. The mystery, the paradox, is that the Goddess is not "she" or "he"—or she is both—but we call her "she" because to name is not to limit or describe but to invoke. We call her in and a power comes who is different from what comes when we say "he" or "it." Something happens, something arises that challenges the ways in which our minds have been shaped in images of male control. The hum of bees drowns the sound of helicopters.

A liberation psychology, based on the acknowledgment of the inherent worth of each person, views each person's truth and emotions with respect, sees resistances as evidence of strength, and knows that each process of change proceeds at its own pace.

When we see spirit as immanent, we recognize that everything is interconnected. All the beings of the world are in constant communication on many levels and dimensions. There is no such thing as a single cause or effect, but instead a complex intertwined feedback system of changes that shape other changes. The destruction of the Amazon rain forest changes our weather. The murder of a health-care worker in Nicaragua by the Contras affects our health. And so our health, physical and emotional, cannot be considered out of context. To change ourselves, we must change the world; to change the world we must be willing to change, ourselves.

When the sacred is immanent, the body is sacred. Woman-body, man-body, child-body, animal-body, and earth-body are sacred. They have an inherent integrity and inherent worth. All of our bodily processes, especially the deep, pleasure-giving force of our sexuality, are sacred processes. A psychology of liberation is not one of repression, nor does earth-based spirituality call us to asceticism. The times may demand courage and self-sacrifice, but we have no spiritual need for martyrdom. The celebration of life is our value.

With the AIDS epidemic threatening so many lives, it is more important than ever to assert the sacred value of the erotic. Caution about transmitting AIDS may restrict some aspects of erotic expression, but AIDS does not change the sacred nature of our sexuality any more than it invalidates the medical use of blood transfusions.

Society's response to AIDS reflects our fear and hatred of sexuality. The disease is used as an excuse to tell us, once again, that sex is dirty, nasty, and wrong—especially when not done in the approved manner. Out of fear of AIDS, people can be manipulated to accept schemes for concentration camps, identity cards, and other forms of social control. Punishment is our central social metaphor: we are eager to see AIDS as some form of divine or cosmic punishment, to blame instead of assuming the responsibilities of caring. In a culture that valued the erotic, a disease that attacked our free expression of love would be a top research priority. Instead, we see funds diverted or denied. In a culture that valued the inherent worth of every being, no disease would lead us to shun the sick or deny them treatment, care, or dignity.

By shoving our noses in the face of death, one of the great mysteries, AIDS can be a powerful teacher. The largescale breakdown of immune systems warns us that our environment is dangerously overloaded with toxins. The disease challenges us to speak publicly and graphically about sexual practices, ending hypocritical censorship. Most of all, AIDS challenges us to mobilize the erotic force of love to create communities of healing and care.

Earth-based spiritual traditions are rooted in community. They are not religions of individual salvation, but of communal celebration and collective change. Community includes not just the human but the interdependent plant, animal, and elemental communities of the natural world, and is both a model of and limit to what we can become. A psychology of liberation is one whose primary focus is the communities we come from and create. Our collective history is as important as our individual history. A liberation psychology is more concerned with how structures of power shape and bind us than with the particular events of our individual childhoods. Those events are important, but to focus on them outside of the context of the whole is misleading. Individual therapy may be helpful, and sometimes necessary, but a liberation psychology is more concerned with ways of creating communal healing and collective change. For it is our responsibility to bring into being a culture that will nourish, heal, and sustain us in freedom.

The model we use is not one of health or sickness, but one of personal power. We each strive to increase our power-from-within, and this growth in power is beneficial as long as we remain centered and in balance. Many roads lead to power-from-within: among Witches, some of the traditional ways have been through knowledge of nature, through healing practices, through ritual, through trance, through the erotic, through the provision of food, through divination. Among Native Americans, magic, war, healing, peacemaking, and the vision quest can be roads to power. Pathways to power may be extraordinary or very ordinary. Sister José Habday, a Native American teacher and Franciscan sister, speaks of being called to power by the road of giving gifts to those who don't deserve them.[10]

The Yoruba term for personal power is *ache*. Luisah Teish writes, "Replenishing the 'ache' is a prime reason for the existence of individual and group rituals and the use of charms."

"There is a regulated kinship among human, animal, mineral and vegetable life. Africans do not slaughter animals wholesale, . . . nor do they devastate the fields that serve them. It is recognized that they have been graced with the personal power to hunt, farm and eat; but it is also recognized that they must give back that which is given to them."[11]

Personal power, *ache*, power-from-within, depends on a moving, living balance of the energies that sustain interconnected life. To misuse it is to lose it. Energy, like water, has power to shape only when it is in motion. Dammed, it stagnates and evaporates.

In Witchcraft, the model of balance is the magic circle that we cast by calling four directions and four elements, which each correspond to qualities within a human being. Correspondences vary among different groups, but in the tradition I learned, East corresponds to air and the mind, South to fire and energy, West to water, emotion, and sexuality, North to earth and the body. We need to be in touch with all aspects of ourselves. Each informs, but none controls, the others. When we develop personal power, we learn to move freely around the wheel, and in and out of the center—to evoke the aspect of ourselves that we need, to become whole.

The Principles Of Magic

Magic, as I have said, can be called the art of evoking power-from-within. Art implies skill and knowledge that empowers us to create. The skills of magic are the techniques of moving and shaping energy, of work, celebration, and ritual, of making the proper offerings and giving the right gifts. The knowledge magic teaches is that reality is deeper, more complex, more intricate, than it appears. We can swim, but not measure, its depths.

What we call magic is a body of knowledge compiled from many sources, and a tool that has been used to build many systems, some of them as hierarchical as any construction of mechanistic science. A liberation psychology understands the principles of magic and uses its tools to challenge hierarchies that keep us unfree and create structures that embody values of immanent spirit, interconnection, community, empowerment, and balance.

Magic teaches that living beings are beings of energy and spirit as well as matter, that energy—what the Chinese call *chi*—flows in certain patterns throughout the human body, and can be raised, stored, shaped, and sent. The movements of energy affect the physical world, and vice versa. This is the theory that underlies acupuncture and other naturopathic systems of healing, as well as the casting of spells and magical workings.

Energy can be formed; "structures," stable patterns, can be created by focused visualization. Energy structures influence physical reality. Physical beings are energy structures. Events in the physical world shape energy into patterns that in turn shape events that themselves move energy. The material world and the nonmaterial world are a mutually influencing system, a continuous feedback loop.

Of course, our power to shape reality has limits. Reality also has the power to shape us, and its power is usually stronger than ours. We do not say, as do some fashionable New Age philosophies, that we create our own reality. Such an idea can only conceivably make sense for white, upper-middle-class Americans, and then only some of the time. It is clearly senseless and becomes a form of victim blaming when applied, for example, to a Nicaraguan peasant child murdered by the Contras. We come into a reality that is already a given; within those sets of circumstances, we can make choices that will shape our future, but reality is a collective event and can be changed only by collective action. The peasants of Nicaragua did collectively shape their reality. Many individual changes in consciousness eventually sparked the actions that led to revolution. For action, ultimately, shapes reality. A change in consciousness changes our actions, or it is no true change. Only through action can magic be realized. And when we have acted, our actions shape a new reality that in turn shapes us, as the revolution in Nicaragua, in turn, changed individuals' ideas of who they were and what they could be.

Energy is directed by visualization, by imagining what it is we want to do. What we envision determines how we act. Our vision is distorted if we discount any aspect of reality. We cannot ignore the political, the spiritual, the social, the physical, the emotional, or any dimension of our lives. Again, the goal is balance, the image that of the magic circle where all forces come together equally.

Energy is erotic. Erotic energy is a manifestation of the sacred. Our mysteries draw on the erotic; respect our drives and know that they have their own rhythms and cycles, their own regulatory principle. Control of sexuality by others is a primary way in which our sense of worth is undetermined, and is a cornerstone of the structures of domination.

The tangible, visible world is only one aspect of reality. There are other dimensions that are equally real although less solid. Many cultures acknowledge other realms of existence, and there are many different systems for naming them. Ron Evans, a Native American shaman, identifies eight worlds—the Inner World, the Outer World, the Mist World, the Pollen World, the Dawn World, the Dusk World, the Dream World, the Dark World—each of which has a precise use and is entered by a different type of drumming. The Western theosophists spoke of different planes of existence. Witches, also, speak of different worlds, and read myths and symbols as maps to other dimensions. Tir-Na-Nog, the Land of Youth in Irish mythology, is not a metaphor nor archetype—it is a real place that can be visited, but its reality is not a physical one and the visits do not take place in the physical body.

Beings also exist in those other realms. The Goddesses, Gods, the ancestors, the Beloved Dead are more than symbols; they are powers, consciousnesses, intelligences, perhaps of a different order than our own, but nonetheless real. When we name them, call them, we open a doorway and power enters, for we are naming the great patterns that move and shape life.

"The African observed the voluptuous river, with its sweet water and beautiful stones and surmised *intuitively* that it was female. They named the river *Oshun*, Goddess of Love. They further noticed that a certain woman carried the flow of the river in her stride . . . so they called her the daughter of Oshun. They know that the river came before the woman, and that the woman's stride is affected by the flow of the river."

The gods themselves may be shaped by how we perceive them. Our images of the gods in turn influence our acts. When our Goddess is voluptuous, flowing, erotic, so will be our dances, the rhythms of our drums and chants, our bodies. When the Inquisition became obsessed with the devil, it performed acts of evil, torturing and murdering suspected Witches. To say the Goddess is reawakening may be an act of magical creation.

Just as individuals have an identity, a form, and a corresponding energy form, so do groups. The idea of a "group mind" or a "group soul" is, again, not just a metaphor but a reality in subtler dimensions than the physical.

To expand our vision of reality does not diminish the immanent value of the material world. The ancestors are revered, but not more so than the living. The Goddess, the Gods, the great powers, are the material world, are us. If they extend beyond us they do so like the sun's corona flaring beyond its core. No power is entirely separate from our own power, no being is entirely separate from our own being.

The Dare

Any psychology, to be useful, must look at two basic questions: How did we get into this mess? and How do we get out of it? A psychology of liberation, rooted in the magical description of the world, sees that the process of getting into our mess is long, complex, and historic; that we are in pain because we live in psychic and social structures that destroy us.

Our way out will involve both resistance and renewal: saying no to what is, so that we can reshape and recreate the world. Our challenge is communal, but to face it we must be empowered as individuals and create structures of support and celebration that can teach us freedom. Creation is the ultimate resistance, the ultimate refusal to accept things as they are. For it is in creation that we encounter mystery: the depth of things that cannot be wholly known or controlled, the movement of forces that speak through us and connect us at our core.

To value the mysteries we must describe the world in ways that make possible encounter with mystery. When we view the world through the lens of that description, the old systems and structures may themselves be revealed as distortions.

The core of the mysteries is the understanding that truth is always deeper and richer than any description of it. To change lenses and face a fuller spectrum of that truth can be frightening, shattering. It requires daring.

And so I have named this book after the game of Truth or Dare, a favored pastime in groups suffering enforced boredom or confinement. I have played it waiting in traffic jams and in holding cells after being arrested. The rules are simple. One person is "it." Anyone else in the group can ask that person a question, preferably intimate, sometimes embarrassing. "What would you like to do sexually that you can't ask for?" "What is your most exciting fantasy?" "Who in this room do you find most attractive?"

When you are "it," you are required to tell the truth—or else you must face the dare. No one knows what the dare is, but everyone knows it will be worse than the question.

So the game becomes an endlessly fascinating stripping process, a collective demand to speak the unspeakable, reveal what we have always been warned not to reveal. Secrets become common knowledge. Love affairs are sparked.

In the process, we learn something important about our own secrets: that they too, like the great mysteries, are common. What shames us, what we most fear to tell, does not set us apart from others; it binds us together if only we can take the risk to speak it.

"Let everything private be made public" was a Situationist slogan of the sixties.

The slogan and the core of these encounters with common mysteries is this:

Truth is the dare.

Notes

1. The Christian devil is a construct of Christian theology. To believe in the devil or worship Satan, one must, therefore, be a Christian. Pagans do not believe in the devil.
2. Actually, this seems to me a perfect example of what Mary Daly calls the "reversals" of patriarchy. By rights, the word *Witch* should ring with associations of noble martyrdom, healing, and goodness, and the word *Christian* should be the one we fear. Not that there aren't good, loving, and noble Christians—but after all, who burned whom?
3. For more information about the basic history, philosophy, and practice of Witchcraft, see Starhawk, *The Spiral Dance: A Rebirth of the Ancient Ritual of the Great Goddess* (San Francisco: Harper & Row, 1979). For a discussion of the Witch persecutions, see Starhawk, *Dreaming the Dark: Magic, Sex and Politics* (Boston: Beacon Press, 1982), 183-219.
4. Alice Miller, *Thou Shalt Not Be Aware: Society's Betrayal of the Child*, trans. Hildegarde and Hunter Hannum (New York: Farrar, Straus & Giroux, 1984), 20.
5. Ibid., 19-20.
6. The Fall/Redemption model is not the only one in Christianity. In Christian theology, as in Judaism, a current of religious thought has always existed that stresses and celebrates the sacredness of creation. For a full discussion of the creation–centered tradition in Christianity, see Matthew Fox, *Original Blessing: A Primer in Creation Spirituality* (Santa Fe, NM: Bear & Co., 1983). For examples of earth–centered Jewish celebration, see Arthur Waskow, *Seasons of Our Joy: A Celebration of Modern Jewish Renewal* (Toronto: Bantam, 1982).
7. Margery Wolf, "Chinese Women: Old Skills in a New Context," in *Woman, Culture and Society*, ed. Michelle Z. Rosaldo and Louise Lamphere (Stanford, CA: Stanford University Press, 1974).
8. Audre Lorde, "The Master's Tools Will Never Dismantle the Master's House," *Sister Outsider* (Trumansburg, NY: Crossing Press, 1984).
9. Gertrude and Rubin Blanck, *Ego Psychology: Theory and Practice* (New York: Columbia University Press, 1974), 101.
10. Personal communication, Sister José Habday, August, 1984.
11. Luisah Teish, *Jambalaya: The Natural Woman's Book of Personal Charms and Practical Rituals* (San Francisco: Harper & Row, 1985), 63.

Pages 326-335 from *Weaving the Visions: New Patterns in Feminist Spirituality,* edited by Carol P. Christ and Judith Plaskow. Copyright © 1989 by Carol P. Christ and Judith Plaskow. Reprinted by permission of HarperCollins Publishers, Inc.

6.3

Ritual as Bonding

Action as Ritual

Starhawk

Rituals are part of every culture. They are the events that bind a culture together, that create a heart, a center, for a people. It is ritual that evokes the Deep Self of a group. In *ritual* (a patterned movement of energy to accomplish a purpose) we become familiar with power-from-within, learn to recognize its *feel,* learn how to call it up and let it go.

The pattern of the movement of energy in a Craft ritual is based on a very simple structure. We begin by grounding—connecting with the earth. Often we use the Tree of Life meditation. Then we cleanse ourselves, perhaps with a meditation on salt water or a plunge into the ocean, taking time to release our pain and tensions through movement or sound. The circle is cast: separating the ritual space and time from ordinary space and time, as we invoke the four elements. We invoke the Goddess and the God, and whatever other powers or presences we wish to greet.

Then we raise power by breathing, meditating, dancing, chanting. The power is focused through an image, an action, or a symbol. We may enter a trance together, taking a journey together into the underworld. After the power has reached its peak, we return it to the earth, grounding it through our hands and bodies. Then we celebrate with food and drink and take time to relax and be together. Finally, we thank all the powers we have invoked and open the circle, returning to ordinary space and time.

Rituals create a strong group bond. They help build community, creating a meeting-ground where people can share deep feelings, positive and negative—a place where they can sing or scream, howl ecstatically or furiously, play, or keep a solemn silence. A pagan ritual incorporates touch, sensuality, and humor. Anything we truly revere is also something that we can ridicule respectfully. The elements of laughter and play keep us from getting stuck on one level of power or developing an inflated sense of self-importance. Humor keeps kicking us onward, to go deeper. . . .

In a large group, especially one consisting of people who do not know each other well, we cannot reach the same level of closeness—nor can the power flow as smoothly—as in a small group. Yet larger rituals can also build community, and they have an excitement and an air of festivity that small coven meetings cannot attain. When bonding occurs in a larger group, and a Deep Self is formed, the energy may move by itself in the same way it moves in a small group. . . .

There are many factors we have learned to be aware of in planning large, open rituals. A ritual can alienate as easily as it can empower.

The first element to plan carefully is grounding. For a ritual to be powerful, we must start grounded, stay grounded, and end grounded, because the power that we raise comes into our bodies through the earth, and then returns to the earth.

We always begin a ritual, or any act of magic, by breathing together, by visualizing our connection to the earth and our connection to each other. Most often we use some variation of the Tree of Life. One of my favorite visualizations follows:

Tree of Generations

Breathe deeply, from your belly. Let yourself stand loosely but firmly planted on the earth. Straighten your spine, and release the tension in your shoulders.

Now imagine that your spine is the trunk of a tree that has roots that go deep into the center of the earth. Let yourself breathe down into those roots, and let all the tensions and worries you bring with you flow down with your breath and dissolve into the earth.

Feel the way our roots connect under the earth, how we draw power from the same source. The earth is the body of our ancestors. It is our grandmothers' flesh, our grandfathers' bones. The earth sustained the generations that gave birth to us. As we draw on their power, the power of the earth, as we feel it rise through the roots in our feet and through the base of our spines, let us speak the names of our ancestors—of the ones who came before us, of the heroines and heros who inspire us . . .

And feel the energy of the earth rising into our bellies as we draw it up with our breath, feel it rise into our hearts and spread out from our hearts up through our shoulders and down through our hands. Feel it move around the circle through our hands—feel how it connects us through our breath. As we breathe together—breathing in, breathing out—we link ourselves together, and we speak our own names . . .

And feel the power rising up through our throats, and out the tops of our heads like branches that sweep up and return to touch the earth again, creating a circle, making a circuit. And the branches are our children and grandchildren, the generations that come after us, and we feel them intertwining above our heads, and we know that they are not separate from us, and that, like us, they too will return to earth. And we speak their names . . .

And through the branches, through the leaves, we feel the sun shining down on us, and the wind moving, and the moon and the stars shining down. And we can draw in the power of that light, draw it in as a leaf draws in sunlight, and feel it spread down through all the twigs and branches, down through the trunk, down through the roots, until we are filled with light, and as the light reaches the roots, we feel them push yet deeper into the earth.

And as we relax, we feel the connection, the ground beneath our feet, and we know that we cannot lose that ground.

Whenever energy is raised, we ground it, return it to the earth, by touching the earth. Sometimes we place our palms on the ground; sometimes we crouch down and release the power through our entire bodies. We may ground the energy periodically during a ritual, and we are careful to ground it thoroughly after the cone of power is raised. Otherwise, we are left feeling nervous, anxious, unfinished—and the excess energy easily turns to irritation with each other.

The cone of power is raised at the point in the ritual when the energy we have drawn up through our bodies spirals upward into a cohesive whole, reaches a peak, and then dies down. In a large ritual, the energy needs a clear focus, something easily seen or heard, and understood.

Not everyone in an open ritual will be familiar with the techniques of moving energy. However, if a few strong people shape the power, others will sense its rise and fall. The cone can be directed visually if we throw our arms up in the air. When some people do this, others will instinctively do the same thing, and the energy will follow everyone's body movements. When we touch the earth to ground the energy, others will naturally imitate these actions too. Again, the flow of energy will follow our movements.

In a large, open ritual, language is also crucial. Words that are abstract and New-Age buzz-words drain power, and they cause people's lips to curl. Far better to say, "Let's hold hands and breathe together" than, "Let us have an attunement." William Carlos Williams's famous dictum to poets, "No ideas but in things," is a good guide for ritual-makers as well—since magic is the language of *things*. The metaphors we choose reveal both our spirituality and our politics. We should be careful not to reinforce dualism by focusing on light to the exclusion of dark.

If we wish people to participate in chanting and dancing, then the songs we use must be so simple that they can easily be picked up on the spot. The words must be understandable; nothing drains energy more than a large number of people fumbling with an unfamiliar name, unless it is stopping the momentum of the ritual to instruct people.

When ritual is used in a situation that is not religious, such as a political demonstration, we need to be sensitive to the different needs and perspectives of all the people who may be involved. Religious trappings, the Goddess's names, even the word *Goddess* itself may offend many people and cause dissension. But if we speak of the *things* and people that embody the Goddess, that are manifestations of power-from-within—the earth, air, fire, and water, natural objects, each other—we speak a common language that can touch everyone, no matter what her/his philosophy or ideology.

Rituals at the Diablo Canyon Blockade

The rituals my affinity group, Matrix, facilitated in camp and in jail at the blockade attempting to prevent the opening of the Diablo Canyon nuclear power plant in

California put everything I knew about open rituals to the test. We wanted to share the power of ritual to create a group bond, but we were also aware that most people in camp were not Goddess-worshippers, or interested in becoming Witches. We were very sensitive about not *imposing* our religion on anyone—yet we did want to *share* the experience of magic.

Rose and I were the first members of Matrix to arrive at the blockade, the day after the alert was called. For several days, affinity groups gathered at the campsite, waiting until enough people were present to begin the blockade in force. During the waiting period, we took part in nonviolence trainings, helped with the work of the camp, and facilitated informal workshops in ritual. At one workshop, we planned a ritual collectively for the night of the full moon. It was very simple in structure. The main symbolic act would be to join our hands together in the center of the circle, reflecting the image on our camp buttons: joined hands across a stylized nuclear power plant, surrounded by a red circle that was crossed by a diagonal line (the international symbol for *no*).

We knew that because the underlying structure of the blockade was circular and nonhierarchical, no ritual we attempted to lead could work. Although we had a plan, we knew that, at most, we could facilitate and channel the group's strong, spontaneous energy if it arose.

As always happens, things did not go according to plan, yet everything we intended happened. The full moon rose while people were cooking and eating dinner. It was so fat and beautiful over the hills that everyone began howling, chanting, and banging on pots and pans. We had planned the ritual for much later, but friends came and told us that people were gathered down in an open field, waiting for the ritual to begin.

We went down, announcing the ritual as we went. I found myself deeply grateful for Rose's presence. In a structure so strongly oriented toward collectives, no one person alone could have worked a ritual. I am by nature a shy, introverted person (although I have often been accused of overcompensating), and my first instinct in large crowds is to wish I could disappear. Rose, however, has flair for the dramatic. She combines a warm heart with a striking appearance. She has very short, hennaed hair, clothing in bright, contrasting colors, and a resonant voice. Together, we made an effective team.

In the field a crowd of more than a hundred people was gathered, singing, and some musicians played guitars. We had, of course, no lights, no sound system. We could not even have candles because of the extreme danger of fire—there were no props.

Our plan had been to start with a Tree of Life meditation, and build this into a visualization of a circle of protection that would surround each person, each affinity group, the camp as a whole, and even the police and workers we would face on the blockade. We were going to invoke the elements with a simple chant, do a spiral dance, and build power.

However, the power was already built before we began. We asked the musicians to get people into a circle, thinking that this would quiet them so we could begin. But as soon as the circle formed, people began dancing inward in a spiral. I looked at Rose, and she looked at me. We both realized that we needed to abandon our expectations. I knew that if I could put myself in the silent place that I can find in my own coven, and let the inspiration arise, the ritual would work. I also knew that I couldn't relax that much. But the dance was moving inward—and we had to do something. So we joined it. As it became a tighter spiral, and the musicians ducked outside it to avoid being squeezed to death, we began a Native American chant to the elements:

> The earth, the water, the fire, the air
> Returns, returns, returns, returns.

People picked up the chant; it grew in power, becoming an expression of our purpose at the blockade, our commitment to a return of the balance of the elements. Someone picked up the beat with a drum. Suddenly, spontaneously, *everyone* joined hands and moved together, just as Rose had envisioned in our planning. We were swaying and chanting with our hands entwined, and I slipped into the twin consciousnesses that a priestess develops, let myself go into the power, lose myself in it—in the exhilaration of it—and yet consciously remain grounded in order to keep the power grounded. In fact, I finally began to sing a Tree of Life vision above the chanting. Rose also began to sing a vision, and soon others' weaving voices carried words and melodies above the chant.

At last we grounded. As people sat on the ground, we led the meditation we had planned, and then we asked people to speak of their visions for the blockade. Although hearing people's visions can be moving, after a while the descriptions usually begin to deteriorate into spiritual or political catch-phrases. When we felt the energy begin to dissipate, we thanked the powers we had invoked, and started the group singing. The faithful musicians kindly led the singing as we slipped away. The ritual was over.

Chaotic and backward as it was, Rose and I loved it. While some people who took part were frightened by the intensity of the energy, I suspect that most people also loved it as one loves a big, shaggy, clumsy dog who is terribly good-natured but cannot be trusted near breakable china. Certainly, people seemed to want more exposure to ritual. Weeks later, after a long, painful, all-day meeting, the decision by consensus to end the blockade included an agreement to have a closing ritual.

The closing ritual took place at the new moon. Members of the non-violence trainers collective asked me to facilitate. Most of the original members of Matrix had gone home, including Rose. This ritual followed the usual structure more closely, although three weeks on blockade had made me an expert at letting go, and I was prepared, I thought, for anything.

We met in an open space under the central parachute. The trainers rigged solar-powered lights so we could see each other. We sang while people were gathering, and then grounded with a Tree of Life meditation.

"In my tradition," I said to the gathered crowd, "we begin by calling in the four directions and invoke the elements of earth, air, fire, and water. I'd like to do that if it's okay."

The group murmured its agreement.

"Shall we do it formally, or just by chanting?" I asked.

"Formally," several people cried out. I then called for volunteers to call in each direction. These four people spoke the invocations. Two seemed to be from pagan traditions, and two from Native American traditions. Yet together they cast the circle. Again, I realized how easily the traditions fit together. The words and symbols may differ, but the thought-forms are the same.

We began a spiral dance, singing:

> She changes everything she touches,
>
> And everything she touches, changes.

As I began to unwind the spiral, I felt an impulse to make it a kissing spiral, one in which we kiss each person with whom we come face-to-face as we dance. We rarely do this in large, open groups, because many people find it threatening. That night it seemed right because I thought there were about fifty people gathered—a good size for a kissing spiral.

However, while we were invoking and dancing, the spiral had grown. What I didn't realize, until we began unwinding, was that there were about two hundred people in the dance.

We danced, and chanted, and kissed and danced and kissed until we were nearly dizzy or half-way into some other state of being. The situation was funny, but the hilarity only seemed to deepen the power. The spiral unwound, snaked, opened out, and threaded back. The chant went on and on. I began to fear that the energy would dissipate before it could be drawn into a cone. Then it changed. We began to sing:

> We are changers,
>
> Everything we touch can change.

The chant affirmed our purpose, affirmed the strength of the groups going out the next morning, on the last day of the blockade. The power built. We drew together in a tight spiral again, swaying, chanting, and singing in free-form melodies and wordless harmonies until the power peaked. After we grounded, we sang the names of the affinity groups who were present. Again the singing was both funny and beautiful. Chanting, "Mother Earth," can be solemnly spiritual; chanting, "No nukes, Hold the Anchovies," demands an appreciation of the absurdities of life. . . .

THE EQUINOX RITUAL

The oak trees of the back country around Diablo Canyon are the oldest oaks in the world. I don't know who told me that, or where the information came from, but I believe it. The oaks stretch around us and above us, high and sheltering. There are about eighty of us hiking on a secret path in the back country near the plant, a path that our guides have scouted. We are dressed in our darkest clothes, greens and blues, so that we can blend into the brush when helicopters fly over.

I am tired. Or rather, I am in a state beyond tiredness, between waking and sleeping, brought on by broken sleep and bad food. I am sustained now by energy that is no longer physical. In this state, the trees, the earth, come alive. They speak. They are angry, and we can let ourselves be pulled by the currents of their deep earth power. This must truly have been a sacred place to the Indians, for it feels like an open crack between the worlds, a place where even in bright daylight we are half in the underworld.

In my haze, I begin to see the whole blockade as a giant hex on the plant, an elaborate ritual. It has its own rite-of-entry, nonviolence training. Our way to the camp was secret—like the secret of the labyrinth. First we checked in at a site in the nearby town; then we were handed a map that guided us in a roundabout, circular fashion to camp. . . .

A group of us hike into the back country. In a surprise action on the morning the Nuclear Regulatory Commission is scheduled to grant the low-power testing license to the plant, some of us will block the seven-mile-long road that leads from the main gate to the plant at its midpoint. This will catch both the workers and the police off-guard. When the first contingent of thirty people is rounded up, another thirty will appear suddenly a little further down the road.

Some of us are climbing up the hill because the next day is the eve of the autumnal equinox, and we are determined to celebrate it within sight of the plant. Our ritual will be a political action, a threat to the plant's security, an expression of defiance. It will assert—on a day when we know hundreds of our people will be arrested—that we are still here, that we are loud, and strong, and will come back in force. . . .

For two days, we hike intermittently, eating cold foods because fires are both a security and a fire hazard in the back country. We sleep huddled together under thin blankets because the police are confiscating property and not returning it, and we do not want to lose our good sleeping bags. We hike in the dark and in the hot sun, as the logistics of our secret journey requires.

Finally, as dusk is falling on the eve of the Equinox, the guides lead us over a hill onto an open ridge. The fog-dipped coastal hills roll softly away from us. Below us lies the plant, square, hard-edged, and out of place, like a bad science fiction fantasy cartoon imposed on the landscape. In this place where the earth stretches out her arms and rears her soft breasts, this plant is the emblem of our estrangement, our attempts to control, to impose a cold order with concrete and chain links.

The sun is setting. We sit on the hill and eat our meager dinner, chanting:

> We are all one in the infinite sun
> Forever, and ever, and ever.

A helicopter flies by. It does what can only be called a double take, and returns. On the third pass, some members of the group moon it. That seems to be the signal to start the ritual.

We gather in a circle on the ridge. The helicopter flies around it, as if to seal it for us. In the center is a living tree the Sabotniks affinity group has brought to plant in the back country for a member of their group who was killed during the summer in a highway accident. We plant a flag they have made—a black one for anarchy, for the power of the dark, that is embellished with the pentacle of the Goddess. Some of us have brought offerings—I leave an abalone shell on the hillside.

The ritual is loose and wild. Dark falls, and as we feel our power and our anger rise, we break from the circle, line up on the ridge, shine our flashlights down on the plant, and scream. We yell out curses. We want them to know we are here, shining our flashlights down, to draw their searchlights playing over the hills. We are banging on pots and pans, pointing our anger like a spear.

Hiroshima.

Nagasaki.

Three Mile Island.

No Diablo!

We can think of no worse forces to invoke.

The power peaks, at last, as power always does. We send it down to find the plant's weakest spots, the fault lines within its structure-of-being. We ground, and open the circle, and pick our way slowly, silently, in the dark, back to where we have made our camp.

We wake at three in the morning and hike down the hill in the dark, to plant the tree and to climb over the fence onto the grounds of the plant, breaching their security. Again, the police arrest us.

As Kore returns to the underworld, we return to jail. We celebrate the Equinox once more, among women. But just as Kore emerges in the spring, we know that we shall also return to the hills, to this blockade or another one, to whatever action we must take to bring about the renewal of the earth.

Our Equinox ritual was only one small action in the larger ritual of the blockade. It was another step in a dance of many actions, many rituals, many focused powers.

After the blockade ended, new problems were suddenly discovered in the plant. Blueprints had been reversed; structures had been built wrong; equipment had been inaccurately weighed. The safety violations were so grave that the Nuclear Regulatory Commission took back the license it had earlier granted. At this writing, the power company is embroiled in audits and litigation. No fuel rods were loaded, and still the land is uncontaminated.

So the blockade succeeded—not by physically stopping the workers, but by changing the reality, the consciousness, of the society in which the plant exists. Not the blockade alone, but the years of effort and organizing that preceded the blockade, created that victory.

The ritual, the magic, spins the bond that can sustain us to continue the work over years, over lifetimes. Transforming culture is a long-term project. We organize now to buy time, to postpone destruction just a little bit longer in the hope that before it comes, we will have grown somehow wiser—somehow stronger—so that in the end we will avert the holocaust. But though power-from-within can burst forth in an instant, its rising is mostly a process slow as the turning wheels of generations. If we cannot live to see the completion of that revolution, we can plant its seeds in our circles, we can dream its shape in our visions, and our rituals can feed its growing power.

As we see the Goddess mirrored in each other's eyes, we take that power in our hands as we take hands, as we touch. For the strength of that power is in the bond we make with each other. And our vision grows strong when we no longer dream alone.

Excerpts from *The Spiral Dance: A Rebirth of the Ancient Religion of the Goddess, Deluxe 10th Edition,* by Starhawk. Copyright © 1979, 1989 by Miriam Simos. Reprinted by permission of HarperCollins Publishers, Inc.

6.4

The Spiral Dance

A Rebirth of the Ancient Religion of the Great Goddess

Starhawk

Ritual is partly a matter of performance, of theater. Some people delight in this aspect of Witchcraft; others become shy and frozen in front of a group. The quieter coveners, however, may channel power in other ways. Brook, for example, rarely wants to cast the circle or invoke the Goddess, but when she chants, her voice, ordinarily pleasant but unremarkable, becomes an eerie, more-than-human channel for power.

Magical training varies greatly from coven to coven, but its purpose is always the same: to open up the starlight consciousness, the other-way-of-knowing that belongs to the right hemisphere and allows us to make contact with the Divine within. The beginner must develop four basic abilities: relaxation, concentration, visualization, and projection.

Relaxation is important because any form of tension blocks energy. Muscular tension is felt as mental and emotional stress, and emotional stresses cause physical and muscular tension and *dis*-ease. Power trying to move through a tense body is like an electric current trying to force its way through a line of resistors. Most of the juice is lost along the way. Physical relaxation also seems to change brain wave patterns and activate centers that aren't ordinarily used.

Exercise 9: Relaxation

(This can be done in a group, alone, or with a partner, Begin by lying down on your back. Do not cross your limbs. Loosen any tight clothing.)

"In order to know how relaxation feels, we must first experience tension. We are going to tense all the muscles of the body, one by one, and keep them tense until we relax our entire bodies with one breath. Don't clench the muscles so they cramp, just tense them lightly.

"Start with your toes. Tense the toes in your right foot . . . and now your left foot. Tense your right foot . . . and your left foot. Your right ankle . . . and your left ankle . . .

(Continue throughout the whole body, part by part. From time to time, remind the group to tense any muscles that they have slack.)

"Now tense your scalp. Your whole body is tense . . . feel the tension in every part. Tense any muscles that have gone slack. Now take a deep breath . . . inhale . . . (pause) . . . exhale . . . and relax!

"Relax completely. You are completely and totally relaxed." (In a sing-song tone:) "Your fingers are relaxed, and your toes are relaxed. Your hands are relaxed, and your feet are relaxed. Your wrists are relaxed, and your ankles are relaxed."

(And so on, throughout the entire body. Periodically pause and say:)

"You are completely and totally relaxed. Completely and totally relaxed. Your body is light; it feels like water, like it is melting into the earth.

"Allow yourself to drift and float peacefully in your state of relaxation. If any worries of anxieties disturb your peace, imagine they drain from your body like water and melt into the earth. Feel yourself being healed and renewed."

(Remain in deep relaxation for ten to fifteen minutes. It is good to practice this exercise daily, until you can relax completely simply by lying down and letting go, without needing to go through the entire process. People who have difficulty sleeping will find this extremely helpful. However, do not allow yourself to drift off into sleep. You are training your mind to remain in a relaxed but alert state. Later, you will use this state for trance work, which will be much more difficult if you are not in the habit of staying awake. If you practice this at night before sleeping, sit up, open your eyes, and consciously end the exercise before dozing.

Many of the other exercises can be most effectively practiced in a state of deep relaxation. Experiment to find what works best for you.)

Before any ritual there is always a period of purification, during which participants can clear away worries, concerns, and anxieties that may hamper their concentration. Some covens simply aspurge (sprinkle) each member with salt water while casting the circle. At very large rituals, this is the only practical method. But for small groups and important workings, we use a more intense meditative exercise called the Salt-Water Purification.

Salt and water are both cleansing elements. Water, of course, washes clean. Salt preserves from decay and is a natural disinfectant. The ocean, the womb of life, is salt water, and so are tears, which help us purify the heart of sorrow.

Exercise 20: Salt-Water Purification

(This is one of the basic individual meditations that should be practiced regularly. During periods of high anxiety or depression or when undertaking heavy responsibilities, it is helpful to practice this daily.)

Fill a cup with water. (Use your ritual chalice, if you have one.) With your *athame* (or other implement), add three mounds of salt, and stir counterclockwise.

Sit with the cup in your lap. Let your fears, worries, doubts, hatreds, and disappointments surface in your mind. See them as a muddy stream, which flows out of you as you breathe and is dissolved by the salt water in the cup. Allow yourself time to feel deeply cleansed.

Now hold up the cup. Breathe deeply, and feel yourself drawing up power from the earth (as in the Tree of Life exercise). Let the power flow into the salt water, until you can visualize it glowing with light.

Sip the water. As you feel it on your tongue, know that you have taken in the power of cleansing, of healing. Fear and unhappiness have become transformed into the power of change.

Empty the leftover water into a running stream. (Alas, in these decadent times the nearest stream is usually running out of the kitchen faucet and down the drain.)

In the following spells, raise power by breathing or chanting, as in the exercises given previously. You can cast a circle formally or simply by visualizing it. Don't forget to earth the power and open the circle at the end. Names of materials used are given in capital letters, for ease of reference.

Spell casting is the lesser magic, but imagery and symbols are also used in the greater magic of rituals, where they become the keys to self-transformation and the links that connect us to the divine, within and without.

Anger Spell

Visualize a circle of light around yourself.

Cup a BLACK STONE in your hands and raise it to your forehead.

Concentrate and project all your anger into the stone.

With all your might, hurl it out of the circle into a lake, stream, river, or the ocean. Say:

> With this stone
> Anger be gone.
> Water bind it,
> No one find it.

Earth the power.

Release the circle.

(To be done alongside flowing water.)

The Indrinking Spell

(For self-acceptance when you've made a mistake or are filled with guilt or regrets.)

Cast a circle.

Sit facing North, and light a BLACK or WHITE CANDLE.

Hold in both hands your CUP, filled with CLEAR WATER. You should have before you an IMAGE OF THE GODDESS and a GREEN PLANT, in earth.

Visualize all the negative things you are feeling about yourself, the mistakes you have made, the things you have done wrong. Talk to yourself and admit you feel bad. Tell yourself, out loud, exactly what you have done wrong, and why. Let your emotion build energy, and project it all into the cup. Breathe on the water.

Raise power.

Visualize the Goddess as forgiving Mother. Imagine her hands cover yours. Hear Her say,

> I am the Mother of all things,
> My love is poured out upon the earth.
> I drink you in with perfect love,
> Be cleansed. Be healed. Be changed.

Pour out the water onto the plant, and feel your self-hate draining out of you. (It is possible this ritual will kill the plant.)

Fill the CUP with MILK or JUICE.

Raise more power, and visualize yourself as you would like to be, free of guilt and sorrow, changed so that you will not repeat the same errors. Charge the cup with strength and the power to be the person you want to be.

Again, visualize the Goddess. Her hands cover yours, and She says,

> Mine the cup, and Mine the waters of life.
> Drink deep!

Drink the juice or milk. Feel yourself filled with strength. Know that you have changed, that you are, from that very moment, a new person, not bound by the patterns and errors of the past.

Bind the spell.

Earth the power.

Open the circle.

In coven rituals, energy raised is most often molded into the form of a cone, the Cone of Power. The base of the cone is the circle of coveners; its apex can focus on an individual, an object, or a collectively visualized image. At times, the cone is allowed to rise and fall naturally, as in the power chant described in Chapter Three. It may also be sent off in a burst of force, directed by one person, who may be part of the circle, or may stand at its center. When a group is familiar with the exercises given in Chapter Three, the following will prepare members for more advanced energy workings:

Exercise 45: The Cone of Power

All ground and center. Standing or sitting in a circle, take hands. Begin with a Group Breath, and gradually build a wordless Power Chant.

As the energy builds, visualize it swirling clockwise around the circle. *See* it as a blue-white light. It spirals up into a cone form—an upright shell, a cornucopia. Hold the visualization until it glows.

The energy forms we build have a reality of their own. As the power rises, people will intuitively sense the form that takes shape. As the peak is reached, the chant becomes a focused tone. If you have an image that represents your intent for the working, focus on it. Sometimes words or phrases come through. Let the power move until it falls, suddenly or gradually.

Let the energy go, fall to the ground, and relax completely, allowing the cone to fly off to its objective. Breathe deeply, and let the residue of power return to the earth, for her healing.

Rhythm, drums, hand claps, and dance movements may also be used in building the cone. Covens should experiment, and feel free to try many methods. Other words, names, Goddess or God names, or simple incantations can be used to raise power. The energy can also be molded into other forms: for example, a fountain, that rises and flows back on the coveners, a wave form, or a glowing sphere. Possibilities are infinite.

6.5

Roundtable Discussion

Backlash

Starhawk

I sit down to write this at a time of wonderful and terrible contradictions. This year, we have a pro-choice president and a feminist First Lady, but we have seen the violence of the antichoice movement escalate to open murder. In this still-new decade, we've seen the fall of the Berlin Wall, and the resumption of genocide in Bosnia, with rape openly used as a tactic of war. As we move into the next millenium, we have a vice president in office who has a deep and intelligent understanding of environmental issues, and an ozone layer thinning more rapidly than the worst predictions. Certainly the last years have seen women make important steps forward, but when I think back to the issues, agendas and hopes of the feminist movement twenty years ago, when I was newly involved, it sometimes seems as if we have been running in place.

As a woman who has been publicly "out" as a Witch for almost two decades now, I think I know something about backlash. What we call "backlash" is an organized, well-funded and well-orchestrated campaign to preserve the status quo, in particular in relations between women and men. More than that, it is an attempt to radically change the nature of our democracy in the United States, which is founded on the principles of freedom of religion and separation of church and state. The Robertsons and Buchanans of the world would replace religious freedom with theocracy, the rule of a very narrow brand of Christianity, without room for pluralism.

Too often, the response of the feminist movement and other progressive movements has been to abandon the terrain of the sacred to the fundamentalists. Influenced by Marx's condemnation of religion, the Left has been uncomfortable with issues of spirit. An exception has been in the struggles of indigenous people, who have always been clear that their land rights and physical and cultural survival are inseparable from their spirituality. Another exception has been the feminist spirituality movement, which has labored over the last two decades to bring forward questions of the sacred into the larger political dialogue.

Overall, however, the fundamentalists have succeeded in slanting our national dialogue, placing their own frame around such issues as abortion and gay rights. They appear to speak for religion and morality against an opposition that is defined as secular, amoral or immoral, and nonreligious.

Fortunately, the majority of Americans are not ready to accept fundamentalist morality, as the heartening results of the November elections proved. But questions of the sacred are central to the dialogue about social change. What we consider sacred is the metavalue that determines all our values, that defines what we do not want to see defiled, exploited, or compromised. The sacred is what we are willing to take a stand for, to sacrifice for.

When we in the feminist movement ask our society to make profound shifts in its view of the most basic and intimate relationships of power and gender, we must confront issues of deep value. We need to come from a clear position grounded not in amorality but in a different morality from that of the fundamentalists.

For the past five hundred years, if not for millenia, patriarchal religions have defined the sacred as something located outside the living fabric of the world. The patriarchal God creates the world as an object separate from himself, and the closer one gets to God the further one moves away from the world. The desacralized earth and her human, animal, plant and mineral children thus become fair game for exploitation.

Of course, even the most patriarchal religious traditions also contain currents of earth-centered theology and practice. But the positions taken by the fundamentalists come from the most rigid and hierarchical reading of ancient scriptures and teaching. Their God is a sovereign over the natural world.

In contrast, when we see God, or Goddess, as immanent in the world, when we begin to see the cosmos itself as a living, conscious being, our definition of the sacred undergoes a profound change.

The understanding that the earth is alive seems new to us today as it reemerges in our culture, but it is very old. It has always been held by indigenous peoples, and is central to their culture, religion and survival. It is shared by the reemerging Goddess traditions that have sparked much of the feminist spirituality movement. It is gaining recognition by scientists who name it the Gaia hypothesis. It is understood by environmentalists who must contend with the complex interactions of living systems, and intuited by many people who identify with none of these groups.

In this view, the earth is a living being in which we all participate, part of the larger being which is the cosmos. The earth, the moon, sun and stars, the whole fabric of the universe is an organism, dynamic, interactive, complex beyond our ability to analyze and control. We value knowledge but also respect the mystery—we can never know and control all of life.

What is sacred, all around the globe, to earth-based spiritual traditions are the four elements that sustain life—air, fire, water and earth—plus the fifth, essence or spirit, which comes into being when the other four are in balance. Sacredness is embedded in the living world itself, in the cycles of birth, growth, death and rebirth that are continually being enacted in nature, in the cosmic cycles of time, and in human culture.

If we are to counter backlash with forelash, we must clarify and define this conflict of values. And we can certainly expect opposition. For to say that the earth is alive and sacred is to take a truly radical stand. What is sacred cannot be exploited. If the ground we walk on has a sacred character, we cannot allow its soil to become eroded. We cannot clear-cut the old growth forests for profit, for what is sacred cannot be measured against the scales of profit and loss. If we say the river is sacred, we must keep it clean; we cannot sell "polluting rights" to chemical companies. If we say the air is sacred, we cannot blithely run our air conditioners while the ozone deteriorates. If we respect earth-based religions as we do other religions, then we must begin to listen when native peoples claim a particular piece of land as sacred. We cannot strip-mine the sacred mountain and relocate the tribe, build a golf course in a sacred wood, place a geothermal installation in a sacred rain forest, test nuclear weapons on sacred land.

Our stand is also radical because when the earth is alive, God the Ruler is dethroned. For if we are all participants in sacred being, then each of us embodies sacred authority, particularly in the bodily realms of birth, sex and death. This authority might be dangerous were it not universal—I become destructive when I claim authority over you—but if you are as much Goddess as I, I cannot do that. All I can do is claim my sacred right to make my own life-and-death decisions and answer the call of my own conscience.

By virtue of my womb, my potential to bring forth life, I become a priestess of life and death, one charged with making those choices about when to let new life come through and when to keep it back. Regardless of what the fundamentalists may think, all women face these decisions, whether we are happily married wives or single mothers or women who choose not to have children or face infertility, which brings with it a myriad of choices of its own. Women's lives are integrally bound up with this constant choosing, until we become crones, at which time we face equally deep choices around losses, age, and death. We do not merely have the right to choice—we are doomed to choice. To challenge that right is to attack our very being as women, as participants in the great round of birth, growth, and yes, death.

Our sexual morality also arises from our inner authority. Pleasure itself is sacred. For we see the earth as a living being, we are bound to notice what an erotic being she is. If you doubt me, go stand on a hill by the ocean with a spring wind blowing and a profusion of wild irises at your feet. Eat a strawberry, slowly. Or run your hand along the soft, rough bark of a redwood tree. The giving and sharing of pleasure is one of the core purposes of the universe. Each of us has the sacred right to share pleasure in whatever forms our inner being calls us to explore, and with that right come the responsibilities that form our sexual morality, based on equality of power between partners, respect for each other, and safeguarding each other's physical and emotional health and well-being.

When we carry sacred authority within us, then we also have the right to choice at death. Last year the Catholic Church mobilized enormous opposition to California's right-to-die initiative, which would have allowed terminal patients to request a physician's aid in ending their lives. Having recently watched with my mother as she went through a long and painful death, I found it hard to understand why any religion would mandate such prolonged suffering. But the patriarchal God is jealous of all the prerogatives of his rulership, not the least of which is that he and he alone should determine the moment of death. To take that decision into our own hands is to undermine his authority, to imply that our lives might belong to us, not a cosmic master.

Change provokes fear and reaction, so backlash should never surprise us. But if we are to move forward, and not endlessly be forced to regain the same ground, we must frame the issues that clarify the deep questions of value our society is struggling with. We need forelash to counter backlash. And we need vision to counter fear—the vision of a resacralized earth, where the needs of the interconnected web of life forms set our policies, where diversity of genders, races, species, sexual orientations and worldviews is considered a gift, where those who differ can listen and learn from each other instead of attempting to dominate one another, where we can assure for the next generations that the cycles of birth, growth, death, and rebirth will continue to generate new forms and new lives.

7

Introduction to Paula Gunn Allen

Born in 1939 in Cubero, New Mexico, Paula Gunn Allen's ethnicities combine her mother's Laguna Pueblo, Lakota, and Scottish heritages with her father's Lebanese background. She received her M.F.A. in English in 1966 from the University of Oregon and her Ph.D. in American Studies in 1975 from the University of New Mexico. She explains that she never fit in and always has felt uneasy with her place in the world. Her poem "Some Like Indians Endure" speaks to her multicultural background and her attempt to survive in a world in which she, along with many other Native American Indians, never feels at home.

Gunn Allen's work critiques the centuries-long European tradition of misinterpreting all things Native and Indian. In "Grandmother of the Sun: Ritual Gynocracy in Native America," Gunn Allen retells the tradition, explaining that, when told correctly, Indians and spirits are always found together, traditional tribal lifestyles are more often gynocratic than not, and they are never patriarchal. Her poem "Essentially, It's Spring" also speaks to this history of misinterpretation and the pain it has caused for Native American Indians.

Gunn Allen's theories also address questions of alienation and the importance of living in constant connection with others—whether those others are humans, other animals, things in nature, spirits, or even aliens. "All the Good Indians" addresses this exigence as well as the practices and norms that are bringing about extinction for Native peoples. "Haggles" explains the absurdity of Western notions of isolation and the ways that the Western desire to organize everything (or to eliminate that which cannot be organized) leads to alienation, vulnerability, and despair.

7.1

All the Good Indians

Paula Gunn Allen

Yesterday, a student said something that forced me to contemplate a world without Indians. He said that the elder people knew that we were disappearing, and when something is ending, it gets smaller. He said it's like shutter on a camera, the opening grows smaller as it closes. That is why, he said, so many of us have begun to write: to write everything down so that there will be a record.

The student is the second chief of his tribe, the Narragansett; he has been an active and involved Indian, working for his tribe and his people for well over a decade. He is at Berkeley studying Native American studies and anthropology, readying himself to research and record everything he can about his own tribe and others accurately in terms of both perspectives.

The class let out after five o'clock. I left the U.C. Berkeley campus walking down Telegraph toward the parking lot. As I walked I saw people going past me. I saw the shops, the goods on display in the windows. I went by restaurants and coffee houses. Nowhere did I see an Indian, an item produced by or even reminiscent of Indians, a food or beverage for sale that was identified in my mind or in the mind of those others around me, as Indian. Coffee is Indian, but not really. Corn, turkey, tomatoes. Pumpkin, chili, tortillas. So many things. But no Indian visible anywhere, not even me.

Less than 24 hours later, I still haven't begun to deal with his remark.

But walking along Telegraph I remembered a time when I had lived in an Indianless world; I was in Oregon, attending the University in Eugene. For the first year or so I never saw or heard of an Indian. I was the only Indian I knew. That was around 1967. Sometime in 1968, a package arrived in the mail from my parents. It was a signed copy of N. Scott Momaday's *House Made of Dawn*. I believe that book saved my life.

How do you touch extinction?

How do you comprehend that the entire world is about to vanish?

Sitting Bull did that. He comprehended the totality of death. He went with Buffalo Bill's Indian circus, like the last exotic striped quagga goes with the zoo. He told the people to see to it that the children got educated in the white man's schools, and he worked to get schools opened so they could. They left the wondrous way of the Sioux. He left it. They became ranchers and farmers; Christians and bureaucrats, soldiers in the conqueror's armies, welfare recipients. Their life-expectancy was as much as 44 years in the 60s. It hasn't increased.

Crazy Horse chose to fight and to die instead. They bayoneted him when he came to the fort to talk. They bayoneted him because they couldn't shoot him. His medicine was such that he was invulnerable to bullets.

They used to dance the ghost dance. They wept. They knew what they had lost, what was gone. They tried to dance it back.

In Oregon, I didn't know the name of the disease I was suffering from. I was seeing a shrink. I didn't know that I was only grieving and lost. I thought I was mentally ill.

In Oregon I was involved. In the civil rights movement; in the peace movement. I taught and spoke and wrote. I struggled. One night at the local campus bar I was in a conversation with some people—two radical black men, a white man (my husband) and a couple of SDS-types. We were talking about why the movement was important. One black man said I couldn't know how significant it was. That I had no reason to care. He said I was a "groupie," a "voyeur." The other one said that wasn't so; I had at least the same difficulties black people had. I faced the same oppression, repression, depression. "She's a woman," he said. "For her it's even worse." Nobody said, "She's an Indian." Not my husband. Not even me.

It is 1982. I live in California. I teach at Berkeley. In Native American Studies. The Indians I see are in my classes (2 Indians out of 40 students) or in the department's offices. Out of some 30,000 students enrolled at "Cal," something like 160 are American Indian.

Out of 200.6 million people (more or less) in the United States, slightly over 1 million are American Indian.

When I think of the figures, I wonder how I could have lived 43 years thinking the world was *not* bereft of Indians.

But, I think, there are millions of us south of here. In Mexico and Central America, in South America. But just a day or so ago I read that the Guatemalan regime recently massacred 2,500 Indians. A few months ago I read that the Sadinistas massacred several hundred or a thousand Indians. A few years ago I read that they hunt Indians in Brazil with airplanes; when they spot them they bomb them, napalm them, throw nets over them and haul them away to camps where they are raped, beaten to death, starved. Or in the time honored fashion of the invader, they just throw down some bundles that contain poisoned food, pestilence-infected clothing and blankets. Scratch scores, hundreds, thousands, millions of Indians.

Some say that upwards of 45 million Indians lived in what is now the United States on the eve of contact. Government records put our numbers at 450,000 in the 1970 census. The population of Indians in the United States hasn't doubled in ten years; the count was just more accurate.

Some health workers say that over 25 percent of Indian women and 10 percent of Indian men in the United States have been sterilized without their knowledge or consent. Scratch several hundred thousand future Indians. Many Indians "marry out." Go to the cities and get lost. Over two-thirds of all American Indians live in cities now. Maybe more. They walk down Telegraph, or Central, or Market, or Fifth Avenue. They see themselves nowhere they look. Scratch several hundred thousand more. They say, the only good Indian is a dead Indian. There are millions of good Indians somewhere.

Do you remember the child's song, "One Little, Two Little, Three Little Indians?" The first part counts one, two, three, up to ten. The second part counts backwards: ten, nine, eight little Indians, seven, six, five little Indians, four, three, two, little Indians, one little Indian. It's on my mind right now. I learned it in the 40s. I forgot it later. It comes up today.

Lens closing. So light doesn't get through. But the camera leaves a picture for posterity.

I remember the 60s. A time when American hippies discovered Indians, rediscovered Indians. A decade-long Columbus day. In the early 70s a story about that was published in Rosen's *The Man To Send Rain Clouds* anthology. It was written by Simon J. Ortiz. You should read it. It's about an old Pueblo man who goes to San Francisco looking for his granddaughter who has disappeared. He goes to the Indian Center on Valencia Street to see if anyone there has seen her. But there are no Indians there. The building is locked. He is befriended by some hippies. They are practicing to be Indians. They take him back to their pad, hoping he can turn them on to the proper Indian uses of peyote. He doesn't find his granddaughter—they don't know her. A picture, a record, left by an Indian, a Pueblo writer named Ortiz.

And *House Made of Dawn,* another picture. From which the hero, a longhair Pueblo Indian who can't speak, disappears. The only Indian book I read in the 60s was *House Made of Dawn*. At the time, I didn't realize what the end of it meant. I thought Abel ran into life, into tradition, into strength. It was not until the late 70s, when I saw a film rendition of the book made by a group of Indian filmmakers, that I realized that in the end Abel ran into another world; that he reclaimed himself as a longhair Pueblo Indian man by running out of this particular world-frame, this particular universe, this reality. In other words, he died. Abel was a good Indian.

When my student spoke, I thought of *House Made of Dawn,* about what it meant. I understood the record Momaday had made. The one about how the Indian vanishes, with a fine, soundless song; the one that got him the Pulitzer Prize.

And I have known for a long time that what an Indian is supposed to be is dead. But I didn't until just that instant, as my student spoke, understand that what Sitting Bull said was not a statement wrung from him by defeat in a years-long war; it was a statement about who and what Indians are in America. More than forgotten, more than oppressed, more than terminated, relocated, removed; the word for it is extinguished. Dead.

The only book by an Indian I read in the 60s was about the reality of Indianness. Just as the book I began writing in 1970 and finished last spring is. Which I didn't realize until today.

I can imagine a world without Indians. It is a world that has surrounded me most of my life. I only just now recognized it—a world that will have records—pictures, foods, artifacts, heritages of Indians, all transformed into something unrecognizable to an Indian. But it won't matter, I guess. All of us who cannot live in such a world won't, and all of us will be good.

From *The Sacred Hoop* by Paula Gunn Allen. Copyright © 1986,1992 by Paula Gunn Allen. Reprinted by permission of Beacon Press, Boston.

7.2

Grandmother of the Sun

Ritual Gynocracy in Native America

Paula Gunn Allen

I

There is a spirit that pervades everything, that is capable of powerful song and radiant movement, and that moves in and out of the mind. The colors of this spirit are multitudinous, a glowing, pulsing rainbow. Old Spider Woman is one name for this quintessential spirit, and Serpent Woman is another. Corn Woman is one aspect of her, and Earth Woman is another, and what they together have made is called Creation, Earth, creatures, plants, and light.

At the center of all is Woman, and no thing is sacred (cooked, ripe, as the Keres Indians of Laguna Pueblo say it) without her blessing, her thinking.

> ... In the beginning Tse che nako, Thought Woman finished everything, thoughts, and the names of all things. She finished also all the languages. And then our mothers, Uretsete and Naotsete said they would make names and they would make thoughts. Thus they said. Thus they did.[1]

This spirit, this power of intelligence, has many names and many emblems. She appears on the plains, in the forests, in the great canyons, on the mesas, beneath the seas. To her we owe our very breath, and to her our prayers are sent blown on pollen, on corn meal, planted into the earth on feather-sticks, spit onto the water, burned and sent to her on the wind. Her variety and multiplicity testify to her complexity: she is the true creatrix for she is thought itself, from which all else is born. She is the necessary precondition for material creation, and she, like all of her creation, is fundamentally female—potential and primary.

She is also the spirit that informs right balance, right harmony, and these in turn order all relationships in conformity with her law.

To assign to this great being the position of "fertility goddess" is exceedingly demeaning: it trivializes the tribes and it trivializes the power of woman. Woman bears, that is true. She also destroys. That is true. She also wars and hexes and mends and breaks. She creates the power of the seeds, and she plants them. As Anthony Purley, a Laguna writer, has translated a Keres ceremonial prayer, "She is mother of us all, after Her, mother earth follows, in fertility, in holding, and taking again us back to her breast."[2]

The Hopi account of their genatrix, Hard Beings Woman, gives the most articulate rendering of the difference between simple fertility cultism and the creative prowess of the Creatrix. Hard Beings Woman (Huruing Wuhti) is of the earth. But she lives in the worlds above where she "owns" (empowers) the moon and stars. Hard Beings Woman has solidity and hardness as her major aspects. She, like Thought Woman, does not give birth to creation or to human beings but breathes life into male and female effigies that become the parents of the Hopi—in this way she "creates" them. The male is Muingwu, the god of crops, and his sister-consort is Sand Altar Woman who is also known as Childbirth Water Woman. In Sand Altar Woman the mystical relationship between water, worship, and woman is established; she is also said to be the mother of the katsinas, those powerful messengers who relate the spirit world to the world of humankind and vice versa.[3]

Like Thought Woman, Hard Beings Woman lived in the beginning on an island which was the only land there was. In this regard she resembles a number of Spirit Woman Beings; the Spirit genatrix of the Iroquois, Sky Woman, also lived on an island in the void which only later became the earth. On this island, Hard Beings Woman is identified with or, as they say, "owns" all hard substances—moon, stars, beads, coral, shell, and so forth. She is a sea goddess as well, the single inhabitant of the earth, that island that floats alone in the waters of space. From this meeting of woman and water, earth and her creatures were born.[4]

The waters of space are also crucial in the Sky Woman story of the Seneca. Sky Woman is catapulted into the void by her angry, jealous, and fearful husband, who tricks her into peering into the abyss he has revealed by uprooting the tree of light (which embodies the power of woman) that grows near his lodge. Her terrible fall is broken by the Water Fowl who live in that watery void, and they safely deposit Sky Woman on the back of Grandmother Turtle, who also inhabits the void. On the body of Grandmother Turtle earth-island is formed.[5] Interestingly, the shell of the turtle is one of the Hard Substances connected to Hard Beings Woman.[6]

Contemporary Indian tales suggest that the creatures are born from the mating of sky father and earth mother, but that seems to be a recent interpolation of the original sacred texts. The revision may have occurred since the Christianizing influence on even the arcane traditions, or it may have predated Christianity. But the older, more secret texts suggest that it is a revision. It may be that the revision appears only in popular versions of the old mythic cycles on which ceremony and ritual are based; this would accord with the penchant in the old oral tradition for shaping tales to reflect present social realities, making the rearing and education of children possible even within the divergent worlds of the United States of America and the tribes.

According to the older texts (which are sacred, that is, power-engendering), Thought Woman is not a passive personage: her potentiality is dynamic and unimaginably powerful. She brought corn and agriculture, potting, weaving, social systems, religion, ceremony, ritual, building, memory, intuition, and their expressions in language, creativity, dance, human-to-animal relations, and she gave these offerings power and authority and blessed the people with the ability to provide for themselves and their progeny.

Thought Woman is not limited to a female role in the total theology of the Keres people. Since she is the supreme Spirit, she is both Mother and Father to all people and to all creatures. She is the only creator of thought, and thought precedes creation.[7]

Central to Keres theology is the basic idea of the Creatrix as She Who Thinks rather than She Who Bears, of woman as creation thinker and female thought as origin of material and nonmaterial reality. In this epistemology, the perception of female power as confined to maternity is a limit on the power inherent in femininity. But "she is the supreme Spirit, . . . both Mother and Father to all people and to all creatures."[8]

In the nineteenth century, Fr. Noël Dumarest reported from another Keres Pueblo, Cochiti, on Spider Woman (Thought Woman, although he does not mention her by this name). In his account, when the "Indian sister" made stars, she could not get them to shine, so "she consulted Spider, the creator." He characterized the goddess-sisters as living "with Spider Woman, their mother, at *shipapu,* under the waters of the lake, in the second world." It should be mentioned that while she is here characterized as the sisters' mother, the Cochiti, like the other Keres, are not so much referring to biological birth as to sacred or ritual birth. To address a person as "mother" is to pay the highest ritual respect.[9]

In Keres theology the creation does not take place through copulation. In the beginning existed Thought Woman and her dormant sisters, and Thought Woman thinks creation and sings her two sisters into life. After they are vital she instructs them to sing over the items in their baskets (medicine bundles) in such a way that those items will have life. After that crucial task is accomplished, the creatures thus vitalized take on the power to regenerate themselves—that is, they can reproduce others of their kind. But they are not in and of themselves self-sufficient; they depend for their being on the medicine power of the three great Witch creatrixes, Thought Woman, Uretsete, and Naotsete. The sisters are not related by virtue of having parents in common; that is, they are not alive because anyone bore them. Thought Woman turns up, so to speak, first as Creatrix and then as a personage who is acting out someone else's "dream." But there is not time when she did not exist. She has two bundles in her power, and these bundles contain Uretsete and Naotsete, who are not viewed as her daughters but as her sisters, her coequals who possess the medicine power to vitalize the creatures that will inhabit the earth. They also have the power to create the firmament, the skies, the galaxies, and the seas, which they do through the use of ritual magic.

The idea that Woman is possessed of great medicine power is elaborated in the Lakota myth of White Buffalo Woman. She brought the Sacred Pipe to the Lakota, and it is through the agency of this pipe that the ceremonies and rituals of the Lakota are empowered.[10] Without the pipe, no ritual magic can occur. According to one story about White Buffalo Woman, she lives in a cave where she presides over the Four Winds.[11] In Lakota ceremonies, the four wind directions are always acknowledged, usually by offering a pipe to them. The pipe is ceremonial, modeled after the Sacred Pipe given the people by the Sacred Woman. The Four Winds are very powerful beings themselves, but they can function only at the bidding of White Buffalo Woman. The

Lakota are connected to her still, partly because some still keep to the ways she taught them and partly because her pipe still resides with them.

The Pipe of the Sacred Woman is analogous in function to the ear of corn left with the people by Iyatiku, Corn Woman, the mother goddess of the Keres. Iyatiku, who is called the mother of the people, is in a ceremonial sense another aspect of Thought Woman. She presently resides in Shipap from whence she sends counsel to the people and greets them when they enter the spirit world of the dead. Her representative, Irriaku (Corn Mother), maintains the connection between individuals in the tribe as well as the connection between the nonhuman supernaturals and the tribe. It is through the agency of the Irriaku that the religious leaders of the tribe, called Yaya and Hotchin, or hochin in some spellings of the word, (Mother and leader or chief), are empowered to govern.

The Irriaku, like the Sacred Pipe, is the heart of the people as it is the heart of Iyatiku. In the form of the perfect ear of corn, Naiya Iyatiku (Mother, Chief) is present at every ceremony. Without the presence of her power, no ceremony can product the power it is designed to create or release.[12] These uses of the feminine testify that primary power—the power to make and to relate—belongs to the preponderantly feminine powers of the universe.

According to one story my great-grandmother told me, in time immemorial when the people lived in the White Village or Kush Katret, Iyatiku lived with them. There came a drought, and since many normal activities had to be suspended and since the people were hungry and worried because of the scarcity of food from the drought, Iyatiku gave them a gambling game to while away the time. It was meant to distract them from their troubles. But the men became obsessed and began to gamble everything away. When the women scolded them and demanded that they stop gambling and act responsibly toward their families, the men got mad and went into the kivas.

Now, since the kivas were the men's space, the women didn't go there except for ritual reasons. The men continued to gamble, neglecting their ritual duties and losing all their possessions of value. Because they didn't do the dances or make the offerings as they were supposed to, the drought continued and serious famine ensued. Finally one old man who was also a priest, or cheani, became very concerned. He sought the advice of a shaman nearby, but it was too late. Iyatiku had left Kush Katret in anger at her foolish people. She went back to Shipap where she lives now and keeps an eye on the people. The people were forced to abandon the village, which was inundated by floods brought on by the angry lake spirits. So the beautiful village was destroyed and the people were forced to build a new one elsewhere and to live without the Mother of Corn. But she left with them her power, Irriaku, and told them that it was her heart she left in their keeping. She charged them always to share the fruits of her body with one another, for they were all related, and she told them that they must ever remain at peace in their hearts and their relationships.

The rains come only to peaceful people, or so the Keres say. As a result of this belief, the Keres abhor violence or hostility. They are very careful to contain their emotions and to put a smooth face on things, for rain is essential to the very life of their villages. Without it the crops can't grow, the livestock will starve, there will be no water for drinking or bathing—in short, all life, physical and ceremonial, will come to a halt. For ceremonies depend on corn and corn pollen and birds and water; without these they are not likely to be efficacious, if they can be held at all.

II

There is an old tradition among numerous tribes of a two-sided, complementary social structure. In the American Southeast this tradition was worked out in terms of the red chief and the white chief, positions held by women and by men and corresponding to internal affairs and external affairs. They were both spiritual and ritualistic, but the white chief or internal chief functioned in harmony-effective ways. This chief maintained peace and harmony among the people of the band, village, or tribe and administered domestic affairs. The red chief, also known as the war chief, presided over relations with other tribes and officiated over events that took people away from the village. Among the Pueblo of the American Southwest are two notable traditional offices: that of the cacique (a Spanish term for the Tiamuni Hotchin or traditional leader), who was charged with maintaining internal harmony, and that of the hotchin or "war captain," whose office was concerned with mediating between the tribe and outsiders, implementing foreign policy, and, if necessary, calling for defensive or retaliatory forays. This hotchin, whose title is usually translated "country chief" or "outside chief," was first authorized by Iyatiku when she still lived among the people.[13] At that time there was no "inside" chief other than the Mother herself and the clan mothers whom she instructed in the proper ritual ways as each clan came into being. Since Iyatiku was in residence, an inside chief or cacique was unnecessary. The present-day caciques continue even now to act as her representatives and gain their power directly from her.[14]

Thus the Pueblos are organized—as are most gynocratic tribes—into a moiety system (as anthropologists dub it) that reflects their understanding of ritual empowerment as dialogic. This dyadic structure, which emphasizes complementarity rather than opposition, is analogous to the external fire/internal fire relationship of sun and earth. That is, the core/womb of the earth is inward fire as the heart of heaven, the sun, is external fire. The Cherokee and their northern cousins the Iroquois acknowledge the femaleness of both fires: the sun is female to them both, as is the earth. Among the Keres, Shipap, which is in the earth, is white, as was the isolated house Iyatiku dwelt in before she left the mortal plane entirely for Shipap. The color of Shipap is white. The Hopi see Spider Woman as Grandmother of the sun and as the great Medicine Power who sang the people into this fourth world we live in now.

The understanding of universal functioning as relationship between the inner and the outer is reflected in the social systems of those tribal groups that are based on clan systems. It is reflected in ritual systems, as seen in the widespread incidence of legends about the Little War Twins among the Pueblos or the Sacred Twins among other tribes and Nations. The Sacred Twins embody the power of dual creative forces. The potency of their relationship is as strong as that of the negative and positive charges on magnetic fields. It is on their complementariness and their relationship that both destructive and creative ritual power rests.

Among the western Keres, the war captains are the analogues of the Little War Twins, Ma'sewe and O'yo'yo'we. Their prototype appears to be those puzzling twin sisters of the Keres pantheon, Uretsete and Naotsete, who were sung into life by Thought Woman before the creation of the world. These sisters appear and reappear in Pueblo stories in various guises and various names. One of them, Uretsete, becomes male at some point in the creation story of the Keres. Transformation of this kind is common in American Indian lore, and the transformation processes embedded in the tales about the spirit beings and their alternative aspects point to the regenerative powers embodied in their diversity.[15]

When the whites came, the tribes who were organized matrifocally resorted to their accustomed modes of dealing with outsiders; they relied on the red chief (or whatever that parsonage might be called) and on their tribal groups whose responsibility was external affairs. The Iroquois of the northern regions, the Five "Civilized" Tribes of the southern regions, and the Pueblo of the American Southwest—all among those earliest contacted by Anglo-European invaders—had some dual structure enabling them to maintain internal harmony while engaging in hostilities with invading or adversary groups. The Aztecs also had such complementary deities: the internal or domestic god was a goddess, Cihuacoatl, Coatlique, or some similar supernatural woman-being; their external god was Quetzalcoatl, the winged serpent, who was a god of amalgamation or expansion.[16]

Indian stories indicate that a dialogic construct based on complementary powers (an interpretation of polarity that focuses on the ritual uses of magnetism) was current among the Pueblos, particularly the Keres. To the Keres Naotsete was the figure associated with internal affairs, and Uretsete was concerned with maintaining tribal psychic and political boundaries.[17]

Essentially, the Keres story goes something like this (allowing for variations created by the informant, the collector-translator, or differences in clan-based variations): Naotsete and Uretsete were sung into life by Ts'its'tsi'nako Thought Woman. They carried bundles from which all the creatures came. The goddess Uretsete gave birth to twin boys, and one of these boys was raised by the other sister, who later married him. Of this union the Pueblo race was born. Some tales (probably of fairly recent origin) make Uretsete the alien sister and Naotsete the Indian sister. Other stories, as noted earlier, make Uretsete male at some undetermined point (but "he" always starts as female). The Indian sister Uretsete is later known as Iyatiku, or Ic'city, and is seen as essentially the same as her. But it is reasonable to conjecture that Uretsete is the prototype for the hotchin, while the cacique (town chief) is derived from the figure of Naotsete. Certainly the office of hotchin is authorized by Iyatiku, who counsels the Tiamuni hotchin, Chief Remembering Prayer Sticks, to keep the people ever in peace and harmony and to remember that they are all her children and thus are all entitled to the harvest of her body/thought.[18] She in turn is empowered by Thought Woman, who sits on her shoulder and advises her.

While the tribal heads are known as cacique and hotchin—or town chief and country chief, respectively—the Keres do not like fighting. War is so distasteful to them that they long ago devised ritual institutions to deal with antagonism between persons and groups such as medicine societies. They also developed rituals that would purify those who had participated in warfare. If a person had actually killed someone, the ritual purification was doubly imperative, for without it a sickness would come among the people and would infect the land and the animals and prevent the rainfall. The Warrior Priest was and is responsible for seeing to the orderly running of Pueblo life, and to some extent he mediates between strangers and the people. In this sense he functions as the outside chief. The inside chief maintains an internal conscious awareness of Shipap and the Mother, and he advises, counsels, and exhorts the people to the ways of peace.

Traditional war was not practiced as a matter of conquest or opposition to enemies in the same way it has been practiced by western peoples; it is not a matter of battling enemies into a defeat in which they surrender and come to terms dictated by the conqueror. Warfare among most traditional American Indian tribes who practiced it (went on the war path) was a ritual, an exercise in the practice of shamanism, and it is still practiced that way by the few "longhairs" left. Its outcome was the seizure of a certain sacred power, and that outcome could be as the result of defeat as well as of victory. The point was to gain the attention of supernatural powers, who would then be prevailed upon to give certain powers to the hero.

The Navajo have a ceremonial and an accompanying myth that commemorate the gain of such a gift as the result of a battle with some Pueblos. The hero in that tale is a woman who journeys to the spirit world with Snake Man, where she is initiated by Snake Man's mother. After she has passed the tests provided for her learning, she is given particular rites to take back to her people. Along with this ceremonial, which is called Beautyway, is a companion ceremonial, Mountainway. Its hero is a woman who accompanies Bear Man into the spirit world and is also taught and tested. Like the Beautyway hero, she returns with a chantway or healing ceremony to give her people. In a more contemporary version of these tales, the battle is World War II, and an even later tale might be about Vietnam. The exact war is not important. What is important is that from warfare comes certain powers that benefit the people and that are gained by a hero who encounters and transcends mortal danger.

So the hotchin is a medium for the regulation of external ritual events, and the cacique is the medium through whom Iyatiku guides, guards, and empowers her people and keeps them whole. Each is responsible for maintaining the harmonious working of the energies on which the entire existence of the people depends, and they are necessarily men who must be careful how they use the energies at their disposal.

III

As the power of woman is the center of the universe and is both heart (womb) and thought (creativity), the power of the Keres people is the corn that holds the thought of the All Power (deity) and connects the people to that power through the heart of Earth Woman, Iyatiku. She is the breath of life to the Keres because for them corn holds the essence of earth and conveys the power of earth to the people. Corn connects us to the heart of power, and that heart is Iyatiku, who under the guidance of Thought Woman directs the people in their affairs.

It is likely that the power embodied in the Irriaku (Corn Mother) is the power of dream, for dream connections play an important part in the ritual of life of the Pueblos as of other tribes of the Americas. As the frightening katsina, K'oo'ko, can haunt the dreams of uncleansed warriors and thus endanger everything, the power that moves between the material and nonmaterial worlds often does so in dreams. The place when certain dreams or ceremonies occur is said to be in "time immemorial." And the point where the two meet is Shipap, where Earth Woman lives. Corn, like many of its power counterparts is responsible for maintaining linkage between the worlds, and Corn Mother, Irriaku, is the most powerful element in that link. John Gunn describes the Irriaku as "an ear of corn perfect in every grain, the plume is a feather from every known bird."[19]

This representative of Iyatiku is an individual's link and the ceremonial link to medicine power. Of similar power is the Sacred Pipe that White Buffalo Woman brought to the Lakota. This pipe is called waka*n*, which means "sacred" or possessing power.

The concept of power among tribal people is related to their understanding of the relationships that occur between the human and nonhuman worlds. They believe that all are linked within one vast, living sphere, that the linkage is not material but spiritual, and that its essence is the power that enables magical things to happen. Among these magical things are transformation of objects from one form to another, the movement of objects from one place to another by teleportation, the curing of the sick (and conversely creating sickness in people, animals, or plants), communication with animals, plants, and nonphysical beings (spirits, katsinas, goddesses, and gods), the compelling of the will of another, and the stealing or storing of souls. Mythical accounts from a number of sources illustrate the variety of forms the uses of ritual power can take.

According to the Abanaki, First Woman, who came to live with a spirit being named Kloskurbeh and his disciple, offered to share her strength and comfort with them. Her offer was accepted and she and the disciple of Kloskurbeh had many children. All was well until a famine came. Then the children were starving and First Woman was very sad. She went to her husband and asked him to kill her so she could be happy again. When he agreed, she instructed him to let two men lay hold of her corpse after she was dead and drag her body through a nearby field until all the flesh was worn away. Then, she said, they should bury her bones in the middle of the field and leave the field alone for seven months. After that time, they should return to the field and gather the food they would find there and eat all of it except for a portion that they should plant. The bones, she said, would not be edible; they should burn them, and the smoke would bring peace to them and their descendants.

As the tale is recorded in one source, the narrator continues.

> Now have the first words of the first mother come to pass, for she said she was born of the leaf of the beautiful plant and that her power should be felt over the whole world, and that all should love her. And now that she is gone into this substance, take care that this, the second seed of the first mother, be always with you, for it is her flesh. Her bones also have been given for your good; burn them, and the smoke will bring freshness to the mind, and since these things came from the goodness of a woman's heart, see that you hold her always in memory; remember her when you eat, remember her when the smoke of her bones rises before you. And because you are all [related], divide among you her flesh and her bones—let all shares be alike—for so will the love of the first mother have been fulfilled.[20]

Worth noting in this passage are the ideas of kinship that requires peacefulness and cooperation among people and of the centrality of the woman's power, which is her gift to the disciple. Because she is sacred, her flesh and bones are capable of generating life; because she is embued with power, she can share it with human beings. When she came among them the first time, First Woman told Kloskurbeh and his disciple that she was "born of the beautiful plant of the earth; for the dew fell on the leaf, and the sun warmed the dew, and the warmth was life," and she was that life.

Another important point is that the love of the first mother carries several significances. The love of a mother is not, as is presently supposed, a reference to a sentimental attachment. Rather, it is a way of saying that a mother is bonded to her offspring through her womb. *Heart* often means "womb," except when it means "vulva." In its aspect of vulva, it signifies sexual connection or bonding. But this cannot be understood to mean sex as sex; rather, sexual connection with woman means connection with the womb, which is the container of power that women carry within their bodies. So when the teacher Kloskurbeh says that "these things come from the goodness of a woman's heart,"[22] he is saying that the seeds of her power are good—that is, they are alive, bearing, nourishing, and cooperative with the well-being of the people.

The tobacco that she leaves to them is connected also with her power, for it is the "beautiful plant" that was her own mother, and its property is clear thought. She was born of clear (harmonious) thought (for beauty and harmony are synonymous among Indians) that was empowered by water (dew) and heat (sun). (Dew is a reference to vaginal secretions during tumescence.) Tobacco smoke is connected to water, for it imitates clouds in appearance and behavior. It is used to evoke spirits as well as a sense of well-being and clearheadedness and is often a feature of religious ceremonies. That First Woman is connected to water is made clear in another passage of the same account: First Woman (who had referred to both Kloskurbeh the teacher and his nephew the disciple as "my children") had said that she was born of the beautiful plant. The famine had made her very sad, and every day she left home and was gone for long periods. One day the disciple followed her and saw her wade into the river, singing. "And as long as her feet were in the water, she seemed glad, and the man saw something that trailed behind her right foot, like a long green blade."[23]

Among medicine people it is well known that immersing oneself in water will enable one to ward off dissolution. Bodies of apprentices, sorcerers, and witches are subject to changes, including transformation from corporeal to spirit. Immersion also helps one resist the pull of supernatural forces unleashed by another sorcerer, though this does not seem to be what occurs in this story. But the connection of First Woman with water is clear: in the water she is happy, centered, powerful, for she is deeply connected to water, as is implied by her birth story. If she was born of the beautiful plant, then she is in some basic sense a vegetation spirit who has taken a human body (or something like it) to further the story of creation. Her "sacrifice" is the culmination of her earthly sojourn: by transferring the power she possesses to the corn and tobacco (her flesh and her bones), she makes certain that the life forms she has vitalized will remain vital. Thus, one aspect of her power is embodied in the children, while another aspect is embodied in the corn and tobacco. In their mutuality of energy transfer, all will live.

In Zia Pueblo version of the Supernatural Woman, Anazia Pueblo, Utset wanted to make certain that the people would have food when they came up from the lower world (previous world and underworld). As their mother (chief), Utset was responsible for their well-being, so she made fields north, west, south, and east of the village and planted in it bits of her heart (power). She made words over the seeds she had planted: "This corn is my heart and it shall be to my people as milk from my breasts."[24] In a Cherokee version of how food was given to the people to guarantee their provision and their connection to the goddess, Sel*u* (Corn Woman) similarly made the first food from her own body-seed, as does Grandmother Spider in a Kiowa version.

According to Goetz and Morley's rendering of the *Popul Vuh*, the sacred myth of the Quiché Mayans, the heart is related to the power of creation. In the beginning the makers (grandparents) were in the water (void) hidden under green and blue feathers. They were by nature great thinkers or sages. "In this manner the sky existed and also the Heart of Heaven, which is the name of God (the All Power)."[25] The grandparents, called feathered beings (Gucumatz), meditated, and it became clear that creation of the earth that human beings inhabit was imminent. "Thus it was arranged in the darkness and in the night by the Heart of Heaven who is called Huracán."[26] The Gucumatz or Bird Grandparents were so called because the flashes of light around their thinking-place resembled the bright wings of the bird now known as quetzal but known to the ancient Mayans as gucumatz. In their appearance they resemble the Irriaku, and in their characterization as Water Winged Beings they resemble the Water Fowl who saved the Iroquois Sky Woman from her fall through the void (designated as water in some versions of that myth). They also resemble representations of Iyatiku as a bird being, as she appears on a Fire Society altar. In a drawing an informant made of her, Iyatiku appears as a bird woman, with the body of a bird and the head of a woman. Her body is spotted yellow "to represent the earth," and centered on her breast is "a red, arrow-shaped heart" which "is the center of herself and the world. Around her is a blue circle to represent the sky, while an inner arc represents the milky way; above it are symbols for sun, moon and the stars."[27]

One of the interesting features of this depiction of Earth Woman is her resemblance of Tinotzin, the goddess who appeared to the Indian Juan Diego in 1659 and who is known as Our Lady of Guadalupe today. The Virgin Morena (the dark virgin), as she is also called, wears a salmon-colored gown that is spotted yellow to represent the stars. She wears a cloak of blue, and her image is surrounded by fiery tongues—lightning or flames, presumably.

Certainly the Keres Fire Society's goddess was made to represent, that is, to produce, medicine power, and the arrow-shaped heart she exhibited spoke to the relationship between the ideas of "heart" and "strength," or power.

A Mayan prayer connected with Huracán, or the Heart of Heaven, that refers to her as "grandmother of the sun, grandmother of the light":

> Look at us, hear us! . . . Heart of Heaven, Heart of Earth! Give us our descendants, our succession, as long as the sun shall move . . . Let it dawn, let the day come! . . . May the people have peace . . . may they be happy . . . give us good life . . . grandmother of the sun, grandmother of the light, let there be dawn . . . let the light come![28]

Certainly, there is reason to believe that many American Indian tribes thought that the primary potency in the universe was female, and that understanding authorizes all tribal activities, religious or social. That power inevitably carries with it the requirement that the people live in cooperative harmony with each other and with the beings and powers that surround them. For without peacefulness and harmony, which are the powers of a woman's heart, the power of the light and of the corn, of generativity and of ritual magic, cannot function. Thus, when Corn Woman, Iyatiku, was about to leave the people and return to Shipap, she told the cacique how to guide and counsel the people:

> I will soon leave you. I will return to the home whence I came. You will be to my people as myself; you will pass with them over the straight road; I will remain in my house below and will hear all that you say to me. I give you all my wisdom, my thoughts, my heart, and all. I fill your head with my mind.[29]

The goddess Ixchel whose shrine was in the Yucatán on Cozumel Island, twenty miles offshore, was goddess of the moon, water childbirth, weaving, and love. The combination of attributes signifies the importance of childbirth, and women go to Ixchel's shrine to gain or increase their share of these powers as well as to reinforce their sense of them.

Ixchel possesses the power of fruitfulness, a power associated with both water and weaving and concerned with bringing to life or vitalization. Also connected with Ixchel is the power to end life or to take life away, an aspect of female ritual power that is not as often discussed as birth and nurturing powers are.[30] These twin powers of primacy, life and death, are aspects of Ixchel as moon-woman in which she waxes and wanes, sometimes visible and sometimes invisible. Similarly, her power to weave includes the power to unravel, so the weaver, like the moon, signifies the power of patterning and its converse, the power of disruption. It is no small matter to worship the goddess Ixchel, as it is no small matter to venerate Iyatiku, Thought Woman, or White Buffalo Woman. Their connection with death and with life makes them the preponderant powers of the universe, and this connection is made through the agency of water.

Pre-Conquest American Indian women valued their role as vitalizers. Through their own bodies they could bring vital beings into the world—a miraculous power whose potency does not diminish with industrial sophistication or time. They were mothers, and that word did not imply slaves, drudges, drones who are required to live only for others rather than for themselves as it does so tragically for many modern women. The ancient ones were empowered by their certain knowledge that the power to make life is the source of all power and that no other power can gainsay it. Nor is that power simply of biology, as modernists tendentiously believe. When Thought Woman brought to life the twin sisters, she did not give birth to them in the biological sense. She sang over the medicine bundles that contained their potentials. With her singing and shaking she infused them with vitality. She gathered the power that she controlled and focused it on those bundles, and thus they were "born." Similarly, when the sister goddesses Naotsete and Uretsete wished to bring forth some plant or creature they reached into the basket (bundle) that Thought Woman had given them, took out the effigy of the creature, and thought it into life. Usually they then instructed it in its proper role. They also meted out consequences to creatures (this included plants, spirits, and katsinas) who disobeyed them.

The water of life, menstrual or postpartum blood, was held sacred. Sacred often means taboo; that is, what is empowered in a ritual sense is not to be touched or approached by any who are weaker than the power itself, lest they suffer negative consequences from contact. The blood of woman was in and of itself infused with the power of Supreme Mind, and so women were held in awe and respect. The term *sacred,* which is connected with power, is similar in meaning to the term *sacrifice,* which means "to make sacred." What is made sacred is empowered. Thus, in the old way, sacrificing meant empowering, which is exactly what it still means to American Indians who adhere to traditional practice. Blood was and is used in sacrifice because it possesses the power to make something else powerful or, conversely, to weaken or kill it.

Pre-contact American Indian women valued their role as vitalizers because they understood that bearing, like bleeding, was a transformative ritual act. Through their own bodies they could bring vital beings into the world—a miraculous power unrivaled by mere shamanic displays. They were mothers, and that word implied the highest degree of status in ritual cultures. The status of mother was so high, in fact, that in some cultures Mother or its analogue, Matron, was the highest office to which a man or woman could aspire.

The old ones were empowered by their certain knowledge that the power to make life is the source and model for all ritual magic and that no other power can gainsay it. Nor is that power really biological at base; it is the power of ritual magic, the power of Thought, of Mind, that gives rise to biological organisms as it gives rise to social organizations, material culture, and transformations of all kinds—including hunting, war, healing, spirit communication, rain-making, and all the rest.

At Laguna, all entities, human or supernatural, who are functioning in a ritual manner at a high level are called Mother. The story "Arrow Youth, the Witches and the K'a·'ts'ina" is filled with addresses of this sort.[31]

The cacique is addressed as mother by the war captain as well as by Arrow Youth. The Turkey-Buzzard Spirit is greeted as mother by the shaman who goes to consult him. When the cacique goes to consult with the k'apina shamans, he greets them saying, "How are things, mothers of everyone, chiefs of everyone." After he has made his ritual offering of corn pollen to them, he says, "Enough . . . mothers, chiefs."[32] He greets them this way to 'acknowledge their power, a power that includes everything: long life, growth, old age, and life during the daytime. Not all the entities involved in the story are addressed in this fashion. Only those who command great respect are so titled. Yellow Woman herself is acknowledged "the mother of all of us" by the katsina chief or spokesman when he pledges the katsina's aid in her rescue.[33] Many more examples of the practice exist among tribes, and all underscore that motherness is a highly valued characteristic.

But its value signifies something other than the kind of sentimental respect for motherhood that is reflected in Americans' Mother's Day observances. It is ritually powerful, a condition of being that confers the highest adeptship on whoever bears the title. So central to ritual activities is it in Indian cultures that men are honored by the name mother, recognizing and paying respect to their spiritual and occult competence. That competence derives entirely from Mother Iyatiku, and, through her, from Thought Woman herself.

A strong attitude integrally connects the power of Original Thinking or Creation Thinking to the power of mothering. That power is not so much the power to give birth, as we have noted, but the power to make, to create, to transform. Ritual, as noted elsewhere, means transforming something from one state or condition to another, and that ability is inherent in the action of mothering. It is the ability that is sought and treasured by adepts, and it is the ability that male seekers devote years of study and discipline to acquire. Without it, no practice of the sacred is possible, at least not within the Great Mother societies.

And as the cultures that are woman-centered and Mother-ritual based are also cultures that value peacefulness, harmony, cooperation, health, and general prosperity, they are systems of thought and practice that would bear deeper study in our troubled, conflict-ridden time.

Notes

1. Anthony Purley, "Keres Pueblo Concepts of Diety," *American Indian Culture and Research Journal*, vol. 1, no. 1 (Fall 1974), p. 29. The passage cited is Purley's literal translation from the Keres Indian language of a portion of the Thought Woman story. Purley is a native-speaker Laguna Pueblo Keres. Shipapu is the underworld where the dead go, where the Great Mother in her various aspects and guises lives, and from whence she confers to the caciques the authority to govern. Shi wana are the rain cloud spirits. They come from Shipapu by way of southeastern or southwestern wind currents. They are the dead, or the ancestors, who are obliged to bring rain to the pueblo in the proper season. Cha-yah-ni (cheai) are medicine men or holy people. The word may also have the connotation of medicine or ritual power. Kopishtaya or Kupistaya is the Laguna word for Spirits; it, like its allied terms katsina or koshare, is a collective noun.
2. Purley, "Keres Pueblo Concepts," pp. 30-31.
3. Hamilton A. Tyler, *Pueblo Gods and Myths, Civilization of the American Indian Series* (Norman: University of Oklahoma Press, 1964), p. 37. Evidently, Huruing Wuhti has other transformative abilities as well. Under pressure from patriarchal politics, she can change her gender, her name, and even her spiritual nature, as this passage from Tyler suggests:

   > Something of the vastness of the changes in concepts which have taken place can be seen if we recall a statement quoted earlier. There a man of our generation mentions that the roads to the village are closed "to clear the spiritual highway which leads from there to the rising sun. This is a road over which they walk to offer their prayers to the Great Spirit." It will be recalled that the closing of the roads was in actuality a part of an All Souls ceremony for the dead, and in it, Masau'u (the major supernatural of this fourth world and of death, but in no way a creator-god) who has now become the Great Spirit, was most certainly connected with the dead and the underworld, rather than with the sun. The new arrangement is not made out of the whole cloth, however, as the idea is old, but it belonged to the initiation of a new village chieftain. Since the town chief was supposed to be on good terms with the cloud-people, or spirits of the dead, a Kwan man closes the ceremony with these words: "Now I make you a chief and now I give you a good path to lead us to the Sun. Now you are our father."
   >
   > From now on we will hear very little of death, or even of fertility, and much of a sky god who is a supreme being. In the *Hopi Hearings* . . . , old and new attitudes are combined. Simon Scott, whose name hides a Hopi, at one point says: "This supreme being who is over all of us is here with you and listening to all of us in this meeting and will be with us until this meeting is adjourned." Despite the Christian tone, the statement is not far removed conceptually from the remark Stephen quoted, but some days later the same Hopi leader added a few ideas: "It is the Executive Supreme Being who created the world and created a human for a holy purpose. It is this Executive Supreme who made two humans. One has a white flesh and the other is red." Since he was referring to Masau'u, the latter statement contains something quite new: as every Hopi knows, the world was created by Huruing Wuhti, Hard Beings Woman, and in all the accounts we have head there is no suggestion that Massau'u was the creator, either of the world or of mankind. Furthermore, the god has been changed by the competition of white politics as well as white religion. Our Chief Executive must have been an appealing idea, both in phrasing and thought content. (p. 82)

4. Tyler, *Pueblo Gods*, p. 93.

5. For one version of this myth, see "The Woman Who Fell from the Sky: A Seneca Account," *Literature of the American Indians*, ed. Thomas E. Sanders and Walter W. Peek (New York: Glencoe, 1973), pp. 41-43. Cf. "Creation Story: A Mohawk Account," in the *1982 Akwesasne Notes Calendar* (Mohawk via Roosevelt, N.Y.: Akwesasne Notes, 1982).
6. Tyler, *Pueblo Gods*, p. 93.
7. Purley, "Keres Pueblo Concepts," p. 31.
8. Purley, "Keres Pueblo Concepts," p. 31.
9. Fr. Noël Dumarest, Memoirs: *Notes of Cochiti, New Mexico*, vol. 6, no. 3 (Lancaster: American Anthropological Association, 1919), p. 227. Cited in Tyler, *Pueblo Gods*, p. 91.
10. John G. Neihardt, *Black Elk Speaks* (Lincoln: University of Nebraska Press, 1961), and Joseph Epes Brown, *The Sacred Pipe* (Baltimore: Penguin, 1971), p. 44.
11. Alice Baldeagle, personal correspondence, May 8, 1978.
12. See Franz Boas, *Keresan Texts* (New York: Publications of the American Ethnological Society, 1928), especially "P'acaya Nyi," vol. 8, pt. 1, pp. 13-16. According to Elsie Clews Parsons, who gives an account of a healing done by one of the katsina organizations, the she'kine, the healer, set up at the alter, color-coded for the ritual and graced with Irriaku, and uses a crystal to locate the heart of the patient, which has been stolen by someone wishing evil on the patient. Holding a bear's paw, the healer rushes out of the house in pursuit of the heart, and when it is found, the war captains take it. At this juncture, the healer loses consciousness and is revived by female relatives. Mentioned by Boas, *Keresan Texts*, pp. 118-122.
13. Mathew W. Stirling, "Origin Myth of the Acoma and Other Records," *Bureau of American Ethnology Bulletin* 135 (Washington, D.C., 1932), p. 32.
14. See the story "The Cacique Who Visited the Dead" in *Tales of the Cochiti Indians*, ed. Ruth Benedict (Albuquerque: University of New Mexico Press, 1981), pp. 30-31; cf. Benedict, p. 255.
15. Anthony Purley, like Granz Boas, believes that the trend to refer to Uretsete as male is a late development and may reflect a Keres gesture to white tastes in deity. Uretsete is not always male, even in present-day narratives or sacred myths, but changes gender midstream, as it were.
16. For more on this, see Fred Eggan, *Social Organization of the Western Pueblos* (Chicago: University of Chicago Press, 1950), pp. 283-284; Boas, *Keresan Texts*, p. 94; Elsie Clews Parsons, *Notes on Ceremonialism at Laguna*, Anthropological Papers of the American Museum of Natural History 19, pt. 4 (New York: Kraus, n.d.), pp. 109-112; and Tyler, *Pueblo Gods*, p. 106.
17. Boas, *Keresan Texts*, p. 285, says that war captains are the representatives of Ma'sewe and O'yo'yo'we. He adds, "It seems therefore twin heroes must be considered helpers and assistants of all these supernatural beings and that they are types rather than individuals. In the pueblo the twin heroes are represented by the war captains, the 'out of town chiefs.' They are in charge of all public functions. They take care of the shamans, accompany them on their ceremonial visits to Mt. Taylor; they attend curing ceremonials; they are in charge of the rabbit hunt; they make prayer-sticks for hunters and sacrifice for them; they act as town criers; they take part in the ceremonial dance of the warriors (op'i)" (p. 286).
18. Boas writes, "The head religious officer, the so called cacique, is called Tyi'amun'i ho:tc'am u nyo, the chief leader, because he led the people from the place of Emergence. In tales he is always called *ho·tc'anyi ha'tcam'uy k' ayo·k' ai* (chief prayer stick holding), that is, 'always remembering the prayer sticks.' (In the beginning I misheard *k'ayo'ka* for *k'ayo'kai*. The former means 'broken'.) The cacique may belong to any clan. The office has been extinct for a long time [at Laguna]. The last caciques are still remembered . . . The cacique does no everyday labor. He makes prayer-sticks, carries them up the hill near the village, north, west, south, east in this order, and prays

for the people. He may not be a shaman but he must know how to pray. He must be serious-minded and must not have a quick temper . . . The people attend to the cacique's field and the woman cook for him . . . In tales the cacique is the only one who is allowed to make prayer-sticks for the katsina . . . In many cases he himself appears as a town crier, giving notice to the people of his orders" (pp. 288-289).

19. John M. Hunn, *Schat Chen* (Albuquerque, N. Mex.: Albright and Anderson, 1917), p. 218.
20. Natalie Curtis, recorder and editor, *The Indians' Book: Songs and Legends of the American Indians* (New York: Dover, 1950), p. 6.
21. Curtis, *Indians' Book*, p. 4.
22. Curtis, *Indians' Book*, p. 5.
23. Curtis, *Indians' Book*, p. 6.
24. Matilda Coxe Stevenson, "The Sia," *Eleventh Annual Report, 1889-90*, Bureau of American Ethnology (Washington, D.C., 1894), p. 39.
25. Sylvanus G. Morley and Delia Goetz, *Popul Vuh: The Sacred Book of the Ancient Quiche Maya*, from the translation of Adrian Recinos (Norman: University of Oklahoma Press, 1950), p. 82.
26. Morley and Goetz, *Popul Vuh*, p. 82.
27. Stirling, "Origin Myth of the Acoma," pl. 10, fig. 2, and 121n.
28. William Brandon, *The Last Americans: The Indian in American Culture* (New York: McGraw-Hill, 1974), p. 52.
29. Stevenson, "Sia," pp. 40-41.
30. Kay Turner, "Contemporary Feminist Rituals," in *The Politics of Women's Spirituality: Essays on the Rise of Spiritual Power Within the Feminist Movement*, ed. Charlene Spretnak (New York: Anchor, 1982), p. 228.
31. Boas, *Keresan Texts*, pp. 64-65.
32. Boas, *Keresan Texts*, pp. 56-75.
33. Boas, *Keresan Texts*, pp. 62.

From *Life is a Fatal Disease* by Paula Gunn Allen, 1997, West End Press. Reprinted with permission.

7.3

Some Like Indians Endure

Paula Gunn Allen

i have it in my mind that
dykes are indians

they're a lot like indians
they used to live as tribes
they owned tribal land
it was called the earth

they were massacred
lots of times
they always came back
like the grass
like the clouds
they got massacred again

they thought caringsharing
about the earth and each other
was a good thing
they rode horses
and sang to the moon

but i don't know
about what was so longago
and it's now that dykes

make me think i'm with indians
when i'm with dykes

because they bear
witness bitterly
because they reach
and hold
because they live every day
with despair laughing
in cities and country places
because earth hides them
because they know
the moon

because they gather together
enclosing
and spit in the eye of death

indian is an idea
some people have
of themselves
dyke is an idea some women
have of themselves
the place where we live now
is idea
because whiteman took
all the rest
because father
took all the rest
but the idea which
once you have it
you can't be taken
for somebody else
and have nowhere to go
like indians you can be
stubborn

the idea might move you on,
ponydrag behind

taking all your loves and
children maybe downstream
maybe beyond the cliffs
but it hangs in there
an idea
like indians
endures

it might even take your
whole village with it
stone by stone
or leave the stones
and find more
to build another village
someplace else

like indians
dykes have fewer and fewer
someplace elses to go
so it gets important
to know
about ideas and
to remember or uncover
the past
and how the people
traveled
all the while remembering
the idea they had
about who they were
indians, like dykes
do it all the time

dykes know all about dying
and that everything belongs
to the wind
like indians

they do terrible things
to each other
out of sheer cussedness
out of forgetting
out of despair

so dykes
are like indians
because everybody is related
to everybody
in pain
in terror
in guilt
in blood
in shame
in disappearance
that never quite manages
to be disappeared
we never go away
even if we're always
leaving

because the only home
is each other
they've occupied all
the rest
colonized it; an
idea about ourselves is all
we own

and dykes remind me of indians
like indians . . . dykes
are supposed to die out
or forget
or drink all the time
or shatter
go away

to nowhere
to remember what will happen
if they don't

they don't anyway—even
though the worst happens
they remember and they
stay
because the moon remembers
because so does the sun
because the stars
remember
and the persistent stubborn grass
of the earth

From *Life is a Fatal Disease* by Paula Gunn Allen, 1997, West End Press. Reprinted with permission.

7.4

Essentially, It's Spring

Paula Gunn Allen
—*for David Halliburton*

They noticed abstraction and called it evolution,
Plato's trick, or Socrates',
who drank his last salute to history

so we are not allowed to speak of beauty,
causality, essentiality, signs,
but only graphs, charts, numbers, and revolution.

But it is coming spring on the high plateau;
last week's pink and white brilliance blooms
arrested, curled dingy brown in untimely frost,

though the cottonwoods are hopeful, and the elms,
the willows in their fragile, cherished green—a mixed burden,
spring. One hardly knows whether to lament or sing.

The passive dead revised with neither thought nor care,
biblically numbered bones beside lost meanings repose—
abstractions from bodies' lives make progress, unmake significance.

What's gone is not ours to study or to keep:
Plato the Greek was not in favor of literacy of the phonetic kind;

he liked boys, gnosis, metaphysics, mystery—
just ask the Egyptian bones stored in universities.

They say there won't be as much fruit this year.
Absent extravagent rains, piñons, mice, and pollen
will be less threat, just ask the unphonetic
Singers, evicted, wise, unlettered, rude.

From *Off the Reservation* by Paula Gunn Allen. Copyright © 1998 by Paula Gunn Allen. Reprinted by permission of Beacon Press, Boston.

7.5

Haggles

Paula Gunn Allen

Where is One Circle . . . ?

Last night Judy and I were talking to some people about this gynosophic gathering in terms of a "kirk," which is a church that is a "circle," interestingly enough. Anyway, we were saying that I was the "pasture" and my daughter said, "Yes, she's outstanding in her field."

It took me four hours to figure out what the joke was! Well, here I am out standing in my field and it's time for another haggle.

I want to talk about balance, complexity, murder, and things like that. The song we just sang said, "Watch our circle grow." If I were writing that song today, I would change it to "Watch our circles grow." I wanted to do an experiment today, but I don't think I will. Instead I'll just talk and you'll have to do the experiment; I want you to see with your body as well as with your eyes what this room looks like right now. *Feel* the other women in the room. All those little moonshapes everywhere . . .

Now we could do what has become a feminist thing to do, and that is to form a big circle around the room. My sense of a big circle around the room is that we have all lost each other when we do that. What happens is that I'll be too far away from most of the people, and each of us will be too far away from most of the people. But the way we are presently seated, around a number of tables, we have little clusters of folks who can chat with each other and as a consequence have a sense of each other as we go into the service. So what we have is a network of interlocking communities here, which is, of course, how life works. Because that is the kind of circle that life is. That's the sacred hoop that the Lakota talk about. It's the dynamic sphere of being, in which everything is held. But everything works in little circles like that, round and round and round . . . so there's not just one circle but many.

Editor's Note: "Haggle: a persuasive speaking that a hag engages in. Nagging (see Mary Daly, *Gyn/Ecology* and *Pure Lust,* for more on these terms)." In the 1980s Paula Gunn Allen delivered haggles (the definition is hers) as part of a weekly series of "gynosophic gatherings" in Oakland, California. The gatherings, held on Sunday mornings at Mama Bear's coffeehouse, were, according to Gunn Allen, a "woman's worship service celebrating the bond of womanness among ourselves and in connection with our sisters on every continent, island, sea, and in the sky."

Those of you who have been coming every Sunday probably recognize that I am on my favorite schtick, or my favorite broomstick, as the case may be. And off I'm going, and, look, there is no such thing as *one*. I can't find a "one," and I've been trying for weeks and weeks, in fact, for years and years. I wrote a poem about this several years ago, and since I wrote it I keep thinking about it. Where is there a one? A one anything? One sun, no, there are millions of suns. One planet? No, there are lots of planets. One rain drop? No, there are lots of rain drops. I can't think of a single "one" anything.

Another thing I just noticed is that we just sang "*The* Rose." Think about that. There's *the* roses and *the* roses grow on *the* rose bush. English is a very funny language, at least as we speak it today. It gives us the impression that isolation is the normal thing, and that connection is abnormal. When we want to feel connected, we begin to exert great amounts of energy. All the energy we are exerting because we don't want to be alone *is* all about being alone, you understand. All the energy we are exerting is saying I don't want to be alone, exert energy, I don't want to be alone. And the message we are conveying is: This is all about being alone. Alone is really important. But if we were to relax and notice ourselves, not to mention this room around us, we would know that *alone* is an absurdity. We don't have to work to be connected. You do have to work at being alone. It's very hard to imagine that you are alone when all of reality around you is continually telling you, over and over, that the last thing you are is alone. You are always *with*, always *with* . . .

I had occasion to see a documentary film and write a response to it or a dialogue with it or whatever. The film was called *Wilderness Journal*. It was to be shown on PBS and then to be used in classroom work in ecology classes. The film finally came, and I went to the viewing room to see it. It was all about how precious wilderness is and how we must protect our wilderness. There were a number of interesting points in the film, but one that was immediately visible was that the only people of color in the film were some Indians. And we all know, of course, uh, that Indians *are* wilderness. Well, it had occurred to the filmmaker (who's a very good man, I'm sure, I don't mean to make fun of him) to have, among the seven or eight men, a Shoshone and a man who had a Hispanic last name and a mild, very mild (mild to my ear, which is sensitive because I was raised in New Mexico) Chicano accent.

But all of these men had the wherewithal to go to the wilderness. They were all middle-class people who thought of the mountain as some kind of park. And what the discussion was about was what kind of park this should be. Some said, "Well, it should be a park where I get to be the guide and take an occasional person with me when it's comfortable to do so, to see the park, and I shouldn't let them use toilet paper because it pollutes the wilderness. . . ." O.K. Some said, "Well, we should use it intelligently, save some, use some; some people should live on it, there should be water interests, logging interests, mining interests." Some people said, "No, no, we can't have that because wilderness is where a man goes to find his connection with the universe." Over and over they said, "It's the only place where a man can be alone."

Now that says something, and it says a number of very odd things. First, it says that being alone is some kind of a privilege; it says that only a certain very privileged few should be allowed to have this privilege. And it says that interest, public interest, should protect those few people's right to be alone. When you examine it, it begins to make a lot of sense because *alone* is not a natural state; you have to go to a great effort to get aloneness. And, in the world we live in, aloneness requires great resources. A great deal of money is what it requires.

On the other hand, the Indians of that particular tribe had recently realized that human encroachment on the wilderness areas within their reservation boundaries was really destructive to the animal balance in the area. So they went back to their ancient tribal way, and they had to name it a tribal law, violation of which would incur penalties. The old way was that, once in a person's life as a small one, a child, he or she would go out into the wilderness and spend a few days. While there, that child would receive a spirit friend and animal friend that would then be with them the rest of their lives. That journey was the only time that the person would ever encroach upon the space of those beings who actually don't like cities and farms and mines and rivers and dams and all those kinds of things.

What the Indians are saying is that they are recognizing the right of wilderness to be wilderness. Wilderness is not an extension of human need or of human justification. It is itself and it is inviolate, itself. This does not mean that, therefore, we become separated from it, because we don't. We stay connected if, *once* in our lives, we learn exactly what that connection is between our heart, our womb, our mind, and wilderness. And when each of us has her wilderness within her, we can be together in a balanced kind of way. The forever, we have that within us. Forever is when we have our guide so we also have our wilderness. But when we leave the wilderness, we leave it to be what it is. That's one thing.

Another thing is that it's the nature of wilderness not to be presbyterian. I use "presbyterian" as a metaphor for organization or over-control. The tendency is to think that somehow everything, or at least everything that I do, has to be perfect. And perfect doesn't mean moving with exhilaration, joy, and the sense of just being together. Instead, it means that anybody who judged what I am doing could not criticize my work. It also means that by trying to be perfect and presbyterian, I am singling myself out in a particular way. You remember the poem read last week of Adrienne Rich's about the musing over the artful thing that is of the woman's making, knowing all the sources of things, where the feathers and the beads and the shells and the cloth all come from. This artful musing is opposed to the "I am going to paint a picture and I am going to have my picture in the blah blah gallery and they are going to recognize my great talent." Which takes a lot of effort and a lot of money. It's a very hard thing to do. But it's a very easy thing to do to make a bit of loveliness that's a musing between yourself and your world. There's a real difference here between what's hard and what's easy.

Where I come from, I was raised with a number of Protestants of the Presbyterian variety, as well as atheists and other sorts of Christians, including Catholics, and Jews. And what I noticed about the Presbyterians was everything always had to be perfect. It had to be not only clean, but every corner had to be dug out. You not only waxed the floor, but you left not one streak, not one place where there was a little more wax than another place, because that's not perfect! You had to do it perfectly. What that does is it creates an enormous sense of isolation. And to emphasize that sense of isolation, you have picket fences around the house. Now picket fences aren't merely joy sticks stuck in the ground to keep the dogs off the lawn or to give the lawn a sense of orderliness. You know what a picket fence is—it's very tightly organized, carefully calibrated line of little soldiers there, deftly placed around the house. And what you have to do with the picket fence is to keep it painted. And if it begins to crack and the paint begins to peel, you have to go out and sand and paint it. That's what you have to do with everything. So, of course, you, well, I don't know about you, but I am overburdened because I can never, never, never catch up, no matter how hard I try.

What I noticed the other day when I had twenty things to do and I was standing watching the laundry do its thing in the washer and trying to sweep the water off the floor because the plumbing leaks and I was thinking about this mountain of things I had to do to be perfect was that this is an entirely out of balance way to think. For one thing, I was imagining that I had to do it all by myself. And for another, I was imagining that *it had to be done*. And I was, of course, assuming that it could never happen, that I'm a failure and I might as well go to bed. That conclusion is rather nice.

Now, I could have started in the beginning and said, "Heck with it, I'm going to bed!" But I realized the amount of resources it takes to be a good presbyterian; it takes a lot of people in your household who are your slaves or servants and who do exactly as you say. And it takes the money to feed and clothe them. Or, alternatively, it takes a great deal of money to buy a bunch of appliances and hire service people to come in on a contract basis to do it for you. Or, perhaps if you had a large family of adolescents who were so totally brutalized that they never whined, complained, or disobeyed, you might be able to use that as an alternative to arrange this kind of thing. Now there is a kind of balance in that and it's this kind of balance: on this side you put in ten pounds of lentils and on the other side you put ten pounds of lead weights. By golly, you *know* you got ten pounds of lentils because the scale isn't tipping to either side.

And that's the kind of balance, the idea of balance, that most of us have in our heads. When we think of balance, we think everything has to be equal. We don't ever think everything has to be equal; we really say everything has to be identical to the standard of measurement we are applying, in this case, ten pounds of lead weights, and nothing must ever move. If nothing ever moves, everything dies. And that is the interesting thing about extreme orderliness in the law and order sense of the word. What happens in fact in a system that demands absolute order is that you get an enormous amount of unnecessary death, a tremendous amount. So people are dying all the time, animals are dying all time, and they are not dying in the natural course of change and transformation; they're dying in the very abnormal course of attempting to hold everything still so I won't have to wax the bloomin' floor again! That's what that kind of balance leads to: it leads to intense efforts to control everything because I'm too tired to wax the floor again. Absolute order means absolute death.

Chaos, on the other hand, means the enormous vibration of energies; so, the more wilderness, the more something is just dancing in such a way that it doesn't have a pattern that we can perceive. That's one kind of balance. The other kind is absolute death. Where our sacred hoop goes is somewhere within all of these. Order, of a balanced sort, of a sacred hoop sort, of a feminist sort, I hope, and of a Native American sort, I know, is the kind of order that expects complexity, that expects all of the particles to be whatever they are at the moment: some birthing, some dying, coming into physical manifestation, going into another kind of manifestation in the natural course of things, in the natural course of seasons and cycles. In that order, the order of the Grandmother Gods, whatever something is at a given moment in relationship to everything else makes it what it is.

The Oglala medicine man Lame Deer puts it this way. "If it weren't for that beetle there," he says, pointing to the beetle on the ground, "I would not exist." And what he means is that all orders of existence depend for their meaning on the context and identity of everything else. That's why there is no such thing as *the* rose. There is no such thing as *a* circle, and there mustn't be. Because if we attempt to make there be, we will cause the unnecessary death of ourselves and other beings.

What we must understand is that balance means equilibration of a huge number of diverse particles/wavicles of energy, stuff, folks of all the orders of the beastly kingdoms, all the orders of the non-physical kingdoms. The interplay of all of these enables us to be, and if that interplay is messed with, is halted, is organized, we die. And everything around us dies.

So maybe next time we sing that song, we will "watch our circles grow. . . ."

Some Underlying Values: Autonomy and Vulnerability

In the western world, after several thousand years of underground community (a community that often seemed to be composed of only two women or even only one), and after nearly a century of a larger community, lesbians have developed a stunning array of customs, opinions, moral values, and beliefs about how the world of women in general, and the world of lesbians in particular, should conduct itself.

These prescriptions for behavior are expressed in terms that refer to political awareness of the community or to personal love relationships, as in: Don't be racist, don't be sexist, don't be classist, don't be sizist, don't be speciesist, don't be . . . what did I forget? . . . ageist. For heaven's sake, don't be ageist; because if you are, it's you you're calling names. That one gets real personal real quick. Or in love relationships: Don't steal another woman's girlfriend.

And while these rules, or rules of this sort, are explicit, they are not particularly embedded in a value matrix and so aren't easily understood or easily followed except in mechanical and often punitive, guilt-producing, blame-laden ways. White man ways. Today I want to meditate with you on some underlying values that I think must be the fundamental basis upon which a feminist, a lesbian ethic, must be based.

The Gynosophic Gathering is, as you know, devoted to the black aspect of the triple goddess Wisdom, Sophia. I went to a conference at U.C.L.A. on the dark Madonna. One of the things that one of the speakers mentioned was that the black aspect of the goddess in ancient times—in Europe, in Mesopotamia, in the Middle East, and so forth—was wisdom, wisdom itself, which is precisely what this poem you've heard gets to. Wisdom arises from experience consciously blended with knowledge, choice, and understanding. It seems to me that knowledge, understanding, and choices depend on two characteristics: autonomy and honesty. Autonomy and honesty depend on vulnerability, on fragility.

Truth, acceptance of the truth, is a shattering experience. It shatters the binding shroud of culture trance. It rips apart smugness, arrogance, superiority, and self-importance. It requires acknowledgment of responsibility for the nature and quality of each of our own lives, our own inner lives as well as the life of the world. Truth, inwardly accepted, humbling truth, makes one vulnerable. You can't be right, self-righteous, and truthful at the same time. You can't recognize the fragility of others, when you are being true, without accepting that their fragilities are your own.

An ethic based on this kind of truth is compassionate and strong. It is supportive of autonomy and of a sense of self based on affirmation of reality rather than on fantasy, because it recognizes the power of vulnerability, the power of fragility, and the danger of denial. Consciousness, which is the midwife of wisdom, the helper of Sophia, requires vulnerability. The invulnerable, the controlling, the tyrannical, the brutal are as far from consciousness as being can be. Consciousness begins in vulnerability. It grows through autonomy and its blossoms are truth, its fruit is wisdom. Externalized knowledge, projected morality, blaming, and guilting lead away from Sophia because they lead away from truth, from understanding, and from self-generated choice.

And what is vulnerability? Just this: the ability to be wrong, to be foolish, to be weak and silly, to be an idiot. It is the ability to accept one's unworthiness, to accept one's vanity for what it is. It's the ability to be whatever and whoever you are—recognizing that you, like the world, like the earth, are fragile, and that in your fragility lies all possibility of growth and of death, and that the two are one and the same.

Are you ashamed of eating? Are you ashamed of being afraid? Are you ashamed of being open to hurt or loss? Are you ashamed of being alive? Are you ashamed of rotting? Do you have to be perfect—slim and youthful and handsome and popular? Supermom. Superdyke. Superwoman. Probably you can be those things for a time, but not for long. On the other hand, if you intend to walk in the shadow of the Great Mother, you can recognize and come to terms with your inability to be god, enjoy the fragility—the fragility that alone will take you home.

8

Introduction to Trinh T. Minh-ha

Filmmaker, composer, and writer Trinh T. Minh-ha seeks to question existing frameworks and boundaries. Her works challenge hegemony—the authority or power of any particular perspective over others. Born in Hanoi, Vietnam, Trinh studied at the University of Saigon and then finished her education in the United States. She earned a B.A. in music and French literature from Wilmington College in Ohio in 1972 and an M.A. degree in French literature in 1973, an M.A. in music composition in 1976, and a Ph.D. in French and Francophone literatures in 1977 from the University of Illinois. Trinh is a professor of women's studies and film studies at the University of California at Berkeley.

Any hegemonic system of thought is troublesome for Trinh because it often goes unnoticed and is confused with what is natural. It thus easily becomes the only way to think about something. In "Yellow Sprouts," Trinh discusses and illustrates the disruption of hegemony. She illustrates one of her most frequent targets of challenge—documentary filmmaking— by the essay, "The Totalizing Quest of Meaning." Any particular presentation of truth, Trinh suggests, inevitably involves manipulation and constitutes a question of ideology. Among the strategies Trinh suggests for disrupting the hegemonic nature of the world are violation of the expectations that audiences bring with them to a text and a deliberate openness to multiple meanings in representing any phenomenon.

Trinh defines feminism as a movement that contributes to the questioning and challenging of established ideological systems because it is a way of thinking outside of established categories and boundaries. Marginalized individuals are most inclined to engage in this type of challenge, as Trinh suggests in "Not You/Like You," because they most easily can adopt a stance of movement, openness, and fundamental instability in the creation of their self-identities.

Reprinted with permission from the author.

8.1

Not You/Like You

Post-Colonial Women and the Interlocking Questions of Identity and Difference

Trinh T. Minh-ha

To raise the question of identity is to reopen again the discussion on the self/other relationship in its enactment of power relations. Identity as understood in the context of a certain ideology of dominance has long been a notion that relies on the concept of an essential, authentic core that remains hidden to one's consciousness and that requires the elimination of all that is considered foreign or not true to the self, that is to say, non-I, other. In such a concept the other is almost unavoidably either opposed to the self or submitted to the self's dominance. It is always condemned to remain its shadow while attempting at being its equal. Identity, thus understood, supposes that a clear dividing line can be made between I and not-I, he and she; between depth and surface, or vertical and horizontal identity; between us here and them over there. The further one moves from the core the less likely one is thought to be capable of fulfilling one's role as the real self, the real Black, Indian or Asian, the real woman. The search for an identity is, therefore, usually a search for that lost, pure, true, real, genuine, original, authentic self, often situated within a process of elimination of all that is considered other, superfluous, fake, corrupted, or Westernized.

If identity refers to the whole pattern of sameness within a being, the style of a continuing me that permeated all the changes undergone, then difference remains within the boundary of that which distinguishes one identity from another. This means that at heart X must be X, Y must be Y, and X cannot be Y. Those running around yelling X is not X and X can be Y, usually land in a hospital, a rehabilitation center, a concentration camp, or a reservation. All deviations from the dominant stream of thought, that is to say, the belief in a permanent essence of woman and in an invariant but fragile identity whose loss is considered to be a specifically human danger, can easily fit into the categories of the mentally ill or the mentally underdeveloped.

It is probably difficult for a normal, probing mind to recognize that to seek is to lose, for seeking presupposes a separation between the seeker and the sought, the continuing me and the changes it undergoes. Can identity, indeed, be viewed other than as a by product of a manhandling of life, one that, in fact, refers no more to a consistent pattern of sameness than to an inconsequential process of otherness. How am I to lose, maintain, or gain a female identity when it is impossible for me to take up a position outside this identity from which I presumably reach in and feel for it? Difference in such a context is that which undermines the very idea of identity, differing to infinity the layers of totality that forms I.

Hegemony works at leveling out differences and at standardizing contexts and expectations in the smallest details of our daily lives. Uncovering this leveling of differences is, thereof, resisting that very notion of difference which defined in the master's terms often resorts to the simplicity of essences. Divide and conquer has for centuries been his creed, his formula of success. But a different terrain of consciousness has been explored for some time now, a terrain in which clear cut divisions and dualistic oppositions such as science vs. subjectivity, masculine vs. feminine, may serve as departure points for analytical purpose but are no longer satisfactory if not entirely untenable to the critical mind.

I have often been asked about what some viewers call the lack of conflicts in my films. Psychological conflict is often equated with substance and depth. Conflicts in Western contexts often serve to define identities. My suggestion to the "lack" is: let difference replace conflict. Difference as understood in many feminist and non-Western contexts, difference as foreground in my film work is not opposed to sameness, nor synonymous with separateness. Difference, in other words, does not necessarily give rise to separatism. There are differences as well as similarities within the concept of difference. One can further say that difference is not what makes conflicts. It is beyond and alongside conflict. This is where confusion often arises and where the challenge can be issued. Many of us still hold on to the concept of difference not as a tool of creativity to question multiple forms of repression and dominance, but as a tool of segregation, to exert power on the basis of racial and sexual essences. The apartheid type of difference.

Let me point to a few examples of practices of such a notion of difference. There are quite many, but I'll just select three and perhaps we can discuss those. First of all I would take the example of the veil as reality and metaphor. If the act of unveiling has a liberating potential, so does the act of veiling. It all depends on the context in which such an act is carried out, or more precisely, on how and where women see dominance. Difference should neither be defined by the dominant sex nor by the dominant culture. So that when women decide to lift the veil one can say that they do so in defiance of their men's oppressive right to their bodies. But when they decide to keep or put on the veil they once took off they might do so to reappropriate their space or to claim a new difference in defiance of genderless, hegemonic, centered standardization.

Second, the use of silence. Within the context of women's speech silence has many faces. Like the veiling of women just mentioned, silence can only be subversive when it frees itself from the male-defined context of absence, lack, and fear as feminine territories. On the one hand, we face the danger of inscribing femininity as absence, as lack and blank in rejecting the importance of the act of enunciation. On the other hand, we understand the necessity to place women on the side of negativity and to work in undertones, for example, in our attempts at undermining patriarchal systems of values. Silence is so commonly set in opposition with speech. Silence as a will not to say or a will to unsay and as a language of its own has barely been explored.

Third, the question of subjectivity. The domain of subjectivity understood as sentimental, personal, and individual horizon as opposed to objective, universal, societal, limitless horizon is often attributed to both women, the other of man, and natives, the Other of the West. It is often assumed, for example, that women's enemy is the intellect, that their apprehension of life can only wind and unwind around a cooking pot, a baby's diaper, or matters of the heart. Similarly, for centuries and centuries we have been told that primitive mentality belongs to the order of the emotional and the affective, and that is is incapable of elaborating concepts. Primitive man feels and participates. He does not really think or reason. He has no knowledge, "no clear idea or even no idea at all of matter and soul," as Lévi-Bruhl puts it. Today this persistent rationale has taken on multiple faces, and its residues still linger on, easily recognizable despite the refined rhetoric of those who perpetuate it.

Worth mentioning again here is the question of outsider and insider in ethnographic practices. An insider's view. The magic word that bears within itself a seal of approval. What can be more authentically other than an otherness by the other, herself? Yet, every piece of the cake given by the master comes with a double-edged blade. The Afrikanners are prompt in saying, "you can take a Black man from the bush, but you can't take the bush from the Black man." The place of the native is always well-delimited. "Correct" cultural filmmaking, for example, usually implies that Africans show Africa, Asians Asia, and Euro-Americans, the world. Otherness has its laws and interdictions. Since you can't take the bush from the Black man, it is the bush that is consistently given back to him, and as things often turn out it is also this very bush that the Black man shall make his exclusive territory. And he may do so with the full awareness that barren land is hardly a gift. For in the unfolding of power inequalities, changes frequently require that the rules be reappropriated so that the master be beaten at his own game. The conceited giver likes to give with the understanding that he is in a position to take back whenever he feels like it and whenever the accepter dares or happens to trespass on his preserves. The latter, however, sees no gift. Can you imagine such a thing as a gift that takes? So the latter only sees debts that, once given back, should remain his property—although land owning is a concept that has long been foreign to him and that he refused to assimilate.

Through audiences' responses and expectations of their works, non-white filmmakers are often informed and reminded of the territorial boundaries in which they are to remain. An insider can speak with authority about her own culture, and she's referred to as the source of authority in this matter—not as a filmmaker necessarily, but as an insider, merely. This automatic and arbitrary endowment of an insider with legitimized knowledge about her cultural heritage and environment only exerts its power when it's a question of validating power. It is a paradoxical twist of the colonial mind. What the outsider expects from the insider is, in fact, a projection of an all-knowing subject that this outsider usually attributes to himself and to his own kind. In this unacknowledged self/other relation, however, the other would always remain the shadow of the self. Hence not really, not quite all-knowing. That a white person makes a film on the Goba of the Zambezi, for example, or on the Tasaday of the Philippine rainforest, seems hardly surprising to anyone, but that a Third World member makes a film on other Third World peoples never fails to appear questionable to many. The question concerning the choice of subject matter immediately arises, sometimes out of curiosity, most often out of hostility. The marriage is not consumable for the pair is no longer outside/inside, that is to say, objective vs. subjective, but something between inside/inside—objective in what is already claimed as objective. So, no real conflict.

Interdependency cannot be reduced to a mere question of mutual enslavement. It also consists in creating a ground that belongs to no one, not even to the creator. Otherness becomes empowerment, critical difference when it is not given but recreated. Furthermore, where should the dividing line between outsider and insider stop? How should it be defined? By skin color, by language, by geography, by nation, or by political affinity? What about those, for example, with hyphenated identities and hybrid realities? And here it is worth noting, for example, a journalist's report in a recent *Time* issue which is entitled, "The Crazy Game of Musical Chairs." In this brief report attention is drawn to the fact that people in South Africa who are classified by race and place into one of the nine racial categories that determine where they can live and work, can have their classification changed if they can prove they were put in a wrong group. Thus, in an announcement of racial reclassifications by the Home Affairs Ministers one learns that nine whites became colored, 506 coloreds became white, two whites became Malay, fourteen Malay became white, 40 coloreds became Black, 666 Blacks became colored, and the list goes on. However, says the minister, no Blacks apply to become whites. And No whites became Black.

The moment the insider steps out from the inside she's no longer a mere insider. She necessarily looks in from the outside while also looking out from the inside. Not quite the same, not quite the other, she stands in that undetermined threshold place where she constantly drifts in and out. Undercutting the inside/outside opposition, her intervention is necessarily that of both not-quite an insider and not-quite an outsider. She is, in other words, this inappropriate other or same who moves about with always at least two gestures: that of affirming 'I am like you' while persisting in her difference and that of reminding 'I am different' while unsettling every definition of otherness arrived at.

This is not to say that the historical I can be obscured and ignored and that differentiation cannot be made, but that I is not unitary, culture has never been monolithic, and is always more or less in relation to a judging subject. Differences do not only exist between outsider and insider—two entities. They are also at work within the outsider herself, or the insider, herself—a single entity. She who knows she cannot speak of them without speaking of herself, of history without involving her story, also knows that she cannot make a gesture without activating the to and fro movement of life.

The subjectivity at work in the context of this inappropriate other can hardly be submitted to the old subjectivity/objectivity paradigm. Acute political subject awareness cannot be reduced to a question of self-criticism toward self-improvement, nor of self-praise toward greater self-confidence. Such differentiation is useful, for a grasp of subjectivity as, let's say, the science of the subject or merely as related to the subject, makes the fear of self-absorption look absurd. Awareness of the limits in which one works need not lead to any form of indulgence in personal partiality, nor to the narrow conclusion that it is impossible to understand anything about other peoples, since the difference is one of essence. By refusing to naturalize the I, subjectivity uncovers the myth of essential core, of spontaneity and depth as inner vision. Subjectivity, therefore, does not merely consist of talking about oneself, be this talking indulgent or critical. In short, what is at stake is a practice of subjectivity that is still unaware of its own constituted nature, hence, the difficulty to exceed the simplistic pair of subjectivity and objectivity; a practice of subjectivity that is unaware of its continuous role in the production of meaning, as if things can make sense by themselves, so that the interpreter's function consists of only choosing among the many existing readings; unaware of representation as representation, that is to say, the cultural, sexual, political inter-reality of the filmmaker as subject, the reality of the subject film and the reality of the cinematic apparatus. And finally unaware of the inappropriate other within every I.

From Minh-ha, T. T., *When the Moon Waxes Red: Representation, Gender, and Cultural Politics.* Copyright © 1991 Routledge, a member of the Taylor and Francis Group. Reprinted with permission.

8.2

Yellow Sprouts

Trinh T. Minh-ha

If darkness induces reverie and is the medium of a diffuse eroticism, nighttime remains for many poets and painters of Asian cultures the moment of quiescence necessary to the dawning of new awareness. Both the time when no thought arises and the time when the primal positive energy stirs into motion are called the moon. A ray shining clear through the night with the intensity of a white light burgeoning in an empty room. *Nothingness produces white snow; quiescence produces yellow sprouts* (Chang Po-tuan).[1] When stillness culminates, there is movement. The living potential returns afresh, the cycles of the moon go on regularly, again and again the light will wane. In the process of infinite beginnings, even immortality is mortal.

With each phase a shift has occurred, a new form is attained, several motions interweave within a movement. Crescent, quarter, gibbous, full: an old form continues to mutate between loss and gain, while every growth from and toward voidness invites a different entry into areas of social dissent and transformation. The new moon, as science duly demonstrates, cannot be seen at all. To speak of the thin crescent moon as being new is to forget that only when the dark half faces the earth is the moon truly new. Politics waxes and wanes, and like a lunar eclipse, it vanishes only to return rejuvenating itself as it reaches its full intensity. In the current situation of overcodification, of de-individualized individualism and of reductionist collectivism, naming critically is to dive headlong into the abyss of un-naming. The task of inquiring into all the divisions of a culture remains exacting, for the moments when things take on a proper name can only be positional, hence transitional. The function of any ideology in power is to represent the world positively unified. To challenge the regimes of representation that govern a society is to conceive of how a politics can transform reality rather than merely ideologize it. As the struggle moves onward and assumes new, different forms, it is bound to recompose subjectivity and praxis while displacing the way diverse cultural strategies relate to one another in the constitution of social and political life.

In Chinese mythology, those who first ascend to the moon—the pioneers of the Apollo flight—are the Moon-Queen Chang E who swallows the pill of immortality, the hare which throws itself into the magical fire to feed Buddha, and the Sun-King who comes to visit his wife Chang E on the fifteenth day of every moon. Now that scientists readily speak of the "Old Moon" being extinct with the advent of the "New Moon," access to the world of the moon becomes at the same time more reachable (for some) and more limited (for others). There has been a time when Western science-fiction writers cherished the possibility of using the moon as a military base for building nuclear missiles. The paradoxical idea of "colonizing the moon" with the aim of coming closer to uniting the earth has constituted an argument that some scientists have not hesitated to advance. "The *Eagle* has landed," was the statement symbolically uttered upon North American Man's arrival on the moon. Since then, Apollo has come and gone. But the fact that a dozen men have walked upon its surface does not make the moon one bit less puzzling to the scientists.

Just as new knowledge cannot nullify previous results, different moments of a struggle constantly overlap and different relations of representation across "old" and "new" can be made possible without landing back in a dialectical destiny. Postures of exclusionism and of absolutism therefore unveil themselves to be at best no more than a form of reactive defense and at worst, an obsession with the self as holder of rights and property—or in other words, as owner of the world. In the renewed terrain of struggle and of deterritorialized subjectivities, no moon-lovers can really claim possession of the soft light that illuminates towns, villages, forests, and fields. *The same moon that rises over the ocean lands in the tea water. The wind that cools the waters scatters the moons like rabbits on a meadow.*[2] The one moon is seen in all waters; and the many-one moon is enjoyed or bawled at on a quiet night by people everywhere—possessors and dispossessed.

It used to be a custom in many parts of Asia that women, regardless of their classes, all came out in groups to stroll on the night of the Mid-Autumn Festival when the moon is at its fullest and brightest. Also parading through the streets are children from all families who moved together in wavy lines, their songs resonating from quarters to quarters, and their moon lanterns flickering in gentle undulations like so many beads of color on the dragon's body. The moonlight walk remains a memorable event, for here in September, the sky is high, the dewdrop clear, the mountains empty, the night lucent. Moon, waves, pearls, and jades: a multitude of expressions founded on these images exists in Chinese poetry to describe feminine beauty and the carnal presence of the loved woman. *Scented mist, cloud chignon damp/Pure light, jade arm cool* ("Moonlit Night," Tu-Fu).[3] Through the eroticization of nocturnal light, she is, as tradition dictates, often all hair and skin: darkness is fragrant, soft, vaporous, moist, mist- or cloud-like, while the glow emanating from her smooth bare arm evokes the sensation of touching jade. Yet, she is not simply night to his day (as in many Western philosophical and literary traditions), she is day in night.

In the realm of dualities where blinding brilliance is opposed to mysterious luminosity, or to use Taoist terminology, where the logic of conscious knowledge is set against the wisdom of real knowledge, she finds no place she can simply dwell in or transgress. Crisscrossing more than one occupied territory at a time, she remains perforce inappropriate/d—both *inside* and outside her own social positionings. What is offered then is the possibility of a break with the specular structure of hegemonic discourse and its scopic economy which, according to Western feminist critiques, circularly bases its in-sights on the sight (a voyeur's *theoria*) rather than the touch. The interstice between the visual and the tactile is perhaps the (nothing-)spiritual conveyed above in the fragrance of mist—at once within and beyond the sense of smell. Within and beyond tangible visibility. A trajectory across variable praxes of difference, her (un)location is necessarily the shifting and contextual interval between arrested boundaries.

She is the moon and she is not. All depends on how the moon partakes of language and representation. Chinese feminists have by now carefully re-read and rewritten the story of goddess Chang E. In their words, the latter was not confined to living solitarily on the moon because she *stole* the pill of immortality from her husband Hou Yi (who later became the Sun-King). Rather, she chose to live on the moon because it was nearest the earth, and she was forced by circumstances to swallow the elixir to *free* herself from the threat of having to belong to a man craving for power and possession who asserted he had killed her husband.[4] As long as the light of the moon is merely spoken of as having its birth in the sun, decreasing in proportion to its distance from the solar ray, and being accordingly light or dark as the sun comes and goes, women will reject Woman. They will agree with feminist writer Ting Lan that: "Woman is not the moon. She must rely on herself to shine."[5] For having occupied such a multiply central role in Chinese arts and culture, the moon has inevitably been the object of much literary controversy. Subjected to a continuous process of re- and de-territorialization, she bears both strong positive and negative social connotations.

Not too long ago, when the fire of the revolution was at its height, some writers decided that to focus on her was to ruin China, therefore the moon had to be liquidated. A person enjoying the mid-autumn moon and eating rabbit moon cakes was either "feudalistic" or "counter-revolutionary." The moon became the property of the conservative leisure class and, again, her sight was thought to be owned by some to the detriment of others. As an ideological instrument in man's manipulative hand, she could easily constitute a means of escapism, hence to sing her praise is, indeed, to "avoid facing reality." Yet, how realistic was it to liquidate the moon? Can women simply leap *outside* the (un-)feminine without falling into the historical model of mastery? The moment was transitional. Today, as the wind keeps on changing direction, the moon can hardly be bestowed with the power to ruin the nation, and again, she proves to be "shared property" among franchised and disfranchised. The moon waxes and wanes in favor of different trends of discursive production, and the war of meaning or what Mao named the "verbal struggle" never really ends. On the social terrain, desire refuses to let itself be confined to the need of ideological legitimation. Whether the moon is scorned or exalted, she continues to be passionately the subject/the passionate subject of discussion. Even when invalidated and stripped bare of her restorative powers, she remains this empty host-center which generously invites its guests to fill it to their own likings without ever being able to arrogate to themselves the exclusive right of a landlord.

Nothing is less real than realism (Georgia O'Keeffe).[6] Insubordinate processes of resistance do not lend themselves easily to commodification. A man convicted for seditious conspiracy, and currently serving his sixty-eight-year sentence in prison for having upheld the liberation of Puerto Rico, remarks that "the struggle is also between one fiction and another. . . . We, crazy people always strive toward the kingdom of freedom (Marx), towards our own idea and conception of Utopia." Rejecting the disabling and reductive logic that one should not engage in the so-called luxury of art when people starve every day, or when revolution is in danger, the man further asserts that without art, "revolution will lose its spirit. And the spirit of any revolution is the widening of freedom, collective and individual, and not one or the other" (Elizam Escobar).[7] To disrupt the existing systems of dominant values and to challenge the very foundation of a social and cultural order is not merely to destroy a few prejudices or to reverse power relations within the terms of an economy of the same. Rather, it is to see through the revolving door of all rationalizations and to meet head on the truth of that struggle *between fictions*. Art is a form of production. Aware that oppression can be located both in the story told and in the telling of the story, an art critical of social reality neither relies on mere consensus nor does it ask permission from ideology. Thus, the issue facing liberation movements is not that of liquidating art in its not-quite-correct, ungovernable dimension, but that of confronting the limits of centralized conscious knowledge, hence of demystifying while politicizing the artistic experience.

The moon breeds like a rabbit. She causes the seeds to germinate and the plants to grow, but she exceeds all forms of regulated fecundity through which she is expected to ensure the system's functioning. In the heterogeneity of the feminist struggle and its plurivocal projects, the impossibility of defining once and for all the condition of being sexualized as feminine and racialized as colored does not result from a lack of determination, but rather, from an inescapable awareness of the sterility of the unitary subject and its monolithic constructs. *For language is in every case not only communication of the communicable but also, at the same time, a symbol of the noncommunicable* (Walter Benjamin).[8] The gift that circulates with non-closures offers no security. Here in the all-meaning circle where there is no in no out, no light no shade, she is born anew. This is the third scenario. When stillness culminates, there is movement. Non-alignment paradoxically means new alliances: those that arise from-within differences and necessarily cut across variable borderlines, for there is no one who is automatically my ally/ because we are the same/ Alliances don't grow wild and unattended/ . . . they grow on two conditions/ that you and I/ both of us/ understand that we need each other to survive/ and that we have the courage/ to ask each other what that means" (Judit).[9]

While the full moon generally represents the conjunction of *yin* and *yang*, of stillness and action, or of beings dear to one another (the cyclic encounter of Hou Yi and Chang E), the autumn Harvest moon connotes more specifically distant presence and desire for reunion. Separated lovers burnt in longing and imbued with the thought of one another, reunite in watching the same moon. *Night follows night, bright luster wanes / Thinking of you, I am like the full moon* (Chang Chiu-Ling).[10] The potential of sharing the seed of a common journey while being apart keeps desire alive; but the lucid tranquility of lunar realizations eventually helps the desirers to find their repose. Lifted in awareness by the light in the calm fragrant night, moon-lovers remain enraptured by its gentle powers while aspiring to quietism in their creations. Such an in-between state of mind does bear the trace of a name: whoever dreams of the simple moon(life) without looking for conscious knowledge is said, in psychoanalysis, to incline toward the "feminine."

At night inhale the vitality of the moon (Sun Bu-er).[11] She is the principle of transformation and the site of possibility for diversely repressed realities. With the moon, the Imaginary She is at once centered and de-centered. Access to proper names as moments of transition (the "moon" is a name) requires that "the imagination also [be] a political weapon" (Escobar). For, there is no space really untouched by the vicissitudes of history, and emancipatory projects never begin nor end *properly*. They are constantly hampered in their activities by the closure-effect repeatedly brought about when a group within a movement becomes invested in the exercise of power, when it takes license to legislate what it means to "be a woman," to ascertain the "truth" of the feminine, and to reject other women whose immediate agenda may differ from their own. In undoing such closure-effect one is bound again and again to recognize "that piece of the oppressor which is planted deep within each of us, and which knows only the oppressors' tactics, the oppressors' relationship" (Audre Lorde).[12]

Changes in the color of the sun or the moon used to be signs of approaching calamities. When the moon waxes red, it is said in Chinese mythology that men should be in awe of the unlucky times thus fore-omened. Today, lunar eclipses are still impressive, but scientists find them "undeniably lovely," for the dimming moon often shows strange and beautiful color effects. The old fox sees to it that everything becomes a commodity. Yet between rational and irrational enslavement there is the interval and there is the possibility for a third term in the struggle. *We are what we imagine. Our very existence consists in our imagination of ourselves. . . . The greater tragedy that can befall us is to go unimagined* (N. Scott Momaday).[13] In the existing regime of frenzied "disciplinarization," such breach in the regularity of the system constitutes the critical moment of disequilibrium and dis/illumination when Buddha may be defined as "a cactus in the moonlight."

Notes

1. *The Inner Teachings of Taoism*, T. Cleary, trans. (Boston: Shambhala, 1986) p. 6.
2. Gerald Vizenor, *Griever: An American Monkey King in China* (New York: Illinois State University and Fiction Collective, 1986), p. 227.
3. Quoted in Francois Cheng, *Chinese Poetic Writing*, D. A. Riggs and J. P. Seaton, trans. (Bloomington: Indiana University Press, 1982), p. 71.
4. See *Women in Chinese Folklore* (Beijing: Women of China, 1983), pp. 29-43.
5. Ting Lan, "Women Is Not the Moon," in Emily Honig and Gail Hershatter, eds., *Personal Voices: Chinese Women in the 1980's* (Stanford: Stanford University Press, 1988), p. 329.
6. Quoted in Elizam Escobar, "The Fear and Tremor of Being Understood: The Recent Work of Bertha Husband," *Third Text*, Nos. 3-4 (Spring-Summer 1988): 119.
7. Quoted in Bertha Husband, "A Deep Sea Diver in the Phantom(ly) Country: Art and Politics of Elizam Escobar," *ibid.*, pp. 113; 116.
8. Walter Benjamin, *One-Way Street and Other Writings* (London: Verso, 1978; rpt. 1985), p. 123.
9. Judit, "Alliances," *Companeras: Latina Lesbians*, ed. Juanita Ramos (New York: Latina Lesbian History Project, 1987), pp. 245-46.
10. Quoted in *Chinese Poetic Writing*, p. 108.
11. Sun Bu-er, "Ingestion of the Medicine," *Immortal Sisters: Secrets of Taoist Women*, ed. and trans. T. Cleary (Boston: Shambhala, 1989), p. 47.
12. Audre Lorde, "Age, Race, Class, and Sex: Women Redefining Difference," *Out There: Marginalization and Contemporary Culture*, ed. Russell Ferguson, et al. (New York: The New Museum of Contemporary Art and M.I.T. Press, 1990), p. 287.
13. Quoted in Gerald Vizenor, "Socioacupuncture: Mythic Reversals and the striptease in Four Scenes," *Out There*, p. 419.

From Renov, M. (Ed.), *Theorizing Documentary*. Copyright © 1993 Routledge, a member of the Taylor and Francis Group. Reprinted with permission.

8.3

The Totalizing Quest of Meaning

Trinh T. Minh-ha

There is no such thing as documentary—whether the term designates a category of material, a genre, an approach, or a set of techniques. This assertion—as old and as fundamental as the antagonism between names and reality—needs incessantly to be restated despite the very visible existence of a documentary tradition. In film, such a tradition, far from undergoing a crisis today, is likely to fortify itself through its very recurrence of declines and rebirths. The narratives that attempt to unify/purify its practices by positing evolution and continuity from one period to the next are numerous indeed, relying heavily on traditional historicist concepts of periodization.

Nothing is poorer than a truth expressed as it was thought.

—Walter Benjamin[1]

In a completely catalogued world, cinema is often reified into a corpus of traditions. Its knowledge can constitute its destruction, unless the game keeps on changing its rules, never convinced of its closures, and always eager to outplay itself in its own principles. On the one hand, truth is produced, induced, and extended according to the regime in power. On the other, truth lies in between all regimes of truth. As the fable goes, What I tell You Three Times Is True. To question the image of a historicist account of documentary as a continuous unfolding does not necessarily mean championing discontinuity; and to resist meaning does not necessarily lead to its mere denial. Truth, even when "caught on the run," does not yield itself either in names or in (filmic) frames; and meaning should be prevented from coming to closure at what is said and what is shown. Truth and meaning: the two are likely to be equated with one another. Yet, what is put forth as truth is often nothing more than a meaning. And

---

Editors' Note: A shorter version of this article has been published as "Documentary Is/Not A Name," *October*, No. 52 (Summer 1990): 76–98.

225

what persists between the meaning of something and its truth is the interval, a break without which meaning would be fixed and truth congealed. This is perhaps why it is so difficult to talk about it, the interval. About the cinema. About. The words will not ring true. Not true, for, what is one to do with films which set out to determine truth from falsity while the visibility of this truth lies precisely in the fact that it is false? How is one to cope with a "film theory" that can never theorize "about" film, but only *with* concepts that film raises in relation to concepts of other practices?

> A man went to a Taoist temple and asked that his fortune be told. "First," said the priest, "you must donate incense money, otherwise the divination might not be as accurate as possible. Without such a donation, in fact, none of it will come true!"
>
> —"The Words Will Not Ring True,"
> *Wit and Humor from Old Cathay*[2]

Concepts are no less practical than images or sound. But the link between the name and what is named is conventional, not phenomenal. Producing film theory (or rather, philosophizing with film), which is not making films, is also a practice—a related but different practice—for theory does have to be (de)constructed as it (de)construes its object of study. While concepts of cinema are not ready-mades and do not preexist in cinema, they are not theory *about* cinema either. The setting up of practice against theory, and vice-versa, is at best a tool for reciprocal challenge, but like all binary oppositions, it is caught in the net of positivist thinking whose impetus is to supply answers at all costs, thereby limiting both theory and practice to a process of totalization. *I'm sorry, if we're going to use words we should be accurate in our use of them, It isn't a question of technique, it is a question of the material. If the material is actual, then it is documentary. If the material is invented, then it is not documentary.... If you get so muddled up in your use of the term, stop using it. Just talk about films. Anyway, very often when we use these terms, they only give us an opportunity to avoid really discussing the film* (Lindsay Anderson).[3]

In the general effort to analyze film and to produce "theory about film," there is an unavoidable tendency to reduce film theory to an area of specialization and of expertise, one that serves to constitute a *discipline*. There is also advocacy of an Enlightenment and "bourgeois" conception of language, which holds that the means of communication is the word, its object factual, its addressee a human subject (the linear, hierarchical order of things in a world of reification)—whereas, language as the "medium" of communication in its most radical sense, "only communicates itself *in* itself."[4] The referential function of language is thus not negated, but freed from its false identification with the phenomenal world and from its assumed authority as a means of cognition about the world. Theory can be the very place where this negative knowledge about the reliability of theory's own operative principles is made accessible, and where theoretical categories like all classificatory schemes keep on being voided, rather than appropriated, reiterated, safeguarded.

How true is the film theorist's divination? As Sor Juana Ines de la Cruz (a name among many others) would probably defend in her devalued status as a woman in the Church, "true" knowledge has to be separated from its instrumental use.[5] The link between money and fact surfaces in the very instances where it either goes unacknowledged or is adamantly denied. The question of quality in accuracy and truth seems to depend largely on the weight or on the quantity of donation money—incense money, as the priest specifies. Indeed, some of the questions invariably burned in film public debates with the filmmaker are: What's the shooting ratio? What's the budget? How long did it take you to complete the film? The higher the bet, the better the product; the larger the amount of money involved, the more valuable the film, the more believable the truth it holds out. The longer the time spent, the more prized the experience, the more reliable the information. Filmwork is made a *de facto* "low-budget" or "big-budget" product. This is what one constantly hears and has come to say it oneself. "Low-tech," "high-tech," "High-class junk," "low-grade footage." Pressure, money, bigness does it all . . . The widespread slogan in factual and "alternative" realms may claim "the larger the grain, the better the politics," but what exclusively circulates in mass media culture is undoubtedly, the money image. Money as money and money as capital are often spoken of as one, not two. The problem of financial constraints is, however, not only a problem of money but also one of control and standardization of images and sounds. Which truth? Whose truth? How true? (Andy Warhol's renowned statement rings very true: "Buying is much more American than thinking.") In the name of public service and of mass communication, the money-making or, rather, money-subjected eye remains glued to the permanent scenario of the effect- and/or production-valued image.

Documentary is said to have come about as a need to inform the people (Dziga Vertov's *Kino-Pravda* or *Camera-Truth*), and subsequently to have affirmed itself as a reaction against the monopoly that the movie as entertainment came to have on the uses of film. Cinema was redefined as an ideal medium for social indoctrination and comment, whose virtues lay in its capacity for "observing and selecting from life itself," for "opening up the screen on the real world," for photographing "the living scene and the living story," for giving cinema "power over a million and one images," as well as for achieving "an intimacy of knowledge and effect impossible to the shimsham mechanics of the studio and the lily-fingered interpretation of the metropolitan actor" (John Grierson).[6] Asserting its independence from the studio and the star system, documentary has its *raison d'être* in a strategic distinction. It puts the social function of film *on the market*. It takes real people and real problems from the real world and *deals with* them. It *sets a value* on intimate observation and *assesses its worth* according to how well it succeeds in capturing reality on the run, "without material interference, without intermediary." Powerful living stories, infinite authentic situations. There are no retakes. The stage is thus no more no less than life itself. *With the documentary approach the film gets back to its fundamentals. . . . By selection, elimination and coordination of natural elements, a film form evolves which is original and not bound by theatrical or literary tradition. . . . The documentary film is an original art form. It has come to grips with facts—on its own original level. It covers the rational side of our lives, from the scientific experiment to the poetic landscape-study, but never moves away from the factual* (Hans Richter).[7]

The real world: so real that the Real becomes the one basic referent—pure, concrete, fixed, visible, all-too-visible. The result is the elaboration of a whole aesthetic of objectivity and the development of comprehensive technologies of truth capable of promoting what is right and what is wrong in the world, and by extension, what is "honest" and what is "manipulative" in documentary. This involves an extensive and relentless pursuit of naturalism across all the elements of cinematic technology.

Indispensable to this cinema of the authentic image and spoken word are, for example, the directional microphone (localizing and restricting in its process of selecting sound for purposes of decipherability) and the Nagra portable tape-recorder (unrivaled for its maximally faithful ability to document). Lip-synchronous sound is validated as the norm; it is a "must" not so much in replicating reality (this much has been acknowledged among the fact-makers) as in "showing real people in real locations at real tasks." (Even non-sync sounds that are recorded in-context are considered "less authentic" because the technique of sound synchronization and its institutionalized use have become "nature" within film culture.) Real time is thought to be more "truthful" than filmic time, hence the long take (that is, a take lasting the length of the 400 ft. roll of commercially available film stock) and minimal or no editing (change at the cutting stage is "trickery," as if montage did not happen at the stages of conception and shooting) are declared to be more appropriate if one is to avoid distortions in structuring the material. The camera is the switch onto life. Accordingly, the close-up is condemned for its partiality, while the wide angle is claimed to be more objective because it includes more in the frame, hence it can mirror more faithfully the event-in-context. (The more, the larger, the truer—as if wider framing is less a framing than tighter shots.) The light-weight, hand-held camera, with its independence of the tripod—the fixed observation post—is extolled for its ability "to go unnoticed," since it must be at once mobile and invisible, integrated into the milieu so as to change as little as possible, but also able to put its intrusion to use and provoke people into uttering the "truth" that they would not otherwise unveil in ordinary situations.

Thousands of bunglers have made the word [documentary] come to mean a deadly, routine form of film-making, the kind an alienated consumer society might appear to deserve—the art of talking a great deal during a film, with a commentary imposed from the outside, in order to say nothing, and to show nothing (Louis Marcorelles).[8] The event itself. Only the event; unaffected, unregulated by the eye recording it and the eye watching it. The perfectly objective social observer may no longer stand as the cherished model among documentary-makers today, but with every broadcast the viewer, Everyman, continues to be taught that He is first and foremost a Spectator. Either one is not responsible for what one sees (because only the event presented to him counts) or the only way one can have some influence on things is to send in a monetary donation. Thus, though the filmmaker's perception may readily be admitted as being unavoidably personal, the objectiveness of the reality of what is seen and represented remains unchallenged. *[Cinéma-verité:] it would be better to call it cinema-sincerity. . . . That is, that you ask the audience to have confidence in the evidence, to say to the audience, This is what I saw. I didn't fake it, this is what happened. . . . I look at what happened with my subjective eye and this is what I believe took place. . . . It's a question of honesty* (Jean Rouch).[9]

What is presented as evidence remains evidence, whether the observing eye qualifies itself as being subjective or objective. At the core of such a rationale dwells, untouched, the Cartesian division between subject and object which perpetuates a dualistic inside-versus-outside, mind-against-matter view of the world. The emphasis is again laid on the power of film to capture reality "out there" for us "in here." The moment of appropriation and of consumption is either simply ignored or carefully rendered invisible according to the rules of good and bad documentary. The art of talking to say nothing goes hand in hand with the will to say and to say only to confine something in a meaning. Truth has to be made vivid, interesting; it has to be "dramatized" if it is to convince the audience of the evidence, whose "confidence" in it allows truth to take shape. *Documentary—the presentation of actual facts in a way that makes them credible and telling to people at the time* (William Stott).[10]

The real? Or the repeated artificial resurrection of the real, an operation whose overpowering success in substituting the visual and verbal signs of the real for the real itself ultimately helps to challenge the real, thereby intensifying the uncertainties engendered by any clear-cut division between the two. In the scale of what is more and what is less real, subject matter is of primary importance ("It is very difficult if not impossible." says a film festival administrator, "to ask jurors of the documentary film category panel not to identify the quality of a film with the subject it treats"). The focus is undeniably on common experience, by which the "social" is defined: an experience that features, as a famed documentary-maker (Pierre Perrault) put it (paternalistically), "man, simple man, who has never expressed himself."[11]

The socially oriented filmmaker is thus the almighty voice-giver (here, in a vocalizing context that is all-male), whose position of authority in the production of meaning continues to go unchallenged, skillfully masked as it is by its righteous mission. The relationship between mediator and medium or, the mediating activity, is either ignored—that is, assumed to be transparent, as value free and as insentient as an instrument of reproduction ought to be—or else, it is treated most conveniently: by humanizing the gathering of evidence so as to further the status quo. (Of course, like all human beings I am subjective, but nonetheless, you should have confidence in the evidence!) Good documentaries are those whose subject matter is "correct" and whose point of view the viewer agrees with. What is involved may be a question of honesty (vis-à-vis the material), but it is often also a question of (ideological) adherence, hence of legitimization.

Films made about the common people are furthermore naturally promoted as films made for the same people, and only for them. In the desire to service the needs of the un-expressed, there is, commonly enough, the urge to define them and their needs. More often than not, for example, when filmmakers find themselves in debates in which a film is criticized for its simplistic and reductive treatment of a subject, resulting in a maintenance of the very status quo which it sets out to challenge, their tendency is to dismiss the criticism by claiming that the film is not made for "sophisticated viewers like ourselves, but for a general audience," thereby situating themselves above and apart from the *real* audience, those "out there," the undoubtedly simple-minded folks who need everything they see explained to them. Despite the shift of emphasis—from the the world of the upwardly mobile and the very affluent that dominates the media to that of "their poor"—, what is maintained intact is the age-old opposition between the creative intelligent supplier and the mediocre unenlightened consumer. The pretext for perpetuating such a division is the belief that social relations are determinate, hence endowed with objectivity. *By "impossibility of the social" I understand . . . the assertion of the ultimate impossibility of all "objectivity" . . . society presents itself, to a great degree, not as an objective, harmonic order, but as an ensemble of divergent forces which do not seem to obey any unified or unifying logic. How can this experience of the failure of objectivity be made compatible with the affirmation of an ultimate objectivity of the real?* (Ernesto Laclau).[12]

The silent common people—those who "have never expressed themselves" unless they are given the opportunity to voice their thoughts by the one who comes to redeem them—are constantly summoned to signify the real world. They are the fundamental referent of the social, hence it suffices to point the camera at them, to show their (industrialized) poverty, or to contextualize and package their unfamiliar lifestyles for the ever-buying and donating general audience "back here," in order to enter the sanctified realm of the morally right, or the social. In other words, when the so-called "social" reigns, how these people(/we) come to visibility in the media, how meaning is given to their (/our) lives, how their(/our) truth is construed or how truth is laid down for them(/us) and despite them(/us), how representation relates to or *is* ideology, how media hegemony continues its relentless course is simply not at issue.

> There isn't any *cinéma-vérité*. It's necessarily a lie, from the moment the director intervenes—or it isn't cinema at all. (Georges Franju)[13]

When the social is hypostatized and enshrined as an ideal of transparency, when it itself becomes commodified in a form of sheer administration (better service, better control), the interval between the real and the image/d or between the real and the rational shrinks to the point of unreality. Thus, to address the question of production relations as raised earlier is endlessly to reopen the question: how is the real (or the social ideal of good representation) produced? Rather than catering to it, striving to capture and discover its truth as a concealed or lost object, it is therefore important also to keep on asking: how is truth being ruled? *The penalty of realism is that it is about reality and has to bother for ever not about being "beautiful" but about being right* (John Grierson).[14] The fathers of documentary have initially insisted that documentary is not News, but Art (a "new and vital art form" as Grierson once proclaimed). That its essence is not information (as with "the hundreds of tweeddle-dum 'industrials' or worker-education films"); not reportage; not newsreels; but something close to "a creative treatment of actuality" (Grierson's renowned definition). *If Joris Ivens has made the most beautiful documentaries that anyone has ever seen, that's because the films are composed, worked out, and they have an air of truth. Sure the documentary part is true, but all around the documentary sections there's an interpretation. And then you can't talk about cinéma-verité* (Georges Franju).[15]

Documentary may be anti-aesthetic, as some still affirm in the line of the British forerunner, but it is claimed to be no less an art, albeit an art within the limits of factuality. (Interpretation, for example, is not viewed as constituting the very process of documenting and making information accessible; it is thought, instead, to be the margin all around an untouched *given* center, which according to Franju is the "documentary part" or "documentary section.") When, in a world of reification, truth is widely equated with fact, any explicit use of the magic, poetic, or irrational qualities specific to the film medium itself would have to be excluded a priori as non-factual. The question is not so much one of sorting out—illusory as this may be—what is inherently factual and what is not, in a body of *pre-existing* filmic techniques, as it is one of abiding by the conventions of naturalism in film. In the reality of formula-films, only validated techniques are *right*, others are de facto wrong. The criteria are all based on their degree of invisibility in producing meaning. Thus, shooting at any speed other than the standard 24-frames-per-second (the speed necessitated for lip-sync sound) is, for example, often condemned as a form of manipulation, implying thereby that manipulativeness has to be discreet—that is, acceptable only when not easily perceptible to the "real audience." Although the whole of filmmaking *is* a question of manipulation—whether "creative" or not—, again, those endorsing the law unhesitantly decree which technique is manipulative and which, supposedly is not; and this judgement is certainly made according to the degree of visibility of each. *A documentary film is shot with three cameras: 1) the camera in the technical sense; 2) the filmmaker's mind; and 3) the generic patterns of the documentary film, which are founded on the expectations of the audience that patronizes it. For this reason one cannot simply say that the documentary film portrays facts. It photographs isolated facts and assembles from them a coherent set of facts according to three divergent schemata. All remaining possible facts and factual contexts are excluded. The naive treatment of documentation therefore provides a unique opportunity to concoct fables. In and of itself, the documentary is no more realistic than the feature film* (Alexander Kluge).[16]

Reality is more fabulous, more maddening, more strangely manipulative than fiction. To understand this, is to recognize the naivety of a development of cinematic technology that promotes increasing unmediated "access" to reality. It is to see through the poverty of what Benjamin deplored as "a truth expressed as it was thought" and to understand why progressive fiction films are attracted and constantly pay tribute to documentary techniques. These films put the "documentary effect" to advantage, playing on the viewer's expectation in order to "concoct fables." (Common examples of this effect include: the feeling of participating in a truth-like moment of reality captured despite the filmed subject; the sense of urgency, immediacy, and authenticity in the instability of the hand-held camera; the newsreel look of the grainy image; and the oral-testimony-like quality of the direct interview—to mention just a few.)

The documentary can thus easily become a "style":it no longer constitutes a mode of production or an attitude toward life, but proves to be only an element of aesthetics (or anti-aesthetics)—which at best and without acknowledging it, it tends to be in any case when, within its own factual limits, it reduces itself to a mere category, or a set of persuasive techniques. Many of these techniques have become so "natural" to the language of broadcast television today that they "go unnoticed." These are, for example: the "personal testimony" technique (a star appears on screen to advertise his/her use of a certain product); the "plain folks" technique (a politician arranges to eat hot dogs in public); the "band wagon" technique (the use of which conveys the message that "everybody is doing it, why not you?") or the "card stacking" technique (in which prearrangements for a "survey" shows that a certain brand of product is more popular than any other to the inhabitants of a given area).[17]

You must re-create reality because reality runs away; reality denies reality. You must first interpret it, or re-create it. . . . When I make a documentary, I try to give the realism an artificial aspect. . . . I find that the aesthetic of a document comes from the artificial aspect of the document . . . it has to be more beautiful than realism, and therefore it has to be composed . . . to give it another sense (Franju).[18] A documentary aware of its own artifice is one that remains sensitive to the flow between fact and fiction. It does not work to conceal or exclude what is normalized as "non-factual," for it understands the mutual dependence of realism and "artificiality" in the process of filmmaking. It recognizes the necessity of composing (on) life in living it or making it. Documentary reduced to a mere vehicle of facts may be used to advocate a cause, but it does not constitute one in itself; hence the perpetuation of the bipartite system of division in the content-versus-form rationale.

To compose is not always synonymous with ordering-so-as-to-persuade, and to give the filmed document another sense, another meaning, is not necessarily to distort it. If life's paradoxes and complexities are not to be suppressed, the question of degrees and nuances is incessantly crucial. Meaning can therefore be political only when it does not let itself be easily stabilized and when it does not rely on any single source of authority, but rather, empties it, or decentralizes it. Thus, even when this source is referred to, it stands as one among many others, at once plural and utterly singular. In its demand to *mean* at any rate, the "documentary" often forgets how it comes about and how aesthetics and politics remain inseparable in its constitution. For, when not equated with mere techniques of beautifying, aesthetics allows one to experience life differently or, as some would say, to give it "another sense," remaining in tune with its drifts and shifts.

> It must be possible to represent reality as the historical fiction it is. Reality is a paper-tiger. The individual does encounter it, as fate. It is not fate, however, but a creation of the labor of generations of human beings, who all the time wanted and still want something entirely different. In more than one respect, reality is simultaneously real and unreal. (Alexander Kluge)[19]

From its descriptions to its arrangements and rearrangements, reality on the move may be heightened or impoverished but it is never neutral (that is, objectivist). *Documentary at its purest and most poetic is a form in which the elements that you use are the actual elements* (Lindsay Anderson).[20] Why, for example, use the qualifying term "artificial" at all? In the process of producing a "document," is there such a thing as an artificial aspect that can be securely separated from the true aspect (except for analytical purpose—that is, for another "artifice" of language)? In other words, is a closer framing of reality more artificial than a wider one? The notion of "making strange" and of reflexibility remains but a mere distancing device so long as the division between "textual artifice" and "social attitude" exerts its power.[21] The "social" continues to go unchallenged, history keeps on being salvaged, while the sovereignty of the socio-historicizing subject is safely maintained. With the status quo of the making/consuming subject preserved, the aim is to correct "errors" (the false) and to construct an alternative view (offered as a this-is-the-true-or mine-is-truer version of reality). It is, in other words, to replace one source of unacknowledged authority by another, but not to challenge the very constitution of authority. The new socio-historical text thus rules despotically as another master-centered text, since it unwittingly helps to perpetuate the Master's ideological stance.

When the textual and the political neither separate themselves from one another nor simply collapse into a single qualifier, the practice of representation can, similarly, neither be taken for granted, nor merely dismissed as being ideologically reactionary. By putting representation under scrutiny, textual theory-practice has more likely helped to upset rooted ideologies by bringing the mechanics of their workings to the fore. It makes possible the vital differentiation between authoritative criticism and uncompromising analyses and inquiries (including those of the analyzing/inquiring activity). Moreover, it contributes to the questioning of reformist "alternative" approaches that never quite depart from the lineage of white- and male-centered humanism. Despite their explicit socio-political commitment, these approaches remain unthreatening—that is, "framed," and thus neither social nor political enough.

Reality runs away, reality denies reality. Filmmaking is after all a question of "framing" reality in its course. However, it can also be the very place where the referential function of the film image/sound is not simply negated, but reflected upon in its own operative principles and questioned in its authoritative identification with the phenomenal world. In attempts at suppressing the mediation of the cinematic apparatus and the fact that language "communicates itself in itself," there always lurks what Benjamin qualified as a "bourgeois" conception of language. *Any revolutionary strategy must challenge the depiction of reality . . . so that a break between ideology and text is affected* (Claire Johnston).[22]

To deny the *reality* of film in claiming (to capture) *reality* is to stay "in ideology"—that is, to indulge in the (deliberate or not) confusion of filmic with phenomenal reality. By condemning self-reflexibility as pure formalism instead of challenging its diverse realizations, this ideology can "go on unnoticed," keeping its operations invisible and serving the goal of universal expansionism. Such aversion for self-reflexibility goes hand in hand with its widespread appropriation as a progressive formalistic device in cinema, since both work to reduce its function to a harmlessly decorative one. (For example, it has become commonplace to hear such remarks as "A film is a film" or, "This is a film about a film." Film-on-film statements are increasingly challenging to work with as they can easily fall prey to their own formulas and techniques.) Furthermore, reflexibility, at times equated with personal view, is at other times endorsed as scientific rigor.

> Two men were discussing the joint production of wine. One said to the other: "You shall supply the rice and I the water." The second asked: "If all the rice comes from me, how shall we apportion the finished product?" The first man replied: "I shall be absolutely fair about the whole thing. When the wine is finished, each gets back exactly what he puts in—I'll siphon off the liquid and you can keep the rest."
>
> —"Joint Production,"
> *Wit and Humor from Old Cathay*[23]

One of the areas of documentary that remains most resistant to the reality of film as film is that known as anthropological filmmaking. Filmed ethnographic material, which was thought to "replicate natural perception," has now renounced its authority to replicate only to purport to provide adequate "data" for the "sampling" of culture. The claim to objectivity may no longer stand in many anthropological circles, but its authority is likely to be replaced by the sacrosanct notion of the "scientific." Thus the recording and gathering of data and of people's testimonies are considered to be the limited aim of "ethnographic film." What makes a film anthropological and what makes it scientific is, tautologically enough, its "scholarly endeavour [to] respectively document and interpret according to anthropological standards."[24] Not merely ethnographic nor documentary, the definition positively specifies, but scholarly and anthropologically. The fundamental scientific obsession is present in every attempt to demarcate anthropology's territories. In order to be scientifically valid, a film needs the scientific intervention of the anthropologist, for it is only by adhering to the body of conventions set up by the community of anthropologists accredited by their "discipline" that the film can hope to qualify for the classification and be passed as a "scholarly endeavour."

The myth of science impresses us. But do not confuse science with its scholasticism. Science finds no truths, either mathematized or formalized; it discovers unknown facts that can be interpreted in a thousand ways (Paul Veyne).[25] One of the familiar arguments given by anthropologists to validate their prescriptively instrumental use of film and of people is to dismiss all works by filmmakers who are "not professional anthropologists" or "amateur ethnographers" under the pretext that they are not "anthropologically informed," hence they have "no theoretical significance from an anthropological point of view." To advance such a blatantly self-promoting rationale to institute *a deadly routine form of filmmaking* (to quote a sentence of Marcorelles once more) is also—through anthropology's primary task of "collecting data" for knowledge of mankind—to try to skirt what is known as the salvage paradigm and the issues implicated in the "scientific" deployment of Western world ownership.[26] The stronger anthropology's insecurity about its own project, the greater its eagerness to hold up a normative model, and the more seemingly serene its disposition to dwell in its own blind spots.

In the sanctified terrain of anthropology, all of filmmaking is reduced to a question of methodology. It is demonstrated that the reason anthropological films go further than ethnographic films is because they do not, for example, just show activities being performed, but they also *explain* the "anthropological significance" of these activities (significance that, despite the disciplinary qualifier "anthropological," is de facto identified with the meaning the natives give them themselves). Now, obviously, in the process of fixing meaning, not every explanation is valid. This is where the role of the expert anthropologist comes in and where methodologies need to be devised, legitimated, and enforced. For, if a non-professional explanation is dismissed here, it is not so much because it lacks insight or theoretical grounding, as because it escapes anthropological control; it lacks the seal of approval from the anthropological order. In the name of science, a distinction is made between reliable and non-reliable information. Anthropological and non-anthropological explanations may share the same subject matter, but they differ in the way they produce meaning. The unreliable constructs are the ones that do not obey the rules of anthropological authority, which a concerned expert like Evans-Pritchard skillfully specifies as being nothing else but "a scientific habit of mind."[27] Science defined as the most appropriate approach to the object of investigation serves as a banner for every scientistic attempt to promote the West's paternalistic role as subject of knowledge and its historicity of the Same. *The West agrees with us today that the way to Truth passes by numerous paths, other than Aristotelian Thomistic logic or Hegelian dialectic. But social and human sciences themselves must be decolonized* (E. Mveng).[28]

In its scientistic "quest to make meaning," anthropology constantly reactivates the power relations embedded in the Master's confident discourses on Himself and His Other, thereby aiding both the *centri* petal and *centri* fugal movement of their global spread. With the diverse challenges issued today to the very process of producing "scientific" interpretation of culture as well as to that of making anthropological knowledge possible, visually oriented members of its community have come up with an epistemological position in which the notion of reflexivity is typically reduced to a question of technique and method. Equated with a form of self-exposure common in field work, it is discussed at times as *self-reflectivity* and at other times condemned as individualistic idealism sorely in need of being controlled if the individual maker is not to loom larger than the scientific community or the people observed. Thus, "being reflexive is virtually synonymous with being scientific."[29]

The reasons justifying such a statement are many, but one that can be read through it and despite it is: as long as the maker abides by a series of "reflexive" techniques in filmmaking that are devised for the purpose of exposing the "context" of production and as long as the required techniques are method(olog)ically carried out, the maker can be assured that "reflexivity" is elevated to that status of scientific rigor. These reflexive techniques would include the insertion of a verbal or visual narrative about the anthropologist, the methodology adopted, and the condition of production—in other words, all the conventional means of validating an anthropological text through the disciplinary practice of head-and footnoting and the totalistic concept of pre-production presentation. Those who reject such a rationale do so out of a preoccupation with the "community of scientists," whose collective judgment they feel should be the only true form of reflection. For an individual validation of a work can only be suspicious because it "ignores the historical development of science." In these constant attempts at enforcing anthropology as (a) discipline and at recentering the dominant representation of culture (despite all the changes in methodologies), what seems to be oddly suppressed in the notion of reflexivity in filmmaking is its practice as processes to prevent meaning from ending with what is said and what is shown—as inquiries into production relations—thereby to challenge representation itself while emphasizing the reality of the experience of film as well as the important role that reality plays in the lives of the spectators.

Unless an image displaces itself from its natural state, it acquires no significance. Displacement causes resonance. (Shanta Gokhale)[30]

After his voluntary surrender, Zheng Guang, a pirate operating off the coast of Fujian, was to be given an official post (in return for surrendering). When a superior instructed him to write a poem, Zheng replied with a doggerel: "No matter whether they are civil or military officials they are all the same. The officials assumed their posts before becoming thieves, but I, Zheng Guang, was a thief before becoming an official."

—"The Significance of Officialdom,"
Wit and Humor from Old Cathay[31]

As an aesthetic closure or an old relativizing gambit in the process nonetheless of absolutizing meaning, reflexivity proves critically in/significant when it merely serves to refine and to further the accumulation of knowledge. No going beyond, no elsewhere-within-here seems possible if the reflection on oneself is not at one and the same time the analysis of established forms of the social that define one's limits. Thus to drive the self into an abyss is neither a moralistic stricture against oneself (for future improvement), nor a task of critique that humanizes the decoding self but never challenges the very notion of self and decoder. Left intact in its positionality and its fundamental urge to decree meaning, the self conceived both as key and as transparent mediator, is more often than not likely to turn responsibility into license. The license to *name*, as though meaning presented itself to be deciphered without any ideological mediation. As though specifying a context can only result in the finalizing of what is shown and said. As though naming can stop the process of naming—that very abyss of the relation of self to self.

The bringing of the self into play necessarily exceeds the concern for human errors, for it cannot but involve as well the problem inherent in representation and communication. Radically plural in its scope, reflexivity is thus not a mere question of *rect*ifying and *just*ifying. (*Subject*ivizing.) What is set in motion in its praxis are the self-generating links between different forms of reflexivity. Thus, a subject who points to him/her/itself as subject-in-process, a work that displays its own formal properties or its own constitution as work, is bound to upset one's sense of identity—the familiar distinction between the Same and the Other since the latter is no longer kept in a recognizable relation of dependence, derivation, or appropriation. The process of self-constitution is also that in which the self vacillates and loses its assurance. The paradox of such a process lies in its fundamental instability; an instability that brings forth the disorder inherent to every order. The "core" of representation is the reflexive interval. It is the place in which the play within the textual frame is a play on this very frame, hence on the borderlines of the textual and extra-textual, where a positioning within constantly incurs the risk of de-positioning, and where the work, never freed from historical and socio-political contexts nor entirely subjected to them, can only be itself by constantly risking being no-thing.

A work that reflects back on itself offers itself infinitely as nothing else but work... *and* void. Its gaze is at once an impulse that causes the work to fall apart (to return to the initial no-work-ness) and an ultimate gift to its constitution. A gift, by which the work is freed from the tyranny of meaning as well as from the omnipresence of a subject of meaning. To let go of the hold at the very moment when it is at its most effective is to allow the work to live, and to live on independently of the intended links, communicating itself in itself like Benjamin's "the self is a text"—no more no less "a project to be built."[32] *Orpheus' gaze... is the impulse of desire which shatters the song's destiny and concern, and in that inspired and unconcerned decision reaches the origin, consecrates the song* (Maurice Blanchot).[33]

Meaning can neither be imposed nor denied. Although every film is in itself a form of ordering and closing, each closure can defy its own closure, opening onto other closures, thereby emphasizing the interval between apertures and creating a space in which meaning remains fascinated by what escapes and exceeds it. The necessity to let go of the notion of intentionality that dominates the question of the "social" as well as that of creativity cannot therefore be confused with the ideal of non-intervention, an ideal in relation to which the filmmaker, trying to become as invisible as possible in the process of producing meaning, promotes empathic subjectivity at the expense of critical inquiry even when the intention is to show and to condemn oppression. *It is idealist mystification to believe that "truth" can be captured by the camera or that the conditions of a film's production (e.g. a film made collectively by women) can of itself reflect the conditions of its production. This is mere utopianism: new meaning has to be manufactured within the text of the film.... What the camera in fact grasps is the "natural" world of the dominant ideology* (Claire Johnston).[34]

In the quest for totalized meaning and for knowledge-for-knowledge's sake, the worst meaning is meaninglessness. A Caucasian missionary nun based in a remote village of Africa qualifies her task in these simple, confident terms: "We are here to help people give meaning to their lives." Ownership is monotonously circular in its give-and-take demands. It is a monolithic view of the world whose irrationality expresses itself in the imperative of both giving and meaning, and whose irreality manifests itself in the need to require that visual and verbal constructs yield meaning down to their last detail. *The West moistens everything with meaning, like an authoritarian religion which imposes baptism on entire peoples* (Roland Barthes).[35] Yet such illusion is real; it has its own reality, one in which the subject of Knowledge, the subject of Vision, or the subject of Meaning continues to deploy established power relations, assuming Himself to be the basic reserve of reference in the totalistic quest for the referent, the true referent that lies out there in nature, in the dark, waiting patiently to be unveiled and deciphered correctly. To be redeemed. Perhaps then, an imagination that goes toward the texture of reality is one capable of playing upon the illusion in question and the power it exerts. The production of one irreality upon the other and the play of nonsense (which is not mere meaninglessness) upon meaning may therefore help to relieve the basic referent of its occupation, for the present situation of critical inquiry seems much less one of attacking the illusion of reality as one of displacing and emptying out the establishment of totality.

Notes

1. *One-Way Street and Other Writings* (London: Verso, 1979), p. 95.
2. J. Kowallis, trans. (Beijing: Panda Books, 1986), p. 164.
3. Quoted in G. Roy Levin, *Documentary Explorations: Fifteen Interviews with Film-Makers* (Garden City, NY: Doubleday & Company, 1971), p. 66.
4. Benjamin, *One Way Street*, pp. 109; 111.
5. See Jean Franco's re-reading of her work in *Plotting Women: Gender and Representation in Mexico* (New York: Columbia University Press, 1989), pp. 23-54.
6. In *Grierson On Documentary*, Forsyth Hardy, ed. (1966; rpt., New York: Praeger, 1971), pp. 146-47.
7. "Film as an Original Art Form," in *Film: A Montage of Theories*, R. Dyer MacCann, ed. (New York: E. P. Dutton, 1966), p. 183.
8. *Living Cinema: New Directions in Contemporary Film-making*, trans. I. Quigly (New York: Praeger, 1973), p. 37.
9. In Levin, *Documentary Explorations*, p. 135.
10. *Documentary Expression and Thirties America* (1973; rpt., New York: Oxford University Press, 1976), p. 73.
11. Quoted in *Living Cinema*, p. 26.
12. "Building a New Left: An Interview with Ernesto Laclau," *Strategies*, No. 1 (Fall 1988): 15.
13. In Levin, *Documentary Explorations*, p. 119.
14. *Grierson on Documentary*, p. 249.
15. In Levin, *Documentary Explorations*, p. 119.
16. *Alexander Kluge: A Retrospective* (The Goethe Institutes of North America, 1988). p. 4.
17. John Mercer, *An Introduction to Cinematography* (Champaign, IL: Stipes Publishing Co., 1968), p. 159.
18. In Levin, *Documentary Explorations*, pp. 121; 128.
19. *Alexander Kluge: A Retrospective*, p. 6.
20. *Ibid.*, p. 66.

21. This distinction motivates Dana Polan's argument in "A Brechtian Cinema? Towards a Politics of Self-Reflective Film," in B. Nichols, ed., *Movies and Methods*, Vol. 2 (Los Angeles: University of California Press, 1985), pp. 661-72.
22. "Women's Cinema as Counter-Cinema," in B. Nichols, ed., *Movies and Methods*, Vol. 1 (Los Angeles: University of California Press, 1976), p. 215.
23. Kowallis, *Wit and Humor*, p. 98.
24. Henk Ketelaar, "Methodology in Anthropological Filmmaking: A Filmmaking Anthropologist's Poltergeist?" in *Methodology in Anthropological Filmmaking*, N. Bogaart and H. Ketelaar, eds. (Gottingen: Herodot, 1983), p. 182.
25. *Did the Greeks Believe in Their Myths? An Essay on the Constitutive Imagination*, P. Wissing, trans. (Chicago: University of Chicago Press, 1988), p. 115.
26. See James Clifford, "Of Other Peoples: Beyond the 'Salvage Paradigm,'" in *Discussions in Contemporary Culture*, Hal Foster, ed. (Seattle: Bay Press, 1987), pp. 121-30.
27. See *Theories of Primitive Religion* (Oxford: Clarendon Press, 1980).
28. "Récents développements de la théologie africaine," Bulletin of African Theology, 5:9. Quoted in V. Y. Mudimbe, *The Invention of Africa: Gnosis, Philosophy and The Order of Knowledge* (Bloomington: Indiana University Press, 1988), p. 37.
29. Jay Ruby, "Exposing Yourself: Reflexivity, Anthropology and Film," *Semiotica*, 30, 1-2 (1980): 165.
30. In *The New Generation. 1960-1980*, Uma da Cunha, ed. (New Delhi: The Directorate of Film Festivals, 1981), p. 114.
31. Kowallis, *Wit and Humour*, p. 39.
32. Benjamin, *One-Way Street*, p. 14.
33. *The Gaze of Orpheus and Other Literary Essays*, P. Adams Sitney, ed., L. Davis, trans., (Barrytown, NY: Station Hill Press, 1981), p. 104.
34. Johnston, "Women's Cinema as Counter-Cinema," p. 214.
35. *Empire of Signs*, R. Howard, trans. (New York: Hill & Wang, 1982), p. 70.

9

Introduction to Sally Miller Gearhart

How change happens is the primary question that motivates the life and work of Sally Miller Gearhart. Because Gearhart sees feminism as the means by which the system of domination can be transformed into one that is life affirming, it is an integral part of her efforts to investigate this question. Born in Virginia in 1931, Gearhart earned a B.A. in drama and English from Sweet Briar College in 1952, an M.A. in theater and public address from Bowling Green State University in 1953, and a Ph.D. in theater from the University of Illinois in 1956. Most of her academic career was spent in the Speech Communication Department at San Francisco State University.

Gearhart initially considered rhetoric—traditionally defined as persuasion—as a primary means for changing society, and she used persuasion in her activism on behalf of causes such as justice, peace, and the environment. Gearhart then came to understand persuasion as violence, a perspective she explains in "The Womanization of Rhetoric." In "Notes from a Recovering Activist," Gearhart announces she no longer will engage in activism and proposes an alternative to a rhetoric of persuasion.

At the center of Gearhart's new theory of change are certain assumptions: that the purpose of communication is understanding, change happens when individuals choose to change, and changing oneself creates societal change. The translation of these assumptions into communication is illustrated in two works of speculative fiction by Gearhart. One is a chapter, "The Gatherstretch," from Gearhart's book, *Wanderground*, set years in the future when women left the oppression in the cities and moved to the hills, where they have gained telepathic, flying, and healing abilities. The second is a short story, "The Chipko," in which women prevent trees from being logged using alternative techniques of defense. For Gearhart, such fantasies create reality because they allow individuals to experiment with alternative modes of being.

Previously published in *Women's Studies International Quarterly*, Vol. 2, pp. 195-201, 1979. Reprinted with permission.

9.1

The Womanization of Rhetoric

Sally Miller Gearhart

I

My indictment of our discipline of rhetoric springs from my belief that any intent to persuade is an act of violence. In this first section I'd like briefly to review our culpability as teachers of persuasion, explore the distinction between change and intent-to-change, and finally describe a culture-wide phenomenon, the conquest/conversion mentality, in which I find public discourse to be but one of many participants.

The patriarchs of rhetoric have never called into question their unspoken assumption that mankind (read 'mankind') is here on earth to alter his (read 'his') environment and to influence the social affairs of other men (read 'men'). Without batting an eye the ancient rhetors, the men of the church, and scholars of argumentation from Bacon, Blair and Whately to Toulmin, Perelman and McLuhan, have taken as given that it is a proper and even necessary human function to attempt to change others. As modern critics and practitioners of public discourse we have been committed to the improvement in our students of the fine art of persuasion. In fact, our teaching, even if it were not the teaching of persuasion, is in itself an insidious form of violence. The 'chicken soup' attitude or the 'let me help you, let me enlighten you, let me show you the way' approach which is at the heart of most pedagogy is condescending and acutely expressive of the holier-than-thou mindset. Void of respect and openness, it makes even the informative lecture into an oppressive act.

Until the last few decades speech or rhetoric has been a discipline concerned almost exclusively with persuasion in both private and public discourse; it has spent whole eras examining and analyzing its eloquence, learning how to incite the passions, move the will. Over the centuries rhetoric has wearied itself in the ancient and honorable act of finding the available means of persuasion, the better to adapt a discourse to its end. Of all the human disciplines, it has gone about its task of educating others to violence with the most audacity. The fact that it has done so with language and metalanguage, with refined functions of the mind, instead of with whips or rifles does not excuse it from the mindset of the violent.

The indictment of the profession is not an attack on the tools of rhetoric; nor does it suggest that we, its practitioners, serve the world best by forsaking education or committing suicide. With our expertise in persuasion, rhetoricians and rhetorical theorists are in the best position to change our own use of our tools. The indictment is of our *intent* to change people and things, of our attempt to educate others in that skill. The indictment is of our participation in the conquest/conversion mindset that sends us now as a species pell-mell down the path to annihilation.

It is important to know that we can and do change each other daily. Our physical bodies respond to energy; even without our will they react in measurable ways to objects or people generating high energy. We are constantly being changed by each other. Further, we come closer each day to a recognition in our lives of the meaning of Einstein's reduction of matter to energy. It is only in density that the energy fields surrounding each of us differ from the solid energy that is our physical bodies; it is only in density that the energy we generate in our minds or our psyches differs from our auras. As Kurlian photography tracks down revolutionaries by the energy exuded from their very bodies and as Western medicine adopts techniques of visualization and fantasy in the curing of cancer, we realize that to thrust a sword into another person does not differ significantly from wishing them ill or from fantasizing a sword thrust into their heart. Our physical being, our movement, our thoughts, our metaphors: all are forms of energy in constant and infinitely varied exchange.

It is important that we recognize the communication that takes place between entities as well as between humans and entities that we do not count as human. Just as the lunacy of 'talking to yourself' has now become a highly recommended technique of intrapersonal communication, even so has the lunacy of 'talking to your plants' become recognized as an exchange of energy that revitalizes both communicators. (Here in the Bay Area of California you are thought taciturn if you do not talk to your plant and plants have been known to resent such neglect.) We have been human chauvinists too long, calling consciousness our own, cornering the market upon it, setting ourselves above everything nonhuman because of our 'higher awareness.' Chimpanzees and porpoises more and more frequently make mockery of the Crown of Creation we have thought ourselves to be.

To change other people or other entities is not in itself a violation. It is a fact of existence that we do so. The act of violence is in the *intention* to change another. The cultural manifestation of that intention makes up the pages of our history books. It is the *conquest* model of human interaction. More significantly, it is the *conversion* model of human interaction, a model more insidious because it gives the illusion of integrity. In the conquest model we invade or violate. In the conversion model we work very hard not simply to conquer but to get every assurance that our conquest of the victim is really giving her what she wants. In fact, a lot of excitement and adventure would go out of our lives if conquest were the only model. It is conversion that gives us our real kicks; it is the stuff of all our pornography, the stuff of Hollywood, the stuff of romance.

Our history is a combination of conquest and conversion. We conquered trees and converted them into a house, taking pride in having accomplished a difficult task. We conquered rivers and streams and converted them into lakes, marvelling in ourselves at the improvement we made on nature. We tramped with our conquering spaceboots on the fine ancient dust of the Moon and we sent our well-rehearsed statements of triumph back for a waiting world to hear. We'd like to think that much as the Moon resisted us, she really, down deep, wanted us—her masters—to tame her and to own her.

We did not ask permission of trees, river, Moon. We did not in any way recognize the part of the victim in the process. They were the conquered. We were the conquerer. The more 'fight' they gave us and the more difficult the task, the more exhilarating was the contest and the more arrogant we became at winning over them. Many of us have heard it too often: 'I like a woman who gives me a little fight.' While there is satisfaction in conquering, the real rush comes if she resists and then gives in, if you make her want you, if you convert her, if the trees are big, if you fail the first few times to harness the river, if the Moon is hard to get to.

Since the middle ages scholars have been fond of classifying rhetoric into three bands: that which flows from the pulpit, that which is found at the bar of justice, and that which rings out on the senate floor. All three efforts demonstrate precisely a violence not just of conquest but also of conversion, whether it be conversion of the sinner, the jury, or the worthy opposition. Preachers, lawyers, and politicians may congratulate themselves that they are men of reason who have chosen civilized discourse above fighting. Yet where the intent is to change another, the difference between a persuasive metaphor and a violent artillery attack is obscure and certainly one of degree rather than of kind. Our rational discourse, presumably such an improvement over war and barbarism, turns out to be in itself a subtle form of Might Makes Right. Speech and rhetoric teachers have been training a competent breed of weapons specialists who are skilled in emotional manoeuvers, expert in intellectual logistics and, in their attack upon attitude and belief systems, blissfully ignorant of their violation of nature or her processes.

Somewhere in a dark corner of human history we made a serious evolutionary blunder. We altered ourselves from a species in tune with the Earth, with our home, into a species that began ruthlessly to control and convert its environment. At that point, when we began to seek to change any other entity, we violated the integrity of that person or thing and our own integrity as well.

Political speculations about the origin of alienation, theological agitations about the beginning of evil, psychological ruminations about the birth of 'the other' and philosophical explorations of the mind-body split—all have shown us the futility of trying to determine the cause of our violence as a species. Was it our coming to consciousness? Or some leap from our subjective ego to the recognition of another subjective ego? The drive to civilization or the drive to death through civilization? Perhaps the creative urge or the birth of language itself or the first time someone claimed private property? Did it occur when men discovered that they had some role in conception and got so carried away that they organized the patriarchy? Is the violence inherent in the nature of the human being, a product of the natural urge to compete or of the hierarchical mindset? Did it occur from something so practical as the planning ahead for survival through the storing of surplus goods? Or from something so ontological as the realization of death and the planning ahead against its occurrence?

The evidence is plain that somehow our energy has gone haywire, that we are riding roughshod over the biosphere, that we have no species consciousness, that we produce, reproduce and consume in a constantly expanding pattern that is rapidly depleting our natural resources and driving us to the destruction of each other and of the planet which sustains us. 'Rape of the Earth' is not simply a metaphor, or if it is a metaphor it is one so strong that it brings into sharp relief both the reality of the female/male relationship in Western culture and the separation of ourselves as a species from the original source of our being. The earth seems now to be giving us clear and unmistakeable signals that she will not endure our rule over her much longer, that we are a renegade civilization, a dying civilization which may have passed up its opportunity for survival. We need to come to a halt and reawaken ourselves, to refresh and resource ourselves at the lost wells of our own origin. Already it may be too late.

II

To pose the value question, 'Can it be an act of integrity to seek to change another person or another entity?' is to open the door to alternatives to persuasion. I will explore here a non-persuasive notion of communication and show how I believe our discipline has been moving toward that notion in the recent past. Finally I will draw connections between recent understandings of communication and the womanization of culture that I believe is necessary for the survival of the planet.

If we are not to attempt to change our world, then is the alternative to sit forever in a quiet and desperate passivity? Must we choose between being an invader, a violent persuader, and a patient Griselda twiddling our thumbs and curbing our energy in the hope that some miraculous process will do it all for us? Surely it is of value to seek to alter injustices, to change oppressive societal institutions. Is there a way to relate to each other, to other entities, in acts that participate in the changing of our world but which do not themselves recapitulate our heritage of violence? Is there a difference between wanting circumstances to change and wanting to change circumstances?

Mao Tse Tung in his essay 'On Contradiction' gave us the metaphor of the egg and the stone. No one can change an egg into a chicken. If, however, there is the potential in the egg to be a chicken—what Mao called the 'internal basis for change'—then there is the likelihood that in the right environment (moisture, temperature, the 'external conditions for change') the egg will hatch. A stone, on the other hand, has no internal basis for hatching into a chicken and an eternity of sitting in the proper conditions of moisture and temperature will not make possible its transformation into a chicken.

If we think of communicative acts not as attempts to change others or even as attempts to inform or to help them, then perhaps we can understand Mao's metaphor. Communication can be a deliberate creation or co-creation of an atmosphere in which people or things, if and only if they have the internal basis for change, may change themselves; it can be a milieu in which those who are ready to be persuaded may persuade themselves, may choose to hear or choose to learn. With this understanding we can begin to operate differently in all communicative circumstances, particularly those wherein *learning* and *conflict encounter* take place.

What might take place in the learning circumstance could be best understood as a mutual generation of energy for purposes of growth; what would take place in the conflict encounter is best described for lack of a better word as dialogue. In either case, persons entering the interaction would be certain

(1) that no intent to enlighten or to persuade would be made but rather that each party would seek to contribute to an atmosphere in which change for both/all parties can take place;

(2) that there are differences among those who participate—in the case of learning, differences of degree and quality of knowing specific subject matter, and in the case of conflict genuine disagreements between/among people;

(3) that though there are differences, the persons involved feel equal in power to each other;

(4) that communication is a difficult achievement, something to be worked at, since the odds are great that moments of miscommunication will outnumber moments of communication;

(5) that each participant is willing on the deepest level to yield her/his position entirely to the other(s).

If the circumstance is one of learning then instructors must genuinely prepare to learn, prepare to be changed with students in the mutually created setting. As we observe from changes already taking place in classrooms across the country, the number of words spoken by any one individual—teacher or student—in such an atmosphere is far less important than the manner and the intentionality with which they speak the words.

If the circumstance is one of conflict, then all that we are already learning about dialogue comes into play. Somehow the mind-body split experienced by rhetoric or speech communication as well as by other disciplines will have to be bridged in the process of dialogue. Some unity will have to occur there of personality differences with the principled advocacy of positions; some techniques of interpersonal clarification and openness will have to blend with the use of good reason in the controversy. We functioned from Socrates to the 1950s with reason as our standard; then, with the advent of sensitivity training and small group communication, we seemed almost to exchange the tyranny of the mind for the tyranny of the emotions. What we now know is that, in any conflict circumstance, there are positions and arguments, but there are as well the multi-levelled dynamics of human personalities at work.

It is at this point, when we address emerging notions of learning and dialogue that we appreciate the recent changes of the rhetoric and public address that have occurred within the discipline of rhetoric and public address. It is fair to say that until the 1950s speech-making has been practiced and taught on the conquest/conversion model, on a very male chauvinist model, one that not only implied but explicitly assumed that all the power was in the speaker, just as we believed at one point in history that all power was in the sperm. He stood before the crowd, one hero, one persuader. He believed that he did it all, and unfortunately, his audience believed the same thing. His was the message, his the act of converting his hearers; his was the enlightened truth which sought a womb/audience in which to deposit itself and grow. Little attention was paid to the listener, and even less to the circumstances or the environment of the persuasive process.

In the last decades, however, the listener has come into her own. By drawing our attention away from the masses transfixed by one orator and toward the interactions that transpire in our daily lives, by sitting more often in groups or in dyads and less often in lectures, we have come to realize that in its more common and more natural setting communication does not have to be an invasion of enemy territory but can at least be a two-way street. We have begun to admit the listener's presence, perhaps even her participation in the speechmaking process. And the field of *rhetoric*—persuasion—has broadened into the field of *communication,* a change which in itself is a symptom of the change in our concerns.

In recent semantic and communication theory we move closer to the concern for environment, for climate; particularly is this true in a general systems approach and transactional models. Though the term is only beginning to be used, it is important that the whole communication environment be understood as a *matrix,* a womb. A matrix is that within which or from which something takes form or begins. A matrix 'produces' a seed (like the sperm) only we call it an egg. Yet the matrix is not simply a generating substance. It is also a nurturing substance, the atmosphere in which growth and change take place. In terms of communication it is an atmosphere in which meanings are generated and nurtured. We could even say, 'The meaning is the matrix.'

It is a new thing that we do in this century: to turn again toward the wholeness of the communication process instead of separating ourselves out from it, to think in terms of an organic atmosphere that is the source of meanings instead of waiting for an outsider who will, like a god, give us the meanings. We are perhaps on the brink of understanding that we do not have to be persuaders, that we no longer need to intend to change others. We are not the speaker, the-one-with-the-truth, the-one-who-with-his-power-will-change-lives. We are the matrix, we are she-who-is-the-home-of-this-particular-human-interaction, we are a co-creator and co-sustainer of the atmosphere in whose infinity of possible transformations we will all change.

Modern communication theory has not yet articulated its own process of change. With all of its extensive research into human behavior, with all its imagination and creative models, modern communication theory still is concerned almost exclusively with the how and the *what* of communication, how it works and what its definition is. At best it asks questions about the role of values in attitude change and fails as yet to ask essential value questions about its own intent.

The conquest/conversion rhetoricians of the first 2400 years of our discipline constantly asked questions of value: can virtue be taught? Can we allow a dangerous enemy to speak to the masses? What does a lie do to the speaker's credibility? Should teachers of rhetoric take fees for teaching? They too failed to ask the crucial value question, 'Can we with integrity intend to change another?' But at least they reflected on their actions in the light of ethics. We recall, though, that rhetoric has always found its home in the humanities where value questions are the norm. Modern communication theory participates more readily in the social sciences where questions of value hide under the search for objective reality. Until such theory begins to entertain those ethical questions or until communicators in the humanities challenge modern theory on just such questions, we will be little better off than with our commitment to the old conquest/conversion assumptions.

In what is called the second wave of feminism, the rise of the woman's movement in the sixties and seventies of this century, there are threads that may connect a society presently violent to a nonviolent past and to a nonviolent future. One of the threads is an understanding of communication as essentially the womanlike process we have been describing.

Feminism is at the very least the rejection of the conquest/conversion model of interaction and the development of new forms of relationship which allow for wholeness in the individual and differences among people and entities. At the same time it means some sense of how that infinite variety thrives within a unity. Feminism is an ideology of change which rises out of the experiences of women, out of the experiences of our bodies, our experiences of our conditioning both in our individual lives and over the centuries.

It is important to the field of communication that biologically and historically we women have been thought of and think of ourselves as receptacles, as listeners, as hearers, as holders, nurturers, as matrices, as environments and creators of environments. It is important to the field of communication that, though we women now begin to discover what the suppression of our violence has meant to us, violence has been associated almost exclusively with men in our culture. The change in the discipline of speech from the concentration on speaker/conqueror to an interest in atmosphere, in listening, in receiving, in a collective rather than in a competitive mode—that change suggests the womanization of that discipline.

Many of us in the speech field, women and men alike, will be uncomfortable with that idea: that communication, like the rest of the culture, must be womanized, that in order to be authentic, in order to be nonviolent communicators, we must all become more like women. We have all learned that though women are okay they are somehow lesser human beings. It is a blow to the ego to suggest that we may be like a woman. It will be hard for men to think of changing because never having been environments they need lots of practice in becoming so. It will be hard for women in the field to think of changing because though we have been environments, we've spent most of our professional careers trying not to be so, trying not to be women, trying instead to scale ourselves to the conquest/conversion model of the speechmaker, the speech teacher.

We have all diligently studied our Aristotle and learned how to persuade others, how to enlighten them. We have all enjoyed the rush of power that has come with that. How can we forsake all this and think of ourselves not as bearers of great messages but as vessels out of whose variety messages will emerge? We have been practising conquer-and-convert for centuries, struggling for survival in a self-perpetuating system of violence and power conflicts. There is reason, good reason, for us to be uncomfortable with such a 'weak' and 'yielding' model of communication. There is reason enough to be insecure about giving up our desire to change others since our entire identity has been bound up in our power to change others. When all we've done for centuries is to penetrate the environment with the truth we've been taught to believe is ours alone, then it is difficult to enjoy being just a listener, just a co-creator of an atmosphere. Yet that is precisely the task.

Feminism is a source, a wellspring, a matrix, an environment for the womanization of communication, for the womanization of Western civilization. It calls for an ancient and deep understanding and ultimately for a fundamental change of attitude and perspective. In its challenge to history and to the present social order feminism in this, its second wave, feminism this time around, in this century, is playing for keeps for all of us—for women, for men, for children, animals and plants and for the earth herself. The stakes are that high.

From *The Wanderground: Stories of the Hill Women* by Sally Miller Gearhart. Reprinted with permission.

9.2

The Gatherstretch

Sally Miller Gearhart

"Gatherstretch. Tonight after ministrations."

Zephyr was in her nest grace-making when the message came from Pbila. She responded immediately. "What cause?"

"The gentles want to meet with us."

Zephyr absorbed the message. "Shall I reach others?"

"No. I'm free and will continue to stay as center-reach here. Needing you I'll come back to you."

"Come again if so," Zephyr sent.

"Always." Pbila's touch dropped away.

The gentles, Zephyr thought. They had never met with the gentles, at least not so formally. Zephyr shook off the interruption, setting aside thoughts of the gatherstretch so she could return to her grace-making. That setting aside was not for her a simple process but a conscious discipline. Zephyr's natural bent called her to remain with anything that caught her attention until something else reached out and snagged her. Thus, if she let her natural flow control her, she'd be forever shifting from one thing to whatever else might come along. Or, untouched by any outside demand, she might dwell for hours in the intricate pattern of a fungus growth—totally captivated by it, totally wrapped in its complexity. Either way, she rarely felt in control of her life; more frequently she felt she was a slave—albeit a happy slave—to her environment.

"A matter took me," she often apologized when she came late to an appointment. The hill women, understanding and honoring Zephyr's struggle, made their mindstretches to her brief, except when both they and Zephyr had a clear wish to visit. Usually, too, except when she was badly needed, they assured her that their message was strictly informative and not meant to call upon her to *do* anything. Even so, Zephyr waged a constant battle with herself; to complete what must be done—task number one, and, task number two—to dwell no longer with its doing.

Now. Back to the grace-making. She had been centering upon Seja today, paying close attention to an envisioning of the other woman, noting in her mind every detail of her memory of Seja, dwelling with care upon Seja's temperament, upon her behavior, upon her intentions. She closed her eyes and turned her awareness to each aspect of her sister. She felt herself fill with appreciation. She let the feeling overflow like clear water from a cup. She made a wide stream of the water and let it run over Seja's head, drenching her with respect and care. When she came upon the parts of Seja that she could not like—her boundless high energy, for instance—she addressed them directly, attempting to establish contact with those parts, however unpleasant they were to her. To them she said simply, "I see you and I don't choose to praise you. As you are a part of Seja I offer you, too, the care I send to her."

All the while she worked she was careful not to enfold Seja, not to ask for her attention. It was not a mindstretch that she sought but instead the creation of a gift for the other woman, a gift of love and strength that Seja could reach for in a crisis. Seja had been having a number of crises lately, Zephyr mused, and could use a little grace.

This was the grace-making, the creation of extra attention and love, either toward one woman or toward a number of them. Zephyr did not understand what *grace* meant; it was now an archaic word which some equated with good fortune. It was not always a purely pleasant concept, she had heard, and yet it spoke well the principle that was a part of all their sustenance: if each woman offers attention beyond what is needed, then caring energy will always be available to each of us. The trick, she knew, was to offer the attention only when it came from her own fullness, never from duty or obligation. "If I do not give from my overflow, then what I give is poison," she reminded herself.

There was some closure now on her attention to Seja. She last-held her image of the other woman, leaving final warmths and soothes over her whole body. Then with her readiness on tiptoe for another task, she opened her eyes. They fell upon a pile of broken and damaged clay pots. "Got to get those out of here," she thought, as she moved immediately toward the pots and began dragging them to the door of her nest. Herva and Gynia and Su would be here for ministrations and could join her for the gatherstretch. It would be nice to have a little more room. She'd meant for months to address herself to the stacks of pots, boxes, boards, crates, papers, and unidentified paraphernalia which constantly occupied a large portion of any nest she lived in. The stacks would enlarge, space would grow limited, things would be more closely crammed together and then inevitably she would have to take extreme measures—like hauling it all out-of-doors to be exposed to the weather.

Outside her nest the prospect was similar. Covering the premises were layers and stacks of unused, overused or useable articles and materials, most of which had at one time or another enjoyed the priority space inside her nest. Prominent among them now that she viewed them with an eye to placing the pots were: the pile of smooth stones, each carted with good intent from the river for the chimney she had not yet gotten to; odd forms of driftwood, some large and some medium or small, scattered like sea dust over the entire yard; a hand-carved box of tools, open but gradually being covered with the gentle growth of ground roses; a long bannister railing which leaned reluctantly on the hood of the ancient auto for whose uniqueness Zephyr had chosen her nest site; finally the broken potter's wheel that peeped out from behind brown sacks of walnuts and tiers of abalone shells. Surrounding it all was the infinite variety of all the items Zephyr kept collecting and could not throw away.

As she contemplated the scene with some desperation, she wiped her brow with her handless arm. Then she resolutely hauled out one box of the pots to the pile of stones, leaning them back against the side of the hill toward the sun. It occurred to her as it frequently did that she ought to learn toting skills—she in particular who had one less hand than her sisters with which to move things in her hardself and who, among all her sisters, seemed always to be rescuing things and groups of things from some otherwise wasted fate.

"Someday," she determined.

That ritual word of hers was suddenly surrounded by an enfoldment. When she responded she found Pbila again.

"I need your help in reaching the Outposts, Zephyr."

"Good," Zephyr replied.

"Mostly assurances," Pbila went on. "Earlyna, Chthona, and Egathese have probably roused all those along the fringes of the Wanderground. We simply double-check those on watch to see that the news has travelled. We reach Blase, Koe, Rhylla, Ono, and Christa. Then Arlino and Pru. Ready?"

Though they had never touched channels in first-reach before, Zephyr found that she joined easily with Pbila, a comfortable fit with no loose ends or thin edges. She was grateful for Pbila's strong field, for her openness and her steadiness. As they drew together, Pbila's comfort in its turn reached Zephyr so that the first-reach was a fortunate coupling. They stretched the combined offering of their vitality and their spirit to women far over mountains and valleys, to women at the very edges of all safety. Every hill woman would want to know of the gatherstretch. Probably all would want to join.

In winter, darkness came suddenly upon the Western Ensconcement. Zephyr had drawn a special torpor around the nest for the evening, wrapping it in layers of lamb's wool and a bright spring sunshine. She and her visitors had let the wood fire burn low.

Though it was not yet her bedtime, three year old Gynia had fallen asleep in Zephyr's lap and was now snug in the loft. Even the excitement of gatherstretch couldn't keep her awake. "She must have had a rough day," Zephyr observed as she descended the ladder.

Su was smoking what old Artilidea called "that foul pipe." "She did," Su short-stretched. "She and Shuto waited all afternoon for the bear. It never came. She's more disappointed than tired."

Herva was filling Zephyr's tea cup. "We'd better start," she stretched. "I'll need to touch both of you. I always become terrified."

"So do I," Zephyr said. "It's got to be trouble."

"Big trouble," Su joined. "Come, Zephyr." Su was pointing to the mat beside her and moving pillows about so the three of them could sit comfortably and at the same time remain in physical contact with each other. When finally they settled, Herva was leaning against the center post with her feet and legs entwined with those of the women on the mat. Amid some giggles that were more nervous than lighthearted, the three began to move their centers together, breathing separately at first and then, with some effort, in unison. At least, as they linked their energy sources, eyes closed, they breathed effortlessly together.

Zephyr felt herself vaulted in slow motion toward a new awareness, not simply of Herva and Su, though the first-joinings there had been overwhelming at the outset. She was further aware that most of the women from the western hills were coming together. Probably only those on watch would stay away this evening, she calculated. She stood now in the pathway of a tremendous sweep of power. She was both in its channel and anchored by it. She could not locate the source of the sweep; it came from inside herself, from Su and Herva, from a hundred gathering vessels, from everywhere. "The power of women," she said to herself.

"The power of women," the echo came from all directions. One-by-one, two-by-two, three-by-three, ten-by-ten, the women from the Western Ensconcement channel-linked, gathering together in another presence which was itself created by their coming together. Already Zephyr felt her own curiosity and her apprehension intensify. Yet as each group joined she felt more deeply grounded, more vital, more steady, more nearly at home. She waited with ease for the movement that would bring together those gathered here with those gathered from the Eastern Ensconcement. Then there would be the final movement of joining with the women from the Outposts and the Kochlias. It was the same pattern on a far larger scale that the Long Dozen experienced nightly.

The Long Dozen. The women who had called this gatherstretch. Who were they this term? She made herself remember: Doceturva, Beula, Chelyssa, Three-Fold from here, from the Western Ensconcement; Troja, Orino, Batya, Three-Fold from the Eastern Ensconcement; Nova, Li, Annatoo, Three-Fold from the Kochlias; Earlyna, Egathese, Chthona, Three-Fold from the Outposts. The Long Dozen—long because there was always another created—came together across the hills every evening of their term. They brought to each other for sharing or decision all the woman-matters, from threats of external danger to work rotations or the discovery of a covey of quail at a meadow's edge. From her own time of serving as one of the Three-Fold Zephyr knew the extent of the happiness and the depth of the pain that went with being one of the Twelve. In her head she could hear the gathering chant, just as she had heard it each evening a few years ago:

> *There will come:*
> *Three from disquieted Dangerland's edge,*
> *Three who at work will first see the sun's rise,*
> *Three who at work will last see the sun's set.*
> *Three whose long labors see no sun at all*
> *Rise from the shadows, from deep earth to call*
> *To the west,*
> *To the east,*
> *To the far Dangerland,*
> *Saying*
> *It is the eventide, it is the coming time.*
> *Meet now the three on three on three on three.*
> *Meet now the three on three on three on three.*

Were the Long Dozen already together, Zephyr wondered, or did each Three-Fold come to a gatherstretch with its quarter? She did not know. There had been no gatherstretch during her time with the Dozen. There had been some since, though. The last one had been during the spring when waters threatened the grain fields. Apparently the matter of the gentles was calling forth far more women than the floods had.

With growing astonishment Zephyr felt the gathering rhythms lengthen, the tempo slow to a heavy lazy rate, as more and more groups joined the Quarter-Fold. If this was happening in each of the other quarters then the gatherstretch would be the largest ever. Fear struck her. What if it were too big? What if the combined energy were too great? What vast consequence could occur if hundreds of women inhaled together and then released their spirit into the biosphere beyond themselves? She shook. That prospect, she knew, could be a reality someday. All the women were preparing for that—those learning in the Kochlias, those hiding in the City, those patrolling the borders of the Wanderground, those sustaining life in the ensconcements and smaller breakaways, even those living in the deserts thousands of miles to the south and those gathered in communities all over the continent of whom the hill women had only small knowledge—all of them were preparing for the time when it would be possible to gather their power, to direct it, and to confront whatever murderous violence threatened the earth. Many hoped it would not be necessary, that the violence would continue to be contained in the cities, but all held in common the knowledge that even if unnecessary, such an energy-gathering must be made possible. Now was not that time, Zephyr knew. "We are far from ready for that," she reminded herself. "We don't know enough yet and we haven't practiced long enough. We don't care enough yet and we're still the victims of our own violence."

Then why was the movement so vast this evening? Like a handclasp she felt Herva asking the same question. As if to underscore the question the movement shifted. There was another texture, another taste, another tempo abroad now in the common knowing of the women. Zephyr felt turned upside down. Her head swam in a sea without center. In the distance a cry began, tiny as a pinpoint but expanding as it came forward, drawn down a long corridor of silence. The voices of women burst from isolation into joy. The cry filled the corridor, it fell upon Zephyr's whole history and carried her forward with it into tomorrow's tomorrow. She felt her own voice joining the cry. She gave herself up to it, hung suspended in its swells of volume and pitch. Gradually her head righted itself.

"A fortunate joining." She felt rather than heard the greeting of the women from the Eastern Ensconcement. Her own response with that of all the western women reached to touch a presence beyond the low mountains and over the cool river. Enfolding that presence she touched her own center. "At home," she smiled. It was like slipping into old forgotten boots, like curling into sleep after loving, like settling spoons into each other or fitting together every piece of a broken cup so that there is no sign of a break. At home.

Zephyr was not ready for the final movement into the Full-Fold when it came. She began to perceive all over her body dangerously increasing vibrations. The image of a coiling snake filled her mind; a shortening, a tightening of rhythms, a hastening of the tempo as if in preparation for some outward thrust. But the outward motion never came. Instead, the tightening continued, increasing its inward-moving direction and growing hotter and lighter with each moment. None of the hill women was ready for what was happening. Zephyr encountered now all around her a startled and rampant fear rushing through every one, a deepening vortex of terror encircling the common center of the power that they had sought.

It was moving too fast now, moving swiftly inward and out of control. The final joining, the coming together of all the quarters, was too vast for its speed. The gatherstretch was teetering on the brink of implosion.

Then without warning and in the midst of the frenzy a chanting of words began. It came from nowhere, from everywhere:

> *Slow sisters,*
>
> *Slow sisters,*
>
> *Help us move slow.*
>
> *Slow sisters,*
>
> *Slow sisters,*
>
> *Give us your pace.*

Zephyr heard her own voice join the chant. As it did so she brought her attention to her slow sisters, to all the women and girl-children she knew who walked slowly—with a cane, with a crutch, with a limp—or who walked not at all, the women who discovered wonders that moderate walkers rarely saw and that runners overlooked entirely. Zephyr addressed them now. "Your pace must be ours," she said. "Show us."

Over the rhythm of the chant the roaring madness flashed forth for an instant with a renewed force; Zephyr was certain in that moment that they would all be whipped to the center, sucked in, seared by their own speed, and doomed to spin forever in some internal cavern of paleness-and-white-light where none would know another or that another knew her not.

Then the motion broke. As if some raging buzzing motor had suddenly ceased, a silence smote the air and hung there with relief until the chant emerged again, this time soft and slow, this time with gratitude, this time bringing with it a measured manageable pace for the linking of the power of the women. The colors cooled. The wind eased. The chant became more joyous. Somehow the slow sisters had worked their magic—or, attending to the ease and patience of slow sisters, all the women had worked the magic.

The joining was at last complete. The vast presencing of all the women to each other shifted and turned and adjusted until comfort settled on them all. The presence was finally seated in herself. With a keen awareness of the peril they had just escaped, women from every quarter began to draw themselves now into careful attention. Every quarter drew itself to that same attention. Zephyr struggled before she could bring herself to the business at hand. She had found a vision in the deep returning rhythms of that final joining—or was it a memory?—a vision of a green world filled with laughter far beyond the stars. She made herself be present. The listening had begun.

Drawing her own presence to the center of the gatherstretch, Li, from the Kochlias Three-Fold, brought the question before them. Li did not address an audience but instead herself became a hearer as she wove back and forth in her memory between narrative and reflection, description and evaluation, attempting the throw open to all the women the information that had come to the Long Dozen and the work in thinking that the Dozen had done with the knowledge: how Evona from the City carried a request from the gentles that the hill women meet them less than one week hence; how the place of the meeting had been changed; how certain recent apprehensions among the hill women seemed to correlate with the fear of the gentles, fear that changes in the City would soon affect the hill women.

As Li laid open to the presencing of them all the considerations of the Twelve, the sense of curiosity and concern was gradually disturbed by an irritation. The disturbance rose into the presencing from a number of vessels. It was an opposition, a mixing of fire and water. Even before the discomfort was offered up in any formal fashion Zephyr knew its nature: to some of the women it did not matter that the gentles were men sworn to isolate themselves from women; if they were men then there was no reason for concourse with them. Zephyr was impatient. Such an old story. Such ignorance, she felt. The hill women needed the gentles. Women from rotation could say how much. Why always these purists, why always the moralists? She called herself up short. She relaxed her impatience. Far more than she herself wanted to hear, she wanted the dissenting women to be heard. She sighed, then she moved her own presence toward the center of the gatherstretch.

"I name an opposition that lies with us," she sent. "It's the belief that we must have nothing to do with men. Will you own it now, you who believe it?"

"I own it." "And I." "And I." "I own it." "It is mine." Immediate responses came from individual women in all quarters. They came with varying degrees of intensity. As Zephyr and the others waited in silence more women joined the owning until altogether more than fifty women declared their opposition to any negotiation with men.

Zephyr offered her presence once more. "Thank you for owning."

"Thank you, Zephyr, for naming it." Wal-Kara, one of the dissenters sent.

Zephyr continued. "Before we address the dissent I want to hear from women who feel a special danger in these days and I want Evona to share with us her understanding of the gentles' request." From all around her, even from those disagreeing, Zephyr felt the same desire.

The sharing began—small tales and long tales of separate matters, each not so grave in itself but which when taken together lent an ominous tone to the last few months. Troja catalogued her vain attempts to reach Rula-ji who had intended to stay in close touch on her travel to the desert. Rowena reported stories from the Dangerland and even the Wanderground of useless killings, particularly of deer and particularly the further beheading of does. Alaka repeated the observations of the birds that angry men were abroad again outside the City. Women who scanned the heavens and those who read raindrops or the bottoms of tea cups—any who on any occasion had discovered some danger sign—listed and described the omens. There were more of them than anyone found comfortable.

Ijeme's story, known to those of the Eastern Ensconcement, brought questions. Was the woman who fell to her death testing Ijeme? What changes had she, Ijeme, detected in city routine? There was, as well, a moment of standing-with and affirming Ijeme's grief and her feelings of helplessness. Seja's telling of Margaret's rape caused most consternation; Margaret herself was still being cared for in the caves of the mothers, her madness still often upon her, her silence still virtually complete.

Evona was carefully heard. She told of the closer watches on everyone in the City, of even more security measures, of the growing scarcity there of some goods—particularly luxuries like tobacco—of the increased danger there for the women trying to pass as men. She assured them that Ijeme's escape was not known; she felt that Ijeme's experience was isolated, not necessarily connected to other growing pressures. She recounted the urgency of Fabian, the gentle, who had reached her at her work in the City, how they spoke in an elaborate code, prefacing every message word with some ancient religious symbol. Fabian had been for a long while an established contact for hill women just coming into rotation. She trusted him. She trusted the anguish as well as the urgency that she saw in him.

Rumors were, he had said, that some men had discovered that they could be potent again outside the City, even if only for very short periods of time. There was an undercurrent of speculation among the groups of city men. Most would give no serious overt attention to the information, implying by their lack of concern that though they'd never been outside the City to try it they were sure they'd have no trouble being cocksure there or anywhere else they so desired. Others, more daring, were venturing into the countryside for short jaunts, sometimes taking their women with them to test out the rumors, sometimes hunting for solitary women—like Margaret—who were surviving in the country or in a ghost town. No one could say for sure whether or not the rumors of country potency were true; if they were then it was clearly a matter of rare occasions that it was so; otherwise men would have been flooding out of the cities to recapture the whole earth again.

So far none of the gentles outside the City could confirm the rumors but, as Evona reminded them, that was no real test. The country gentles had long since found it a relief not to be sexually active—that's why they were able to be in the country—and probably could not perform sexually even in the heavy energy of the City.

Machines outside the City, continued Evona, were working no better than usual. Breakdowns were still consistent—planes faltered after less than an hour's flight, trains and autos ground to a stop after short bursts of speed, sails and oars were still the only means of progress over water. Natural-grown food was still a luxury, the chemical substitutes still the standard. Communication with any other surviving city was limited to runners. Horses and mules and other beasts-of-burden still refused male riders or drivers.

Evona knew very little more. In answer to questions: yes, she felt the meeting with the gentles was essential; no, she could not explain the change of the meeting place but she trusted the combined mindstretch of Betha and Mito who had made the correction; yes, she would be willing to be one of those who would meet with the gentles if there were a clear wish to do that. The questions came less frequently, then fell away entirely.

There was a long but very full silence in the gatherstretch. No one moved to center, yet all listened to each other, to themselves. It was a time of assimilating, of understanding the news. Zephyr was aware of raw emotions surrounding her, predominantly outrage and fear. She felt the hot responses of many of the women, herself included. They were having visions of manslaying, of manmangling, fantasies of swooping down upon the City and crushing tall buildings with their feet, uprooting miles of pavement with their bare hands. The pictures were bloody and vicious.

Some women were sad and then angry and then despairing. Some were nauseous. In a few a high pitched terror resonated and amplified itself. Others drew on it, added their own to it. For a few moments they let the fear seize them all. Then, having faced it, they found no more fear to yield to. Silence descended again.

Still opening herself entirely to the presencing, Zephyr discovered more sophisticated variations now on the rage and the fear: grim determination, resignation, lingering incredulity, impatience, wry cynicism. It seemed an eternity that the chaos of emotions rolled and tossed over the presencing of the women.

Then the silence began to part. Someone would speak. Earlyna moved to center. "Do we have a clear wish? Shall we meet with the gentles?" For a moment Zephyr dared to hope that a clear wish was upon them. Then the rumblings began again. "Why do we need the gentles? Let us prepare our own battles." "Why not withdraw from the City entirely? Let us wait here and gather our power. By the time they attack we will be ready." "Let us wipe the City out now. One directed gatherstretch..."

Evona's presencing strode to center in a reassurance. "The gentles have some plan—" She was not heard to her finish. Wordless angry objections replaced her center presence. It was Earlyna who threw herself open and vulnerable into the growing heat.

"I ask for the Regard of Tui!" her opening said.

Silence. Miraculous silence. The remembering of who they were. Tui. A moment for the hope of agreement. A moment for the readiness to struggle, a moment for re-commitment to care, whatever the eventual outcome would be. Gradually the presencing grew strong again. Some unity, some bonding on a fundamental level struck an ultimate sense in every gather-stretching woman. It went as deep as their female nature and spread as wide as their infinitely varied temperaments. All leaned together toward the image of woman-on-woman, women-on-women, toward the sameness and toward the differences that mark any two or any two thousand women. All moved toward the gentle holding of two calm lakes, each one of the other.

Earlyna asked for the First Acknowledgement: "Can we, on both sides of the matter, yield?" "The hardest question of all," Zephyr thought. She looked hard at her conviction. Would she be willing to refuse the gentles? Yes. If it came to that. And that was all that was required of her—not that she yield, but that she be willing to yield. Every woman in the gatherstretch was examining herself for that willingness. It took a long time. It took particularly long for Wal-kara and others who dissented to find their willingness to go along with a meeting with the gentles. Finally the acknowledgement came: every woman open, every woman willing.

It was Li who asked for the Second Acknowledgement. "I am called to remind us that at any moment we can cease to be one body. No woman has to follow the will of any other. Always we must know that we can separate, even splinter or disperse one-by-one, for a little while or forever. We rest our unity on that possibility. Do we acknowledge this?" "No," thought Zephyr, "I was wrong. This one's the hardest question of all." Breaking away, separation, the lack of clear wish in the gatherstretch: it was all threatening, even sickening to her. Yet she knew it was vital. So did all others. The acknowledgement came.

In its ending the Regard of Tui broke into words:

> *I embrace the possibility: I may yield.*
> *I may not. Yet I may.*
> *I embrace the possibility: We may not be together always.*
> *We may not. Yet we may.*
>
> *I may not. Yet I may.*
> *We may not. Yet we may.*

It was Li who opened the way for the return. "I need a catalogue of reasons from those who now wish to refuse the gentles."

The long arguments began. First women poured out to the open gathering their mistrust of men, their loss of hope for their ever being truly human or life-loving, their fear that woman energy might again be drained as it had been for millenia before the Revolt of the Earth, their sense that the gentles were not needed, their anger and apprehension, their pride and hatred, their sadness and care. They were heard.

Then came the arguments for the meeting. Women spoke the loyalty of the gentles, the need for the continuing rotations of women to the City, the urgency of the present, the inadequacy of alternatives. They too were heard.

The to-ing and fro-ing went deep into the night, far into the morning hours. At one moment Zephyr felt certain that fifty women would withdraw from the rest, withdraw and have no more to do with any quarter. She knew from the remember rooms that that had happened on at least two occasions in the past. It could happen again.

"They need us. We don't need them." Wal-kara's impassioned extending was urging. "Let them die if they cannot sustain themselves. We do not have to nurture them any longer. What else has our hill history meant if not that?"

The anger was hot; accusations and counter-accusations raged. A bone-deep weariness spread among the women. It seemed that no clear wish could be reached. It was then that Tulu came to the center. There was a hush, a renewed interest, for Tulu had lived many years with the gentles before joining the hill women. She of them all understood the ways of those unmanly men. Her message lay open to the gathered women:

"I shall be going to Earlytown at the appointed time. I shall meet with whatever gentles are there. I shall speak only for myself. I shall return to my quarter and share—in gatherstretch or with whichever sisters wish to know—whatever I then understand the gentles to want from us. Only I, Tulu, will be bound by my words with them. They will understand that, I will welcome the company of any woman who wishes to come with me." Tulu ceased. No one responded. No objection was raised. Zephyr sensed that little more could be said.

Wal-kara brought herself to the center. "Go well, Tulu. I won't try to stop you. Remember, you don't speak for me."

"I don't speak for you or for any of us. I speak only for myself."

Wal-kara continued. "I ask for still another gatherstretch when Tulu returns."

Li addressed the whole presence. "Is that a clear wish, that we gatherstretch again?"

It was a clear wish.

Zephyr could hardly believe it was ending. Where was the characteristic lift, the usual surge of warmth and love which would carry her back into her daily routine? There was no closure, lots of rough edges. Things hung suspended and without proper form. She felt battered, angry, disappointed, and deprived of something she had been promised—or had promised herself. Were they going to move away from gatherstretch feeling this unsettled, this dissatisfied?

Old Artilidea came to center. Her presencing lay open for any who would join. "There was once an infant," she was saying, "not yet used to the world or to the hurts and aches that the world could inflict. One day, after a particularly hard attempt to function with those outside herself, she felt bruised and bloody, cut to the bone in parts of her tiny body. She needed holding. Stroking. Easy and long. Easy and long."

Zephyr took the vision inside herself. She folded herself into a round ball. She began to cry.

"We bend ourselves around her to protect her, to stroke her," Artilidea's message went on.

Zephyr stroked the tiny child.

"We feel her bend around us. She holds us, protects us," said Artilidea.

Zephyr snuggled into the warm arms, was the warm arms.

The mindreach of hundreds of women, sad and sore, battered and disappointed, hung in the air above the northern mountains where, just a ridge or two beyond, the coast hills meet the sea. They created the presence which held them, held and rocked, held and stroked, held and soothed.

"Take your rest. Take your rest. Take your rest."

Gynia came down from the loft and crawled upon the mat among three sleeping women, all nestled close, all holding one another. She curled up among them and atop them, a breast for a pillow and a shoulder for a blanket. They sprawled together in outrageous tangles, soaking up warmth and comfort.

"Like a kitten pile," Gynia thought as she found her dreams again.

This story was anthologized in *Love, Struggle, and Change: Stories by Women* (1988) and in *Finding Courage* (1989), both edited by Irene Zahava, for the Crossing Press. Reprinted with permission.

9.3

The Chipko

Sally Miller Gearhart

Garland was squatting over a shallow hole in the carpet of pine needles, contemplating the woes of the human species and trying to face her own possible impending death. Shitting was not only good civil disobedience protocol—in case they brought in sonarbowel units; it also called up in her the creatively philosophical, and particularly so now that dying seemed such a sudden and extreme reality. As usual, she had begun her morning contemplation with the immediate material circumstances: the dark predawn sky, the cool woods, the nearby preparations for a violent confrontation, her own present—rather strained—position in the scheme of things. And as usual she had leapt immediately to broad overarching universal concepts (good-and-evil, motion-and-rest, being-and-nothingness) that forced her this time to take refuge in HAMLET. She pushed her sphincter muscle hard trying to force out the dregs of yesterday's rice and sprouts, then tightened it again beginning the series of clean-up contractions. The prince of Denmark accompanied her. " . . . Their cur. Rents turn. A wry. And lose. The name. Of ac. Tion." She uttered the last words aloud and, wiping herself with a sheaf of broadoak leaves, rose triumphantly to pull up her pants and step to the side of the hole. There was just enough light to guide her proper covering of her accomplishment.

She picked her way carefully back to the temporary camp that crowded the small meadow. Beyond it over a rise lay the gentle hillside they would be defending in a few hours. She could make out the slow moving forms of other early risers—or un-sleepers—pulling them erect, bulky shadows trying to tiptoe through still-filled sleeping bags. The group had grown even during the night. The expanse of bedrolls covered the whole eastern end of the clearing and extended itself well into the trees.

As she watched the camp come to life she wondered how many times in this world's history it had been women who had awakened early on the day of a battle and stood in a quiet dawn to dread or hope or remember or wonder. For there were mostly women and children here for this chipko, just as there had been twenty-five years ago when the first whole forest had been saved by such a demonstration. Most of the weave-schemes called for ultimate protection of anyone under twelve, but a surprising number of six- and seven-year-olds had refused to be banished from the action; Garland wasn't convinced that either they or their mothers knew how nasty this confrontation was going to be.

"So are you any good with dogs?" Ellen was behind her, holding out to her a mug of something steaming.

"Okay. No better than the next person. Why?"

"They heard we were spiking trees. It's not true, but they're royally pissed anyway. So they're bringing dogs today. Maluma just found out. Said to pass the word."

"I heard it was going to be whirley-birds." Garland sipped her tea and then set it aside to stretch her back and her legs. "Have they ever used air support here?"

"No. And I doubt that they will. The only thing they could drop that would wilt us and not the loggers is mace bags and even Champion International's not going to spring for gas masks for all those loggers." Ellen flung tea dregs onto the clumps of low-growing feeder grass and rested her cup on a stump. "I don't know what could stop helicopters. Unless maybe the flying furies could scare the bejesus out of them."

Garland looked up. She didn't know Ellen well enough to discern a joke in her manner. "You believe in them? Women who can fly?"

"I'd like to. Wouldn't you?"

"When we heard about this chipko, we sent word about it to women in western Michigan. Never heard back from them. There are supposed to be flying furies down there."

"Well, if there are flying furies anywhere it would be in western Michigan. I think it's one big fantasy, myself. I only talk about them to keep my spirits up."

"Yeah," Garland said. Then she drew her oakheart fighting stick from its six-foot cotton sheath. "I'm not sure I'm ready for this," she mused. "The only chipkos I've done were mild compared to what they described last night. Nobody got hurt bad, much less killed."

"So the bluffs have been called and the peaceful parts are over. The jacks are more desperate. They're pushed to feed their kids. 'I'm just following orders, ma'am,' as he pulls his starter cord. They won't use the battery-driven chainsaws. Not enough snarl. The gentlemen we'll be seeing today got their contrachipko training from the N.R.A. Here, let me show you the routine."

She took up her own long inch-round stick, silently addressed it by name, and assumed an alert-rest fighting stance. She moved swiftly then into a series of quick sword-strikes with high blocks. Bending almost to a squat she established an internal pattern of low reverses and knee-breakers, then climaxed with a wide shoulder-high backhand sweep. She ended in the classic absorption stance with her stave extended at head level in the Embrace of the Enemy. The seducement of that energy drew even Garland off-balance and in toward Ellen's center.

Garland bowed and spoke silently to her stick, addressing it by name, and stroking its familiar smoothness. "Obeah, Fear-Striker, you are wood to protect wood today." She crossed a whole ocean and half a continent to remember the island grove where the stick had its origin. What a contrast to today's wholesale cutting! There had been prayers, rituals, consultations (inter- and intra-species) before any tree could be cut. And when the moment came, what tears, what lamentations! Then what celebrations of the new trees planted in the shadow of the fallen! She stepped behind Ellen. "Once more, por favor."

They spent the dawn rehearsing the stickmatrix moves, those precise coordinated attacks designed to rob woodcutters of their machines without seriously injuring the woodcutter. The stickmatrix was the only element of chipko strategy that could be called offensive. Characteristically it went into action only after a tree (or a person) had actually been touched by a faller or a saw, but its preliminary kata, done in unison at the first moment of real threat, was distinctly aggressive and often formidable enough—like the maw of a great whale, some suggested—to give even the largest saw a sputter. More than one crew of loggers had succumbed before any blow was struck to the vision of twelve women (the Goddess made thirteen, and the sticks made them seem like a legion) advancing toward them in a wave of mysterious open power. It was this kata that Garland practiced with Ellen until dawn became sunrise, and until some unnamed figure refilled their cups with a strong nightshade tea for the last time.

Close to a hundred women and children, with a few men, were exiting the meadow and slipping into the woods over the rise, a peace-obsessed army, moving almost noiselessly to the shelter of an oak grove.

The Weavers, the main body of the company, took their assigned places on the perimeter of the cutting site, just across from the clearing on the other side of the road where a yellow crane, its boom towering upward, sat on a large flatbed. Another flatbed held a Number 8 Cat. On the ground, a smaller bulldozer waited patiently to do its task. It was there in the clearing that the trucks would draw up to discharge the logging crews. The Weavers, in groups of friends, lovers, or families, surrounded sets of trees, intertwining their anger, their passion, their love, their stubbornness. From that phalanx rose a protective shield that extended toward the as-yet-empty road.

A group that had come to be called the Stillers mingled with the Weavers but differed in their task. They were to reach out mentally to the oncoming fallers, calming anger, damping unpredicted actions individual men often resorted to. Garland had once seen a logger, crazed by his thwarted attempts to cut the women's fighting sticks, actually turn his revved chainsaw on one of his fellow loggers. Stillers had saved the near-victim's life in that instance—and perhaps that of the attacker. The Stillers certainly didn't give the impression that they were participating in the confrontations. Usually they hovered behind the Weavers looking tranced-out. Most chipkos, however, and for that matter most operative nonviolent groups, refused these days to do an action without some Stillers, so much had they come to depend on them.

Both Stiller and Weaver maintained maximum flexibility in their positions so they could accommodate any shifts in the direction of the attack. And both Stiller and Weaver were committed to the oldest strategy of all, if it came to that: hugging individual trees, there to stay until that tree's life was no longer threatened.

Moving back and forth among them all was Maluma, a strange kind of military genius, clad practically in boots and soft cotton from toe to chin and wearing from her chin up a headdress of brightly colored birdfeathers. "Though maybe that's battle dress, too," Garland reminded herself. Maluma quizzed her lieutenants on plans and counterplans, carried babies from one parent to another, hugged or joked with her troops, and recited with one or another of them: "I protect these trees. I protect myself. I protect my comrades. I protect him who attacks us. I will not be moved." Over the decades those words had become chipko weavers' haunting chant.

Garland had forgotten that she was going to die today. Instead she was fascinated all over again by the steadiness, the assurance, of these weaponless warriors and their leader. Her own adrenaline was already lifting her high, making her feet move up and down in soft stomps of anticipation. Deliberately she closed her eyes. "Broad. Low. Easy. Slow," she told herself. Obeah pulsed with her as she retarded her rhythm.

An old Yamaha geared down over its driver's shouts that eleven pickups and jeeps plus panel trucks and a string of larger rigs were less than nine minutes away from the west, an estimated thirty loggers. And more could be expected from the east. There was a stir among the waiting Weavers and Stillers. As she stepped through roadside briars Garland found herself scanning the early morning blue. Her mind conjured a skyful of pairs of Amazons flying side by side, a war cry on their lips, descending upon the forest. "Hope springs eternal," she muttered grimly.

Clarion was collecting fighting sticks for the blessing, her actions now shot through with a sense of immediacy. Thirteen women were gathered around her, more than those needed for the katas, but not enough to form a semimatrix. The three extras would probably stand with the Weavers as replacements for the matrix when it was moving as a unit. They would join actively when the matrix broke for any individual fighting.

Garland failed to calm her racing heart as she entered the ring of women next to Ellen, adding her own stick to the ones that Clarion was holding on end in the center of the circle: fifteen wooden staves of varying lengths, hues, textures, and degrees of use, each with stories to tell, each marked in some indelible way with the identity of the woman whose spirit extended through it.

Garland joined her hands to the battle sashes of the women beside her and her voice to the rising incantation. They called up the rage of the earth, the suffering of every beaten woman, the death of every witch and that of her familiar, the agony of burning faggots, the strength of roots, trunks, limbs, buds, leaves, and fruit of every tree from alpha to omega. They upturned the gathered rods and set them vertical again, then addressed their destined paths according to the four directions, eight planes, and seven modes of swiftness. They sang for the moment of Quickening in the conflict, the moment at which they would know that the birthing of victory, however pained, would be sure and sweet. They thanked the wands for their protective power, prayed that any injury they brought would heal around a seed of change, and reclaimed their weapons with a shout that Weavers and Stillers joined.

The sound of the first motor came just behind the last three scouts. "The dogs are in the panel trucks," one reported, drawing her bike behind the line of Weavers. A wave of consternation passed over the gathering. One woman and two small crying girls withdrew to the top of the hill. The women in the stick matrix assumed a first form position standing with their staves at rest.

Trucks of all sizes begun pulling into the clearing. The sheriff tumbled out of one pickup, a journalist with a tape recorder from another. A man in a grey workshirt with rolled-up sleeves lurched out of the lead truck. He took off his Big Tar cap and shifted his clipboard to wipe his brow.

"Who's in charge?" he called out, stepping toward the trees he wanted to cut. When only silence greeted him he motioned to one of the other drivers. "Roy!" Then to the lines of humans standing between him and his livelihood he said, "I want to talk with your head woman. And don't give me any of that equal stuff."

Maluma pulled away from the Weavers and advanced toward him. Growling trucks and slamming cab doors drowned out what they said to each other. Garland saw the big man gesturing toward Roy, and Roy speak to Maluma. Maluma shook her head. One of the men kicked a chainsaw on. A burst of raucous laughter charged the air. "Guys, cut it!" shouted Grey Shirt. The chainsaw died. Maluma turned and walked back to the lines of Weavers.

Grey Shirt raised his voice in the growing silence. "This is your last chance, all of you. We have to get to these trees and we have a court order that backs us. I'm asking you once to leave quietly. Go back home and have some breakfast."

No one moved, including Grey Shirt. Then he jerked his head toward the men behind him and sliced the air with his clipboard. The loggers broke into action. Doors to the panel trucks were flung open and pairs of large fighting dogs began straining on leashes. Chainsaw motors tore into the silence. More trucks heaved into view from the east side of the hill. They too spilled out waves of shouting men, saws at the ready. Now from both edges of the cutting site dogs were goaded into snarls and rough barks. They converged on the human barrier confronting them and filled the morning with fury.

Garland felt rather than saw the wave of activity surging toward her. Then she was lost in the swirl of the matrix as it began its move, internally at first, and then with concentrated overt focus. A contingent of women with spinning wands danced in unison into the road intoning a barely audible hum. Startled woodsmen and their dogs hesitated and then drove forward again toward the matrix only to halt when the women broke into a concave double semicircle of raised sticks: the Embrace of the Enemy. For a second the chaos of barks and motors ceased. The forest and all its occupants stood in tiptoe anticipation. Then in the throat of the matrix the hum grew to full voice, a ki-ay growing louder threatening at last to split the silence. Just short of its climax, one of the fallers shouted "Don't fall for it, men! It's a trick! Move! They can't sustain it! Move, I tell you!"

The spell broke, and with its shattering a new roar of cacophony descended. Dimly, Garland was aware that the chaos sounded different, but before she could decide the reason a sixteen-inch chainsaw whipped up and toward her. She sidestepped, driving Obeah's far end into a soft solar plexus. Her attacker doubled over at an angle precisely designed to let her slip her stick into the brake guard and lever the machine out of his hands. To her left Ellen delivered a kneebreaker to the advance of another logger, this one reaching with outstretched blade to a forward standing juvenile oak. All around her a set-to raged. Men shouted, saws roared, Weavers chanted, dogs—no, there were no dogs barking! That was the difference! Dogs, in fact, had simply stopped moving. They sat or lay in the road in an almost reverent silence, regarding the women. No amount of hauling or kicking could stir them. Dobermans, Shepherds, and Pit Bulls, expensively and ruthlessly trained to be ferocious, were refusing to attack. Garland noted a single exception: one Shepherd was actually wagging its tail and attempting to drag its leasher toward the loud-chanting Weavers.

Fallers who were not angrily and futilely urging stolid animals into action were shouting twice as loud, and advancing with redoubled determination toward the scattered matrix and beyond it toward the oaks. In a shift of strategy, two would force a Weaver from a tree, holding her helpless or at times immobilizing her with ropes while a third attempted a jump cut on the rough old trunk. He would be foiled by another body that immediately wrapped itself around the tree. And again: pull her away, rev the idle, step to cut, and find another body inches from the blade. And again and again throughout the forest.

Garland, with other stick-fighters attempting to stave off the onslaught of men with saws, looked when she could toward the Weavers and their attackers. In an instant before he attempted to cut, she saw one faller trying by force of long experience to keep his blade from nearing human flesh. His face rang a host of changes—contempt, braggadocio, conflict, fear, anguish, frustration, and finally rage and dogged determination. He brought the spinning chain a centimeter from a bare shoulder and then jerked it high above his head as he shrieked, "Get her AWAAAAAAAY!"

A constant flow of chanting Weavers was appearing from nowhere to replace those dragged back from the trees. Those dragged back, once released, flung themselves around yet other trees. Garland found herself praying that the good luck would hold, that they would continue to see no blood, that the fallers would give up . . . that the figure stalking toward her with raised and revved saw would go for her outflung stick and not for her belly button.

The man in fact went for the stick, a wild concentration propelling him onward, an ugly smile marring his face. Garland pushed her breath into Obeah, focusing entirely upon the slow drawing of her attacker around, around, and yet further around until she saw his intent to charge. At that moment she swung the stick behind her, twirling tightly and executing the perfect veronica. The logger lunged and stumbled. Then with a frantic scream he toppled to the ground, twisting so that he saved his chest but not his forearm from the still fully throttled spinning chain. Garland got the blood full in her face, and shocked herself by licking and savoring its saltiness before she dropped upon the ignition switch to kill the motor.

The man was shrieking, and jerking in uncontrolled spasms that flung his truncated limb repeatedly against her breast. She determined to ignore what lay before her eyes: a shirtsleeve that couched a severed wrist. Instead she grabbed the flailing stump securing it against her. Then with her full torso she covered him and blocked out the noise and chaos that pounded around them. Gently she held the unresisting body below her and pushed slow extensions into it. The body eased. Garland eased. She looked up then to call for help only to discover above her the forms of two large men. Without conscious thought she reached for her stick. She stopped her motion as one man shook his head. "We'll take him," he said.

"You need to stop the blood," she said, shifting to her feet.

He nodded. "We'll take him," he said again.

In the rising midmorning light, in the interstices of a two-stroke heartbeat and over the inert body of one fallen in the fray, three people searched each other's faces for signs of understanding. Then one of them, partly to hide the rising of inappropriate tears, turned and plunged toward the jungle of sound where lines were clearly drawn.

Garland had just joined an embattled Clarion and two other sick fighters in their defense of a tree called Big Mama Oak when she realized that there had been a distinct change in the whole encounter. Her heart sank when she saw why. The men, almost as many now as those who opposed them, had begun imprisoning the nonresistant women in huge army trucks so that slowly the number of those who returned to protect the trees was dwindling. Garland could see a cordon of guards surrounding the trucks. "Come on!" Garland shouted, pulling Clarion toward that scene.

They clashed head-on with two men trying to force Maluma into a truck. Garland rejoiced to see that Weaver and Stiller tactics had changed now from pure passive nonresistance to an active effort to get back to the trees. She rejoiced a second time when

Maluma released a wild cry that stunned her keepers and gave Clarion a chance to thrust her stick across one man's Adam's apple, thus pinning him against the side of the truck.

Clarion and Maluma were trying to get near the long bolt that imprisoned the people in the truck and Garland was about to throw an attacker who had conveniently grabbed her stick. But all of them froze like statues at the sound of a collective shout of joy. It ascended from a wedge of loggers slowly approaching Big Mama Oak. Already the twenty or so remaining Weavers and Stillers were being seized and tied. Toward the center of the grove the remaining matrix fought a losing battle against a mass of men who moved over them, disarming them, securing them to trees with their own battle sashes.

Intoxicated by such promise of success the men in the wedge were laughing now, pushing forward behind a confident logger who led the way toward the old oak. "Take the big old one first, Pierre! Let 'em see her fall!" "Watch, ladies, watch. She'll make such fine paneling for your house!"

As Garland leapt forward, large men closed in. As she lost her stick she managed to duck her chin and avoid a neck lock. She relaxed into a low energy-gathering stance and with all of Mother Earth beneath and within her she raised her hands in front of her face, dragging with them the protesting arms of the man who held her from behind. She knelt, and with a surge of power swept her assailant over her head and into the path of another oncoming man, thus leaving her own arms free to receive and dispatch her third attacker. But there was a fourth. And a fifth. And a tenth.

She broke beneath their weight and sank to the ground. With what she knew would be her last free breath she hurled a curse at the cordon of men approaching the unprotected tree. As the mass of logger flesh descended on her breathless body she discovered a chink that gave her a view of the ultimate defeat.

She saw Pierre raise his chainsaw. His company of men cheered. He placed its blade close by the bark of the old oak. He revved the motor and began the slanting bite into the wood.

A rock the size of a fist struck the chainsaw from Pierre's hands and drove it into the dirt. The cordon of loggers was peppered with a rain of human bodies. The men fell back, overwhelmed by a sudden foe.

From out of nowhere a war cry split the air. And Garland felt her burdens lift. As man after man was pulled from atop her, as breath after blessed breath went coursing through her hungry lungs, she craned her neck upward toward the midmorning sun.

The sky was full of women.

9.4

Notes from a Recovering Activist

Sally Miller Gearhart

Hi. I'm Sally, and I'm an activist. In my time I've taken to the streets for feminism, lesbian/gay/bisexual pride, civil rights, sexual freedom, disability dignity, AIDS education, peace, jobs, justice, nonhuman animals, Central American solidarity, clean air, Jesse Jackson, the constitution, the redwoods, and the union. I've marched and rallied and picketed, raged and wept and threatened, crusaded and persuaded and brigaded. Even now when I hear chants or songs or the rasp of a bullhorn, my heart leaps up and I have to hold myself back from donning my old Kangaroos (with the zip pocket for a key and a quarter) and stepping into the action. Sometimes I can't resist. Sometimes one chorus of "Union Maid" or the sight of a rainbow banner or the exhilaration of many-colored many-abled many-aged people with arms and bodies entwined is enough to sweep me right out of retirement and back into the streets. It's particularly hard to stay away from a debate or a confrontation, any situation where the adrenaline is bound to be high and violence a distinct possibility. Activism is still for me very heady stuff, a keen sweet poison.

But I'm giving it up. Cold turkey. I'm not going to be an activist anymore. Don't mistake me: I feel more passionately than ever about issues of justice and peace and environmental health. And I do still backslide occasionally into speaking out or letter writing—just so I can get a good night's sleep, I tell myself. But I'm going about my life in a different way—a way, in fact, that I've scorned for 25 years. It's less effort *[lazier?]*. And more detached *[plain old don't-care-ism?]*. And it fairly reeks of Pollyanna-individualism. *[I'm beyond rescue, I'm afraid, having already dropped into the abyss of New Age metaphysics.]*

I'm approaching daily encounters with totally different assumptions. First, I'm assuming that *trying to change other people doesn't work*, that such agitation only muddies the waters and usually makes me feel rotten, particularly when I fail; second, I'm assuming that *cleaning up my own act is the best contribution I can make to any cause*; third, I'm assuming that *what I put out into the world returns to me in like quantity*. *["Oh please, Gearhart, spare me," I'd have said to myself a year ago.]* I'm astounded at the changes that are taking place in my life as a result of these assumptions. *[Whether the world is changing or not is still an open question, in case that matters.]*

For instance, five years ago when I'd see a logging truck loaded with redwoods or old oak, I'd shoot the driver a finger. He'd (could it ever be a she?) shoot one right back at me and then go home and put a bumper sticker on his truck that would read, "Hey, Environmentalist, try wiping your ass with a spotted owl!" Three years ago, I was a shade more gentle. I would stop dead in my tracks, glare at the driver of a logging truck and make sure he read my lips: "Fuck you, mister." Then he'd go home and add another bumper sticker to his truck: "Earth First! We'll log the other planets later!"

Two years ago, I moved from belligerence to tolerance. That is, I began surrounding the driver of a logging truck with love, affirming his probable good will, and prescribing specific changes for his enlightenment—i.e., I wished on him the pain of the trees he was hauling and envisioned him coming to understand the excesses of the logging industry so that he would vow never to participate in the cutting of another tree and begin immediately to retool himself for another profession. One day, shortly after I adopted this tactic, a hard-driving logging truck ground to a stop to let me cross the street. The driver leaned out the window to smile at me and wave.

These days, I'm going the whole nine yards: I'm practicing acknowledging loggers as "fellow travellers on Planet Earth," as Trudy the bag lady would say, doing what they do just as I do what I do; I'm laying off any attempt to change or even judge them, and I'm trusting that that acknowledgment of our kinship can make a positive difference in the texture of all of our lives. *[I can't believe I just said that.]*

I do realize that "what loggers do" is not benign. And what the Religious Right does isn't benign either. Nor is greed or fascism or exploitation. To nod my head and sweetly acknowledge these atrocities, these crimes against life, must be to condone them. These are things I must resist, defend against, declare war upon, fight.

Or must I? Is it possible to *acknowledge* a circumstance even though I abhor its existence? Are the hard-core pacifists right, that by fighting I am simply using the "enemy's" tools and, thus, enhancing his or her strength? Even more horrifying, what if I keep playing this game (of friends/enemies, win/lose, perpetrator/victim, right/wrong) only because without the game I would have no identity? What would I do if I did not have my crusade? Who would I be? Apparently, Gorbachev told Reagan in the mid '80s that the U.S.S.R. was about to do the most devastating thing possible to the United States: it was about to deprive us of an enemy. And sure enough, since communism quit the international scene, our government has been in a bustle of activity trying to find a new threat, some new terrifying "other" upon whom to focus the nation's fears.

These days, I'm taking a cue from Audre Lorde who suggested that the master's house will never be dismantled by the use of the master's tools. In fact, I'm not even thinking much about dismantling anything. When I meet an erstwhile "enemy," instead of moving immediately into horse posture or splitting the scene entirely (fight or flight), I find myself standing my ground but identifying some seemingly irrelevant third thing upon which to focus my attention. Usually the confrontation is dissipated or made unnecessary.

The "third thing" that I have decided to focus upon whenever I meet an erstwhile "enemy" is *whatever interests or concerns we have in common.* I look for the joining point, the place where we are the same, where we can meet each other as beings who share the experience of living together on this planet. I introduce that into the conversation, and we talk about the thing that belongs to both of us. *[This sounds disgustingly like a version of "How to Work a Room" or "How to Charm HIM" from some handbook for nice southern ladies. But I have to admit that that's what I'm doing. Happily.]* So I talk with the cockfighter about the beauty of his fighting birds; and with the woman who pickets abortion clinics I compare notes about the arrangements to be made (clothes, phone numbers, children, cats) before going to a demonstration; the NRA member militantly against gun control lets me hold and appreciate his Vietnam Commemorative M14. *[And the Klansman? What, Gearhart, will you chat with the Klansman about? Perhaps the Oxydol sparkle of his white sheet?]*

When I can't find any common ground upon which to stand with some "enemy," like a logger, then I ask him to take me into his world for a day or two so I can hear him and his buddies talk about what it means to be out of work in a poor country with a family to feed.

And so I can learn what it feels like to sit in the box of a huge hook-crane and, with my own movements, lift and load freshly cut redwoods onto a truckbed. *[It was an incredible rush!]* Or so I can drive a Number 8 Cat and manipulate the blade as it uproots whole tree stumps and moves around a mountain of fresh earth that once was a forest. *[I loved it. I hated myself and I loved it, all at the same time. Every repressed instinct to dominate that I'd ever had—call it yang; call it topping; call it machismo; for sure, call it political heresy—rose up in a flood of exhilaration at last released. I was giddy with the feeling. They couldn't get me down from that machine for hours. And during those days I understood anew what a huge sacrifice feminism is asking of men: that they give up that power, that thrill. These guys can get that rush every day of their lives, many times a day, in their big machines, conquering the earth, exercising their hard-won skills, doing a difficult job well. And we're saying to them, "Oh no no, you mustn't do that." In that moment, because of the excitement I was feeling inside my very own self, I despaired of my feminist goal: that as a species we can eradicate the will to dominance. More to the point, I wasn't sure I wanted us to.]*

This decision to join rather than confront "wins" nothing, at least not immediately. The cockfighter is still trying to legalize the "sport"; the woman from Operation Rescue still tries to close down abortion clinics; the NRA man still proudly displays the bumper sticker on his pick-up: "My wife? Yes. My dog? Maybe. My gun? Never!" And the loggers and road men still rev their chainsaws or bulldozers and enthusiastically vote Republican.

The story goes that when Androcles was facing death in the Roman arena, he survived because the lion he was thrown to turned out to be an old friend he had helped to heal in the forest some years before. Roman citizens witnessed a joyful reunion rather than a devouring. Is that what I'm doing? Am I just hoping that sometime in the future when the chips are down, these people I'm joining with now will somehow spare me because we've shared a magic moment? I doubt it.

Or is this simply another form of denial, the refusal to see the danger that this person holds for me, for others, for the planet? Is this my "codependency" acting out, trying to please others at whatever cost to myself? Is it a way to feel good without having to confront the real issue? Am I kidding myself that I'm acting from a place of love and peace when the fact is I'm just a coward, rolling over and baring my throat at the first hint of conflict?

When all's said and done, I measure these encounters by my feelings. I *like* "joining" better than fighting or running away, better even than marching for or rallying to a cause. I feel warm and light, sometimes even high, floating inches off the ground. The reactions I get from erstwhile "enemies" suggest they feel something similar. One man said to me, "I still don't like your politics and I'm not sure I even like you, but you're sort of a family member that I'll always protect." When I really let that statement sink in, I am bowled over by its implications.

I've learned a lot. I've learned that it is never *[right, read "never"]* individual men/people who are my "enemy" but complex systems of exploitation that have emerged from centuries of alienation and perpetuation of violence; it is these systems and that consciousness—not the people—that I can, with integrity, *hope* to change. I've learned that my pain, anger, and/or hatred accomplish nothing except to render me ineffectual and to increase the problem by adding to the pain, anger, and hatred that already burden the world. I've learned that whole parts of my identified "enemy" are really my own self, walking around in different costume. And in the moments where we've found some joining space, I've learned that, though I still may not choose to spend time with him, I do feel kinship or love for that killer, that exploiter. *[Where has my rage gone, not to mention my good sense?]*

Is it crazy to participate in some kind of ministry of love to the "enemy?" Am I nuts to believe that if, by my psychic embrace of him, a big-time hunter or an advocate of Proposition 187 feels better about himself—more at peace, less angry, less under attack—then he will be less likely to join the madness of the annual wolf hunt or temper his resentment of "aliens?"

Maybe. I don't know. I do know that last week when I stepped between a man and the dog he was kicking, I was pretty sure he would bite me next. When I said, "What did the dog do?" I learned that he was trying to keep it from attacking the other two dogs that he also had on leash. I could understand that. And I could also see that the dogs were just a bit healthier and better-spirited than he was. I told him how well-cared for and basically friendly they seemed to be. He shifted from hostility toward me to pride in his dogs. We ended up sitting together on the sidewalk in front of the Circle K sharing canine kisses and hints on flea control. He's a panhandler. Sometimes when he finds a free phone, he calls me up and we talk.

I also remember recently finding a shoeshine stall in the San Francisco airport. The man with the buffers and polish told me in one look that no woman should be wearing such butch boots, much less getting them shined. He turned up the hymns from his Christian radio station and, as I took my seat above him for the shine, moved his open Bible closer to his side as if for protection. He was rough and surly with the applicator. I said, "What's your favorite Bible verse" He squinted at me and then quoted the passage about how narrow the gate is to righteousness, how wide the path to destruction. "Judge not, that ye be not judged," I said. He smiled and quoted the Lord: "I am the way, the truth, and the life. No man comes to the Father but by me." I grinned at him and said, "There is neither Jew nor Greek, slave nor free, male nor female, for ye are all one in Christ Jesus." We carried on like this for a good while. Then suddenly his eyes rolled back and he began speaking in tongues, punctuating the obscure words with snaps of the cloth over my boots. When he "came back," I asked him what happened when he did that. He said most folks thought he was crazy but that it was the Holy Spirit speaking through him. We hugged when we parted. I gave him a good tip and said, "Thank you, Alvin." "You're welcome, Sally," said he.

Probably the most popular story about "joining" involves a young American student of aikido who was eager to use his carefully honed skills of inviting the attacker's energy so that that very energy could be the attacker's downfall. One day, on a train in the Japanese countryside, he at last had his chance. Onto the train, terrorizing the passengers, lurched a very big, very drunk Japanese man. He swung down the aisle toward the student, shouting and pushing people into one another. Our hero, the young American, knew just how he would handle this bully. Catching the big man's eye, he delicately threw him a kiss. As he hoped, the drunken man raged in response and started to leap toward him. At that moment, the hand of a small man reached out from one of the intervening seats and tapped the attacker. "Hey," said the small man's voice, "What're ya drinkin'?" The big man's attention was caught. "Saki!" He roared. "Great drink," said the little man. Then, to the amazement of the aikido student, the big man began talking with the little man about how he and his wife used to make saki but now that she had died, he only wanted to drink it. The drunken man sank down into the seat beside the little man and began to tell him, through many tears, about his wife. Everybody was out of danger.

To tell the truth, I don't regret a single day of my past as an activist. I figure that the desire to stop injustices and heal the earth is an honest and an honorable one. It's a big part of who I have been as a being incarnated on this planet. That's why I've been here: to speak out and confront, to crusade and fight, to be involved in those struggles up to my eyeballs. I wouldn't know what I know, and probably wouldn't be making the changes I'm making, without those experiences of activism. But right now, I'm getting clear and unmistakable signals that it's time for another approach. If I can still hold strong to my standard of what is just and decent and appropriate behavior for human beings and yet go about my life with a new awareness, with joy in the process instead of my former debilitating pain, and if I can do all this without creating and maintaining "enemies," then I have to try it.

Just this once, I need to alter our closing: May All That Is grant me the serenity to acknowledge that I cannot change others, the courage to change myself, and the wisdom, in any conflict, to find a third path. So be it.

10

Introduction to Sonia Johnson

Sonia Johnson's work and life are directed to creating and living women's world, a strong contrast to her upbringing in the Church of Latter Day Saints (LDS). Born in Idaho in 1936, Johnson earned her B.A. in English from Utah State University in Logan in 1959 and an M.A. in Education in 1964 and an Ed.D. in 1965 from Rutgers University. She raised four children and taught English as she followed her husband to various teaching positions around the world until the family settled in Virginia.

Johnson's conversion to feminism came with the LDS opposition to the Equal Rights Amendment to the U.S. Constitution, which she describes in the first selection, an excerpt from *From Housewife to Heretic*. Her activism on behalf of the ERA culminated in a 45-day fast before the Illinois legislature and ultimately led to her excommunication from the Church. These experiences convinced her that seeking to end patriarchy's oppression of women by resisting it was ineffective. She turned her attention to envisioning and living women's world as ways to bring the world she wants into being. Feminism shifted from an effort to secure equal rights in a patriarchal world to a total life engagement, a new habit of mind designed to create women's world. The excerpt from *Wildfire* describes her understanding of how to begin to create such a world.

Johnson is committed to questioning every aspect of the world in patriarchy, including relationships, and three chapters from *The Ship That Sailed Into the Living Room* illuminate this process. In contrast to her activism on behalf of the ERA, she finds resistance not only to be ineffective but actually counter-productive in that it gives power to that which is not desired. Her rhetorical options begin with the notion that the means are the end—that what individuals are doing in the present is what they attain in the future. To reach women's world, then, requires turning away from patriarchy and living women's world. Johnson herself has adopted this strategy; she no longer writes or lectures because she believes that how to live women's world is an individual choice. She now trusts in women's competence—they can and will figure out what is best for their lives.

Excerpt from From Housewife to Heretic, 4th edition, *by Sonia Johnson, 1989, WildFire Books. Reprinted with permission.*

10.1

The Bursting of the File

Sonia Johnson

Not long after we settled in Virginia, which was—and at the time of this writing still is—a very, very unratified state, I began hearing about the Equal Rights Amendment. The place I heard about it was church, and everything I heard was bad.

This disturbed me. Not because I cared about the ERA—I didn't even know what it was for a long while—but because I found that hearing politics being discussed so much in our most sacred church services interfered with my feelings of reverence and worship. It was disorienting to me for sacrament meeting to change suddenly, right in the middle, from a religious meeting to a precinct meeting. And, too, I liked the *name* of the amendment. I couldn't help feeling uneasy that the church was opposing something with a name as beautiful as the *Equal Rights* Amendment.

At that time, the church was also resisting racial equality by continuing its refusal to allow black males entry to the priesthood. Hazel had told me with disgust how church members in Alexandria had fought tooth and nail against integration of Alexandria schools. I had been troubled for a very long time about the race issue, ever since I had known Karl at the University of Minnesota, but I had been quietly troubled, with firm faith that everything would work out as it should. But this was different. Women were the issue, and I was a woman. This time we were talking about *me!* Without knowing much about the ERA, I felt directly implicated and involved. And the church would not let me forget, but kept the issue before my eyes, forcing my attention back to it week after week.

I would like to have forgotten about it, frankly, because in being driven by the church's vehemence to study, and growing more and more positive about it the more I studied, I was also growing more and more miserable: guilty about not being able to agree with the Brethren (as we call the leaders of the church) and seriously perplexed about why they had taken another such obvious anti-human-rights stand. I had never been in any serious opposition to the church's policies or doctrines, and I wanted nothing more than to preserve that record to the end of my life. And to teach my children to do likewise.

But instead of lessening, the political excitement, talk, and activity in the church only intensified over the next year or so, until I was in serious emotional distress about the issue. So I was pleased when, in the spring of 1977, it was announced one night in church that after sacrament meeting the next Sunday evening, our stake president (roughly equivalent to a Catholic bishop) was coming to our ward to explain the church's opposition to the ERA. I didn't know this stake president—he was new—but I was impressed by his credentials. Not just that he was a local church authority, which always impressed me in those days, but that he had, some years before, been the Project Director of the Army's Jet Propulsion Laboratory for the manned exploration to the moon!

I was still so naïve, I thought that meant something about his intellect.

So I rushed home and called Hazel and Ron, who were also suffering about the church's anti-ERA stance. "You people have to come out to my ward next Sunday night," I commanded. "The Project Director for the manned exploration to the moon is going to be there to explain why the church is against the Equal Rights Amendment. *Finally* we're going to hear something intelligent on the other side of this issue!"

That was before I knew that there *wasn't* anything intelligent on the other side.

The next Sunday night when the Project Director got up to speak, nine of us pro-ERA Mormons (in a group of twenty or thirty of the other kind) sat hoping that he would help us understand why our church, the Church of Jesus Christ, had taken what seemed to us such an *un*-Christlike stand. But he wasn't halfway through his first sentence before he had murdered that hope.

He had not, he informed us, prepared anything to say that night. And while he was on his way to the church, he had begun to get a little nervous about this ("I should think *so!*" I whispered to Rick). In the midst of his growing alarm, he suddenly remembered someone's telling him there was an article about the ERA in the latest *Pageant* magazine ("That woman's magazine," he called it, which did little to halt my plummeting estimation of the Army's Jet Propulsion Lab since *Pageant*, now deservedly defunct, was a C-grade *Reader's Digest*). So when a 7-11 store miraculously appeared on the horizon, he had dashed in, bought a *Pageant* and, while we were having our opening song and prayer, read that article. Now, he announced triumphantly, he was ready to talk to us about the ERA.

This confession, which he seemed to regard as charming, dumb-founded me, and a fury like none I'd ever felt before anywhere for anyone—to say nothing of in church and for a church official—began to boil up inside me. On my recommendation my friends had driven an hour to get to this meeting. In our small pro-ERA group alone, there were three doctorates and three master's degrees, and *Pageant!* Really! *Pageant* magazine. Such an insult, and not only to us. It was a slur on the mind of every person in that room, none of whom was feebleminded.

Looking incredulously at the bland, empty, smiling face of the Project Director, I knew the answer to the biblical question: "Which of you, if your child asked for bread, would give her a stone?" The answer was, "My church leaders." We had come hungering and thirsting for help, for a reason to believe that the leaders of our church were inspired, for a reason not to have to become renegades. We had come asking for thoughtful answers, for good sense, for concern, for comfort. And he had given us a stone. We had brought him our pain and our longing to believe, and he had given us *Pageant*.

In all our asking of church leaders since, the women and men of the church who by the thousands are troubled by the church's anti-female activity have systematically been given stones.

As I watched him I realized that if he had been speaking on an issue that affected *his* civil rights—*men's* human rights—he would have prepared very thoroughly indeed. But like all other leaders of the church with whom I have spoken or whose words I have read or heard since, he obviously considered women's issues so trivial, so peripheral, that he did not feel any need to inform himself about them before going forth to teach and work against them. Women's problems do not need to be taken seriously. Women must continue to put their needs and desires last for the sake of the kingdom, which belongs to and benefits men. Women's pain does not matter as long as the institution prospers. In his infinite ignorance and insensitivity and lack of love, the Project Director of the manned exploration to the moon stood before us as a true representative of the leaders of our church. It was a heart-stopping revelation. I began to be in serious spiritual pain.

But it accomplished good things. It helped me begin to free myself from the bonds of Mormon leader worship. Since then, leaders in the church have had to prove themselves worthy of my respect before I give it; I no longer automatically bestow it upon them because of their positions, as I did for the first, incredibly naïve forty-two years of my life.

And few, very few—almost none—have proved to deserve it.

How can I have any respect for them? Men who can not accept that women are anything but child bearers and caretakers, who refuse to see women as full, competent, strong human beings who do not need to be told by men what is best for them but who know this themselves, being fully offspring and heirs of God in every sense men are—these men have not grown to maturity; they are emotional and spiritual adolescents. We may like them, as we do children, but we cannot respect them, because they are not children. And we certainly cannot trust them.

Then the Project Director made his second critical mistake with me: he read the short and beautiful text of the Equal Rights Amendment: *Equality under the law shall not be denied or abridged by the United States or by any state on account of sex.* Although Hazel and I had often talked about it, and although I had felt very positive toward it despite my lifetime desire not to oppose the opinions of church leaders, when he read those words in that hostile room that night, they took hold of my heart like a great warm fist and have not let go for one single second, waking or sleeping, since.

I don't claim to understand the dynamics of that. Perhaps it was like being born again.* All I know is that every time I hear someone describe the born-again experience, I am reminded of the night of the Project Director.

Then, after he had converted me heart and soul to the Equal Rights Amendment, the Project Director began to read the letter from the first presidency of the church explaining their opposition. It was then that I had an experience of a sort I had been teaching college students about for years, but had never experienced personally,

---

*I saved a church bulletin from that time, on which I had written:

Is it possible that
first birth was this stunning?
I wake and feel the fell of
womanhood.

or known anyone else who had. I'd even begun to think only characters in books had epiphanies—but I was wrong, because I had one that night, and I don't recommend it as a way to come into the women's movement. Far better to move slowly, if you can, an inch at a time, getting used to it, as you would to very cold, very invigorating water.

I say an epiphany because it was a profoundly enlightening and spiritual experience, but I don't think there was anything supernatural about it. I can explain it best by analogy.

All day and all night, as long as we are sentient beings, each of us is bombarded constantly by stimuli, countless bits of information that register upon us though we deal consciously with only a few. In fact, we have to be very selective about which and how many we acknowledge or we would soon be overwhelmed. So we select from this immense smorgasbord of continually accumulating data only those bits we need to appear sane and reasonable to our friends, and we file the other bits away for future reference or for oblivion. But though we consciously deal with only a minute portion of the incoming data, the experts tell us that we never lose any of it. So what we have in effect, each of us, is miles and miles of underground corridors full of filing cabinets in which we busily file away mountains of data every day.

Somewhere in these endless subterranean storage cabinets, women have a unique file entitled "What it means to be female in a male world," and from the moment we are born female and a voice says, "It's a girl," we begin dropping pieces of data into it. For some women, this file is readily accessible; they can look into it whenever they wish, and it often offers its contents to them spontaneously. For still others, this file opens only infrequently and is so threatening that it is quickly closed, though the owner knows and remembers what she has glimpsed there. There are all degrees of awareness and willingness to cope with this file until at the other end of the continuum are women like the woman I was, traditional women, deeply male-oriented and patriarchal in our view of the world and ourselves. Our file is buried deep, deep under all the others, and our defenses against its contents intruding themselves upon us of a sudden are inordinately powerful. We, more than other women, fear the knowledge that file contains, so much so that even when we are forced to look, we deny what we have seen, we distort the data to make it fit the myth patriarchy teaches women to live, and we thrust the file deeper, down into the bottom corridor and underneath stacks of files we never open. No matter. This subterfuge does not fool our unconscious sorter. Data about being female under male rule still drops at an alarming rate into that file, and the file grows fuller and fuller—there is so much data!—until the seams begin to crack. We reinforce them frantically (perhaps by fighting the ERA). Finally, however, no matter how strong that file—and patriarchal women have almost bionic files—there comes along the one piece of data that breaks it wide open.

Not everyone responds identically to the bursting of the file. Women who have no faith in themselves, who are totally dependent upon approval of both patriarchal men and women—as is classically the case in fundamentalist church settings—and whose feelings of self-worth have been almost totally crushed, these women must still deny what their now open file tells them is the truth. But in order to deny now, in the very face of the truth, they must distort reality so much that they become ill: emotionally, physically, and morally. Not facing their file data is the way to self-destruction, which women choose more or less deliberately rather than face the implications.

Depressed women, women with psychogenic illnesses—backaches, headaches, chronic fatigue—these women are still acceptable to their institutions. Even insane women are more acceptable than free women.

The woman who faces the contents of her file chooses the way to health, inner strength, and peace. This woman—and she is multiplying until one day she will fill the earth—is a threat to patriarchy because she has faced and accepted the great secret whose discovery is taboo: *women are oppressed and have been since the dawn of recorded history.* This is the knowledge women hide from themselves in that file, and would often rather die, or at least live miserable half-lives, than know. Because to know is to be in danger of having to do something about it, of having to *be,* and patriarchy trains women to believe that they cannot *be* except through men and male institutions; only through patriarchy. That is the great deception, which keeps women enthralled.

That night, when the Project Director read the letter from the first presidency, my forty-two-year-old file, which had been absolutely bulging before, had just been stretched to the breaking point by that very large piece of data called *Pageant.* The seams, repeatedly and desperately mended, glued, and clamped, were trembling under that strain when two more little bits of data fluttered from his lips, finally breaking the file's back. In a tremendous psychic explosion my defense gave way, and there it all lay before me.

The miraculous part of an epiphany is that when the file bursts, and all the file data flood into the conscious mind, they are perfectly organized; they present one with conclusions. I knew instantly what the women's movement was all about; I knew it in my very bones. It hit me like a ten-ton truck. I knew where women were in this society and where they had been for thousands of years, despite the rhetoric to the contrary, and I thought I would die of knowing. It was the largest lump of pain I had ever been handed at one time, and I found myself concentrating during the remainder of that meeting simply on surviving it. Hazel says that (and this is bizarre behavior in a Mormon meeting) I was shaking my head back and forth and saying in a loud voice, to the great consternation of everyone else in the room, "Oh no! Oh no!"

That is probably the moment my estrangement from members of my congregation began, for I was oblivious to them. Finally I was faced with all I had kept from myself for forty-two years. Before that night, I had thought I knew a good deal on the subject of being a woman, but I had only begun to prepare myself to know. I had discovered my true feelings about patriarchy, I had found that being female was the central conundrum of my life—as it is for all females in patriarchal cultures—and I had read the writings of the great women leaders of our time. But until that night, feminism with all its implications and reverberations had never struck my soul. Everything had been encompassed in my head. Intellectualizing had kept me from making many necessary connections. Until ideas touch the quick of emotions, they are only facts; they may be hurtful facts, but they can never be cataclysmic; they can never revolutionize our lives.

I did not want to stop loving the church. Despite everything, I meant to hold on, I meant to endure to the end.

And so it was not until that night, in full view of the Sterling Park Ward, that I came together, heart and mind. I began to be born—not a woman, but a human being. A painful, beautiful birth.

When I reveal the two little pieces of data that caused my file to explode, you may be disappointed and wonder how two such small things could have done such a great deed, but you must remember the state of my file—how very bulging it was, how cracking and straining at the seams, how trembling with the pressure of its contents: how *ready* I was to know.

The first presidency's letter, which the Project Director read, began with a reminder of how the men of the church have always loved us. Although I had heard that rhetoric for forty-two years, until that night I had refused to hear how condescending, how patronizing that language is. I realized that the women of the church would never write a letter to the men telling them how much we loved them. We simply are not in a position to—what?—*matronize?*—them like that. Women are the condescended to. We are the patronized.

The letter went on to say how Mormon women have always been held in an exalted position. I can explain best what I knew this meant by describing a banner I saw the next July as, one hundred thousand strong, we marched in Washington, D.C., for an extension of the time limit for ratification of the ERA. The banner stretched most of the way across Constitution Avenue, and was all white except for a big deep hole painted right in the center. Down in the bottom of the hole were painted two little pedestals and on the pedestals were painted two little bitty women. Way up on ground level you could see the big heavy boots of the men walking around in the real world. And down in the hole, one little woman has turned to the other and is saying, "I'm getting tired of this exalted position!"

As Hazel says, "What you learned that night, Sonia, is that pedestals are the pits!". . .

Today, many feminist theorists are fulfilling an essential and invaluable function by providing women with language that describes our basic feelings and experiences and that can therefore unite us. Mary Daly does this in naming the pedestals-are-the-pits syndrome "patriarchal reversal." As I understand it, this theory says that as the rhetoric about women in a patriarchal institution or society escalates, as it becomes fuller of praise, more lush and purple, more elevated, more *exalted*—women are copartners with God; women are more pure and holy than men; women are more than equal: they are superior; women have never had it so good! As this rhetoric becomes more and more elevated on the one hand, on the other, in the real world where women actually experience their lives, the lid of oppression is *descending* at the same rate that the rhetoric is *ascending*. The language is a deliberate attempt to distract women from noticing what is really happening to them in their lives. It is a deliberate attempt to manipulate our perceptions so we will believe what it benefits men to have us believe. Because men are regarded as the authorities in this world (notice any TV ad) and set themselves up as the authorities on women as far back as we can see, women take their self-serving rhetoric at face value and *are* distracted from noticing the truth about their own and other women's experience. Despite oceans of evidence to the contrary, they persist in believing that all is well, has never been better for women, *because men say so.*

We are living in a time of extreme patriarchal reversal. All around us today we hear that women have never had it so good, that things are constantly getting better for them. But why, if this is true, is it that the gap between what men and women earn for doing the same work widens every year? Women made 61¢ for men's dollar in the mid-sixties; it has now fallen to 59¢. Why, if things have never been better, is it that there are fewer women in tenured positions in universities today than in the 1930s and 1940s? Why is it that women with university degrees make less than men with eighth-grade educations? Why is it that of the 28 million people living in poverty in this country, 24 million are women and children? (By the year 2000, if the trend continues—which it will without the ERA—100 percent of the Americans living in poverty in this country will be women and children.* Why is it, if things are so good for women and we really are men's equals or even superiors, that the United Nations reported that though women do two thirds of the world's work (put in two thirds of the working hours), they make—what? Two thirds? One half? How about one fourth, or even one fifth? No, women make *one tenth* of the world's money, and own—not two thirds, not even one tenth, not even one fiftieth, but *one hundredth* of the world's property.

These are not the statistics of oppression. They are the statistics of slavery. Women are the dispossessed of the earth. . . .

Nowhere is this more true than in the Mormon church, which in fact provides a classic and impeccable example of patriarchal reversal, as I realized that night listening to the Project Director.

That night in April, 1977, when I finally allowed myself to see through their rhetoric to the pervasive and profound sexism of the leaders of my church, I was such a mass of emotions when I left that meeting that I am surprised I didn't atomize on the spot, that I couldn't be seen for miles. I felt betrayed, because I had been betrayed, because all women have been betrayed. And I felt ashamed and humiliated that I, who should have known better, had been so easily duped for so long. Humiliation makes one angry, and I felt a fury that I had never dreamed possible. But most of all I felt an incredible sorrow. Sorrow for the lives women have lived for as long as we have record, sorrow for my grandmothers' lives, my mother's, my own. I thought I couldn't bear the pain for fifteen more minutes, let alone for the next forty years, of knowing what it has meant all these centuries to be female.

On the way home I turned to Rick and said, finally, what I had been resisting saying for a long time. "I am a feminist. In fact, I am a *radical* feminist!" I didn't even know what that meant, but I knew that radical meant "at the root" and I knew that at the very roots of my soul I had been changed, that I would never be the same, nor would I wish to be. I knew what women have to know, I felt what women have to feel, to become fully human.

Feminist. The word felt lovely, true, and delicious on my lips. Since then, I have never been ashamed or reluctant to say it. Thank God I finally and truly became one!

Not long afterward, I wrote to a Mormon woman in Maine who was distressed about my position: "I'm a feminist to the core and will be until I die . . . fiercely, passionately, reverently, and totally committed to justice for my sisters on this earth. I feel, frankly, as if I had been born in this time because I have always felt this way—even in the preexistence. This is the right time for me. I feel as if I have come home."

When Rick and I reached home that night, I was ready to explode with emotion, and needing to, and no longer afraid to. If I was going to live, I had to. And soon. So I made sure Rick and the kids were safely in bed on one side of the house and I went over to the room above the garage, locked myself in, and let God have it.

I told him what I thought of a supreme being who had made women so full, so rich, so talented and intelligent, so eager for experience and so able to profit by it, and then put us in a little box, clamped the lid on tight and said, "Now stay there, honey!" I told him that was the most vicious, the ugliest, and ultimately the most evil thing that had ever been done, and that if I could get hold of him I would kill him.

---

*Washington *Post,* October 19, 1980.

I know this is shocking. But I was coming to grips with the ugliest, most insidious and damaging aspect of my enculturation. In our patriarchal world, we are all taught—whether we like to think we are or not—that God, being male, values maleness much more than he values femaleness, that God and men are in an Old Boys' Club together, with God as president, where they have special understandings, figurative secret handshakes, passwords. God will stand behind the men, he will uphold them in all they do because he and they, being men and having frequent, very male, very important, business dealings, know what they know, a large part of which is that women must be made to understand that females are forever outside their charmed circle, forever consigned to the fringes of opportunity and power. Forever second-best, and a poor second at that. I had been taught as we all have, not in so many words but nonetheless forcefully, that in order to propitiate God, women must propitiate men. After all, God won't like us if we don't please those nearest his heart, if we don't treat his cronies well.

Believing such unutterably hurtful nonsense, which is the foundation of patriarchy, no wonder I was furious. No wonder I considered God villainous and treacherous in the extreme. Since such a God is eminently hateful, my hatred and rejection of him, though perhaps shocking, was perfectly appropriate. One of my first signs of health was my beginning to make appropriate responses.

For two solid hours I raged at him at the top of my lungs, screaming and sobbing. I think you must understand that this was quite unlike my usual parlance with God. I have a naturally quiet voice and am not given to raising it in anger, to say nothing of screaming. In addition, I grew up in a family where God was much respected (by my father) and much loved (by my mother). Despite what Nancy Friday says, I always wanted to be just like my mother, and because her most salient characteristic was her deep faith, from my earliest years I had tried to establish the same close, loving relationship with heaven that she had. I saw what comfort and strength she found in prayer, and though I did not understand then why she needed it, that it is one of women's only possible recourses in misogynist society, I determined to have it also. And so, despite the serious handicap of envisioning God as the Old Testament tyrant, which is the way he is portrayed in Mormon scripture and worshipped in the church, I had come to love and trust him because I loved and trusted my mother. And I had also read the scriptures, and knew that people who did not respect God got zapped. There is a lot of zapping in the Old Testament (and in the Book of Mormon). I respected that kind of power.

But that night I didn't care if I *did* get zapped. I figured I didn't have anything to lose—that I *had* been zapped, that all women have been zapped; and I even felt that it might be a relief to be hit by a bolt of something, because what was I going to do with this horrendous stuff out of my file? It hurt so much I didn't know how I was going to live from one moment to the next. How was I going to go from day to day knowing what I knew, seeing so clearly? I didn't know how long a person could feel so much pain and keep from dying, and I wasn't sure I wanted to find out. But nothing happened except that my frenzy continued and my horror spilled out into the night.

The only frustration I felt through the whole wild scene was that my vocabulary was not potent enough for the job. I had led such a sheltered existence that I just did not have the appropriate verbal ammunition; when the best you can do is, "You rotten old rascal!" or "You son of a gun!" it leaves a lot to be desired. But I made up in volume what I lacked in vocabulary, and fought God with all the might of my accumulated pain and rage and sorrow.

When my vocal cords and lungs finally gave out and I found myself reduced to an exhausted perspiration-and-tear-soaked heap, I discovered to my amazement that I felt wonderful—absolutely euphoric. I even got the fanciful impression that up in heaven there was general jubilation at my coming of age, that my friends there were saying to me, "Well, Sonia, it took you long enough! Forty-two years and you're just figuring it out! We thought you never would. But we don't mean to scold. Congratulations on coming around at last. And now don't waste any more time. Get busy and do something for women!"

From *Wildfire: Igniting the She/Volution* by Sonia Johnson, 1989, WildFire Books. Reprinted with permission.

10.2

Who's Afraid of the Supreme Court?

Sonia Johnson

After one of my workshops at the Michigan Women's Music Festival in the summer of 1987, a woman came up to talk to me. She told me she had been working frantically day and night for the preceding two months to keep Bork off the Supreme Court. She had been writing letters and organizing others to write, holding public meetings, distributing flyers, talking to the media, setting up telephone networks—desperately doing everything she could think of. Her panic drove her into insomnia and depression and began to affect her health.

So she had come to Michigan to try to relax and rest but until my workshop had not been able to do so. As she listened to me, however, she thought, "What if she's right? What if it really doesn't matter who's on the Supreme Court?" Immediately, she felt as if an enormous burden had fallen from her shoulders. Her body felt light and buoyant, full of energy and zest. Feeling as if she hadn't breathed for two months, she filled her lungs with clear rain-washed air. The world that had appeared a uniform gray for so many weeks now glowed richly with color. She felt peaceful and happy—and this worried her.

"Do you think I'm just being *irresponsible?*" she asked nervously.

I know there are feminists who would have answered without hesitation, "Yes, I think you are!" But it seemed obvious to me that this woman, by daring to open herself to a seemingly fantastic possibility, had slipped through a crack in her programming and lived for a few precious moments in a free, nonpatriarchal world. I understood that for as long as she could stay outside her old beliefs and remain in the feeling of freedom she would be engaged in the actual creation of that new world. I told her I found her behavior eminently responsible, perhaps the only responsible behavior possible for women at this time in history.

It seems to me that to understand this, much depends on how we view the nature of reality. One of the most insistent messages from my inner voice in the last few years reaffirms the feminist revelation that among the myriad hoaxes of men, the biggest and most basic is what we are socialized to perceive as real. Since every second of my life is focused upon transforming "reality," I have had to think long and hard about that lie.

As I have asked myself: how does reality come into being? Why does it persist or die? I have known, of course, that there have always been voices among us insisting that what we perceive as reality has no objective existence. Though I have found this interesting, I didn't understand how it translated into daily life until I came across the following story.[1]

Several hundred years ago, Magellan and his men sailed into a harbor in the Tierra del Fuego islands in their tall ships, put down their anchors, and rowed ashore in rowboats. A few days later, the shaman called the islanders together and she[2] said, "I'm going to tell you something preposterous, so get ready. Those men couldn't have come across all that open sea in the little boats they landed on our beach in. That means—and this is the preposterous part—that there have to be big, *big* boats out there in the harbor." Everyone turned to look—and got goose bumps; all they could see was the shimmering blue water. "Really?" they asked. "Really," she answered.

Because I am tired of using examples about men from men's books, I occasionally ask women in my audiences to give me another example of this phenomenon, one with women as its main characters. Here is a Lesbian story with the same theme:

Heather and Ruth (not their real names) had lived together as lovers for many years in an otherwise straight neighborhood. Because of their jobs, they had chosen to remain deeply closeted. Even those neighbors with whom they were close believed they were merely house-mates.

For their bang-up fifteenth anniversary celebration, Heather hung a huge sign *in lights* above the front door, a sign so big and dazzling that it nearly bowled the arriving guests over: "Ruth darling, 15 wonderful years together! I love you. Heather."

Heather and Ruth's property was surrounded by a fence that blocked a view of the shining love letter from the street and from their neighbors' places. But that night, their married friend from next door, not realizing they were having guests over, decided to come around for a chat. She walked up the path to the front door, knocked, and found herself in the midst of a party. It soon became apparent that she wasn't just pretending out of embarrassment, she really did not even *suspect* the reason for the celebration. The woman who told me the story assured me that it was fact that the neighbor had looked directly at the blazing sign for 50 yards as she came up the walk, had stood ringing the doorbell directly beneath it, and *hadn't seen it at all.*

Of course we ask how the Tierra del Fuegans could *not* see the ships, with their tiers of white sails sparkling in the sun, billowing in the wind? How could Heather and Ruth's neighbor *not* see their sign? The ships, the sign—they were so obvious, so "real."

But they were not real to those who had no place for them in their world view. They could not see them because reality is what people *expect* to see in the harbor or on the front of their neighbor's house. Reality is what we *believe* we will see when we look there, what we think is possible, what we have been told to believe is true, very strong, inevitable, unchangeable, irrevocable. Reality is what we are conditioned to value, and therefore *what we pay attention to.* Reality is what we are taught to think god plunked down in front of us and we have no choice but to learn to live with the best we can. It is what is called "natural."

Reality, then, is an internal construct, and it is defined and controlled by the dominant group.³ The moment we internalize men's propaganda, their reality comes to live in our hearts and minds. Then, projecting it out onto our external screen, out onto the harbor or our friend's front door, we proceed to interact with it in ways that make it concrete, that institutionalize it, that real-ize it. In order for it to continue, all of us have to wake up every morning and project again what we believe is real out onto our external screen and immediately begin again to connect with it in reciprocal ways. This is how we are intimately and every moment involved in its creation and perpetuation.

The implications of this are that by interacting with a totally different world right now, we can bring *it* into focus. Women's world never left this planet. It is still here, right in front of our noses. We recreate it as we learn to see it and to live in it.

Though a basic lie of patriarchy is that "reality" is outside us, that it is someone else's creation and that therefore someone else has to change it, my hunch is that we along with every living thing in the universe (and all is alive), are the creators of the world and that we daily recreate it from the stuff of our expectations and beliefs, from what we perceive as possible.

The question of the existence of "objectivity" is now before the worldwide scientific community. I have been much entertained by the uproar. For several hundred years now science has been almost synonymous with the Newtonian/Cartesian model of the world as machine—an object external and independent of us, ticking along like a great clock. The job of science has been to discover, describe, and use to advantage the laws by which the clock operates—laws, it has been assumed, that are entirely unaffected by human desire.

Now, of course, some scientists out on the fringes of credibility (but perhaps less and less so) are recognizing that results of experiments thought to be free of investigator bias are, in fact, *dictated* by that bias. That what develops in a petri dish, for instance, does not reveal the laws that govern the substances therein so much as it reveals the investigator's expectations and beliefs about what must inevitably develop there under certain conditions. In short, scientists are whispering with wide eyes that objectivity doesn't seem to be possible.

Sitting on a plane reading this, I smiled and murmured under my breath, "No kidding!" Women, who have always been belittled for our lack of "objectivity," have known in some deep, intuitive, and conclusive way that objectivity was a figment of men's fevered necessity to be in all things "not women," a phantom spawned by their panic to find their own male and superior ways of verifying truth, a way of being in control.

If the genesis of all reality is internal and subjective, all systems are internal systems, including patriarchy. Patriarchy does not then have a separate existence outside us; it exists inside us and we project it daily onto our external screen, onto our harbor the world, and then interact with it in ways that keep it functioning as we are taught to believe it must inevitably function.

The wonderfully hopeful part of this is that reality's being within us obviously makes it very much under our control. So much under our control, in fact, that the instant patriarchy dies in our hearts and in our minds, it dies everywhere. When women cease to believe that patriarchy is very strong, when we stop being afraid of it, when we stop believing that we must do everything through and in relation to men and their system, when we stop thinking of men's control as power, when we deprogram ourselves from the belief that we cannot build a new world without first getting men's approval (trying to get them to legislate it for us, for instance), and when we stop believing that we have to do any piece of our lives as society dictates, then patriarchy is over. The instant enough of us detach from patriarchy and stop facilitating it, that is the instant tyranny will cease.

We are learning how to look, how to see. We are not on our way to a new world, we are there already and must simply recognize it. Though we began by seeing our oppression, now we must see beyond it, see that our freedom is as real as our bondage, and that we can—and often do—live in it right now.

Once, to a group of friends, I talked about how, with my current understanding of my role in perpetuating patriarchy and because of my love for myself and women and all life, I had to let go, to detach, to cut the umbilical cords of belief and feeling. To illustrate what I meant, at least in part, I quoted my friend Sheila Feiger:

> I'm not interested in doing less than changing the world. But I've been in the movement—in NOW—for 12 years. I've carried the picket signs and gone to the conferences, been in the demonstrations, and spoken, and written letters, and watched Congress, and worked for candidates, and done all the things we thought would change the world. And I know that that is not the way to change the world and I'm not going to do those things anymore.

"And neither am I," I said to my friends.

"Oh, Sonia," one of them sighed, "that's just not practical!"

"Practical," I repeated thoughtfully. "Isn't that an interesting word." I thought to myself how for 5,000 years women have been resisting patriarchy in all the ways that have been called practical, resistance itself held to be the only practical avenue to change. Some say that women weren't always aware enough to resist or didn't know anything was wrong. But I say that if we want to know how women were down through the centuries, all we have to do is look at ourselves. *We* are how women have been: brilliant, brave, strong—magnificent. All through history women have known, intuitively when not cerebrally, that patriarchy was deadly to everything we loved, and we have *always* resisted it in every way, overt and covert, private and public, that presented itself—the most creative, inventive, imaginative ways possible (and there are countless ways to resist, as we know) on all its levels. Women have resisted patriarchy with unsurpassed cunning, craft, and passion for at least 5,000 years.

I don't want to be hasty, but it seems to me that 5,000 years is long enough to try any method, particularly one that doesn't work. Women want above all else to be fair, and we have given resistance a fair trial. In all fairness then, it is time to try something different.

It should have been obvious to us, and would have been if we hadn't been so deeply conditioned to believe otherwise, that resistance *doesn't* work. When we look at the world, what we see is patriarchy at its nadir, in its decadence, patriarchy most fully itself, so ripe it is rotten. I think this is not *despite* women's resistance but *because* of it. There are women who want to believe that if we had not resisted, patriarchy would be even worse, that our resistance has been a sort of holding action. But nothing can be put on "hold"; all is constantly changing, as patriarchy grown obscenely, putrescently patriarchal, attests.

Then these women say, "My life is so much easier because of the women who fought before me. How can I not do the same for my sisters?" But men give starving women crumbs to distract us from their escalating violence. They point out how they have improved women's lot. How women can now get men's jobs, can now attend the universities. What they are saying is that they have seen to it that we have a larger stake in their system. It is called co-optation.

What if the women who went before us had, instead of fighting against patriarchy, made a different world? If they had, the heritage they would have left us would be *no patriarchy at all.* That's the heritage I'm interested in leaving behind. More than that, that's what I want for myself right now.

From the field of Neuro-Linguistic Programming comes a useful rule for resisters: "if you always do what you've always done, you'll always get what you've always got. So if you want change, do *anything* else!"[4]

As I thought about resistance being the most powerful, albeit the most subtle, form of collaborations possible, and speculated about the mechanics of it, into my mind sprang a picture of a fortress on a hill—patriarchy!—with its pennants flying, its great bulwarks, its massive gate, and all the men ranged behind its walls being male-ly supreme.

Looking down the hill a short distance, I saw the women, thousands of them, a huge battering ram in their arms, crying "We've got to get through to the men! We've got to make them stop! We've got to get them to understand that they're destroying everything!" They run at the gate with the ram: Whoom! And again: Whoom! Over and over again, for five long millennia: Whoom! Whoom! Whoom! Some women are pole-vaulting over the walls, shouting as they leap: "If we can just get in there, we can change everything!" Through the centuries, women fall by the way but others quickly take their places and the desperate siege goes on, Whoom! Whoom!

With my mind's eye, I looked to see what was happening *behind* the gate during all this and I could see it as clearly as if I were actually there: the men, drunk with adrenalin, are being spurred by the assault to incredible heights of creativity. They have invented bionic metals to reinforce the gate and walls wherever the ram reveals a weak spot, gradually making the fortress impregnable, impenetrable—ah, the sexual terms we have in English for not being able to get through! The assault, by forcing them to strengthen, refine, and embellish the original edifice, serves to entrench patriarchy further with every Whoom!

I should have learned from this image—and from my experience of being a woman in patriarchy—what Susan Horwitz called to my attention about this scenario. "It's obvious," she said, "that resistance is an acknowledgement and an acceptance of powerlessness. And if we perceive ourselves as powerless, presto, we *are* powerless."

Motherhood should have taught me that resistance only causes deeper entrenchment. Any woman who has had teenagers will testify that when kids are doing something they shouldn't be doing and Mother nags about it, lectures about it, pleads about it, attacks it—in short, when she makes a federal case of it—the behavior only gets worse, often very creatively worse. Mothers finally learn that resistance is not the way to change kids' behavior. But being the least credible people in patriarchy, to ourselves as well as to others, we have a hard time believing that we, in our lowly kitchens, have stumbled upon a principle of human interaction that has cosmic implications.

Talking to my friends that day about disengaging, part of what I knew was that if I were serious about "disappearing" patriarchy, I could never again work to get laws passed in the system. I finally understood that men, who own all laws—since they make, interpret, and enforce them—will never manipulate their legal system in a way that threatens their privilege.

I remembered what happens when women finally *do* persuade men to pass laws for us: how women's hard work in California, for instance, finally produced a no-fault divorce law that, though it quickly proved disastrous for them, they couldn't get rid of because it was so profitable for men; how women in many states, by dint of extraordinary dedication and labor, got child support payment laws passed only to see them succeed primarily for men in extorting child support from *women;* how the same holds true for custody laws—men are using the laws we worked for to take our children away from *us*. Men use the laws we get them to pass as daggers to stab us in the back. How many lessons do we need before we learn the simple facts of gender-based control? I have decided not to be an accomplice in my own oppression any longer, never again to hand men weapons with which to kill me.

Often when I say that laws are not worth warm spit[5] in patriarchy, those women who are frightened by the revolutionary implications of that statement often counter with the argument that *Roe v. Wade* is incontrovertible evidence that women *can* go through men and their system to win freedom. I reply that, unfortunately, *Roe v. Wade* is incontrovertible evidence not of freedom but instead of one of the most blatant co-optations, or reenslavements, of women by patriarchy in its history. I go on to tell them how I think *Roe v. Wade* saved and continues to serve patriarchy.

I wasn't a feminist at the beginning of the second wave of feminism in this country in the late 60s and early 70s, but I have talked with hundreds of women who were. From them and from the literature written then, I can almost *feel* the incredible excitement of the Movement in those days. Despite, or perhaps partly because of, very legitimate and healthful anger, women were fairly bursting with energy and enthusiasm. Euphoria and elation might best describe the general atmosphere. It was a very heady time. Every woman I have spoken to who was an active feminist then looks back at that time with nostalgia: those were the halcyon days, the Golden Age.

There were many reasons for that feeling but chief among them, it seems to me, was that liberation seemed not only possible, but imminent. In addition, many feminists had a basic understanding of women's enslavement that has since been lost in a general way: that women are men's colonized lands; that just as the English "colonized"—a racist euphemism for conquered—Nigeria and India, for instance, men have colonized women. The English declared themselves owners of these countries and their people, made all the laws that governed them, and pocketed the profits themselves. Britannia "ruled" by plundering and raping the colonials and their lands.

The Indians, the Nigerians, the other "colonized" peoples of the world (and colonization takes firmest hold in the feelings and perceptions of a people) tried to make the usurpers' system work for them. They struggled to get laws passed that would give them more leeway, and they managed in some instances to infiltrate low- and even middle-level government echelons and to attain a few managerial and supervisory jobs in the industrial/corporate world. A token handful got into the educational institutions reserved for the masters. Some of them regarded these inroads as progress.

But enough of them eventually realized that it did not matter what else they seemed to achieve, if they did not have home rule, they could never be free. They came to the understanding that freedom was simply not possible for them—ever—in the colonial system. Freedom meant owning themselves, owning their own lands, using their resources for their own enrichment, making their own laws. The revolution began with their feelings and perceptions of themselves as people who not only *should* but *could* govern themselves.

Women were the first owned, the first "ruled" people in every race and class and nation, the first slaves, the first colonized people, the first occupied countries. Many thousands of years ago men took our bodies as their lands as they felt befitted their naturally superior, god-like selves and our lowly, animalistic natures. Since this takeover, they have made all the laws that governed our lands, and have harvested us—our labor, our children, our sexuality, our emotional, spiritual, and cultural richness, our resources of intelligence, passion, devotion—for their own purposes and aggrandizement. These have been men's most profitable cash crops.

Occasionally, some feminist objects to my insistence that men literally own women. I usually discover that as she was growing up her family were Protestants—e.g., Methodist, Presbyterian—or Unitarians, or atheists, or liberals of some stripe, and that therefore as a child and young woman she didn't hear with her actual ears the sort of propaganda those of us reared in Fundamentalist religions heard.

I remember clearly, for instance, visiting girl cousins in another town when I was little and taking a bath with one of them under her mother's supervision. As we were washing, my aunt carefully instructed us not to touch our genitals but instead to spread our legs and with one hand repeatedly splash water upon them. When we asked her why, since that seemed a very ineffective way of getting clean, she answered that we had to save those parts for our husbands, for marriage.

My husband at the time was about five years old and living in Wisconsin. I'm sure he had no interest whatever in the fact that he owned some little girl's reproductive organs in Utah. But I can remember the feeling that experience gave me about my relationship with my body, and I can best describe it as housesitting until the landlord comes home. When one is housesitting someone else's property, one does not rummage through his private things, intimately handle his personal possessions. One behaves circumspectly, carefully, respecting the invisible "no trespassing" signs.

After my speech at the International Women's Book Fair in Montreal in the summer of 1988, Margaret Hecimovich, a young ex-Catholic woman from the midwestern United States, told me that her childhood conditioning had been much fiercer even than mine. When she was a little girl, she was forbidden to *see* herself naked, even in the bathtub. Saving herself for her future lord and master, she washed her body under cover of a long flannel nightgown.

Although most women apparently did not hear the words spoken, every woman born gets the message subliminally, repeatedly and strongly, from her earliest days that she does not belong to herself. And the evidence that we have believed it until now has been our acceptance that men had a right to control our bodies and our lives. Every time we lobbied them for the right to choose whether or not we will have children, we acknowledged that men owned us.

The burgeoning women's health movement of the early 70s was evidence of women's awareness of our physical colonization and of our realization that no matter what else we did, no matter how many laws we got men to pass, no matter how many low-echelon government and corporate positions we won, like the Nigerians and the Indians and all other colonized peoples, unless we had home rule, everything else we did to try to free ourselves was meaningless.

So we were saying "howdy" to our cervixes for the first time in our lives, our own and our friends'. We may have been the 17th person to see them and the first 16 may have been men, but finally we were meeting them face to face. In doing so, we realized that it didn't take a man's eye to see a woman's cervix, it didn't take an American-Medical-Association, male-trained mind to diagnose the health of our reproductive organs or to treat them. We were shocked to remember how "natural" it had seemed to go to male gynecologists, and realized that, in fact, men's being gynecologists was *perverted*, gross, and sick and that our accepting them as experts on our bodies—when they had never had so much as one period in their lives, never experienced one moment of premenstrual psychic clarity, never had one birth pain, never suckled one child—was evidence of our ferocious internalized colonization. It began to appear as obscene to us as it truly is.

As obvious as this may seem now, it hadn't *been* obvious for a very long time.

So in learning to examine our own sexual organs, to diagnose and treat our own cervical and vaginal ailments, to do simple abortions, to deliver babies, and in beginning to think seriously about developing our own safe, effective, natural contraceptives and getting the word out, women were moving out of colonization, out of slavery. We were taking back and learning to govern our own countries.

In those days, the movement was called The Women's Liberation Movement, and that, in fact, was what it was. Women were breaking the contract that exists between all oppressed people and their oppressors, in our case our agreement to allow men to own us and to exploit us as their resources. Though we agreed to it under the severest duress imaginable,[6] in order, we thought, to survive, we nevertheless agreed.

Those who do not understand how the thirst for home rule among women at the beginning of the second wave of our Movement in this century rocked the foundations of patriarchy worldwide simply do not understand the necessity of women's slavery to every level of men's global system. Perhaps even many of the women at that time did not fully understand the revolutionary nature of what they were about. But in establishing a new order in which women owned our own bodies and were not men's property, they were destroying the very foundation of patriarchy. Since any power-over paradigm is totally dependent upon those on the bottom agreeing to stay there, men's world organization was in grave peril. If women would not be slaves, men could not be masters.

The men who control the world are not intelligent, as is evident to even the most casual observer, but they are crafty, particularly about maintaining privilege through control. Over their thousands of years of tyranny, they have acquired a near-perfect understanding of the psychology of the oppressed—if not consciously, then viscerally. They knew precisely what to do when women began refusing to honor the old contract, and I am absolutely convinced that their move was conscious, plotted, and deliberate.

They sent an emissary after the women as they were moving out of the old mind into a free world. Hurrying after us, he shouted, "Hey, girls! Wait up a minute! Listen! You don't need to go to all this trouble. We already know how to do all the things you're having to learn. We know your bodies and what is good for you better than you do. Trying to learn what we already know will take too much of your time and energy away from all your other important '*issues.*'"

Then he used men's most successful lie, the hook we had always taken in the past because men are our children and we need to believe they value us, that we can trust them. "You know we love you and want your movement to succeed," he crooned. "So do you know what we're prepared to do for you? If you'll come back, we'll *let* you have legalized abortion!"

How could we refuse such a generous, loving offer? We had listened to men's voices and trusted them for so long—in the face of massive evidence that they had never been trustworthy, had had so little practice in hearing and trusting our own, that we lost our tenuous bearings in the new world and turned around and walked right back into our jail cell. We allowed them to reduce liberation to an "issue." We forgot that anybody that can *let* you, *owns* you.

So the men let us have legalized abortion. Some women protest that women *won* the right to it, forgetting that the legal system is set up to keep patriarchy intact, which means to keep women enslaved, and that men *own* the law. They will never use it to free us. As Audre Lorde states clearly, "The master's tools will never dismantle the master's house."[7]

You know how pityingly we have looked at the benighted woman who says, "I don't need the Women's Movement. My husband *lets* me do anything I want." But our pity has been hypocritical: *Roe v. Wade*, the "glory" of the movement, is exactly the same sad phenomenon—our husband the state *letting* us, and our feeling grateful for it. But, of course, like a husband the men "let" us not because it is good for us but because it is necessary for them. It keeps us colonized, our bodies state property and our destinies in their hands, and it rivets our attention on them.

So the men let us have legalized abortion, and almost instantly the energy drained from the movement, like air from a punctured balloon. Instead of the Women's Liberation Movement, we became simply the Women's Movement, because liberation is antithetical to letting men, *depending* upon men to, make the laws that govern our lands. For the last 15 years we have been nailed to the system by *Roe v. Wade*, our mighty energy and hope and love channeled into begging men in dozens of state and national bodies not to pare away cent by cent the truly miserable allowance they promised us for abortions for poor women.

If we hadn't trusted them again, if we had kept on going in the direction we were headed, with the same time and money and energy we have since expended on groveling, we could by this time have had a woman on every block in every city and town who is an expert on contraceptives, women's health, birthing, and abortion. We could have educated the women of this country in countless creative ways about their bodies and their right to rule them. We would have learned how to govern ourselves, discovering a whole new way for women—and therefore everyone—to be human.

And, significantly, a Bork could have been appointed to every seat of the Supreme Court, men could have been spewing laws aimed at controlling our bodies out of every legal orifice, and all their flailing and sputtering would simply be irrelevant. Having removed ourselves from their jurisdiction, we would have settled the question of abortion and birth control, of women's individual freedom, blessedly and for ages to come. When the Nigerians and Indians got ready to rule themselves, the English had no choice but to go home. Tyranny is a contract. Both parties have to stick to it.

But in the early 70s women hadn't had time to complete the necessary internal revolution in how we thought and felt about ourselves that was necessary for us to be free. Evidence of this is that we took as models for our movement the movements that had preceded ours, all of which were reformist because they involved men. Since our own internal, authentic women's voices were still very weak and difficult to hear and when heard still without sufficient authority, we didn't take seriously enough the fact that women and men are in wildly different relationships to the system. We didn't realize that since the entire global system of laws and governments is set up with the primary purpose of keeping women of every color and class enslaved by men of their own color and class, and often by other men as well, talking about civil rights for women was oxymoronic. We had still to learn how colossally brainwashed we are by patriarchy to do in the name of freedom precisely those things that will further enslave us.

Roe v. Wade was very smart politics for the men; now, regardless of what party is in power or who is on the Supreme Court, the groundwork has been laid. The hopes of thousands of dedicated feminists are bound firmly once more to the husband-state. And we are all a dozen years further away from trusting women and finding a lasting non-male-approval-based solution to the problem of our physical and emotional colonization.

It is time for us to remember that no one can free us but ourselves. Time not to try to get the men to do it for us—which reinforces their illusion of godhood and ours of wormhood and perpetuates the deadly power-over model of reality—but to do it ourselves. Time for thousands of us to learn to perform abortions and to do all that needs to be done for one another in so many neighborhoods throughout the country that our liberation cannot be stopped. Time to manage our own bodies, heal our own bodies, own our own bodies. It is time for home rule.

This is how I want women to spend our prodigious intelligence and energy.

Obviously, *Roe v. Wade* doesn't stand alone; it simply models patriarchy's subversive tactics most clearly.[8] Almost all segments of our Movement have suffered such co-optation. Many women who have been active in the shelter movement for years, for instance, have pointed out to me the similarities in strategy and effect between *Roe v. Wade* and government funding for shelters.

To obtain funding for shelters in the first place, women must tone down their feminism and conform to male officials' standards and expectations. To keep the money, the women who work in the shelters as well as those who come there for help are required to do masses of paper work, the purpose of which seems to be to keep women from helping and receiving help. In some areas, when women are in crisis and call a shelter, before their feelings and needs can even be addressed they must be asked a dozen questions and informed at length about the conditions under whic the shelter will accept them (they can have no weapons, for instance).[9] Many women simply hang up in total frustration and anger. In other instances, funders won't allow discussions of racism or homophobia or of battering among Lesbians. They also often control who is hired. Funders regularly split women's organizations apart by clouding the issues of who is going to define the group, what their work is, what their analysis is, and even what the issue is.[10]

In addition, nearly every funder's prerequisites are designed to keep women powerless, thinking and behaving as victims. One state, for example, requires shelters to use only professional counselors, specifically prohibiting peer counseling. Peer counseling, I am told by women with much experience, is the only counseling that has yet been seen to have any significant effect upon battered women.

Because of the scope and depth of the subversion of our purposes by funders, local and national, many shelter workers agree with Suzanne Pharr who concluded her brave speech at the 1987 National Lesbian and Gay Health Conference in Los Angeles with these words; "From my experience, my strongest urge is to say, DO ANYTHING—BEG, BORROW, STEAL—BUT DON'T TAKE GOVERNMENT FUNDING!"[11]

Trapped in the victim/rescuer/persecutor loop,[12] we continue to believe that men will rescue us—even knowing that among the men who grant funds for shelters and rape crisis lines are many who rape and brutalize their wives, daughters, and other women. "But that's just the point," some women expostulate. "Those are precisely the ones who *should* be paying for shelters!" But we can never forget for a moment that such men will only pay guilt money in a way that ensures their violent access to women. I think we have to be constantly aware that, like other colonized people, we cannot get free, we cannot change our oppressed reality, through the colonists' system.

"Well, then, Sonia," women say to me at this point, "if trying to change laws, or to amend the Constitution [the greatest document for freedom *for men* in the history of the world], and if civil disobedience and protests and lobbying and campaigns and voting[13] aren't the ways to change reality, then what is? What *shall* we do?"

Notes

1. Lawrence Blair, *Rhythms of Vision: The Changing Patterns of Belief.* Schocken Books: New York, 1975, p. 22.
2. This is the only change I've made in the story, but the men changed it first; I am merely restoring authenticity.
3. Andra Medea, "Medea's Laws of Conflict," from the text of a speech given at the 1987 annual Chimera conference and teacher training in Chicago, p. 9. This material is the basis of a forthcoming book tentatively titled *The Corporate Chimera*.
4. Correspondence from Rain On The Earth, Clearlake, CA, January 6, 1988; also letter from Kate Martin, St. Louis, Mo, January 15, 1988.
5. Suzette Haden Elgin's so-apt phrase in her short story, "Lo, How An Oak Ere Blooming," *Fantasy and Science Fiction,* February 1986, p. 109.
6. It is instructive about men that they call the three hundred years in European history during which they massacred nine million women the "Renaissance." The inquisition concluded the process of taming women. Until now we have been good draft horses as Marilyn Frye so brilliantly points out to us in *The Politics of Women's Reality: Essays in Feminist Theory* (The Crossing Press· Trumansburg, NY, 1983, p. 58) and good prostitutes in our marriages, our churches, and our political systems. But now as fear leaves our hearts, the fires of our passion and power have space to blaze unimpeded *inside* us. Our sisters the elements are at last able to befriend and aid us, instead of as in former times made to turn against and destroy us, as all things female and biophilic have been terrorized to turn against and destroy one another.
7. Audre Lorde, essay by that name in *Sister Outsider.* The Crossing Press: Freedom, CA 1984, p. 110.
8. I use war terms such as "strategy" and "tactic" only when talking about actual war, as I am here in addressing men's war against women.
9. I learned much about this situation in a meeting with women law students in Madison, Wisconsin, April 1988.
10. Suzanne Pharr, director of the Women's Project in Little Rock, Arkansas, "Do we want to play faust with the government? Or, how do we get our social change work funded

and not sell our souls?" speech at the March 1987 National Lesbian and Gay Health Conference in Los Angeles.
11. Suzanne Pharr, speech at the March 1987 National Lesbian and Gay Health Conference.
12. Diana Rabenold, *Love, Politics, and "Rescue" in Lesbian Relationships,* Lesbian-Feminist Essay Series, No. 2, HerBooks: Santa Cruz, CA.
13. Women didn't even *get* the vote until it no longer mattered. One of the major characteristics of a hierarchy is that it goes pyramidally up and up until there are only a few at the top. A handful of men—totally behind the scenes—already owned the world by 1920 and no matter who anyone voted for after that, those few men won. As the bumper sticker sums it up, "If voting could change things, it would be illegal."

Excerpt from *The Ship that Sailed Into the Living Room: Sex and Intimacy Reconsidered* by Sonia Johnson, 1991, WildFire Books. Reprinted with permission.

10.3

Ship Ahoy

Sonia Johnson

Sometime during the day that Susan and I decided to have a relationship, we heard a knock at the door. Rushing from different places in the house to answer it, we opened the door together. To our amazed delight, there on our doorstep rode a magnificent ship. No ordinary ocean-going vessel this but a luxury liner tiered with staterooms, looking for all the world like a great floating wedding cake. "Our relation Ship!"[1] we cried joyously in unison.

We could hardly believe our senses, but there it was on our front porch, its fresh white paint and miles of polished brass sparkling in the sunshine, its rows of spiffily uniformed crewmen standing at attention on its gleaming decks, and its regal flags triumphant against the sky.

Giddy with excitement, we stepped back and watched it sail through the hall and up the stairs into our living room where it put down its mighty anchor and came majestically to rest. We walked reverently around it, hand in hand, gazing up at it in awe from every angle. One fact was certain: Neither of us had ever before seen such a Ship, certainly not in the living rooms of anyone we knew. Proudly we congratulated ourselves on having one of the grandest relation Ships in the world, a Ship so superior to everyone else's that we were flooded with pity for the rest of human kind.

How disappointing it must be to enter one's drawing room every day to be confronted by a mere yacht. How humiliating to live—as so many of our friends did—with sooty tugboats chugging about their living rooms. How tragic that even more multitudes existed with lowly canoes moored to their lamps, or life preservers bobbing under their coffee tables. Surveying our glorious Ship, we were deeply grateful for our good fortune.

But unbeknownst to us, even as it was steaming up Second Street looking for our address, our Ship had known it would have the upper hand in our home. It was well aware that from birth both Susan and I had been profoundly socialized to believe that a relation Ship was the one acquisition absolutely essential to our happiness. It also knew that by the time it sailed at last into our lives we would be so saturated with this assumption that we would feel it as a fact of life: Natural, inevitable, unarguable. We would so passionately believe that we *must* have it that a Ship could do with us just about as it pleased.

And it did. The instant it dropped anchor in our living room it began bossing us around.

"Now hear this! Now hear this!" the officer on the bridge shouted at us through his megaphone. "Don't just stand there gawking. Get to work on your relation Ship!"

We had expected this, of course, knowing that serious responsibilities accompanied Ships. So I dutifully fell to and began scraping a stray barnacle off one side of the hull while Susan ran way around to the other side and began polishing the brass.

I waved at her every once in a while, whenever I caught a glimpse of her—or at least when I thought it was her; there was so much Ship between us I could barely make her out—and sometimes I was sure I could see her waving back. So what if the huge hull of the Ship prevented us from communicating with each other? What if we weren't able to be close or alone together? We expected to have to make sacrifices for a good relation Ship, and we were prepared to do whatever was necessary to keep ours riding at anchor forever in our house.

As it turned out, we were never to be close or alone together again. Unbelievably plastic, our Ship changed shapes to stay between us from that moment on. Becoming short and stubby, it sat between us in the car, or flattening itself out, separated us on walks, issuing commands the while.

But stretched out long and thin and lying between us in bed it was particularly dictatorial. "Now hear this!" the officer on the bridge began shouting at us almost at once. "You two had better have sex tonight. Sex is your Ship's basic survival need. So if you don't want it to sail out of your lives, rip those clothes off and start moving!"

Thus terrorized, we made love. Without asking ourselves whether we really felt like it, to keep the Ship happy we made love.

Equally compliant about its hundreds of other demands, we lived together, slept together every night, spent most of our spare time together, compromised and negotiated. At its command, we ceased being individuals and became instead one entity all-too-significantly called "a couple."

We stopped asking ourselves what we really wanted, how we genuinely felt. Instead we asked what would be best for our Ship, how we could keep it happy and safe and permanently ours. Like so many others, we had fallen under the deep hypnotic spell of the voice from the bridge.

Though Susan and I were regarded as one entity by our relation Ship, I was of course always only me. Trapped in my own skin, I was never Susan for even a moment—never thought with her mind, never felt with her heart. So this is my story—as it must be—not Susan's.

Nevertheless, I never forget as line after line of my writing focuses on my experience that Susan was living her own story at the same time every bit as passionately and courageously as I felt I was living mine. I want to be very clear that though I cannot attempt to portray her point of view—except when I quote her directly—I accept its validity and respect it utterly. I think, however, that it would be both fair and useful to say that this was probably not the experiment she would have chosen at this time. She was examining other—to her more disturbing and urgent—areas of experience and facing other very difficult facts. Since her world was spinning anyway, I surmise that she may have wished for stability in her life with me.

But this is only a guess. Despite our discussions, I have little real notion how she currently views that time in any of its particulars. If she were to write her impressions, they might bear little or no resemblance to mine. But like witnesses to an accident whose accounts wildly diverge, both of us would be telling the truth.

For many reasons, both parties in a relation Ship rarely want to investigate the same possibilities at the same time. This spells pain, and there was pain aplenty at 3318 Second Street South that year. It intensified each time I wrenched at the Ship's anchor and Susan strove to keep her equilibrium on the pitching deck.

Though we are each doing well now, in retrospect my heart aches for us both and blames neither. Above all, in writing the following account of my life and thought, I want to avoid the implication that the one in a relation Ship who chooses change in a way and at a moment that frightens the other is somehow smarter, righter, nobler, or more advanced than the one who, bravely confronting a dangerous and uncertain world every day, tries to salvage what happiness is at hand. But neither do I wish to suggest that the rebel is less sensitive or compassionate or loving. People are on their own individual paths, paths that are non-parallel and non-linear. Words such as "ahead" or "more advanced," and "behind" or "less advanced"—linear concepts—are meaningless on the infinite spiral that is our lives.

The most accurate judgment I can make, therefore, is that the time came when Susan and I chose different tasks. What task she chose is hers to name. As for me, after half a lifetime of stuporous loyalty to Ship dogma, I began to stir in my relationsleep. Some glimmering of my servitude began to filter through the blinds of my understanding, some budding suspicion that the Ship wasn't the Ark of the Covenant after all but just a big bossy boat. A big bossy *menacing* boat.

Realizing this, I chose mutiny.

Note

1. I've chosen to make relation Ship two words when I use it as a noun and one word—relationShip—when I use it as a verb, adjective, or adverb. I know this choice may be confusing to others but for some reason it satisfies me. This clarification is for those who would otherwise be annoyed at what they perceived as my carelessness and inconsistency.

Excerpt from *The Ship that Sailed Into the Living Room: Sex and Intimacy Reconsidered* by Sonia Johnson, 1991, WildFire Books. Reprinted with permission.

10.4

Meet My Needs, Make Me Happy

Sonia Johnson

So far every detail, every feature of OurBS [Belief System] that I'd ferreted out, was more disheartening than the last. This pattern persisted now as I looked at the next bit of encapsulated programming: Being lovers means that we should meet each other's needs and make each other happy.

I knew full well by this time—nobody better—that obeying "shoulds" was lethal to integrity. I also knew that obeying these particular "shoulds" was the point in the relationShip poem where we most give up our power. "Shoulds" do us as much damage as any of the conditioned responses in the coupling program.

Like most women, I was bombarded from birth with messages about what a "good woman" is, many of which in my culture are about what a "good woman" wants.

Since a good woman's happiness comes from making others happy, she puts their needs first. A good woman believes that her wants and needs are incompatible with what is good for other people, and therefore that she would be immature and anti-social if she did and had what she wanted. In addition, everyone would be very angry, call her a bad woman, and not love her. A good woman thinks that it is legitimate to have what she wants only after everyone else has everything they want. But since everyone else never has everything they want and it is therefore never legitimate to have what she wants, she never really has to risk in her own behalf.

A good woman has focused so hard and so long on never giving in to "selfishness" that early on she ceases to ask herself what she wants. This becomes such a habit that she loses the ability to tell how she feels and what she wants, and mistakes conditioned relationShip beliefs for her own genuine idiosyncratic desires.

A good woman is convinced that pleasure weakens individual and societal character. She believes that the nature of life is such that, for the smooth functioning of relation Ships, families, countries, and all other institutions, everyone has to do many things they would prefer not to do. She believes that she is morally strengthened by doing these less-than-pleasant things, and is certain that any woman who does only what she wants to do is outrageously selfish, hedonistic, and unloving—a bad woman.

I realized now as I looked at relationShip commandments that my "good woman" habits of thought had caused me to view my feelings as really very much out of my direct control. I saw that I had come to believe that they were externally determined, that other people's behavior and opinions, situations, even objects, were what "made" me feel certain ways. If someone said something unkind to me or I failed an exam, my assumption was that of course I would feel bad. It was simply cause and effect. Having been taught that certain feelings were appropriate—by implication, "natural"—to certain situations and that others were not, this had not appeared to be a matter in which I had conscious choice.

So I felt powerless to change my feelings, out of my own control and at the mercy of every thing, every person, every situation on the planet. Since a large part of who I am is how I *feel*, where then was my Self if everyone and everything but I could determine how I felt at any given moment? There's no better definition of Self-lostness and powerlessness.

Most of what I now know about my power I figured out as a mother. It seems to me that a significant piece of patriarchy's Motherhood Belief System (MomBS?) is that a good mother's feelings are determined by how her kids are feeling and what they are doing. If her kids are suffering, a good mother suffers. If her kids are worried or behaving foolishly, a good mother worries. Only if her kids are happy and well can a good mother be happy without guilt.

Several years ago,[1] [when my third child was seventeen, he and I had a clash in the kitchen one night, one of a great many throughout his adolescence, this time about drugs. He stormed downstairs to his room and slammed the door, leaving me standing in the middle of the room feeling wretched and powerless.

Even having already reared two adolescents, I had no more idea how to get the present one to do what he should than I had had with the first two. The task seemed impossible. I had lived in terror for years—terror that they would be unhappy, that they would do drugs, that they would self-destruct—and doing everything I could think of to prevent these disasters had neither lessened the fear nor changed their behavior. Although the first two had made it through somehow, I wasn't at all sure if or how my actions had helped or hindered those outcomes, and the trial-and-error of it had nearly undone me. I couldn't imagine, standing there that night, how I was going to live through two more adolescences.

Suddenly, I began to feel very angry—in my experience always a first sign of returning health. I realized that I was furious at the anguish I had suffered so long as a mother and the misery that seemed still to stretch so endlessly before me. I felt as if I couldn't wait to be happy until all my kids were over thirty and safe. (Besides, mothers of over-thirty's had told me that their kids were still never safe.) I'd been the best mother I'd known how to be for over twenty years and I deserved to be happy. What's more, I deserved it *now!* I was nearly fifty years old. When had I thought I was going to begin?

Then, thinking of my tyrant son sulking down in his room, and feeling an unaccustomed invulnerability, a new firmness at the center, I thought, "That kid can go to hell in a handbasket! I would be sorry, because I love him, and I'll do what I can to prevent it—but not like before. I can't live his life for him: I can't make him do what

I want him to do. He's just going to have to decide for himself whether he's going to self-destruct or not, and I'm going to have to be happy no matter what he decides."

I felt as if I had been holding his heel as he hung upside down over the abyss. One cannot live one's own life while holding someone else's heel. I decided I needed to love and be true to myself first, do what was best for me, assuming that whatever is best for me is best for everyone around me.

Though I didn't understand for a long time the scope of my change that night, and though I still had much work to do to make that change permanent, looking back it is clear that I was finally beginning to understand the dynamics of how I gave away my power. I was getting hold of a basic principle of power, that when we make our feelings of well-being or security or safety dependent upon someone else's behavior, we hand them the opportunity, even the invitation, to destroy us.

I realized that night that I would never have control of my life if I continued to make my internal climate contingent upon whether or not my children or anyone else outside me did what I wanted them to do. It had become unmistakably clear in that flash that because I couldn't control anyone or change anyone but myself, it was emotional suicide to put the responsibility for my happiness in someone else's hands.

In some inchoate way that night, I knew that I had to hold *all* responsibility for my feelings in my own hands or I would never be safe or free. Since no one can care about me as much as I care about myself, I would always get hurt, sometimes very badly. I felt as if I could not bear the pain of being a "good mother" another second.

Without knowing exactly what I was doing, but for the sake of survival, I detached myself from my children then as sources of well-being for me, took the responsibility away from them, where I couldn't control it, back into myself where it belonged. At the same time I realized, momentarily at least, that I was not responsible for any other person's well-being or security or safety either; that there comes a time when we must each learn to put our own lives first, realize that no one else can or will or should consistently bear the burden of making us feel safe and loved, and find our source of satisfaction and safety *within ourselves*. In any other thinking, disaster looms.

That night in my kitchen these ideas were largely still feelings—strong, internalized feelings of love of myself and a dedication to my own happiness, the basis of power.

With these feelings full upon me, without thinking of a plan, without asking, "What shall I *do?*" I went down and confronted my son. I have no idea what I said; there is a limited repertoire in such situations. Certainly I didn't say or do anything I hadn't said or done a dozen times before. I couldn't have put into words the change I'd just gone through enough to articulate it to myself let alone to him.

The difference was in how I *was*. The instant he reluctantly opened his door to me, he knew the old game was over. He knew he was standing in the presence of New Mom, Mom who could not be manipulated or bullied, Mom in her power. Regardless of what his ears were picking up, all his antennae were quivering with the message that had become a part of my being, of my aura: I had let go of his heel. He knew without conscious thought that whether or not he plunged to his death in the abyss below or decided to change his course was now entirely up to him. I was handing him back the responsibility for his life.

Overnight—and I mean that literally—the chronic disquiet in our home disappeared. My son's life changed dramatically in the direction I had been trying to get it to change for years, and it has stayed changed. Of course, he could have chosen to self-destruct, though most people, given the responsibility and the choice, do not. But even if he had made that choice, I would have been all right. I would have grieved terribly, but my heart's fire would not have been extinguished with guilt as it would once have been.]

That night I had realized that since at any given moment at least one of my kids might very well be wretched about something, If I were a "good mother" I could look forward to continual misery until the day I died.

So I decided to be a bad mother. Being a bad mother meant that I could be sorry when my kids had sad times, but *I* wouldn't be sad. Their being sad was already enough sadness. They could be in trouble and suffer, and I would commiserate and help in whatever appropriate way I could, but *I* would not suffer.

That day I chose power. I chose to feel how I wanted to feel no matter what was happening to others, no matter how others behaved toward me, no matter the situation. I chose not to be, victim-like, at the mercy of external circumstances, but instead to be potent in magnifying the joyful, free spaces in my soul. I made a deliberate choice to jettison from my beliefs the nonsense that it is nobler to suffer—particularly as long as any other living thing is suffering anywhere on the planet—than to be at peace in spite of everything. I accepted accountability for being who I wanted to be.

When I had believed that my feelings were contingent upon others—not only Susan and my children and friends, but bishops, pornographers, legislators, rapists, judges, and presidents—I had to try to get them to do the things that would "make" me feel the way I wanted to feel—safe, worthy, lovable, intelligent, important. I had to manipulate situations in the same way, since I had also granted them the power to determine my well-being. It was a big job and took lots of time and energy. So it was with great relief that I gave up my struggle to make external circumstances yield up what I needed and concentrated upon accepting and using my own considerable power in behalf of my own beloved Self.

So being in my power came to mean taking total responsibility for feeling the way I felt every minute—whether I liked how I felt or not—and for feeling the way I wanted to feel all the time, despite everything. I noticed that the more I lived in this internal security that I knew was power, the more I could allow other women to be themselves, without my having to try to change their beliefs or behavior. Knowing that I wasn't responsible for their feelings or beliefs or behavior any more than they were for mine, I could also be more myself around them without fear of what they might say, what they might do.

I realized that when I wasn't covertly relying on or expecting anyone else to act in certain ways or to do certain things to make me happy—when I chose friends freely, no strings attached—I saw that our loving one another didn't depend on what we did for each other.

I discovered that I liked others most when I was being most myself. This encouraged me to continue to dare to be that way. I wanted to experience the freedom to be myself that only disinterested affection offered, caring that didn't need to control because it wasn't a means to something else, had no agenda but itself. I was learning the truth that I was totally lovable just as I was, that other women were lovable just as they were, without having to *do* anything.

As this change was taking place in me, I tried to articulate it to Susan. "I would love you even if you never got me another speaking engagement, never took care of Noel[2] another second. I appreciate what you do for me, but it does not *make* me love you. I love you because you are smart and brave. I love you because you sit like that in the chair with your foot up and your hair shining in the lamplight. No, none of that's right. It doesn't matter how you look or act. What I love is your *Susanness,* the essence of you that remains the same no matter how much you change." I would add now, "The more I love myself and am willing to provide myself with all I need, the more I am able to let you simply be that wonderful Susan."

I vowed never again to see any woman as an object, as a means to certain ends—such as filling up my emptiness, giving me feelings of security, keeping me from loneliness, or "making" me happy in dozens of other ways. In addition to exploiting women, it was a tragic lie that any other woman could do this for me. I promised myself instead to see truly *who she was* and to be most pleased when she was most herself, to love *her* so that she didn't have to *do* anything to be lovable to me except to be herself.[3]

When I stopped depending on other women to meet my needs, I affirmed my supposition that if I were no longer obscuring their real faces with my projected needs, I could "see" them more clearly, begin genuinely to know them. Because I understood that getting my needs met and feeling the way I wanted to feel all the time had nothing to do with them, when they were around me they didn't have to do anything special or be anything but exactly what they wanted to do and be. And I didn't have to do anything but really see and hear them. When I was in my power, other women's simply *being* in my presence gave me the purest of all my life's many pleasures.

What a gigantic relief, too, to give up the obligation of critiquing other women's political correctness, not to have to decide whether they were being patriarchal in any way—racist or elitist or agist or able-bodiest—and oppressing them about it, trying to force them to stop. I knew that pressure or coercion of any kind for any purpose—even purposes I might perceive as crucial—was always part of mensgame, always oppressive, always sadomasochistic, and could change nothing except for the worse. I knew that I couldn't change anybody but myself for the better. And I also trusted that other women were doing the best they could at the moment, as I was, and that, like me, all they needed from others in order to get on with their personal work was to be unconditionally accepted as the experts on their own lives.

I could only give them this when I felt it for myself, when I loved and accepted myself completely, so I assumed that they could only give this kind of freedom to me when they were also in their power. From observing myself become less and less critical, I knew finally that all critical feelings toward others are motivated by a lack of self-love, by self-denigration.

At the same time that I stopped looking to other people to meet my needs, I stopped feeling responsible for meeting theirs. I realized that there comes a time when learning how to meet our own needs becomes more important than having them temporarily met by others. I didn't want to disable other women by stepping in—assuming the one/up position and forcing them into the one/down. I had to believe that they could be depended upon to get what they wanted.

Part of what this came to mean to me was that none of us is on this planet to meet any other person's needs, including children's. This is not the reason for being. Like rainbows, we are here simply to be. Everyone understands that a rainbow just is, that it has no extrinsic purpose. No one demands that a rainbow meet their needs; they simply enjoy its presence.

That we have *had* to fill others' needs, even children's, that we have been coerced into putting their needs first *whether we felt like it or not, wanted to or not* at the moment, is evidence of the gross, and I think deliberate, mis-organization of society into nuclear family units based on ownership. There isn't a woman living who couldn't design a model more freeing and humane, and it's a good thing. Because in order to have a new world, we must figure out how everyone's needs can be completely filled without any of us doing a single thing we don't really want to do, *without even the smallest sacrifice.*

The denial of Self and life, the lack of integrity and power inherent in sacrifice, is deeply disfiguring to all of us, children and adults alike. Children are damaged—just as we are—by having their needs met by slaves, by people who are not making free choices out of love but are instead acting much of the time out of the despotic coercions of apparent necessity and guilt and needs for approval and desire to control. From this, kids internalize all life-hating, joy-destroying messages of manunkind and start on their own progression into numbness and robotitude.

What if every piece of clothing we put on, every tool we handled, every bit of food we ate were made, grown, or prepared by someone who chose freely to do it because they so enjoyed the actual doing of it? Imagine eating food prepared by someone who loved preparing it, who chose to do it right then for her own enjoyment. Imagine how infused with her integrity and power, how much more tasty, more nourishing and wholesome such food would be than that cooked by someone primarily because she knew it had to be done.

It is true that the woman who chooses to cook because she feels like it right now also gets great pleasure from watching others enjoy it. But this is not the reason she does it. That there is no linear time signifies that the means are the ends, making the journey truly the destination. Therefore, since she chooses to be alive—to act out of the integrity of her real feelings at the moment—the cook's food preparation is both means and end. She does not project her pleasure along a fictitious line into a non-existent future and fix food for the purpose of enjoying others' enjoyment of it in an hour or so. Being true to her Self every moment is her source of life-stuff. It is freedom.

She can and of course does still care very much about others' well-being, even more deeply perhaps because she cares so very much about her own. She often feels like surprising and delighting others, and helping them when it is appropriate. But her overriding motive for doing anything for others remains that the actual doing of whatever it is gives her pleasure at the time. She knows that when any behavior becomes a means to another end, it carries the genes of oppression in it.

Doing something for another person might incidentally accomplish some goal other than delight—such as making life easier for them for awhile, or proving to them (and to her) that she is a good, caring person with the right politics, or causing them (or her) to think more highly of her, or making them like her better—and that would be fine. But none of these secondary benefits could persuade her to do something she did not, at that moment, actually want to do. No outcome, no matter how worthy in the old social sense, could compensate her for the devastation wreaked in her own and other lives by such betrayal of Self.

Though I was greatly relieved when I realized that I wasn't on the planet to meet anyone else's needs and that no one was here to meet mine, like the woman who loved cooking this didn't mean that I stopped caring about others—their difficulties and pain, triumphs and joys—or that I didn't help or rejoice in whatever non-sacrificial, non-guilt-motivated, non-hierarchal ways I could see. It meant that I recognized other women as able to take their own power as I took mine.

I recognized sacrifice as a virulent form of control. By this time I knew absolutely that power cannot exist in the presence of coercion, under even the merest, seemingly most innocuous, pressure. Just as I facilitated personal power in my children by trusting them to feel their own feelings and live their own lives and by being the best example I could in my own life of how to do this, I knew I had to let go of control in a global sense. I had to stop believing that focusing on other women's problems was desirable behavior, that through my own personal sacrifice I could somehow "save" them.

I had to keep on believing despite massive propaganda that how I helped create a world in which everyone got their needs met was by creating within myself the ability to meet my own; that how I helped create a universe of freedom for everyone was by creating a free inner universe for myself. I had to believe that this was not only the most I could do but that it was abundantly, miraculously enough.

Notes

1. The story that follows—enclosed in brackets—is excerpted from my book *Wildfire: Igniting the She/Volution*, Wildfire Books: Albuquerque, 1989, pp. 89–93.
2. Noel, my last child, was eight years old when Susan and I obeyed the mandate to live together.
3. Back in the days when Joyce Marieb and Linda Barufaldi owned The Amazon Sweet Shop in San Diego, Joyce once wrote out for me on the back of her business card: No amount of hard work, struggle, suffering, or success will make you any more worthy of love than you are right now.

Excerpt from *The Ship that Sailed Into the Living Room: Sex and Intimacy Reconsidered* by Sonia Johnson, 1991, WildFire Books. Reprinted with permission.

10.5

The Bears and Anarchy

Sonia Johnson

The basic feminist view that we should be true to ourselves had been very familiar to me for a long time. But it had taken the trauma of confronting the Relationship Belief System to get me to understand why and how our knowing what we want to do and doing *only* that, knowing who we are and being *always* that, might bring into being a non-relational, non-hierarchical world, a world of peers—women's world.

Groping toward an understanding of how society, not just relation Ships, would change, I first turned for help to my left brain, developing theory to justify the intuitive command that I follow *absolutely and every moment* the desires of my heart.

Men responding to me on talk shows helped. Many of them scornfully contended that if everyone did only what they wanted to do, if there were no rules, no laws, no one in charge, there would be an explosion of crime, there would be total disorder, there would be—horror of horror—anarchy!

"Do you mean," I asked innocently, "that what we are looking at in the world is *not* an explosion of crime? Are you telling me that this is not *already* total disorder?" I wanted to quote Emma Goldman to them, that wild and wonderful anarchist, on the subject of governments and crime:

> The most absurd apology for authority and law is that they serve to diminish crime. Aside from the fact that the State is itself the greatest criminal, breaking every written and natural law, stealing in the form of taxes, killing in the form of war and capital punishment, it has come to an absolute standstill in coping with crime. It has failed utterly to destroy or even minimize the horrible scourge of its own creation.
>
> Crime is naught but misdirected energy. So long as every institution of today, economic, political, social, and moral, conspires to misdirect human energy into wrong channels; so long as most people are out of place doing the things they hate to do, living a life they loathe to live, crime will be inevitable, and all the laws on the statutes can only increase, but never do away with, crime. What does society, as it exists today, know of the process of despair, the poverty, the horrors, the fearful struggle the human soul must pass on its way to crime and degradation?[1]

I agreed with these callers however that, yes, thank goodness, living as I was suggesting *would* mean anarchy. A very different kind of law-and-order than they recognized, but order nevertheless, the order inherent in self-government—total and effortless, fluid, creative, and lusty.[2]

I directed them to observe nature, the perfect anarchy. For billions of years, nature has gone blithely about her business of creating the most extraordinary life systems and forms with awe-inspiring brilliance and efficiency. The stunning fact is that through it all there has been *no one in charge*. No government agencies, no department chiefs, no bureaucrats making laws, demanding triplicates, forming committees to study proposals, holding endless meetings, or funding research. Not even a god.[3]

When left to itself—as unfortunately it has not been since patriarchy's debut—every part of nature simply does what it wants to do all the time, following with integrity its genuine desires, taking full responsibility for itself, and relying on all others to do the same—*needing* all others to do the same. In this way, nature's nearly indestructible ecological web is woven.

When, for example, the river runs where it wants to run and is neither dammed nor turned artificially out of its course, every strand of nature's web, including humankind, benefits. Even granting that rivers flood, floods, too, are necessary for the long-range well-being of the web.

But when rivers are forced to do something that is not in their nature to do, something they do not want to do, widespread disaster follows. For example, when men, who are not rivers and therefore know nothing about *being* rivers, decided that they knew better than the River Nile how it should *be* and dammed it, they shredded the surrounding ecological web for hundreds of miles. Many species of plants and animals died out, disease ran rampant, desertification began its ravages, people who had farmed the rich lands along the Nile's banks, or had lived from its bounty as fisherpeople for thousands of years, were suddenly without means of survival and migrated in calamitous numbers to the cities.

Every living thing must be true to itself, must do what it wants to do, so that all other living things can be free to do the same. This is anarchy, this living in knowledge of total connectedness, and it is perfect order.

The patriarchs do not live in this knowledge and order, and haven't for thousands of years. Because they do not have the spiritual and emotional health that is a precondition for freedom and true power, when they do what they want to do, the rest of us suffer. But when I speak of the desirability of no one ruling anyone else—of no "archy"—I make the assumption that many women are moving, and moving rapidly, toward the soundness of thought and feeling that will make such freedom possible.

Emma Goldman defines anarchy as "the philosophy of a new social order based on liberty unrestricted by man-made law; the theory that all forms of government rest on violence, and are therefore wrong and harmful, as well as unnecessary."[4]

In nature's anarchic design, the denizens of the forest don't stand around watching the bears prepare to hibernate and mutter among themselves: "Look at those lazy louts! What makes them think they can lie around all winter while the rest of us have to work?" They do not then march back and forth in front of the Bureau of Hibernation with their picket signs, chanting, "What do we want? No hibernation! When do we want it? Now!" and demanding, "Wake those bears up and put them to work!"

They don't complain or riot, not only because there is no one in charge that they might influence with such behavior, but I think also because they live every moment in profound understanding of the absolutely crucial connections among us, a wisdom that mensgame has programmed out of us. They know that in order for the web of life to stay intact and healthy, every living thing must be every moment as much what it truly is as possible, must have the individual power that springs from wholeness, and must have the freedom—most wildly, most expansively, most ecstatically—to create from moment to moment an ever new and unique Self.[5]

I think they know that because all living things are intimately connected, when the bears are true to themselves, when they are being as bearful as they can possibly be, everything that lives is more free to create fully its unique Self.

The bears' integrity is therefore not only good for everything else but *necessary* for the well-being of the whole. When bears are about their life's purpose of being every moment at the peak of ursinity, experimenting with the parameters of bearishness, *creating* bearness—and the more bearish the more joyful—all life rejoices. One filament of the web pulsing with creativity and power sends creativity and power zinging through the entire network.

In my past conventionally activist life, I acknowledged this fundamental connection in a negative way by agreeing that when any of us is oppressed, we are all oppressed. I know now that the positive of this is equally true: When any of us is free, we are all free.

But some argue that the case for doing only what we want to do—for anarchy—cannot be supported by analogy with the natural world. All is not cozy cooperation there, they say. Animals, for instance, are violent. They stalk, kill, and eat one another. Maybe the woodland folk are happy to see the bears hibernate, not because in this way the ecological balance necessary for life will be maintained, but rather because for a few merciful months bears will be out of circulation, freeing the forest of their menace.

This argument ignores our growing understanding of the complex and complete interconnection among all living things. Since all of us are interdependent in life's web, and everything that affects any one of us affects us all, it is unthinkable that animals can have remained unchanged by the truly immeasurable male violence of the past 5,000 years on this planet. How can we presume to know their true natures when for millennia they have lived, as we have, in a reality of perpetual terror? We have no more seen a "free" or "natural" animal in the past few thousands of years than we have seen a "free" or "natural" woman, or a "free" or "natural" anything.

The bible, however, as a history of the systematized genocide of the goddess people, inadvertently offers us a glimpse into their pre-patriarchal world, a world of other possibilities for animals as well as for ourselves. Courtesy of that eerily familiar world-mind comes the image of the lamb lying down with the lion. Totally alien to patriarchal thought, this remnant of goddess culture hints evocatively that all is not as it seems, that other ways of being are always open to us.

When we are all free, I will observe animals and say, "This is how they behave in anarchy, in perfect freedom, in total self-government, in absolute love. This is therefore how they truly are." Until then, I am reserving judgment about their nature, as I am reserving judgment about yours and mine.

Though the bear story is an analogy, not an argument, and can be taken only so far, a basic assumption about our experience as humans can be made from it. We are part of nature's mystical, magical latticework, totally interdependent.

When I am in a big city surrounded by enormous buildings, I often look up at the thousands of windows signifying thousands of offices and hundreds of thousands of workers and think, "What can they all possibly be *doing* in there?" I know that there is actually little that needs to be done, and that anything beyond that is destructive—to the human spirit and to the soul of the planet. So I know that most people working in those offices are doing work that is dangerous to them and others.

But I also know that the greatest danger is that most of them are not enjoying the work they're doing. Most of them don't want to be in those offices and many are absolutely wretched there, but they are enslaved by their belief that they have no economic alternative.

The consequences to every living being of this massive unhappiness, this vast spiritual and physical bondage, are incalculable. Because we are connected to one another on every level as if by shining silver cords, the strands of our lives woven inseparably together into the web, the suffering of any one of us vibrates through every filament and is felt by us all. When any one of us betrays our Selves, does what we don't want to do, what is not in our natures to do, what causes us to live less powerfully, less creatively, less joyfully, the quality of every life on the planet is damaged. When we are not true to ourselves, we seriously endanger the health not only of our own but of everyone else's spirit on Earth. There is no way for any of us to live as fully as we are capable as long as so many others are sending distress to our souls through the threads of life's tapestry.

Like the other animals, to the degree that each of us is whole and living in our power—that is, knows who and how valuable we are, how we feel, what we want, and, honoring and loving ourselves, acts totally out of the desires of our hearts every moment—no one can control us, neither can we nor would we wish to control anyone else. Tyranny cannot exist when self-loving beings act with integrity.

Anarchy is the name for this ecology of the spirit. A new social and economic order, it requires that we love and trust ourselves, and are totally accountable for our own feelings and behavior. It requires that we dare to believe that when we have done enough of our internal cleansing from patriarchy, when we are whole again for the most part and sane, then doing what we desire to do all the time will bless us and all other living things.

For obvious reasons, the men who control the world tremble at the word anarchy. If everyone valued themselves, if they took full responsibility for themselves, if they knew exactly how they felt and did what they wanted to do every moment, they would be ungovernable. None of them could be forced to work eight hours a day at mind-numbing, soul-destroying jobs. The system could not survive for five minutes without the capitulation of people who absolutely believe that human beings have no choice but to do many things in life that they don't want to do, people who surrender responsibility for their lives to mensmachine.

The fact that the word anarchy has so much power to terrify the tyrants should put us on alert, since we know that patriarchy reverses the truth. In this light, its insistence that violence and disorder are inherent to anarchy makes it safe for us to assume the opposite: That given a certain level of emotional and spiritual health among its practitioners, anarchy by its very nature generates peace and order.

Those of us intent upon designing, creating, and living in a literal new world right now want to understand not only the theory but also how in our lives to follow nature's anarchic model. We want to know how we can reestablish the ecology of the spirit among us, and what would happen if we were selftrue.

Although we know we can't envision a new paradigm standing in the thick smog of the old, we can't help but speculate about how we might remake the world by having the courage and insight to live free from manunkind's self-serving assumptions.

What we know is that everything around us would undergo drastic alteration if we adhered fiercely to our desires. Take, for instance, toilets.[6]

Every time I talk about my vision of self-government and freedom based on desire, some woman objects, "But who's going to clean the toilets?" she asks. Sometimes another woman will call out, "I love to clean toilets!"[7] Several others will jokingly urge her to come and live with them. But toilets, both as themselves and as symbols of unpleasant work, remain a problem.

Let us give the toilet problem to a small imaginary community of thirteen women who are experimenting earnestly with the principle of doing only what they want to do all the time. These women live together in one large house or have separate houses and a communal building or some other arrangement that gives them some shared space.

In this shared space is a conventional toilet, and one day one of the women says, "Hey, you gynes! Look at this dirty toilet. Do any of you want to clean it?" Each woman checks out her feelings—and shakes her head. No one wants to. They all stand looking at the toilet and waiting for enlightenment.

But because these women believe that their desires are perfect guides to behavior, none of them says, "It's got to be done. Someone's going to have to do it whether she wants to or not. Someone's got to sacrifice so that the rest of us will be comfortable." Trusting their feelings and knowing that they spring directly from their values, they realize that since none of them wants to clean it, something is wrong with the *toilet*, not with *them*.

The theory upon which they are operating is that if the work that presents itself is in harmony with their values, they will want to do it. If it promotes a world of peace and abundance and joy and love and beauty and health, they will delight in doing it, it will be a pleasure, it will *fit* them. Obviously the converse is also true: If a job is somehow out of sync with their world view, they will find it repugnant *and will not be able to do it*.

Already the experience of thousands of women in the United States bears out this theory. Women are walking out of jobs everywhere, and walking out *before* they have any other economic crutch. The typical experience, as it has been told to me time and time again, goes something like this. One day a woman upon entering her office realizes that she can no longer be there. Though she is frightened, inside herself she feels an enormous rush of optimism and power that propels her through her resignation that day and beyond.

Everywhere, these women—many of whom have still not discovered what they want to do or found other ways to survive financially—tell me that they have never regretted acting on that impulse. They assure me that the instant they decided, despite their economic terror, to stop squandering their precious lives doing merely tolerable, or boring, or infuriating work was the best moment of their lives.

I have learned that living in this way may have benefits I couldn't have dreamed of at first. A friend told me, for instance, that she had seen a talk show—she *thought* it was

Sally Jesse Raphael—where four people who had been certified as having had AIDS, three men and a woman, speculated about why they currently showed no clinical trace of it at all. Though none of them could answer how they had been healed, the friend who watched it noticed that their stories all followed a similar pattern.

When they had been told that they had AIDS, they had each resolved that, since they had so little time to live, they would live exactly as they pleased for as long as they were able. They had then proceeded to do only what they wanted to do and nothing else—in the best of health an incredibly radical, difficult, and transfiguring act.

Already we are beginning, many of us without knowing or even caring why, to stop being ruled by fear, refusing to let it persuade us to be relational, reactionary, stimulus-response-bound. Trusting our desires, we are becoming free from every form of dis-ease in patriarchy.

As soon, for instance, as the women with the dirty toilet realize from their feelings of distaste that something about toilets as they are presently designed does not mesh with women's values, they ask themselves what it is about this object and the way it functions that does not belong in their new world. The answers begin to come at once.

First, they notice that it is too high for most able-bodied women. Humans were meant anatomically to squat while they defecate. Our colons need this added assistance for best cleansing. Next, they realize that it takes marvelous, scientifically unreproducible organic matter, matter that has picked up miracle substances from every organ and gland of the body, and destroys it, losing it to the life cycle for which it is so necessary. Last, they are appalled at its waste of water, the earth's most necessary, most precious resource. Water, they agree, is liquid life, solid light, full of intelligence and wisdom. If there is a tangible goddess, she is water.

The women of this community reach the conclusion that other women have reached before them, that what they need are toilets that fit them—physically and ecologically. What they need are custom-made composting toilets.

As they follow through on this decision, they notice with excitement how it alters their entire living space. Because they can build composters anywhere, inside or out, they don't have to put them in something called a "bathroom." This opens up their minds to possible rearrangements of tubs and wash basins as well. Do these need a separate room? Might the tub not be warmer and sunnier on the south side of the bedroom (if there is such a room!) or in the kitchen, or in the greenhouse or sunroom, or somewhere else? How many bathtubs and showers and composters does the community need, and what would be the best location to allow re-use of water and easy transport of compost? Would covered walkways from living quarters to a central bathhouse or several strategically placed composters cut down the numbers of tubs and toilets necessary, and would these arrangements be comfortable and convenient?

The entire conventional floor plan that has developed out of menstream values is then up for rethinking. As are energy sources, and placement of living areas in accord with natural heat and cool. As are rigidly square corners that abruptly stop the spiraling flow of energy in a room, giving the occupants dis-ease. And so on.

As they follow their desires, the very look of their world radically, marvelously changes to reflect the change in values. Because they are emotionally and intellectually healthy and largely deprogrammed from their conditioning, they can transform their abstract values into concrete reality by fulfilling their desires.

Their toilet experience reinforces these women's understanding of patriarchy as the reaction against, the reverse of, women's ways. Men, trapped in the illusory future by their own linear time deception, begin, for example, with projected goals. They then decide what jobs need to be done and when they must be finished in order for these goals to be reached on time. Their next step is to get other people to do these jobs whether they want to or not—genuine desire is not only irrelevant but actively discounted and discouraged.

The truth is, of course, that people most often don't want to do these jobs and sometimes even intensely dislike doing them. But they are coerced into them by their need for money. Hence the necessity to oppression of an exchange system. How else could men force people into spending most of their precious lives doing things they don't want to do?

However, living in the conscious value-rich present—and the present is all there ever is or will be—decisions about what needs to be done arise out of the desires of women who are in their power. If there is work that no one wants to do, the work itself is scrutinized for its anti-life, anti-freedom properties. The women do not look into themselves for the flaw. Pure desire, the fruit of integrity, can have no flaw.

Even when the women in the community cannot recognize at first why certain work is not desirable to any of them, they still refuse to do it. They refuse because they know that doing it despite their warning that it is not harmonious with their values is treacherous to themselves, subversive to the spiritual ecology of their community, and therefore disruptive to all communities, human and otherwise. They understand that ignoring or resisting their desires will tear this shimmering metaphysical web apart in ways both obvious at once and insidious over time. This keeps them firm in their resolve not to capitulate to old ways of being and thinking, never again to let guilt—the "shoulds" of the fathers—dictate their behavior.

Their belief in the validity of their desires gives them the courage not to do work that no one wants to do even when in the old world such work was believed to be absolutely necessary; the courage not to do it even when they cannot see how to achieve the same result in other ways; the courage to wait and see what happens when that work is not done; the courage to make decisions from that experience rather than from the post-hypnosis-like trance induced by brainwashing.

We are these hypothetical women. Shouldering the responsibility for becoming more fully who we are every moment by recognizing and honoring the desires of our souls, we help restore self-government, peerness, and freedom to all other living things in nature's gorgeous ecological tapestry.

More than this, in believing in our own internal voices we reinvent human nature, we create another, more expansive and inclusive, more interesting, more playful and at the same time more serious, myth of humanness. Guided by our desires, we live moment by moment in richest chaos—that is, at the summit of creativity where every possibility is present at once.

Out of this ripe and exuberant chaos, women are once again creating connections with all that is, animate and inanimate—the heart connections that have been lost for so long and so sadly missed.

Notes

1. Emma Goldman, *Anarchism and Other Essays*, Dover Publications, Inc.: Mineola, NY, 1969, pp. 59–60.
2. As Lucy Frey from Anchorage, AK, wrote in a January 1991 note: "In London at SisterWrite Bookstore, I bought a card that said, 'A woman without a man is like a country without a government.'"
3. Sue Lampson from San Jose suggests that cats are among the best models of anarchy. Cats, she says, always know and do exactly what they want. They live totally in the moment.
4. *Anarchism and Other Essays*, p. 50.
5. I am aware here both of partaking of men's arrogance in believing I know what animals *are* and of anthropomorphizing—and therefore falsifying—animals in order to make my point. I apologize, but I think the point is worth it. I want to make clear, however, that every day I gain more respect for animals, feel more humble in their presence, and am more willing to accept that, in my present gross psychic state, I cannot understand them. But I look forward eagerly to the rapidly-approaching time when we will again be able to communicate with them in direct ways. And the time when we will never kill them, never force them to do anything they do not choose to do. I long for our ancient unity and peerness with them.
6. Alternatives to conventional toilets exist only because our new value system has already begun imposing itself upon our environment.
7. *She* may, but most of us don't. I know I like to *have cleaned* them, I enjoy having them clean. In the past I haven't minded doing the yucky jobs because I saw this work as the means to another end. I believe that all our wants have been deliberately obfuscated by this kind of linearity.

Index

Activism, 266, 270
Adam, 110, 116
Akomfrah, John, 67
Allen, Paula Gunn, 179-211
    control, 208, 209, 211
    disappearance of Native Americans, 181-183
    education of, 179
    ethics, feminist, 210-211
    focus of work of, 179
    interconnection, 207-208, 210
    lesbians as like Indians, 199-203
    perfection, 208-209
    power, myths of female, 184-198
    truth, 210-211
Allen, Woody, 63
Alliance, 91, 223
Anarchy, 304-307
Anthony, Susan B., 42
Anzaldúa, Gloria, 75-104
    Borderlands, 75-76, 85, 100
    Chicano/a culture, 86, 88, 89, 90-95, 103
    education of, 75
    feminism defined, 75
    focus of work of, 75
    identity, 101-104
    lesbianism, 77, 88, 91, 98-99
    men's role, 89-91
    mestiza consciousness, 75-76, 85-91, 104
    writing, 77-84
Architecture, 71, 72
Ardener, Edwin, 19, 21, 22
Ardener, Shirley, 10, 20, 21
Art, 71, 222, 223, 229

Balance, 209, 210
Be-ing/being, 114, 124
Berg, Barbara, 51-52
Billops, Camille, 69
Birth name, 29
Bolinger, Dwight, 16
Borderlands, 75-76, 85, 100
Boundary living, 113-115
    See also Borderlands
Bourne, Jenny, 58, 60
Bridge, 100, 101, 102, 104
Bunch, Charlotte, 56
Burnett, Charles, 64, 65

Callan, Hilary, 20
Capitalism, 50, 55
Carroll, Berenice, 40
Change:
    alternatives to, 244, 286
    as inner process, 92, 157, 159, 239, 270, 299, 300
    as long-term process, 169
    as purpose of rhetoric, 241
    as violation, 243
    focus on systems in, 269
    impossibility of changing others, 266, 270, 285, 301
    inevitability of, 242
    internal basis for, 244
    new theory of, 239
    responses to, 177
    role of intention in, 242, 243
Chicano/a culture, 86, 88, 89, 90-95, 103
Chipko strategy, 259-265
Christ, Carol P., 144
Christianity, critique of, 107-118
Cixous, Hélène, 42
Colonization, 102, 287-289, 291, 292
Combahee River Collective, 60
Common ground, creating, 267-270
Communication:
    among non-human entities, 242
    as label for *rhetoric*, 246

redefinition of, 244
satellite, 35
transformation of, 5
Community, 37, 54, 108, 113, 157, 162-163
Competition, 14, 111
   See also Cooperation
Confession, 61, 62
Conflict:
   as transformative, 100
   difference as replacement for, 216, 218
   strategies in, 245, 267, 270
Conquest, 241, 242-243, 245, 246, 247
   See also Persuasion
Control:
   antithetical to consciousness, 211
   critique of, 34-37
   of life, 299-300
   over-control, 208-209
   sacrifice as form of, 303
Conversion, 241, 242, 245, 246, 247
   See also Persuasion
Cooperation, 14, 49, 191
   See also Competition
Crazy Horse, 182
Crime, 304

Daly, Mary, 39, 105-139, 278
   Christianity, critique of, 107-118, 144
   dictionary, 135-139
   education of, 105, 123-125
   focus of work of, 105
   Outercourse, 130-133
   professional history, 126-129
   Sparking, 121-122
   Spinning, 122, 132-133
   Spooking, 120-121, 128
   women's spaces, 53, 119-122
Dash, Julie, 64, 67, 68
de Beauvoir, Simone, 25, 109
Defamiliarization, 64
Definition, 13
   See also Redefinition
Design, 71-73
Dictionary, 13, 30, 135-140
Difference, 216-218, 222, 245
Dixon, Marlene, 53
Domination, system of:
   as internal, 284-285
   as white supremacist capitalist patriarchy, 45, 50, 71
   characteristics of, 21, 92, 103-104, 107, 117, 126, 129, 152, 153, 176, 269, 310
   eradication of as goal of feminism, 2-3, 45, 48, 49, 52
   maintenance of, 53
   strategies to enforce, 284
   See also Hegemony
Dumarest, Noël, 186

Ehrenzweig, Anton, 144
Eisenstein, Zillah, 49
Elgin, Suzette Haden, 30, 39
Ellmann, Mary, 10
Enemy, 267, 268, 269, 270
Energy, 158-159, 242, 243
Equal Rights Amendment (ERA), 271, 273-275, 276, 278, 279
Equality, 47-48, 49, 50, 53, 56
Ethics, 146, 210-211
Evans, Ron, 159
Eve, 116

Feelings, 268-269, 298, 300, 301
Feminism:
   as collective, 54, 55
   as creation of women's space, 53-54, 108, 113-114, 282, 307
   as lifestyle, 54-55, 58
   as reform movement, 48-49, 50
   as revolutionary movement, 48-49, 55, 110, 222-223
   backlash against, 175, 176, 177
   conversion to, 273-281
   definitions of, 2, 7, 38n, 45, 47, 51-52, 53, 56, 75, 213, 239, 247, 271
   domination by white, middle-class women, 53
   first wave of, 134
   focus on men as enemy, 53
   forelash of, 176, 178
   need for theory in, 56
   personal is political, 52, 56, 57, 59, 60, 61, 62
   political consciousness required for, 52-53, 55, 57, 58, 59
   second wave of, 134, 246, 247, 287
   third wave of, 4
Film:
   anthropological, 233-235
   as mechanism of social change, 66
   documentary, 235-237

representations of black women in, 63, 64-70
Third World, 217-218
Flexner, Stuart, 10
Foster, Brian, 10
Freedom, 287-288, 290, 291, 302, 303, 305, 306
Friedan, Betty, 12

Gaia hypothesis, 176
Gardner, Gerald, 145
Gatherstretch, 248-258
Gearhart, Sally Miller, 239-270
    chipko strategy, 259-265
    disavowal of activism, 266, 270
    education of, 239
    feminism defined, 239
    focus of work of, 239
    gatherstretch, 248-258
    new approach to change, 266-270
    persuasion as violence, 239, 241-243
    proposal for non-persuasive rhetoric, 244-247
Gerima, Haile, 65, 66
Gilligan, Carol, 40
God:
    as synonymous with *Goddess*, 156, 159, 160
    critique of patriarchal conception of, 107-117
    patriarchal conception of, 144, 176, 177, 279-281, 305
Goddess:
    as basis for Witchcraft, 143-148, 150, 151
    as sacred, 156, 176
    black aspect of, 210
    characteristics of, 159, 309
    effects of images of, 160
    embodiments of, 154, 156, 164, 169, 177
    remnant of in patriarchy, 306
Goldman, Emma, 304, 305
Gossip, 154-155
Grace-making, 249
Gross, Jeanne, 50, 53
Gyn/Ecology/Third Passage, 119, 120, 121, 122

Habday, Sister José, 158
Haggle, 206
Harding, Sandra, 40
Harris, Harwell Hamilton, 71, 72
Hartsock, Nancy, 40
Haug, Frigga, 61
Hegemony, 53, 213, 216
    See also Domination, system of
Higginson, Thomas, 11
Home, 101
hooks, belle, 45-73
    education of, 45
    personal is political, 57-62
    feminism defined, 2, 45, 47-56
    focus of work of, 45
    importance of design, 71-73
    intersection of oppressions, 47-48, 50, 53, 54, 55
    representation of black women in film, 63-70
Humor, 22, 135, 162
Hymes, Dell, 16

Identity:
    individual, 215-219
    politics of, 58, 59, 60, 61, 62, 101, 103, 104
    racial, 91, 101
    social, 12
Ideology, 213, 220, 222, 229, 233, 236
Insider-outsider status, 217-218, 221
Interconnection:
    as feminist value, 37
    characteristic of world, 156, 207, 210, 305, 306
    effects of, 307, 310
    effort required to break, 207-208
    nature of, 218
    See also Isolation
Interdependence. *See* Interconnection
Isolation, 179, 207-208, 209, 210
    See also Interconnection
Issue, women's, 289

Jacklin, Carol Nagy, 23, 24
Jaffa, Arthur, 67, 69
Jarmusch, Jim, 63-64
Jespersen, Otto, 10, 28
Jesus, 116, 117, 125, 144
Johnson, Sonia, 271-311
    anarchy, 304-310
    conversion to feminism, 273-281
    education of, 271
    Equal Rights Amendment (ERA), 271, 273-275, 276, 278, 279

feminism defined, 271
focus of work of, 271
living women's world, 272
reality, nature of, 282-285
relation Ship, 294-296, 297-298, 304
resistance, strategy of, 285-287
Roe v. Wade, 287, 289-291
Jong, Erica, 14

Kendall, Kathy, 83
Knowledge, 102, 221, 226
Kramarae, Cheris, 7-44
   critique of control, 34-38
   education of, 7
   feminism defined, 7
   focus of work of, 7
   muted-group theory, 19-26
   need for feminist theories of
      communication, 39-40
   public/private dichotomy, 43-44
   silencing of women, 40-41
   women's exclusion from language,
      10-13
   women's linguistic innovation, 13-15
   writing the body, 41-42

Láadan, 30
Language:
   accessibility of, 3
   castration of, 111
   creates reality, 12, 151, 155, 159
   gender bias in, 10, 11, 12, 13, 15, 16,
      19, 25, 110, 111
   male creation of, 10, 11, 13
   referential function of, 226
   slang, 10
   women's innovation in, 9, 10, 11, 12,
      13, 14, 15, 25, 28, 29, 30, 111, 119,
      135-139
Laughter, 14, 135, 137, 162
Lee, Spike, 67-68
Lesbians and gays:
   at forefront of liberation efforts, 91
   invisibility of, 77
   like Indians, 199-203
   negative responses to, 54, 98-99
   part of all races, 88
   prescriptions for behavior, 210
Listening, 245, 247
Littlebear, Naomi, 80
Lorde, Audre, 36, 155, 224, 267, 290

Maccoby, Eleanor Emmons, 23, 24
Machismo, 89-90, 112
   See also Masculinity
Magic, 147, 149, 151, 155, 158,
   163, 165, 170
Mao Tse Tung, 244
Markovic, Milhailo, 50
Marxism, 41, 50
Masculinity, 90, 145
McRobbie, Angela, 43
Meaning, 225-226, 232, 234-237, 246
Media, industries, 42-43
Memory, 61, 62
Mestiza consciousness, 75-76, 85,
   86-91,104
Metaphor, 156
Micheaux, Oscar, 64
Miller, Alice, 152
Momaday, N. Scott, 181, 183, 224
Moraga, Cherríe, 78, 80, 81, 82, 83, 100
Morphogenesis, 88n
Morton, Nelle, 112
Motherhood, 195, 298
Muted-group theory, 19-26

Native Americans:
   disappearance of, 181-183
   myths of female power among, 184-198
   social structures of, 188-190
   views of motherhood among, 194-195
Needs, meeting, 297-303
New tribalism, 101, 104
New Virtues, 134
Nichols, Patricia, 9, 23
Noguchi, Isamu, 73

Objectivity, 229, 233, 284
   See also Reality
Ortiz, Simon J., 183
Outercourse, 130-133

Paranoia, positive, 120
Parsons, Elsie Clews, 27, 28
Patriarchy. *See* Domination, system of
Perfection, 208-209
Persuasion, 241-247, 287
   as violence, 241-243
Piratic perspective, 123, 131-132, 133
Power:
   as source of magic, 191
   choosing, 299-300

connection to Goddess/Mother,
    149, 151, 163, 169, 187,
    194, 195
connection to tobacco, 192
equality of, 245
in women's spaces, 113-114
lack of, 286, 298
myths of female, 184-198
patriarchal, 113, 268
raising, 162, 164, 165, 174
types of, 152-155, 157-158, 162, 289
warfare as source of, 190
Prigogine, Ilya, 88n
Psychology, liberation, 155-158, 160
Public/private dichotomy, 43-44
Purley, Anthony, 185

Race, cosmic, 85
Radway, Janice, 43
Reality:
    as internal, 283-284
    as objective, 246
    conventions for presenting in film,
        228-229, 230, 231, 232, 233
    effects of lack of labels for, 12
    limits on powers to change, 159
    See also Objectivity
Redefinition, 13
    See also Definition
Reflexivity, 234-236
Reframing, 76
Relation Ship, 294-296, 297-298, 304
Research by women, recovery of, 27,
    28, 29-30, 39-40
Resistance:
    absence as, 114
    as ineffective, 86, 271-272, 285, 286
    creation as, 160
Reversal, patriarchal, 278
Rhetoric:
    definition of, 2
    theorist of, 2
    types of, 243
Rich, Adrienne, 208
Rights, 37
Rituals, 162-174
    grounding in, 162, 163, 164, 166
    in Native American culture, 188,
        189-90, 195
    samples of, 163, 165, 166, 170-174
Roe v. Wade, 287, 289-291

Sacredness, 157, 176-177, 185-186, 191,
    194, 206, 209
Sacrifice, 302, 303, 308
Saffioti, Heleith, 49
Salvation, 116
Sanders, Alex, 145
Sartre, Jean-Paul, 113
Scapegoat, 115
Second Coming, 116
Self-determination, 48, 52, 92, 101,
    299-302, 306-310
Self-love, 299
Semantics, heteropatriarchal, 41
Sex differences:
    explanations for, 24
    in conversation, 30
    in labels for behavior, 16
    in literacy, 40
    in phonology, 23
    in stereotypes regarding speech, 9
    in test results, 24
    in topics discussed, 24
    in verbal skills, 23-25
    in vocabulary use, 28
Sex vs. *gender*, 32, 41
Sexual caste system, 107, 123
    See also Domination, system of
Sexuality, 147, 157, 159, 177
Silence as change strategy, 216-217
Silencing of women, 40-41
Sin, 116, 123, 125, 126, 134
Sisterhood, 108, 111, 122
Sitting Bull, 181, 183
Sparking, 121-122
Speech, women's
    as inarticulate, 20, 22
    conformity to standards, 23
    exclusion from public forums, 29
    inadequacy of public modes for, 22
    stereotypes of, 9, 15
Spender, Dale, 10, 24, 25, 29, 39, 40
Spinning, 122, 132-133
Spooking, 120-121, 128
Stanley, Julia Penelope, 13, 14, 25,
    30, 39, 41
Stanton, Elizabeth Cady, 42, 115
Starhawk, 141-178
    education of, 141
    focus of work of, 141
    Goddess, 143-148, 150, 151, 154,
        156, 164, 169, 176, 177

magic, 147, 149, 151, 155, 158, 163, 165, 170
power, types of,
psychology, liberation, 155-158, 160
rituals, 162-174
truth or dare, 160-161
Witchcraft, 141, 143-148, 150-151, 158
Stone, Lucy, 32, 33n
Strainchamps, Ethel, 14
Structure of realization, 19
Structure, template, 19
Subjectivity, 217, 218, 220
Swidler, Leonard, 116-117

Tajfel, Henri, 12
Technologies, communications, 34, 35, 36, 37, 42
Teish, Luisah, 79, 83, 158
Theology:
  as data for study of sexism, 125
  Christian, 110
  of women's liberation, 109
Theory:
  as distorted, 39-40
  feminist, 39, 40, 56
  significance of, 56
  definition of, 2
Thinking:
  convergent, 86
  divergent, 86-87
Third World:
  access to technologies in, 35
  exploitation of women in, 36
  filmmakers of, 217-218
  tokenization of women of, 79
  women writers of, 77-84
Tillich, Paul, 110, 116
Todasco, Ruth, 13
Tokenism, 79, 112, 127
Trinh T. Minh-ha, 64, 68, 213-238
  challenge to hegemonic representations, 220-224
  difference, 216-218, 222
  education of, 213
  feminism defined, 213
  film, anthropological, 233-235
  film, documentary, 225-237
  focus of work of, 213
  identity, 215-219
  reality as constructed in film, 228-233
Truth:
  as ideological presentation, 213, 225-226, 227, 229, 230, 231, 236
  creates vulnerability, 210-211
  multiple paths to, 234
  relationship to meaning, 225-226
Tyranny, as contract, 290

Vasconcelos, Jose, 85
Vasquez, Carmen, 47
Victimization, 61, 76, 101, 103
Violence:
  against women, 41, 49, 61, 90, 119, 128-129, 130, 152, 291
  among lesbians, 291
  by species, 243, 247
Vulnerability, 211

Walker, Alice, 40
Ware, Cellestine, 48
Williams, Raymond, 11
Williams, Carlos William, 164
Willingness to yield, 245, 256
Witchcraft, 141, 143-148, 150-151, 158
Wolf, Margery, 154
Women's Information Exchange, 36
Wong, Nellie, 83
Wood, Julia, 2
Writing, 77-84, 104
  the body, 41-42

About the Editors

The three co-editors—**Cindy L. Griffin** (Ph.D., Indiana University-Bloomington; M.A., University of Oregon; B.S., California State University, Northridge), **Sonja K. Foss** (Ph.D., Northwestern University; M.A. and B.A., University of Oregon), and **Karen A. Foss** (Ph.D., University of Iowa; M.A. and B.A., University of Oregon)—are well-known in the communication field for their work in the area of feminist scholarship, and all have focused on the reconceptualization of rhetorical constructs and theories from feminist perspectives. They are the co-authors of *Feminist Rhetorical Theories* (Sage, 1999), which won the 2000 Book of the Year Award from the Organization for the Study of Communication, Language, and Gender.

Among their previous books are *Invitation to Public Speaking* (Cindy Griffin); *Rhetorical Criticism, 3/e* (Sonja Foss); and *Inviting Transformation, 2/e, Contemporary Perspectives on Rhetoric, 3/e, Readings in Contemporary Rhetoric,* and *Women Speak* (Karen Foss and Sonja Foss).